A·N·N·U·A·L E·D·

MARKETING

Twenty-First Edition

99/00

EDITOR

John E. Richardson
Pepperdine University

Dr. John E. Richardson is professor of marketing in The George L. Graziadio School of Business and Management at Pepperdine University. He is president of his own consulting firm and has consulted with organizations such as Bell and Howell, Dayton-Hudson, Epson, and the U.S. Navy as well as with various service, nonprofit, and franchise organizations. Dr. Richardson is a member of the American Marketing Association, the American Management Association, the Society for Business Ethics, and Beta Gamma Sigma honorary business fraternity.

Dushkin/McGraw-Hill
Sluice Dock, Guilford, Connecticut 06437

Visit us on the Internet
http://www.dushkin.com/annualeditions/

Credits

1. Marketing in the 1990s and Beyond
Facing overview—© 1998 by PhotoDisc, Inc. 89-92—Photomontages by Lou Beach.
2. Research, Markets, and Consumer Behavior
Facing overview—© Cleo Freelance Photo.
3. Developing and Implementing Marketing Strategies
Facing overview—© 1998 by PhotoDisc, Inc.
4. Global Marketing
Facing overview—© 1998 by PhotoDisc, Inc.

Copyright

Cataloging in Publication Data
Main entry under title: Annual Editions: Marketing. 1999/2000.
    1. Marketing—Periodicals. 2. Marketing—Social aspects—Periodicals.
3. Marketing management—Periodicals. I. Richardson, John, *comp.* II. Title: Marketing.
ISBN 0-07-041175-1   ISSN 0730-2606   HF5415.A642   658.8'005   73–78578

© 1999 by Dushkin/McGraw-Hill, Guilford, CT 06437, A Division of The McGraw-Hill Companies.

Twenty-First Edition

Cover image © 1999 PhotoDisc, Inc.

Printed in the United States of America   1234567890BAHBAH54 21098   Printed on Recycled Paper

iii

To the Reader

In publishing ANNUAL EDITIONS we recognize the enormous role played by the magazines, newspapers, and journals of the public press in providing current, first-rate educational information in a broad spectrum of interest areas. Many of these articles are appropriate for students, researchers, and professionals seeking accurate, current material to help bridge the gap between principles and theories and the real world. These articles, however, become more useful for study when those of lasting value are carefully collected, organized, indexed, and reproduced in a low-cost format, which provides easy and permanent access when the material is needed. That is the role played by ANNUAL EDITIONS.

New to ANNUAL EDITIONS is the inclusion of related World Wide Web sites. These sites have been selected by our editorial staff to represent some of the best resources found on the World Wide Web today. Through our carefully developed topic guide, we have linked these Web resources to the articles covered in this ANNUAL EDITIONS reader. We think that you will find this volume useful, and we hope that you will take a moment to visit us on the Web at **http://www.dushkin.com/** to tell us what you think.

The 1990s are proving to be an exciting and challenging time for the American business community. Recent dramatic social, economic, and technological changes have become an important part of the present marketplace. These changes—accompanied by increasing domestic and foreign competition—are leading a wide array of companies and industries toward the realization that better marketing must become a top priority now to ensure their future success.

How does the marketing manager respond to this growing challenge? How does the marketing student apply marketing theory to real-world practice? Many reach for *The Wall Street Journal, Business Week, Fortune,* and other well-known sources of business information. There, specific industry and company strategies are discussed and analyzed, marketing principles are often reaffirmed by real occurrences, and textbook theories are supported or challenged by current events.

The articles reprinted in this edition of *Annual Editions: Marketing 99/00* have been carefully chosen from numerous different public press sources to provide current information on marketing in the world today. Within these pages you will find articles that address marketing theory and application in a wide range of industries. In addition, the selections reveal how several firms interpret and utilize marketing principles in their daily operations and corporate planning.

The volume contains a number of features that are designed to make it useful for marketing students, researchers, and professionals. These include the *Industry/Company Guide,* which is particularly helpful when seeking information about specific corporations; a *topic guide* to locate articles on specific marketing subjects; *World Wide Web* pages that relate to the listings in the *topic guide;* the *table of contents abstracts,* which summarize each article and highlight key concepts; a *glossary* of key marketing terms; and a comprehensive *index.*

The articles are organized into four units. Selections that focus on similar issues are concentrated into subsections within the broader units. Each unit is preceded by a list of unit selections, a list of key points to consider, which focus on major themes running throughout the selections, Web links that provide extra support for the unit's data, and an overview that provides background for informed reading of the articles and emphasizes critical issues.

This is the twenty-first edition of *Annual Editions: Marketing.* Since the first edition in the mid-1970s, the efforts of many individuals have contributed toward its success. We think this is by far the most useful collection of material available for the marketing student. We are anxious to know what you think. What are your opinions? What are your recommendations? Please take a moment to complete and return the *article rating form* on the last page of this volume. Any book can be improved, and this one will continue to be, annually.

John E. Richardson
Editor

Contents

UNIT 1

Marketing in the 1990s and Beyond

Sixteen selections examine the current and future status of marketing, the marketing concept, service marketing, and marketing ethics.

The concepts in bold italics are developed in the article. For further expansion please refer to the Topic Guide, the Glossary, and the Index.

The concepts in bold italics are developed in the article. For further expansion please refer to the Topic Guide, the Glossary, and the Index.

UNIT 2

Research, Markets, and Consumer Behavior

Eight selections provide
an analysis of consumer
demographics and lifestyles,
the growth and maturation
of markets, and the need
for market research
and planning.

UNIT 3

Developing and Implementing Marketing Strategies

Fourteen selections analyze factors that affect the development and implementation of marketing strategies.

The concepts in bold italics are developed in the article. For further expansion please refer to the Topic Guide, the Glossary, and the Index.

The concepts in bold italics are developed in the article. For further expansion please refer to the Topic Guide, the Glossary, and the Index.

UNIT 4

Y. S.

Global Marketing

Three selections discuss the increasing globalization of markets, trends in world trade, and increasing foreign competition.

The concepts in bold italics are developed in the article. For further expansion please refer to the Topic Guide, the Glossary, and the Index.

This topic guide suggests how the selections and World Wide Web sites found in the next section of this book relate to topics of traditional concern to marketing students and professionals. It is useful for locating interrelated articles and Web sites for reading and research. The guide is arranged alphabetically according to topic.

The relevant Web sites, which are numbered and annotated on pages 4 and 5, are easily identified by the Web icon (⊙) under the topic articles. By linking the articles and the Web sites by topic, this ANNUAL EDITIONS reader becomes a powerful learning and research tool.

TOPIC AREA	TREATED IN	TOPIC AREA	TREATED IN
Advertising	1. Future of Marketing 3. Secret's Out 5. Emerging Culture 16. New Hucksterism 21. Tapping the Three Kids' Markets 22. Culture Shock 28. Making Old Brands New 32. Stores That Cross Class Lines 35. Nostalgia Boom 38. Global Advertising and the World Wide Web ⊙ *1, 5, 17, 19, 26*	**Distribution Planning and Strategies**	4. Envisioning Greenfield Markets 24. Joy of Shopping 26. Discovering New Points of Differentiation 32. Stores That Cross Class Lines 33. Value Retailers Go Dollar for Dollar 34. Retailers with a Future ⊙ *13, 14, 15*
Brands and Branding	3. Secret's Out 8. Customer Loyalty 17. Metaphor Marketing 21. Tapping the Three Kids' Markets 27. What's in a Brand? 28. Making Old Brands New 33. Value Retailers Go Dollar for Dollar 35. Nostalgia Boom 40. Are You Smart Enough to Sell Globally? ⊙ *5, 21, 23*	**Economic Environment**	2. Everything New Is Old Again 5. Emerging Culture 11. Wrap Your Organization around Each Customer 14. Service Is Everybody's Business 33. Value Retailers Go Dollar for Dollar 38. Global Advertising and the World Wide Web ⊙ *7, 28, 29, 32, 33*
Competition	3. Secret's Out 10. Customer Intimacy 11. Wrap Your Organization around Each Customer 15. Whatever It Takes 18. Finding Unspoken Reasons for Consumers' Choices 25. Very Model of a Modern Marketing Plan 26. Discovering New Points of Differentiation 29. Built to Last 30. Taking Guesswork Out of Pricing 34. Retailers with a Future ⊙ *2, 22, 23, 24, 25*	**Exporting**	39. So You Think the World Is Your Oyster ⊙ *27, 28, 32*
		Focus Group	18. Finding Unspoken Reasons for Consumer's Choices 19. New Market Research 40. Are You Smart Enough to Sell Globally? ⊙ *11, 12, 13, 14, 15, 16, 17, 18, 29*
		Franchising	14. Service Is Everybody's Business 26. Discovering New Points of Differentiation 40. Are You Smart Enough to Sell Globally? ⊙ *1, 2, 26, 29*
Consumer Demographics/ Consumer Behavior	1. Future of Marketing 5. Emerging Culture 8. Customer Loyalty 11. Wrap Your Organization around Each Customer 12. Innovative Service 17. Metaphor Marketing 18. Finding Unspoken Reasons for Consumers' Choices 19. New Market Research 20. Beginner's Guide to Demographics 21. Tapping the Three Kids' Markets 22. Culture Shock 23. What Your Customers Can't Say 24. Joy of Shopping 27. What's in a Brand? ⊙ *1, 3, 12, 15, 16, 17, 18*	**Global Markets**	1. Future of Marketing 4. Envisioning Greenfield Markets 5. Emerging Culture 22. Culture Shock 26. Discovering New Points of Differentiation 29. Built to Last 38. Global Advertising and the World Wide Web 39. So You Think the World Is Your Oyster 40. Are You Smart Enough to Sell Globally? 41. Writing for a Global Audience on the Web ⊙ *6, 8, 11, 18, 26, 28, 29, 30, 31, 32, 33*
		Innovation	2. Everthing New Is Old Again 12. Innovative Service 13. How You Can Help Them 16. New Hucksterism 29. Built to Last ⊙ *1, 6, 8, 9, 23, 25*

1

⦿ Annual Editions: Marketing

The following World Wide Web sites have been carefully researched and selected to support the articles found in this reader. If you are interested in learning more about specific topics found in this book, these Web sites are a good place to start. The sites are cross-referenced by number and appear in the topic guide on the previous two pages. Also, you can link to these Web sites through our DUSHKIN ONLINE support site at *http://www.dushkin.com/online/*.

The following sites were available at the time of publication. Visit our Web site—we update DUSHKIN ONLINE regularly to reflect any changes.

General Sources

1. Krislyn's Favorite Advertising & Marketing Sites
http://www.krislyn.com/sites/adv.htm
This is a most complete list of sites, including information on marketing research, marketing on the Internet, demographic sources, and organizations and associations.

2. Retail Learning Initiative
http://www.cate.ryerson.ca/~csca/rli_link.htm
This series of small business and retail marketing links from Canada connects to many more business links in the United States and to workshops and dialogue forums.

3. STAT-USA/Internet Site Economic, Trade, Business Information
http://www.stat-usa.gov/
This site from the U.S. Department of Commerce contains Daily Economic News, Frequently Requested Statistical Releases, Information on Export and International Trade, Domestic Economic News and Statistical Series, and Databases.

Marketing in the 1990s and Beyond

4. American Marketing Association Code of Ethics
http://ama.org/about/ama/ethcode.htm
At this site you will find the American Marketing Association's Code of Ethics for Marketing on the Internet, and also will be able to link to the Association itself.

5. Energize Your Brand
http://newmedia.com/newmedia/97/07/fea/Energize_Your_Brand.html
This article, from the June 2, 1997, issue of *New Media, The Magazine for Creators of the Digital Future*, is written by Peter Jerram, who says that the Web is breathing new life into product branding. He goes on to discuss how.

6. "Envisioning Tomorrow's Business World Today"
http://www.cba.neu.edu/alumni/m-article29.html
In this article, the author takes advantage of the work of The World Future Society to discuss what the future will hold for business in the next century.

7. "Marketing in the Service Sector Key to Success"
http://www.cba.neu.edu/alumni/m-article17.html
Here is a professor's discussion of the major role that the service sector plays in the U.S. economy and the importance of marketing to the success of small business, often the provider of such services.

8. Melnet/A World Class Business Network
http://www.bradford.ac.uk/acad/mancen/melnet/index.html
Melnet functions as a cooperative for those businesses that are looking to improve their business thinking through the exchange of know-how. One subject the network covers at

this site is the importance of branding. The site also includes the top 10 momentous questions for turn-of-the-century organizations to consider.

9. "New Century Will Bring with It New Challenges"
http://www.cba.neu.edu/alumni/m-article20.html
This discussion of the challenges that the new century will bring to business, especially small business, provides interesting reading about the importance of market research, among other factors, to success.

10. "Small Companies Face Off against Ethical Dilemmas"
http://www.cba.neu.edu/alumni/m-article13.html
The importance of business ethics in the absence of any simple, universally applicable formula for solving ethical problems is discussed in this article. Unethical choices can lead to a company's quick demise.

Research, Markets, and Consumer Behavior

11. CyberAtlas Demographics
http://www.cyberatlas.com/market/demographics/index.html
The Baruch College–Harris Poll commissioned by *Business Week* is used at this site to show interested businesses who is on the Net in the United States. Statistics for other countries can be found by clicking on Geographics.

12. General Social Survey
http://www.icpsr.umich.edu/GSS/
The GSS (see DPLS Archive: *http://DPLS.DACC.WISC.EDU/SAF/*) is an almost annual personal interview survey of U.S. households that began in 1972. More than 35,000 respondents have answered 2,500 questions. It covers a broad range, much of which relates to microeconomic issues.

13. "Identifying Your Appropriate Market Opportunity"
http://www.cba.neu.edu/alumni/m-article21.html
The importance of identifying a proper marketing opportunity or niche is the subject of this article, which also includes a few basic rules for small business entrepreneurs.

14. "Market Research Essential in Determining Firm's Viability"
http://www.cba.neu.edu/alumni/m-article3.html
This article outlines how to obtain market information from government, educational, financial, and other sources.

15. Marketing Tools Directory
http://www.marketingtools.com/directory/
Maritz Marketing Research Inc. (MMRI) specializes in custom-designed research studies that link the consumer to the marketer through information. At this spot on their Web site they offer a Marketing Tools Directory, a comprehensive guide to resources for finding, reaching, and keeping customers. Sections include Demographics, Direct Marketing, Ethnic Marketing, Market Research, and more.

16. U.S. Census Bureau Home Page

http://www.census.gov/

This is a major source of social, demographic, and economic information, such as income/employment data and latest indicators, income distribution, and poverty data.

17. USADATA

http://www.usadata.com/usadata/index.htm

This leading provider of marketing, company, advertising, and consumer behavior data offers national and local data covering the top 60 U.S. markets.

18. WWW Virtual Library: Demography & Population Studies

http://coombs.anu.edu.au/ResFacilities/ DemographyPage.html

Over 150 links can be found at this major resource to keep track of information of value to researchers in the fields of demography and population studies.

Developing and Implementing Marketing Strategies

19. "Advertising Plays Critical Role in Firm's Success"

http://www.cba.neu.edu/alumni/m-article32.html

The importance of advertising to a company's success is explored in this short article, which details the importance of advertising but claims that it is not a panacea.

20. American Marketing Association Homepage

http://www.ama.org/

This site of the American Marketing Association is geared to managers, educators, researchers, students, and global electronic members. It contains a search mechanism, definitions of marketing and market research, and links.

21. Hunt Out the Corporate Inertias That Cause Brand Proliferation

http://www.bradford.ac.uk/acad/mancen/melnet/lj2_9/ e2_9_2.html

This article is adapted from an article by Chris Macrae. It warns against overbranding and umbrella branding.

22. "Marketing Paramount to Company's Success"

http://www.cba.neu.edu/alumni/m-article2.html

A failure to market a company's goods or services effectively is the reason why more than 60 percent of all new businesses fail in their first 5 years of operation. The author explains the importance of marketing and how to get help with it with little or no out-of-pocket expense.

23. Product Branding, Packaging, and Pricing

http://www.fooddude.com/branding.html

Put forward by fooddude.com, the information at this site is presented in a lively manner. It discusses positioning, branding, pricing, and packaging in the specialty food market, but applies to many other retail products as well.

24. "Proper Pricing Plan Is Essential to Company's Success"

http://www.cba.neu.edu/alumni/m-article19.html

The most important element of an effective marketing plan is pricing. The author explores the issue in this article.

25. Welcome to CRUSH

http://www.rtks.com/

This site presents an overview of Real Time Knowledge Systems and its product, CRUSH, a multimedia application for gathering, structuring, analyzing, and presenting competitive information that will help users create winning strategies. Marketing case studies are included.

Global Marketing

26. Asian Advertising & Marketing

http://www.asianad.com/about/index.html

This is the Internet presence of A & M, the leading source of professional information for Asian marketing and advertising.

27. Chamber of Commerce World Network

http://www.worldchambers.net/

International trade at work is viewable at this site. For example, click on Global Business eXchange (GBX) for a list of active business opportunities worldwide or to submit your new business opportunity for validation.

28. CIBERWeb

http://ciber.centers.purdue.edu/

The Centers for International Business Education and Research were created by the U.S. Omnibus Trade and Competitiveness Act of 1988. Together the 26 resulting CIBER sites in the United States are a powerful network focused on helping U.S. business succeed in global markets. Many marketing links can be found at this site.

29. Emerging Markets Resources

http://www.cob.ohio-state.edu/ciberweb/International/ Emergingmarkets/emerging.htm

This excellent source provides resources about the emerging economies, sorted in two ways: general resources and country-by-country resources.

30. International Business Resources on the WWW

http://ciber.bus.msu.edu/busres.htm

This Web site includes a large index of international business resources. Through *http://ciber.bus.msu.edu/ginlist/* you can also access the Global Interact Network Mailing LIST (GINLIST), which brings together, electronically, business educators and practitioners with international business interests.

31. International Trade Administration

http://www.ita.doc.gov/

The U.S. Department of Commerce is dedicated to helping U.S. businesses compete in the global marketplace, and at this site it offers assistance through many Web links under such headings as Trade Statistics, Cross-Cutting Programs, Regions and Countries, and Import Administration.

32. Seven Steps to Exporting

http://www.city.kitchener.on.ca/Kitchener_import_export. html

From the city of Kitchener's Business Self-Help Office comes this page containing seven steps to exporting, an export marketing plan, and an export market analysis checklist.

33. World Trade Center Association On Line

http://iserve.wtca.org/

Data on world trade is available at this site that features information, services, a virtual trade fair, an exporter's encyclopedia, trade opportunities, and a resource center.

We highly recommend that you review our Web site for expanded information and our other product lines. We are continually updating and adding links to our Web site in order to offer you the most usable and useful information that will support and expand the value of your Annual Editions. You can reach us at: *http://www.dushkin. com/annualeditions/.*

www.dushkin.com/online/

Industry/Company Guide

This guide was prepared to provide an easy index to the many industries and companies discussed in detail in the selections included in *Annual Editions: Marketing 99/00*. It should prove useful when researching specific interests.

INDUSTRIES

Unit Selections

Key Points to Consider

❖Dramatic changes are occurring in the marketing of products and services. What social and economic trends do you believe are most significant today, and how do you think these will affect marketing in the future?

❖Theodore Levitt suggests that as times change the marketing concept must be reinterpreted. Given the varied perspectives of the other articles in this unit, what do you think this reinterpretation will entail?

❖The article "The New Hucksterism" reflects how stealth advertising is creeping into a culture saturated with logos and pitches. Are the forms of advertising in this article problematic? Why or why not?

❖In the present competitive business arena, is it possible for marketers to behave ethically in the environment and both survive and prosper? What suggestions can you give that could be incorporated into the marketing strategy for firms that want to be both ethical and successful?

DUSHKINONLINE Links   www.dushkin.com/online/

4. **American Marketing Association Code of Ethics**
   http://ama.org/about/ama/ethcode.htm
5. **Energize Your Brand**
   http://newmedia.com/newmedia/97/07/fea/Energize_Your_Brand.html
6. **"Envisioning Tomorrow's Business World Today"**
   http://www.cba.neu.edu/alumni/m-article29.html
7. **"Marketing in the Service Sector Key to Success"**
   http://www.cba.neu.edu/alumni/m-article17.html
8. **Melnet/A World Class Business Network**
   http://www.bradford.ac.uk/acad/mancen/melnet/index.html
9. **"New Century Will Bring with It New Challenges"**
   http://www.cba.neu.edu/alumni/m-article20.html
10. **"Small Companies Face Off against Ethical Dilemmas"**
    http://www.cba.neu.edu/alumni/m-article13.html

These sites are annotated on pages 4 and 5.

If we want to know what a business is we must start with its purpose. . . . There is only one valid definition of business purpose: to create a customer. What business thinks it produces is not of first importance—especially not to the future of the business or to its success. What the customer thinks he is buying, what he considers "value" is decisive—it determines what a business is, what it produces, and whether it will prosper.

—Peter Drucker, *The Practice of Management*

When Peter Drucker penned these words in 1954, American industry was just awakening to the realization that marketing would play an important role in the future success of businesses. The ensuing years have seen an increasing number of firms in highly competitive areas—particularly in the consumer goods industry—adopt a more sophisticated customer orientation and an integrated marketing focus.

The dramatic economic and social changes of the last decade have stirred companies in an even broader range of industries—from banking and air travel to communications—to the realization that marketing will provide them with their cutting edge. Demographic and lifestyle changes have splintered mass, homogeneous markets into many markets, each with different needs and interests. Deregulation has made once-protected industries vulnerable to the vagaries of competition. Vast and rapid technological changes are making an increasing number of products and services obsolete. Intense international competition and the growth of truly global markets have caused many firms to look well beyond their national boundaries.

Indeed, it appears that during the 1990s marketing will take on a new significance—and not just within the industrial sector. Social institutions of all kinds, which had thought themselves exempt from the pressures of the marketplace, are also beginning to recognize the need for marketing in the management of their affairs. Colleges and universities, charities, museums, symphony orchestras, and even hospitals are beginning to give attention to the marketing concept—to provide what the consumer wants to buy.

The selections in this unit are grouped into four areas. Their purposes are to provide current perspectives on marketing, discuss differing views of the marketing concept, analyze the use of marketing by social institutions and nonprofit organizations, and examine the ethical and social responsibilities of marketing.

The first subsection article reflects the importance of positioning the Internet as a significant influence in the future of marketing. The next five articles provide significant clues about salient approaches and issues that marketers in the decade ahead need to address in order to reach, promote, and sell their products in ways that meet the product and service expectations of consumers.

The five selections that address the marketing concept include Theodore Levitt's now classic "Marketing Myopia," which first appeared in the *Harvard Business Review* in 1960. This version includes the author's retrospective commentary, written in 1975, in which he discusses how shortsightedness can make management unable to recognize that there is no such thing as a growth industry. The next three articles cover the importance of differentiating between customer satisfaction and customer loyalty. The essay "Wrap Your Organization around Each Customer" conveys that successful marketers will focus on the needs of individual consumers.

In the *Services and Social Marketing* subsection, the three subsection articles describe how quality products and exemplary service will be the essential determinants for business survival in the future.

In the final subsection, a careful look is taken at the strategic process and practice of incorporating ethics and social responsibility into the marketplace. In "Whatever It Takes," Michele Marchetti sadly reveals that in the battle to win sales in today's marketplace, ethical behavior is often the first casualty. Then, the article "The New Hucksterism" reveals some subtle and controversial ways in which advertising has been woven into our culture.

Marketing in the 1990s and Beyond

The Future of Marketing

WHAT EVERY MARKETER SHOULD KNOW ABOUT BEING ONLINE

Address by BOB WEHLING, *Senior Vice President Advertising, The Proctor & Gamble Company*
Delivered to the World Federation of Advertisers, Sydney, Australia, October 31, 1995

Over the next half hour or so, we're going to have some fun. We're going to take a test drive—at warp speed—down the information superhighway.

Our destination is the future: the future of marketing, actually, a future where smart marketers will be surfing across the internet into the homes of billions of consumers in hundreds of countries, at the speed of light.

We'll be driving by the virtual storefronts of companies that are already creating this future. Pay attention. Because when our trip is finished, you'll be ready for more than a test drive. You'll be ready to get wired into this exciting future yourself. I know, because that's exactly what happened to me—and to a lot of us at Procter & Gamble—after we took this trip.

Preparing for the New Media Future

Before we get started, let me give you just a little background.

There's been a lot of hype about the Information Superhighway for several years now. P&G got into the fray a year and a half ago when our chairman, Ed Artzt, gave a watershed speech to the American Association of Advertising Agencies.

Here's a brief clip that captures the essence of what he had to say.

"From where we stand today, we can't be sure that ad-supported TV programming will have a future in the world being created—a world of video-on-demand, pay-per-view, and subscription television.

If that happens, if advertising is no longer needed to pay most of the cost of home entertainment, then advertisers like us will have a hard time achieving the reach and frequency we need to support our brands."

That talk created quite a stir. Dick Hopple at DMB&B called it "a seminal speech for the industry." Advertising Age, the New York Times, the Wall Street Journal, and the Financial Times all covered the talk extensively. It was truly a wake-up call that got the industry moving.

The first thing that happened was the creation of CASIE, an industry coalition led by senior advertiser and agency executives from the Four A's and the Association of National Advertisers.

They got to work in several areas. They kicked off a legislative and regulatory game plan both to protect ad-supported broad-reach television and to ensure advertiser access to new media.

They started work to establish common technical standards for new media. The lack of standards is one of the biggest barriers to advertiser participation in new media. Currently, applications developed for one new media provider cannot be used on another, without the advertiser incurring significant reauthoring costs.

But, perhaps most important, they did an inventory of new media research, looking at which new media technologies were closest to commercialization and how their emergence would likely affect consumer behavior.

The Future of Marketing

The most valuable learning that has come from this research is that the technologies that had seemed most imminent when Ed gave his speech—interactive TV, pay-per-view movies, video game channels—are being eclipsed by computer-based media.

This has happened principally because the economics of building and operating interactive TV systems are out of line with what consumers will pay. And furthermore, while only a few thousand households currently have access to interactive TV, more than 20 million people are on the internet today—and that number is growing fast.

As a result, the internet is now positioned to influence the future of marketing as much as—and maybe even more than—any other medium we've ever known.

From *Vital Speeches of the Day*, January 1, 1996, pp. 170–173. © 1996 by City Publishing Company, Inc. Reprinted by permission.

The internet originated in the early '70s as a network to connect university, military and defense contractors. It was an information sharing tool that was never intended for broad public use. But throughout the '70s, as its capabilities were expanded, the network grew.

Then, in 1993, two things happened that dramatically accelerated the net's growth. First, the World Wide Web was created. The Web is the graphical portion of the internet. And, at about the same time, the first, easy-to-use navigation tools were developed. Together, these two breakthroughs turned the internet—or, more specifically, the Web—into a medium that consumers were attracted to and could find their way around.

As a result, the Web has grown—and continues to grow—at extraordinary rates. The number of web sites is doubling every 53 days—that's growth of about 50% per month. Today, millions of consumers are "surfing" the net through online commercial services, like America Online and Prodigy, and through direct connections with navigators such as Netscape.

This is unprecedented. As the Economist pointed out recently, "no communications medium or consumer electronics technology has ever grown as quickly—not the fax machine, not even the PC. At this rate, within two years, the citizens of cyberspace will outnumber all but the largest nations."

What does all this frenetic activity mean for us, as marketers? It means that an entirely new form of marketing—interactive, online marketing—is emerging as a breakthrough way to sell products and services to consumers.

Unprecedented Opportunities for Marketers

There are different types of marketing opportunities online. The most common, on the Web, are corporate sites, or home pages. A home page is a company's online storefront. It's a place where consumers go for product and corporate information. At a minimum, a company's home page can be an extremely effective public relations tool. At its best, a web site captures the personality of the company and presents such useful information and services that consumers not only visit but return again and again.

Another opportunity is "webvertising"—banner ads placed inside editorial or other content in Web-based media. What makes these banner ads so effective is that, by clicking on them, a reader can jump instantly to the marketer's own site.

This is a technology called "hyperlinking." And it works not only for banner ads, but even for straight editorial. For example, the Economist did an article about the internet earlier this year. In the online version of that article, a reader interested in a particular example—say, this reference to Zima beer—could simply click on the word "Zima" and, in an instant, be taken directly to the Zima home page.

No other marketing medium can accomplish this. It elevates the power of right-time marketing to an unparalleled level.

There's one additional marketing niche that's just beginning to evolve on the Web, and that's sponsored programming.

The most common programming right now are celebrity interviews. Oldsmobile, for example, features online discussions with a range of celebrities as a way to attract consumers to its corporate site.

But an even more innovative form of content is the virtual magazine—which, at its best, is far more than an electronic version of a print publication. HotWIRED is a good example. It's a highly-interactive journal of online culture that incorporates banner ads and commercially-supported hyperlinks throughout its editorial. In fact, they reportedly made $2 million in ad revenue last year from these kinds of placements—and you can bet they're just getting started.

As you can see, these are far ranging and very significant new marketing opportunities. Now, to be clear, mass media isn't going away. There will always be a need for the reach and frequency of mass advertising. But online marketing represents the next generation of advertising—and smart marketers are already using it as a powerful new way to create consumer awareness, to stimulate trial, even to sell their products and services.

P&G On the Net

At P&G, we're just getting online. We launched an experimental web site in Germany about five months ago. This site includes information about P&G, it announces employment opportunities and, most important, it contains information about a few of our brands.

For example, consumers can request a handy dispenser for our leading laundry detergent brand, Ariel, and find solutions to common laundry problems. As you can see, this first experiment is pretty basic.

We made our second—and somewhat more sophisticated— venture onto the net just two weeks ago, with our new Word-Slam site tied to the U.S. introduction of Hugo, the new Hugo Boss men's fragrance.

This site is an integral part of our product launch and publicity campaign. The selling line for this new fragrance is, "Don't imitate . . . innovate."

The Hugo page builds on this theme with the first online Spoken Word poetry contest. Spoken Word competitions are a hot trend among Generation Xers and this unique site should attract young "surfers" from around the world. While they're visiting, we'll give them a chance to learn about the new Hugo line of products. We'll invite them to join in online forums and chats with celebrity guests. And we'll provide links to other sites, as well.

We're planning to expand our Web presence over the next several months. One prototype we're experimenting with is for our leading laundry brand in the U.S. We call it the Tide Stain Detective. If you spill red wine on your favorite cotton shirt, you can ask the Tide Stain Detective how to get it out. And he'll give you a fast—and proven—solution. This is the kind of value-added information consumers want, which builds loyalty to our brand.

It's premature for me to talk much more about our plans, but—as we take our test drive into the future—I can tell you some of what we've learned over the past few months while we've prepared to expand our presence on the Web.

So let's get going. We see six core benefits of marketing online.

Instant Access to the World

First, the net is global. It reaches consumers in literally every part of the world. It's hard to get a precise number of users, but we know that there are somewhere between five and six million host computers that provide Web access to at least 20 million consumers in over 100 countries.

The distribution is very uneven—90% of the host computers are in North America and Western Europe—but interest and access is growing around the world.

For example, there are now over 300,000 host computers in Asia/Pacific. In fact, Australia is the third most wired country in the world. In terms of the number of computer hosts per 1,000 people, Australia ranks behind only Finland and the U.S.

In Central and South America, there are only 16,000 hosts—but that's more than double the number that existed just a year ago.

One major restriction to the Web's global growth is language. The net is principally an English-language medium today, which makes it inaccessible to non-English-speaking users. But smart, global marketers like IBM are changing that by providing multi-lingual sites.

IBM offers a unique feature called Planetwide. By clicking on Japan, for example, a user can get information about IBM, its products or its operations in Japan—in Japanese. Or in Italian. Or Spanish.

More than any other I've come across, the IBM site demonstrates conclusively that this is truly a global medium. There is no other medium that enables you not just to reach but to interact with consumers in virtually every country on earth—if you do it right.

And its global reach is not just for the IBMs of the world. Because the price of entry onto the Web is relatively low, a corner flower shop, for example, has the potential to become a global flower powerhouse virtually overnight with the right kind of approach.

Unprecedented Depth of Sale

Second benefit: online marketing is self-selective. You know the consumers who visit your site are interested. They want to know more about your products. Not only does this help identify your highest-potential consumers, it permits a depth of sale that no other medium can provide.

Auto makers have been among the first companies to tap this potential. Virtually every major car company is online today: Ford, General Motors, Toyota, Nissan, Honda, Mitsubishi. They provide a world of information, from a lineup of models to lists of options to comprehensive dealer directories.

But the best among them, from what I've seen, is the Chrysler Technology Center. You can get all kinds of information on Chrysler—the company's environmental record, its financial performance, you can even chat with CEO Bob Eaton.

But most interesting, you can look at cars.

Want to see the cars of the future? Go to the Technology section and look at concept cars. For example, the Plymouth Back Pack—a part utility, part pickup and part sporty coupe that's likely to be a real hit with young buyers.

Or you can go to the showroom and look at the latest cars on the market today. If you're in the market for a Jeep, you've got your choice of three models. Click on the Jeep Grand Cherokee and you can look at the vehicle, pull down specs, compare it feature-by-feature to its main competitors—even read reviews from the auto press.

And that's not all: soon you'll be able to custom price the Jeep of your dreams—or the Chrysler or the Dodge or the Eagle. Choose the features you want and the system will automatically calculate the suggested retail price and even tell you what your monthly payment will be.

Together, these features are the perfect right-time marketing tool: they give you the chance to reach consumers who are interested—when they're interested.

Opportunities to Engage

The third benefit of online marketing is that it is interactive. It enables you to engage consumers in a way that no other medium can. The Chrysler site I just mentioned is one good example. Another is American Express ExpressNet on America Online.

You can apply for a card, check your account status, pull down photos of exciting travel locations, plan a trip and even make reservations. If you're travelling to Asia and want to know what's happening in Beijing this week, you can choose from sports to shopping to restaurants and nightlife. You can order a customized Fodor's travel guide that helps ensure you get to see and do exactly what you want to do no matter where you go.

Whether you're planning a trip or charting your expenses after one, ExpressNet puts you in charge. And reminds you that, no matter where you're going or where you've been, you can always count on American Express.

Fully Integrated Marketing

The fourth benefit is that online marketing is fully integrated. It combines the activities of every marketing discipline, from advertising to PR to direct mail.

Sony, for example, uses its web site to promote new products, from CDs to movies to electronics. It's even being used as a sampling device.

Click on Wiretap and check out the CD from Mariah Carey, one of the biggest recording artists in the U.S. You can even sample the video of her #1 hit, Fantasy.

You can find out where she's touring, enter a contest for a "Fantasy" weekend in New York, or win tickets to her live TV special.

This is truly integrated marketing. There is no other medium in which you can integrate so many different marketing tools at once.

Marketing One-to-One

The fifth benefit of being online is the medium's unique one-to-one marketing capability. This is the most important loyalty-building benefit of online marketing, because it gives you the ability to establish enduring relationships with individual consumers.

McDonald's McFamily, on America Online, is a good example. This site reinforces the idea of McDonald's as a parent's best friend. Parents can get information on the latest Happy Meal or nutritional information about McDonald's products.

But even more valuable is the community McDonald's has created. For not only can parents talk directly to McDonald's, they can also talk with experts and with each other on a whole range of parenting issues—from how to keep the family healthy and safe to how they can spend more quality time with their kids.

McDonald's has proven the benefits of relationship marketing through a number of direct mail programs they've used in recent years. And they believe the interactivity of online marketing will make it even easier to build relationships with consumers. In fact, the level of relationship building they're achieving online would have been almost impossible to create even two or three years ago.

The Virtual Store

Finally, there is one last and very important benefit: you can sell.

A great example of this is right here in Australia—the Flag network of hotels, inns, resorts and apartments. Flag is Australia's largest independent accommodation group with properties in Australia, New Zealand, Papua New Guinea, Fiji, Western Somoa as well as the U.S. and the U.K.

They make it easy to stay at a Flag hotel or inn. A traveler can navigate by map to any of the 450 facilities in the Flag network. If you're on your way to Australia, simply click on the region—say New South Wales—and the city—perhaps Sydney—and you're ready to select your hotel.

You can pull down details and ratings of every Flag hotel in the area and, once you've made a decision, enter your reservation.

Flag will confirm within 24 hours, either by phone or e-mail—whichever you request.

There are other benefits of being online, as well. But these six are the most important, because they demonstrate that everything we do to build consumer loyalty is affected by this new medium: from awareness to trial to purchase and repurchase. It is a major step forward in the evolution of marketing.

Next Steps: Tapping the Net's Potential

The key question, is how do we tap the full potential of this exciting new medium? How do we make it a global bonanza for advertising and a rich source of entertainment, information and community for consumers?

To do this, we have to resolve a number of issues—from the security of online transactions to consumer privacy. But there are a few things, in particular, that I would urge you to focus on most.

Measuring Online Effectiveness

As an industry, we need to establish clear, broadly-accepted standards for measuring the cost effectiveness of the net versus other media.

All the examples I've just shared demonstrate that the Web can be a highly-effective marketing medium. But, for it to become a truly valuable tool for the industry, it must also be highly-efficient. And we need accurate, reliable measures to

gauge that efficiency. CASIE has provided a good starting point. Just a month ago, they presented a set of guiding principles for measurement that I strongly endorse. We have copies of the executive summary in the back, but let me just mention the highlights.

First, audience measurement of interactive media should be directly comparable to the measures used for other media. This is fundamental to the reliability of audience research.

Second, audience measurements should be taken by objective third-party research suppliers and not by the medium being measured. What little measurement there is today rarely follows this principle.

And one more: interactive media research standards must be set by a broad representation of the advertising industry, including advertisers, agencies, media, research companies and industry groups.

In all, CASIE has developed 11 guiding principles. We need to use them to establish clear measurement standards as quickly as possible.

I've been told by some of our agencies that it may take three to five years to iron out the measurement issue. That's too long. We need to do it by next year so we can begin building on and justifying our investments in this new medium.

This is a global issue and it needs broad, global leadership from the advertising industry. So today, I'm calling for the WFA to join forces with CASIE to accelerate the creation and adoption of measurement standards for interactive media.

By this time next year, at the '96 WFA conference, I'd like to see the WFA and CASIE jointly endorse a set of broadly accepted standards that will enable us to measure and compare the effectiveness of interactive media in any part of the world.

Getting Up Close and Personal

In addition to this industry-wide effort, there are a few important things that I encourage you to do as individual advertisers.

First, get up close and personal with the internet.

Any advertising professional who hasn't been online should get online. You simply cannot appreciate the potential of this medium until you've "surfed" it yourself.

In fact, seeing first hand how limited the current online efforts are will convince you that, even if you're not online to-day, you're not that far behind. No one out there—even the best, like those I've mentioned here today—is very far out in front at this point. Now is the time to get online. Not just to catch up but to jump ahead. It's a big opportunity.

Another thing you can do, when you get back home, is to be sure that your governments are not establishing regulations that will inhibit the growth of this medium or advertiser access to it. If that's happening, it is in your interest to try to change it. This is as strategic a public policy issue as any advertiser will face.

Six Questions to Ask Before You Go Online

Now, if you go away from this meeting thinking that Wehling's talk was interesting, but I'm not sure it has anything to do with me, I encourage you to think about it harder. Think about what the Economist said recently: "As a new medium with almost no distribution costs, the internet has the potential to reshape the media world, letting new competitors in and forcing established giants to evolve or die." That's a pretty clear call to action, in my book.

If, on the other hand, you go away from here fired up about the potential of this new medium—convinced that you've seen the future and it works—then I have some parting advice for you.

The key to winning online is content. That's true for any marketing medium, and it is especially true for the internet. And what's important to remember about online content is that it's not just a matter of piping a 30-second ad over the internet or converting printed materials into electronic form. It requires a fundamentally different approach.

My suggestion is to start with the six benefits I listed earlier. They should provide a valuable framework to guide your thinking. Take a look at your marketing messages and at how you're delivering them today. Then ask yourself six questions:

1. How can I make my message global?

2. How can I offer such useful and interesting content that consumers will come back to my site again and again?

3. How can I make it interactive?

4. How can I fully integrate the full range of marketing disciplines into the delivery of my message?

5. How can I make my message more compelling by using the net's one-to-one capability? And,

6. How can I use this technology to sell my products?

I think you'll find that the answers to these questions will provide a creative blueprint as you think about how to tap the full potential of the net.

Find a Way to Get Online

The key is: find a way to get online. Experiment, Learn about it. Get prepared. You may ultimately decide it's not right for your business. But make it an informed decision.

In fact, I echo what the Economist had to say. I believe that—over the long term—marketers who remain unprepared for the sea-change we're about to experience won't survive. Marketers who understand the implications and get ahead of the curve will not only survive, they'll thrive. They'll emerge more competitive than ever and they'll build relationships with consumers that are deeper and more enduring than any we can create today.

The future of marketing is bright and the smartest among us are going to take tremendous advantage of that potential. I encourage you to be among the leaders.

Thanks for the chance to talk with you today. I look forward to seeing you online.

Everything New Is Old Again

With customer-focused innovation, true brilliance radiates

throughout the organization.

by Barton G. Tretheway

EXECUTIVE *BRIEFING*

Yesterday's proven solutions are today's "green's fees," and everyone is once again doing everything the same way. New products and services have been the traditional focus of innovation, but leading organizations are differentiating themselves not only in their product introductions but also in the processes they use to nurture and expand an innovative culture. The most powerful initiatives employ an outside-in-outside process that adds customer value.

The last drops of reengineering are being wrung out of the cost side of the business equation. More and more corporate executives and experts are turning their attention to the demand side of the equation. But as a result of these reengineering efforts, we find ourselves in a much-altered business environment. Organizations are much flatter (an entire level of middle managers no longer exists), leadership is migrating from a control mindset to one of support and sharing, and the 40-hour work week is a fading memory.

Suddenly, time has become the scarce corporate and personal resource. Meeting today's demands with yesterday's solutions is a guaranteed formula for fail-

ure and frustration. To combat these new demands, the emphasis must be on innovation and the ability to tackle problems creatively. Focusing exclusively on new products and services, however, leaves many untapped opportunities. Innovation initiatives can be new processes in manufacturing, warehousing, or distribution; new service or billing paradigms; or new marketing programs. Consider the following examples:

• Chicago's Shedd Aquarium was looking for innovative ways to grow awareness, attendance, and revenues. Officials hit upon the idea of opening their doors for after-hours entertainment and special events. Throughout the last two summers, Shedd has held a jazz concert each Thursday evening, closing three hours later than usual. This has sparked interest among single adults, who now view the events as opportunities to meet people. The success of this innovative program has prompted thoughts of scheduling year-round concerts.

• In 1995, Embassy Suites in Montgomery, Ala., was the first hotel to feature a guest check-in system that

EXHIBIT 1

Innovation pays off

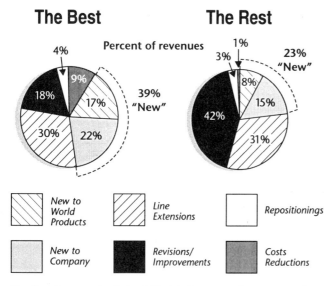

The Best   The Rest

Percent of revenues

New to World Products

Line Extensions

Repositionings

New to Company

Revisions/ Improvements

Costs Reductions

The "best" companies derive 39% of their revenues from new products and services vs. only 23% from the "rest."

Source: Kuczmarski & Associates Inc., Chicago

eliminates the traditional front desk. Four hexagonal podiums, or pods, were installed in the lobby area, incorporating all major functions of a front desk. The pods were designed to facilitate increased interaction between employees and guests and make the check in/out process easier and more personal by eliminating physical barriers. Looking at innovative ways to increase customer satisfaction has made the check-in process more pleasant for hotel guests which, in turn, has helped increase overall customer satisfaction and repeat stays. There are plans to implement a similar pod system in other Embassy Suites.

• The Saturn automobile is an outstanding example of innovation that touched multiple functions within an organization. Not only did GM form a new subsidiary to develop this car, the company also created innovative new technology, manufacturing processes, work force processes, management techniques, and labor-management paradigms. This innovation was spurred by the wide-held belief that the old methods were not working and the time was right for an entirely new approach to manufacturing, selling, and servicing cars. The company's successful results are well documented.

Innovation starts with the individual. It is not a top-down endeavor, but must have the support of senior management and permeate the entire organization. Innovation is a multi-step process and, for it to work, it must be embedded into the organization's culture.

The most powerful innovation initiatives add customer value. It is an outside-in-outside process. Innovation starts with some form of a customer (outside) need. A solution is created (inside) against the need (be it operational, customer service, or a new product) that in some manner adds customer value. Then the solution is rerouted back (outside) to the customer.

Power of Innovation

Innovation is the fuel for organizational growth and survival. The time clock for everything we do in our personal and corporate lives is accelerating at warp speed. To progress demands new thinking in everything we do. Innovation becomes a never-ending quest for new and creative solutions. Although new paradigms usually have the greatest impact, innovation also occurs incrementally, having a cumulative effect over time. The early fax machine was single-copy feed and receive. Later models were multiple-page feed and had the capability to store fax numbers. Today's fax machines are multifunction and go beyond faxing to include copying and scanning features.

Real innovators reinvent themselves or create new markets and industries: Motorola was originally in the car radio business; Boston Chicken is now Boston Market; Apple Computer created a new industry for personal computers in the early '70s; Fidelity Investments redefined the mutual fund and investment business; and Charles Schwab broke new ground in the brokerage business.

Companies like Motorola and 3M are well known for innovation and a willingness to take risks, and the stock market has rewarded them well for their efforts. But, innovation takes on many flavors:

• NationsBank is tailoring technology to meet customer needs and requirements with new service innovations.
• Hershey Foods uses new products as a major growth engine. Management constantly challenges the organization to come up with new products.
• Catalina Marketing focuses on innovative solutions to meet market needs. The firm introduced a new retail phone card that is printed instantly at the retailer's checkout counter.
• Motorola pursues new ventures like Irridium, the global satellite system. Corporate divisions often compete against one another for market supremacy. The organization focuses on customer initiatives and invests heavily in technology.
• Gillette's commitment to research, development, and technical supremacy results in new products that cannibalize current product successes. Risk is encouraged and failure is tolerated; otherwise, market innovation will come from competitors.

A new products and services best practices study we recently completed looked at the results of more than 11,000 new products and services introduced over a five-year time period. Companies were divided into two categories: the "best" and the "rest." Best companies generated nearly twice the proportion of profits from products and services introduced in the past five years, compared with the rest. Additionally, best companies had more than twice as many of those new products still on the market compared to the rest. The study found that companies that continually find new ways to serve the market enjoy better results. The best companies derived 39% of their revenues from new products and services vs. only 23% for the rest (see Exhibit 1).

Another significant finding was that failures are inevitable. The study noted that even the best companies have a 35% failure rate (see Exhibit 2). Tolerating failure and acknowledging that it happens is a very important element in supporting an overall innovation mindset. A national building products company holds semi-annual Failure Parties at which the division head hands out savings bonds to team members who worked on failed projects as a way of acknowledging that growth comes through failure. The message is that taking a risk that doesn't have a successful outcome will not cost you your job.

EXHIBIT 2

Even with successful companies, new product failures are inevitable

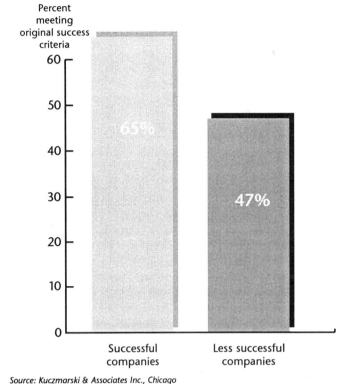

Source: Kuczmarski & Associates Inc., Chicago

Creating Links

Successful innovation depends upon having the right people and a repeatable process that can be embraced and followed throughout the organization. Having an innovation champion is great, but success can't rest on the shoulders of a single individual. Although there is no single, generally accepted innovation process, the model that follows has been successfully applied to numerous organizations. It works because its underlying premise relies on links to the customer and marketplace.

All functional areas of the organization should be part of any innovation initiative.

Forming a cross-functional team to develop the innovation plan sets expectations and builds early buy-in from the entire organization. Keep in mind that, if innovation is to work, it must be embraced by everyone and have solid senior management support and commitment. Once the team has put the innovation plan in place, a steering committee should be established to manage the initiative on an ongoing basis. Someone needs to own (individual or team) innovation within the organization. Having an innovation champion along with a process is a big plus.

Organizational innovation can be described as a six-step program. Vision leads to objectives, which yields to strategy, and that leads to implementation, support and enhancement of the original idea. Innovation does not happen by itself. Yes, pockets of innovation can reside within individuals or groups of individuals, but for it to permeate an organization, a concerted effort must take place.

Innovation can surface in a number of ways. An individual who recognizes the power of innovation might build support for change within the firm; an internal audit of core competencies might flag innovation as a clear weakness; or a major competitor might introduce innovations that revolutionize your industry, producing attrition among your customers. Once support coalesces and senior management makes innovation an organizational initiative, an innovation team needs to be formed. It should be cross-functional in nature, with representatives from each major function of the organization. This team must not be a dumping ground for managers with time on their hands. Ideal team members should be respected and recognized leaders within their functional areas. A players produce A results; B players produce B results at best. With a process in hand, the team needs to develop preliminary goals and secure senior management commitment and sponsorship to move forward.

Step 1: Vision

As with any organizational initiative, the first step to successful execution is to articulate the vision and objectives for what the organization wants to accomplish. Innovation is no exception. The vision sets the tone for what the organization wants to become. It explains how innovation will be used as a catalyst. It should crystallize the desired image the organization wants to project. Importantly, the innovation vision links to and supports the overall corporate vision. Innovation vision elements should include sources for competitive advantage (determined by assessing internal strengths/weaknesses and external interviews that identify customer benefits only your organization can provide) and general areas for innovation focus (specific focus areas will be determined as the organization sets innovation objectives).

The following vision statement from a consumer packaged-goods company incorporates many of these elements: "The (Division) will be a leader in simple solutions that help food taste better by delighting consumers with innovative programs and new products that represent an integral part of the meal occasion. We will drive innovation-centered change by embracing the different perspectives of all our colleagues, knowing where our consumers are going and in some cases leading them there. Using tools of innovation we will anticipate, focus on, and solve key consumer problems as they arise in a Division-wide environment of shared accountability."

> Primary screens are "must pass," secondary screens are "nice to have."

The innovation vision is a good work-in-progress to share with the entire organization. This starts to alert employees that the value of innovation is recognized and it will be given priority within the organization.

Step 2: Objectives

Before setting innovation objectives it is worthwhile to conduct an innovation audit. This is an analytical tool aimed at improving future innovation efforts. It identifies strengths and weaknesses of past innovation efforts. It guides innovation by allowing the innovation team to build on strengths and learn from past efforts. Audits include financial analysis as well as management reviews.

For example, results from a recent audit found one organization lacked a long-term innovation focus and had no funding for innovation efforts. Additionally,

the cost of failure was perceived as too high, there was not enough idea time, the physical environment did not encourage innovation, there was *little account of the customer* and a *noticeable lack of any kind of growth*. It is important not to position audit efforts as a finger pointing exercise but as an opportunity to grow from lessons learned.

Innovation objectives are manifold. They define the purpose innovation should serve within the organization. Both strategic as well as financial objectives are important. The key is to let customers drive innovation as much as possible. What have your customers said about various aspects of the business? Are they happy with customer service? Is there a more creative way to serve them? Do customers continually complain about billing procedures? Is there an innovative approach to enhance the connection with customers? What creative ways can enhance processes? Remember, not all customers are outside the organization; do not forget to respond to internal customers. Financial objectives might include innovative means to cut transportation costs or a new way to manufacture or track product production.

A good way to assess innovation focus is to look at the organization's value chain. A typical value chain for a packaged-good-manufacturer might look like this: Raw materials, production, fixed overhead, product, packaging, warehousing, distribution, retailer/trade, marketing, and sales. Closely examine each link in the chain. Where do the opportunities lie to focus innovation efforts?

Inherent in this process are innovation roles. What role does the organization want innovation to take? Possible roles include:

- Position the organization as leading edge in its market.
- Support a risk-free environment that encourages all employees to seek the next paradigm.
- Increase process effectiveness.
- Reduce trade allowances.
- Identify new innovative productivity opportunities.
- Be first to market with new products.
- Consider new procedures that benefit both internal and external customers.
- Drive revenue growth through new products and services.
- Optimize processes, shorten cycle times.

At some point, hopefully there will be more innovation initiatives on the table than the organization is able to digest. A method of prioritization is in order. Prioritization links back to the roles innovation has been assigned along with any innovation screens that are developed. These innovation screens are a series of minimal thresholds that all innovation initiatives have to pass through to be considered for activation. Screens help the organization increase its likelihood

The Innovation Quiz

How innovative is your company? Here's a self-examination to put organizational innovation in perspective. Score 10 points for each statement you completely agree with and 5 points for those that are partially true.

1. Innovation and creativity are part of everyday conversation.
2. There is an organizational process for innovation.
3. Risk-taking is seen as a positive individual/team/organization attribute.
4. The organization recognizes yesterday's solutions will not fuel future growth.

5. Customers and customer considerations are a key link in innovation endeavors.
6. "Free thinking" is encouraged to explore new ideas and solutions.
7. Employees take time individually and in teams to have fun.
8. Information is shared freely across the organization.
9. Cross-functional teams are recognized for their power to come up with innovative solutions.
10. Senior management recognizes the power of innovation and the positive effect it can have on all stakeholders.

Scorecard:

75+, Awesome. Your organization has a strong, supportive, innovative mindset. This atmosphere should allow you to accomplish great things.

50–74, All Right. Your organization knows about innovation, but still has some work to do to make it a reality.

49 or less, Awful. Your organization does not recognize the power of innovation. Are you sure this is a place you want to work?

—*Barton G. Tretheway*

---

of success by focusing energy, efforts, and resources on those initiatives that represent the highest potential returns and the greatest impact on an organization. At the same time, screening criteria help to filter out less attractive initiatives.

Screens usually come in two flavors: primary and secondary. Primary screens are "must pass," secondary screens are "nice to have." Primary screens might include minimum revenue and/or profit thresholds and desired impact on the customer. Secondary examples might include fit with innovation roles, amount of investment/resources required, and expected return from initiative (either strategic or financial). Determining primary and secondary screens is purely subjective, organizationally specific, and should link to ensuring that innovation roles are met.

Step 3: Strategy

Innovation strategies are the pathway to meeting innovation objectives. There will most likely be a set of strategies to accomplish each objective. Think of strategies as the outline of direction to accomplish objectives. For example, if the goal is to get from Chicago to San Francisco, the objective might be to get there by Saturday and spend no more than $500. The strategy for accomplishing this could be to drive and take a companion, with the tactic being to leave on Wednesday at 6 a.m., take your car, drive Interstate 80 to Salt Lake City, stop for dinner, and so on.

Strategies often offer the most opportunity for creative thinking. This is where the individual or team should push to think "out of the box" and develop new paradigms. This can be accomplished through a variety of means:

- Mine good ideas with the bad ones, then edit.

- Start with a problem statement.
- Accept failure.
- Expose yourself to a wide range of perspectives.
- Work in diverse teams; hire opposites.
- Get out of the office.
- Don't create new ideas, create new solutions to old problems.
- Approach the situation as a first-time user.
- Look at substitutes and what others are doing.
- Aim for quantity, then pare down.
- Forbid negativism during ideation.
- Drive to actionable solutions.

Step 4: Implementation

Once innovation strategies have been set, the next step is to develop specific implementation and support plans. These plans include roles, responsibilities, timing, and resource requirements needed to execute the strategies. This is a very critical juncture in the process and where most innovation plans fall by the wayside. The plan may be the best ever written, but people and organizational structure often are obstacles to implementation.

The key to success is to get buy-in from the entire organization prior to implementation. This takes time; 12–18 months is not uncommon. Implementing new ways of doing business requires multiple and ongoing individual and team meetings. Securing cross functional agreement now, building consensus, and shaping expectations are important. To most managers, knowing their responsibilities in making innovation happen will be just as important as knowing what they can expect to get from it.

Step 5: Support

Few initiatives, innovation included, will succeed without proper support. Support takes two forms. The first is organizational support. This is a relatively quick fix once the issues are identified. Does the organizational structure support innovation? Areas to examine include: communication channels, team resources, reporting relationships, team empowerment, rewards, commitment, project ownership, risk tolerance, organizational framework, and infrastructure.

The second and more challenging requirement is cultural support. Does the organization have the values and norms in place that support innovation? Establishing innovation values and norms enables employees and teams to create a mutually satisfying environment in which to work. Values are shared goals, beliefs and ideals that evoke one's inner convictions. Norms are employee- and team-decided codes of conduct. They are a standard to grade and shape group behavior.

The types of shared values that need to be engendered in the organization's culture will vary, but to illustrate, consider the following:

- Stress innovation and creativity in all we do.
- It's OK to fail.
- Confrontation can be good; issues and problems are resolvable.
- Foster trust and openness with one another.
- Encourage open and direct communication.
- Don't settle for the status quo.

Likewise, common norms and operating behaviors need to be established in the group. Examples include:

- Work only on those activities that add customer value.
- Allocate/dedicate resources to innovation.
- Demonstrate, embrace, and encourage diverging and converging conversation.
- Proper up-front planning should limit crises.
- Realize it's OK to say, "I don't know."
- Celebrate milestones regularly.
- Have fun!
- Walk the talk.

Besides establishing a culture that supports innovation, rewards and compensation plans are key success factors in garnering employee support and buy-in. These rewards fall into two buckets: monetary and motivational. These can be either individual or team based. Monetary rewards include savings bonds, performance bonuses, long-term financial bonus, phantom stock tied to the innovation effort, stock/ownership options. Motivational rewards include peer recognition luncheons, dinners, and breakfasts; senior management recognition such as "gold stars" and pats-on-the-back; paid vacation days; increased budget authority; and educational opportunities. Rewards do not necessarily cost the organization money. When was the last time you sent a note to a colleague telling her what a great job she was doing?

It's been said a fun organization is more likely to be an innovative organization. The atmosphere is open, people support one another, risk-taking is OK, trying something new is encouraged. Developing innovation activators can elevate the success of innovation efforts. Make sure "fun" is mixed in with your efforts. T-shirts, hats, pins, and banners can add some excitement.

Step 6: Enhancement

Once innovation is implemented, there is a need to monitor progress against stated goals and objectives. What is working? What is not working? What can be done to improve innovation efforts?

In the early stages of implementation, innovation efforts must be closely monitored. It is important to begin on a positive note. After the first few months, monitoring and reporting can be spaced to coincide with the organization's review time frame.

The innovation team sets up a tracking matrix based on goals, objectives, and the implementation plan. Those inputs should provide suitable metrics to track innovation progress. Metrics might include number of innovation initiatives in the pipeline, innovation success rate, innovation survival rate, return on innovation, and customer value. Finally, there are the softer issues to monitor. Does the culture and mindset of managers and employees support innovation? Do managers allow employees time to innovate? These can be monitored in interviews and roundtables. Monitoring and tracking these goals will allow for enhancement of innovation efforts. If goals are not met, the causes must be examined and a plan developed to address the situation. Instilling innovation within an organization is not easy. Mistakes will be made, but improvement comes by learning from mistakes.

The innovation team should hold regular meetings to review progress and track success and take any corrective steps. The team should get on senior management's agenda for periodic updates on innovation efforts and success.

After executing the six-step innovation process, it is helpful to develop an overall innovation-plan summary. This brief document serves as the roadmap to innovation success and captures all the important elements of the plan. It also serves as an easy reference for managers and senior managers.

This summary plan should outline the innovation vision; goals and objectives, with revenue and profit targets and strategic targets; roles and screens; priorities for initiatives and opportunities. A useful addendum is the innovation implementation plan worksheet, which details each innovation initiative and the steps to its accomplishment. There should be one sheet for each initiative.

Overcoming Barriers

Innovation does not happen overnight. It is a mindset that must be embraced by and permeate the entire organization. This takes time and a plan. Barriers to innovation usually fall into three general categories: people, time, and resources. Typical "barriers to innovation" comments are:

- "Our challenge is to keep innovation top of mind."
- "We have no time to innovate, we are too focused on the 'now.' "
- "How do we know if we are innovative?"
- "We have no senior management support for innovation."
- "There is no incentive to take risks with new ideas."
- "How do you teach an old dog new tricks?"

Barriers can surface anytime. The first step in eliminating these barriers is to identify, recognize, and be prepared for them as they occur. This can be done through interviews, surveys, and roundtables. Talk about the benefits of innovation and share the company's innovation plan. Get employees to articulate innovation opportunities and how they might play a role. Ask employees what innovation barriers they see.

Next, categorize the barriers (organizational, personal, resources, and so on) and brainstorm tactics to overcome them. The best barrier busters are those that prevent them from being erected in the first place. All too often that is not the case as most organizations prefer the status quo. Successfully instilling an innovation mindset within the organization requires a broad communication of the innovation plan and senior management's support. This support should be observable in management's day to day actions.

Sustaining innovation enthusiasm requires communication. Simple techniques such as an innovation room, innovation walls, innovation breakfasts, idea banks, printed post-its, banners, company newsletter articles, screen-saver messages, e-mail reminders, and celebrations of both successes and failures help. Allowing risk taking is an example of maintaining innovation momentum.

Innovation Best Practices

- Senior management commitment.
- Consistent funding.
- Motivation and rewards.
- Cross-functional teams.
- Dedicated resources.
- Return on innovation measures.
- Customer value-added.
- Systematic processes.
- Innovation goals, objectives, and strategies.
- Innovation roles and screens.

Keep the Spirit Alive

The best way to keep innovation alive is to have a few orchestrated quick hits. Build enthusiasm early and make sure the entire organization knows the results. A national testing service holds monthly innovation breakfasts to discuss and celebrate activities. Their first innovation success was widely communicated to all employees. A Midwest telecommunications company periodically includes new product successes in their daily newspaper.

There is great value in keeping the innovation team alive once the initial process has been completed. Innovation needs to be kept top of mind, strategies have to be monitored and enhanced, priorities set, etc. Continuity of team members is a big plus. If members self-select to "move on," keeping one or two original team members will work. The worst scenario is to form a new team to support ongoing innovation efforts. These new members will have little link or ownership to the work just completed and may in fact start second-guessing decisions.

Senior management support cannot be understated. Reinforcement tools senior managers can use include sending memos and articles to managers on the importance of innovation on a periodic basis, scheduling time to meet with innovation teams, sending out congratulatory letters to team members, avoiding cutting innovation budgets, putting in a system of innovation rewards and compensation, and establishing career paths for those working on innovation efforts.

Senior managers and forward-thinking organizations see innovation as a key corporate strategy. They recognize the value innovation can bring to the table. How long will we have to wait for our first CIO (chief innovation officer) at a major organization? The Bank of Montreal now has a senior manager of creativity and innovation. In Canada, Manitoba tracks innovation province-wide because officials believe that innovative new products and processes are critical in the global, knowledge-based economy that is emerging.

In 1993, Taco Bell nearly tripled profits from the previous five years by redefining itself. Instead of being a company that produced Mexican food, it became a service organization that retails meals and snacks. Kitchens were consolidated to central facilities around the country and an internal software program, dubbed TACO, was developed to process regional data at headquarters every night, leveraging downtime and saving on computing expenses.

Developing a personal innovation contract is a good method to get employees to take personal ownership of innovation. Ask employees what they are willing to commit to making themselves and the organization more innovative: People and organizations who are serious about innovation can make great things happen.

Additional Reading

Kuczmarski, Thomas D. (1996). *Innovation*. Chicago: American Marketing Association and NTC Business Books.

"Winning New Product and Service Practices for the 1990s," a study conducted and published by Kuczmarski & Associates, Chicago.

About the Author

Barton G. Tretheway is a Principal and Managing Director of Kuczmarski & Associates, Chicago. His areas of expertise include innovation, marketing strategies, and growth planning. Barton leads the firm's K&A Skills Transfer training practice (KAST), which focuses on experientially transferring skills in functional and consulting process areas of K&A expertise and experience. Barton also is an Adjunct Professor at Northwestern University's Kellogg Graduate School of Management and has held marketing and merchandising positions at Sears Roebuck & Co., where his duties include buying, merchandising, and marketing in retail and direct response.

the
secret's
OUT

The one marketing rule you absolutely must know for the new millennium

BY JERRY FISHER

WANT TO GROW your small company with the brilliance of a marketer from Mensa? Want a business-building strategy that would have Bill Gates groveling at your feet? Want to pull it off without breaking a sweat or breaking the bank? No problem. Just reach out to your existing customer base—whether that's three customers or 3,000—as *Entrepreneur*'s marketing experts have long recommended. As we begin a new era of more sophisticated company-to-customer interactivity, this approach becomes even more potent as a marketing tool . . . and, we felt, merited a special update to brief you on all the possibilities as we quickly approach the new millennium.

We've all seen and admired examples of marketing genius over the past few decades—like that of Walter E. Diemer, who died recently at age 93 and who sold us on a gooey pink substance called "Double Bubble" chewing gum. And let's not forget whoever talked us into potbellied pigs for pets. But in 2000 and beyond, the golden statuettes for marketing genius will be handed out to entrepreneurs of another sort: those who realize the smartest marketing move is to develop unbreakable relationships with their current customers.

Yes, start-up companies will always need to beat the bushes for new customers. But once you're up and running, selling more goods to fewer people is not only more efficient, it's also far more profitable. Plus, for many companies, old customers are often the best source of new customers. But more on that topic later.

THE HIGH COST OF PROSPECTING

You've heard it before. It costs at least five times as much to get a new customer as it does to keep one you already have—or to reactivate an old one. Yet the majority of companies still spend a fortune chasing after new customers and concentrating on that first sale.

Add it up. You offer deep discounts to get new customers into your bakery. You create loss leaders to increase traffic in your minimart. You offer a duplicate item for just a penny or a dollar more. Or you start giving stuff away: free ice tongs to the adults and face painting for the kids. All this costs money, not to mention the expense of promoting it through advertising. And it's all done without an ounce of assurance that even one new customer is going to pledge allegiance to your business.

On the other hand, staying in touch with your satisfied customers and making them devotees costs you relatively little. The idea to keep in mind is that a happy customer is like a perennial in your garden: With proper care and feeding, you can usually count on it to bloom

If Einsteln Had Been In Marketing . . .

A few brainy ideas businesses can use to generate new income

Business: Auto repair and maintenance

Problem: You get very little drive-by business, and current customers don't come in unless there's a major problem. The small ads you run in local papers don't draw customers.

Solution: Send notes to current customers saying you're going to start making oil-change house calls to make it more convenient for them to service their cars. For an extra $15, they can get the oil and lube service for which they normally can't find time. Of course, some will say no. But many others will appreciate the new convenience and not be concerned with the extra fee.

Extra benefit: If the car owners are having any mechanical problems, the house call can double as a diagnostic visit and mean extra profits.

Business: Beauty salon

Problem: You're booking fewer appointments and find you don't get an increase in business unless you heavily discount. What added value can you offer current customers so they'll come in more regularly?

Solution: Invite customers to a low-cost series of lectures at the shop on "sane weight control" conducted by a local doctor. You get to schmooze and win back inactive customers, and the doctor may get a few new patients.

Extra benefit: Customers tell others about your unique new offering, and you'll book more appointments.

Business: Pizzeria

Problem: Your pizzeria has to go up against the big franchises, and even though you started offering delivery and frequency discounts, they still have the edge in name recognition.

Solution: Start attaching an unexpected reward to each pizza box. Maybe it's an offer for an extra can of soda or a house salad. Any thoughtful surprise gets indelibly etched in the customer's mind. Also, make up a 3-by-5 card about each customer that lists their favorite toppings, so you can say "the usual?" when the customer places an order.

Extra benefit: Again, your generosity gets talked about, and you're recommended by current customers.

Business: Carpet cleaning (or any other home service)

Problem: You're a new franchisee of a carpet-cleaning company that is sending out fliers the franchisor recommended, but you're not booking much business. With few current customers, how can you use relationship marketing?

ILLUSTRATION © SCOTT POLLACK

Solution: Personally visit carpet sellers and make the following proposals: "You'll sell more carpet by offering the first cleaning free, and that's what I can provide. In return, I get that base of customers to cultivate on my own." Start relationships with customers by offering an every-six-months cleaning for a lower cost.

Extra benefit: "Upsell" by calling ahead to ask if customers would like their windows cleaned while you're there.

Business: Chiropractor

Problem: Your practice is not getting a lot of repeat business, and ads are ineffectual unless, by luck, they happen to appear when someone is having a problem.

Solution: A phone call—as simple as it sounds—can work magic. Have your assistant call previous customers to say "Dr. O'Connor asked me to find out how your neck is feeling and if there are any other problems or concerns he can help you with."

Extra benefit: Some customers will respond with a need, plus the call can be an excuse to inform the customer about a new treatment or service.

Business: Catalog sales

Problem: You don't get enough repeat orders, even though your catalog is sent out quarterly to remind customers of special values.

Solution: Think about how many of your customers would consider stocking up on a product of yours they use throughout the year if they could save some money. Research shows a good number of people would be interested.

Extra benefit: You don't lose future sales from people "stocking up." Instead, all your wares are perceived in the same positive light as the great volume discount you gave.

IN THIS INCREASINGLY IMPERSONAL
world, every me-to-you query adds strength to a customer relationship that no amount of discounting from your competitor can weaken.

year after year. When a customer buys from you the first time, he or she is saying "I like you; you have my trust." This is an invitation not just for a sale, but for a relationship.

NEW PROFITS RIGHT UNDER YOUR NOSE

The revelation that it is often costlier to obtain new customers has caused many small-business owners to take a step back and look at their most priceless yet overlooked business builder—their current customer base. And from this enlightenment has sprung a whole new branch of marketing called relationship marketing. It's a field of vast profit opportunity for even the newest entrepreneur, and it's ultra-easy to implement. Best of all, there are a number of experts on the subject whose knowledge can help you maximize your use of relationship marketing.

Martha Rogers, Ph.D., co-author with Don Peppers of *The One to One Future: Building Relationships One Customer at a Time* (Currency/Doubleday), is one of those experts. Rogers, a founding partner of management consulting firm Marketing 1 to 1/Peppers and Rogers Group in Stamford, Connecticut, believes your goal, rather than to increase your customer base, should be to ensure that each customer who buys your product or service buys more of your product or service, buys only your product or service, and is happy always choosing your company over others. In a word, loyalty. In four words, a customer for life.

In the future, says Rogers, more businesses will focus on the "lifetime value" of each customer rather than the short-term profits they can get from new customers. She says creating one-to-one relationships is key and will be helped by evolving interactive technologies that small businesses can take advantage of. Today's fax machines, cell phones and e-mail technology are just the tip of the interactive iceberg that you and your customers can use to stay chummy. And interactive television is just around the bend.

REMEMBER WHEN ...

The key word to etch in your mind, insists Rogers, is "remember." Remember the dress that needs special han-

dling for your regular dry cleaning customer without her having to remind you. (You can note this on your computer or on a 3-by-5 card you make for each customer.) Remember the occasion that prompted your flower shop customer to buy a bouquet so next year you can send a reminder that you'd be happy to send one again. Remember the rattle in the wheel well that your gas station customer was complaining about last time he or she was in, and ask about it the next time that customer comes in for a tune-up. Remember to ask your plumbing customer if that upstairs sink is still leaking and if he or she would like you to take a look at it.

Just as a doctor writes down details of a patient's health on his or her chart, so should you record information about your clients. Then the next time you connect with a client in person or by e-mail (you are routinely asking for their e-mail addresses, aren't you?), ask how the customer's daughter is doing in her first year of college, inquire about that nagging lower lumbar problem he or she previously mentioned, ask if he or she has been happy with that new sport utility vehicle ... Well, you get the idea. In this increasingly impersonal world, every me-to-you query adds strength to a customer relationship that no amount of discounting from your competitor can weaken.

AND THEY TOLD TWO FRIENDS, AND SO ON ...

Another relationship marketing enthusiast is Patrick Daly, who oversees the Customer Care Program for the huge international courier DHL Worldwide Express in Redwood City, California. "Most profits in most companies [are generated] through current customers; new customers cost money to develop," Daly says flatly. However, he points out, the monies come not just from the customers themselves but from others they steer your way.

"Many businesses, such as contractors and other home-service providers, find that referrals from loyal customers account for up to 80 percent of their new business," says Daly. "[Plus,] the 'close rate'—turning a prospect into a client—from loyal-customer referrals is far higher than from new customer leads from advertising." However, Daly warns that just getting a satisfied customer into the fold is not enough to ensure loyalty.

What's The Buzz?

JUST BECAUSE YOU RUN a small business doesn't mean you can't use some of the cutting-edge marketing techniques employed by larger companies. We asked Bradley Johnson, technology editor and columnist for *Advertising Age*, a weekly magazine covering the advertising industry, to clue us in on some of the strategies—aside from relationship marketing—the industry giants use to snare the attention of media-savvy consumers.

❖ **Unbundling media.** In the past, companies used large, established ad agencies to both create the ads and buy the media that would get the message out to consumers. Now advertisers can choose to use smaller, more creative agencies that don't have media-purchasing capabilities; these firms will create the ads, then link up with a media-buying firm to complete the process. The result is often hipper, smarter, more youthful ads that are more likely to take risks to sell the product. "Not surprisingly, the larger ad agencies don't like this idea," says Johnson. "They want to sell the full services of their agency."

❖ **Branding.** Brand messages tell you something about what the brand stands for but nothing about a product, like Apple Computer's iconoclastic "Think Different" TV and print ad campaign, which uses great thinkers (and noncomputer users) like Albert Einstein to suggest that the company designs its products for users who think out of the box. This type of ad works best when the company name is already familiar to the public.

Product messages, on the other hand, tell you about a product and give little or no information about the advertiser. Dell Computer's print ads, which offer nothing but product specifications and a toll-free number, are a good example. In this case, Dell, a direct marketer of PCs, doesn't have the name recognition of Apple, so it must sell the product instead of the name. The ideal ad, according to Johnson, is one that blends both brand and product messages. In general, only larger companies have the budget to produce separate brand and product ads.

❖ **Integrated marketing.** Sending consumers a coherent advertising message requires a unified approach to all your communications. TV and print ads and direct mail should all look like they came from the same company, even if you work with different agencies. All three types of ads should refer customers to the company's Web site, where they will see similar messages with the same logo and graphics. Integrated marketing is becoming increasingly necessary to reach consumers who are bombarded with media messages.

On the Internet:

❖ **Direct response banners.** Banner ads are supposed to attract customers to a company's Web site, but the relatively low response rate indicates that people are reluctant to click on them. Why? Because clicking through a banner ad takes customers out of the Web site they were looking at, forcing them to backtrack to their point of origin. Direct response banners, on the other hand, allow customers to learn about a company without leaving the Web page they're viewing. These banners also allow customers to fill out forms for e-commerce, contests and requests for more information. According to Johnson, this concept is relatively new, so there isn't a lot of data on its attractiveness to consumers, but it seems to address the low-response problem of current banner ads.

❖ **Product placement on the Web.** Nearly every movie made in the United States in the past 10 years has used a brand-name product as "set dressing," and now this subtle marketing technique has reached the Internet. In 1997, Oldsmobile made a deal with NBC to feature its Intrigue model on the network's Web site, which was promoting a show called "The Pretender." By linking their product to the content of NBC's Web site, Oldsmobile received just as much (or possibly more) attention as it would have if it had paid for commercial airtime during the show, at a much lower cost. —*G. David Doran*

"Studies show that even customers receiving good service and good value can't be counted on to stay loyal," Daly says. "Earning loyalty requires the relationship to reach a whole new level of involvement."

Daly recounts that his first lessons in relationship marketing started with his father, Dennis, the owner of a printing company in Sacramento, California. "He was thinking of buying an expensive new press," Daly says, "and he invited his most loyal customers to a luncheon to discuss the pros and cons of buying the equipment. By the end of the lunch, his customers not only reassured him he was making the right decision but gave him enough unsolicited orders to book the press six months in advance."

THE SIMPLE THINGS

Daly offers the following four commandments to develop truly loyal customers:

1. Naming names. In today's detached, "just-give-me-your-account-number" world, nothing is more well-received than individual, personalized attention. Even though you may already be courteous and friendly to customers, greeting them by name is valued 10 times more on the worthy-of-loyalty scale.

2. Custom care. Customers pretty much know what they do and don't want from your company. If you always ask and remember what they want on an individual basis—even if it's something as simple as knowing a dry cleaning customer likes light starch in his collars—then you have in place one of the key elements of a strong loyalty program.

3. Keeping in touch. You can't communicate enough on a me-to-you basis with your customers. And don't just connect to make a pitch. Clip out a newspaper or magazine article that pertains to a customer's business and send it to him or her with an attached note saying "FYI—thought you'd be interested." When customers know you take time to think about them, they don't forget it.

4. "Boo-boo research." Part of any customer loyalty program is taking the time to reach out to lost customers to learn why they went elsewhere. In many cases, just the contact and showing you really care about getting their business will win them back—along with their contribution to your profits.

According to Robbin Gehrke, senior vice president, executive creative director at Russ Reid Co., a Pasadena, California, advertising agency that employs relationship marketing and fundraising, relationship marketing has become the battle cry for a growing number of companies. Gehrke says the activities of her agency are aimed at making clients' customers feel a sense of increasing equity in the company, getting them to believe there was something at risk in abandoning their relationship or changing their loyalty.

BUY FIVE PIZZAS, GET THE SIXTH FREE?

Should frequency rewards—giving extra stuff for getting more business—be the basis for cementing relationships? On a small scale, it can be worth it, says Gehrke, but she warns that such programs can be hazardous. "They're expensive if you don't know what you're doing; they're also high maintenance, and you can get into financial liability that you can't possibly manage." In addition, she adds, "They can be easily matched by a competitor, and then you're left with no advantage."

The more important aspects of a loyalty program are preferential, personal service, Gehrke says, adding that the most powerful secret in relationship marketing is unanticipated rewards.

The idea, according to Gehrke, is to give regular customers some benefit they weren't expecting, whether it's a gift certificate, flowers or some other kind gesture. "Customers remember such thoughtfulness for a long time," she says.

Experts in this field stress the importance of making your relationship marketing endeavors systematic. Make it one of your weekly routines so it becomes second nature to make regular contact with your loyal customers. And don't ever forget the two most meaningful words you can utter to a current customer that, surprisingly, often get left out. Those magic words: "Thank you."

Envisioning Greenfield Markets

How to leverage your core strengths in new businesses.

By Allan J. Magrath

There's an old saying that a rut is just a grave without both ends filled in. For firms that spend too much time in familiar markets, these ruts can get in the way of next-generation growth. It is vital to envision "greenfield" markets: arenas in which a company's core capabilities can thrive anew. These can take the form of an existing market landscape not yet considered, or of a newly emerging vista just bubbling up into view. In either case, finding greenfield markets can be systematic, thoughtful, and creative—and, when done well, can provide new areas for growth, new products, new applications of existing offerings, and incremental profit.

Where the Green Things Are

Four proven strategies exist to unearth new opportunities:

Ask yourself if your products and services can thrive in another location or type of venue. This simple prescription can be enormously powerful in leveraging a company to new horizons. In the early 1990s, McDonald's Corp. was struggling with its U.S. growth formula. Relying on its traditionally large, prime freestanding stores worked fine—until it became difficult to find new sites. In 1991 and 1992, McDonald's U.S. expansion slowed by one-third; it had to look to new spaces to sell

ALLAN J. MAGRATH is director of corporate marketing services and new business ventures at 3M Canada Co., and has contributed writings on strategy to ATB for nearly a decade. His last [Across the Board] article was "Achieving Uniqueness" in September 1997.

its burgers and fries. The answer: innovating with smaller stores in venues that had never seen a McDonald's. So the fast-food giant co-located inside Wal-Mart, alongside pumps at Amoco service stations, in military bases, at truck stops, in sports stadiums, museums, science centers, and other tourist sites; it even went into hospitals and universities and began popping up in small airports. Much of the company's 1990 to 1995 expansion was due to its ability to thrive in different physical settings and grow in other ways besides merely expanding overseas or changing its menu offerings. McDonald's recent slowdown may require it to look for brand-new greenfields of a completely different stripe.

Starbucks offers a similar example with its move into supermarket packaged coffee beans, which could add $250 million in sales, a greenfield market almost 25 percent of the retailer's current $967 million revenue. Of course, the sooner one finds an untapped opportunity before rivals, the better. When Fellowes Manufacturing spotted the "home-office" market as a new place to sell its paper shredders, it got in early with office resellers such as Staples, OfficeMax, Quill, and Wal-Mart. Consequently, its sales skyrocketed.

Ask yourself if you can leverage your growth by finding a new "activity" center to bolster your company's strengths. Recognizing the vast multiproduct opportunities, Nike is moving ahead aggressively in the hockey and golf markets. Honeywell's fastest-growing greenfield business is in control systems for casinos—a growing leisure-activity-based center. Even high-tech Intel has entered the sports-enthusiast market via its stake in Sportsline

From *Across the Board*, May 1998, pp. 26-30. © 1998 by Allan J. Magrath. Reprinted by permission.

USA, the Website owner of CBS Sportsline. This provides Intel a vista on multimedia, a growing application for its next-generation chips.

Ask yourself if a greenfield market could be found based upon a growing compelling need, then segue your offerings to service that need. Novartis' new flea-control drug allows "time-poor" pet owners to solve pet flea problems with less hassle—no more shampoos, powders, collars, sprays, etc. Some needs are specific; others are more universal, such as more "environmentally safe" products. DuPont is aggressively chasing this need-based market opportunity with its new polyester, developed from cornstarch technology.

Another emerging need is for "total solutions" in information and communication systems. Hewlett-Packard has landed a huge contract to supply more than 75 different H-P computing-communication hardware products for the 1998 World Cup in France. These servers, PCs, printers, and local area networks will assist in Internet site data/stat feeds and in intranet feeds to journalists for events in 10 different stadiums across France. Total solution-type marketing programs are proving a boon to distributors who can offer one-stop shopping to large original-equipment-manufacturing customers for factory consumables—Chicago-based W. W. Grainger's growth bears witness to this need.

Ask yourself if a new market opportunity exists in tackling a new-to-you industry, one that you may have previously ignored or shied away from. Procter & Gamble has created a sizable business in pharmaceuticals this way, as has General Electric in broadcasting (with NBC) and Monsanto in biotechnology. Disney will enter the cruise-line industry this year, and Hallmark entered the children's-crayon market in 1984 by purchasing Crayola manufacturer Binney & Smith Co. Rubbermaid turned to a new greenfield market a few short years ago—gardens, decks, and garages. It has generated a whole host of new products, from mobile workbenches to "no-tool assembly" sheds, deckboxes for storage, and plastic workbenches.

While many firms enter these new-to-them industries via acquisition or alliance, others prefer the organic-growth route: Witness Disney's natural segue into retail stores, or Levi Strauss' entry into office casualwear (Dockers, Slates).

One variation on "industry" greenfield spotting is to select national market clusters in which a country has world leadership and then try to match up your core strengths to penetrate such a market (see "Innovating in Market Clusters"). Reuters did this by targeting stock- and investment-fund managers in New York and London with its electronic money-market information services. A variety of U.S.-based market clusters are global leaders, from Hollywood to Silicon Valley; the Detroit auto cluster; the Indiana R/V cluster; and the North Carolina furniture cluster.

How Green Is It?

There are, of course, some criteria worth considering when screening greenfield markets as growth candidates. A greenfield opportunity ought to have an accessible customer base, so the less fragmented the potential customers are, the better. It ought to offer scope to create a sizable impact on the firm—not just in total dollars but also in multiple segments. As GE got into broadcasting with NBC, it also was able to grow in a new segment: cable business news, with CNBC. When Rubbermaid entered the children's-product market, it expanded beyond toys into playground equipment and children's furnishings in multiple settings, such as day-care centers. Nike's choice of the hockey market opened an entire product line—skates, sticks, apparel, equipment—far more than a single product. To expand the overall business, pick markets with high ceilings with lots of segment "headroom."

In addition, a greenfield market ought to provide for healthy margins—otherwise the top line goes up with little to show for it in terms of shareholder wealth. This is where leveraging your core strengths becomes critical: H-P can leverage its engineering skills and broad product line for World Cup '98; P&G leverages branding and marketing skills in pharmaceuticals transferred from its health- and beauty-aid experience; 3M leverages its cross-divisional selling and bundling skills in pursuit of marine markets; and Rubbermaid leverages its channel contacts, new-product savvy, and plastic-resin processing when it targets kids' products.

Opportunities for the Next Millennium

One could conclude that this is all well and good if you're spotting new market-entry strategies for existing industries, but how does one scout out future greenfield opportunities? There are four powerful ways to do this; each requires you to make careful judgments about trends.

Look for trend convergences. Whenever trends converge or collide, the ensuing chaos often sorts itself out into burgeoning new opportunities. Federal Express watched the trend toward globalized freight/trade flows converge with outsourcing demands and the Internet, and invested heavily in fleets and IT to be at the intersection of these favorable developments. Enron is exploiting the convergence of fossil-fuel utility markets such as natural-gas and hydroelectric-power markets, two formerly separate industries. And 3M has been watching the intersection of new-materials usage in appliances, automobiles, and aircraft, along with the need to reduce labor intensity in assembly or finishing to launch its structural adhesives, specialized tapes, micro-finishing abrasives, and vibration-damping product lines.

Look for "fringe" markets that may break into the mainstream. When a fringe activity begins to become more mainstream, demand burgeons. This occurs in a whole host of markets, from sports (rollerblading, snowboarding) to health (vitamin therapy, herbal medicine, self-diagnostics) to fashion (tattoos, body piercing, retro-fashion) to retailing (microbreweries, gourmet coffee bars) to travel (adventure tours, growth in 4X4's, extreme skiing/mountaineering).

Then figure out how legitimizing a formerly fringe activity might create a greenfield market for your firm. American Sensors jumped quickly into manufacturing carbon-monoxide detectors for the home from its main business of smoke alarms and propane/natural-gas detection, when it saw this "fringe" concern become mainstream.

Take a hard look at bottlenecks that exist in the flows of trade or commerce. Often, the company that eliminates them can accrue big dividends. Electronic cash and smart cards help break logjams in the flow of money or checks. High-speed trains boost people flows. Factory farms and aquaculture can solve food-stock flows. Water re-use technology and drip-based irrigation assist in water-flow solutions/shortages. Waste-stream flows are optimized with lower-cost treatment processors that use U.V. processing. Paperwork flows can be solved with online software alternatives or CD-ROMs.

3M has built a formidable greenfield business in solving record-retrieval flows in hospital-patient records with its Health Information Systems business. H-P is charging hard into solving elec-

Innovating in Market Clusters

Concentrations of global industrial leadership often are found inside the borders of specific nations. Holland leads the world in cut flowers (production and trading), Belgium in diamond-cutting, France and Japan in high-speed trains, and Sweden in mining machinery, just to cite a few cases. Israel contains the leading market cluster in irrigation systems for farming, while Germany's Nuremberg region still dominates global leadership in mechanical/scientific pens and pencils.

The origins of such dominance are multiple—sometimes driven by economics, sometimes by history, sociology, geography, or technology. If a firm can target such clusters and find ways to map its products or services within them, it can create growth and discovery. A great many corporations excel at exploiting software produced "to order" from India's Bangalore region, and

any number of companies have succeeded in high-fashion marketing by marrying their firms to Italian textile producers.

Italy, for example, represents a very fertile lighting expertise market cluster for three reasons. First, its designers are top-notch, using novel engineering of light in the architecture of operas, theaters, restaurants, and public roadways in the mountainous north. Second, a large portion of the world's fragile cultural assets—paintings, sculpture, frescoes, manuscripts, and textiles—are fading or in danger from light and heat, and many of these are housed in Italy. Finally, there is a great deal of above-ground traffic in Italy, considering its size. Thus, its 9,000 kilometers of underground tunnels assist the country's infrastructure. 3M has been able to take advantage of this market cluster by marketing various light-management technologies, from light systems that

won't damage works of art to lighted guidance tubes for the underground tunnels.

In France, 3M may target its problem-solving technologies to a little-publicized market cluster in which the French lead the world—water management. Large corporations in France excel at pumping, treating, storing, distributing, and retreating water—including all the specialized engineering required. Lyonnaise des Eaux is a $19 billion, 180,000-person firm that leads this industry and exports its skills to 80 nations worldwide. This expertise will be necessary as Europe, especially France, copes with problems of lead leaching into potable water supplies due to old pipes (and two world wars!). These pipes must be replaced/upgraded to meet tougher environmental-safety guidelines out of Brussels.

—A.J.M.

tronic/commerce issues by building tools to help businesses buy supplies, capital equipment, services, and other nonproduction items by linking extranets and intranets together.

Think deeply about the likely ripple effects of the ascendancy of "new values" on opportunities for a business. Three examples come to mind. One value shift that has occurred is the desire for "immediacy" in transacting business. As a result, new businesses grow up to service this immediacy value, from just-in-time logistics, to EDI, electronic banking, and 24-hour food stores, just to name a few.

Another value emerging is *taking personal charge of one's health.* This value is rippling into new business opportunities in nutrition/vitamin therapy, fitness products, self-diagnostics, and self-help books/seminars. Yet another value is *knowledge is king* (in a knowledge-worker world!). This, too, is propagating itself into CD-ROM encyclopedias, "edutainment" software, a revival of adult night-school courses, video-educational credits for distance learning, groupware for team-based learners to share files, and so forth.

Any new value always plays itself out into a business opportunity—and thinking hard about how this could play out allows a firm to mobilize resources for tomorrow's world. For instance, in Canada a major bank and a movie-theater chain are testing the possibility of issuing movie passes at ATMs in malls or banks so patrons can buy tickets in advance and avoid waiting in line for a hit movie. This new business opportunity is an outgrowth of consumers' need for "immediate" purchase fulfillment, one that is convenient and suits their lifestyle (combine it with their regular shopping or banking and conclude the entire transaction on the spot). This farsighted initiative is a fine example of thinking through "value" shift implications to find greenfield opportunity that leverages a core strength—in this case, the bank's ATM distribution network.

Envisioning greenfield markets for your firm is never easy—it takes effort and creativity to reconceptualize your company's market charter. But by systematically approaching greenfield sources based on new places, activities, or needs, or neglected parts of existing markets—as well as casting an eye on emerging possible markets—you can create new opportunities for the next millennium's marketplace.

THE EMERGING CULTURE

Nearly one in four American adults lives by a new set of values, according to this decade-long study. People who believe in environmentalism, feminism, global issues, and spiritual searching are scattered across the country and found in all social groups. These "Cultural Creatives" tend to be affluent, well-educated, and on the cutting edge of social change. By catering to the new values, businesses can serve the leading edge of many consumer markets.

BY PAUL H. RAY

A major change has been growing in American culture. It is a comprehensive shift in values, world views, and ways of life. It appeals to nearly one-fourth of American adults, or 44 million persons. People who follow this new path are on the leading edge of several kinds of cultural change. They are interested in new kinds of products and services, and they often respond to advertising and marketing in unexpected ways.

This emerging group has been labeled Cultural Creatives by American LIVES of San Francisco. In numerous surveys and focus groups, we have seen that Americans live in three different worlds of meaning and valuing. Each world creates distinctive contexts for a wide array of consumer purchases, political convictions, and civic behavior. And within each world are class divisions that create different subgroups that share the same broader views.

The first world view is Traditionalism. It is the belief system for about 29 percent of Americans (56 million adults) who might also be called Heartlanders. In America, traditionalism often takes the form of country folks rebelling against big-city slickers. Heartlanders believe in a nostalgic image of small towns and strong churches that defines the Good Old American Ways. That image may owe as much to John Wayne and Jimmy Stewart movies as to any historical reality, but for them it is a powerful reminder of how things ought to be.

> In Cultural Creative circles, it's common to meet women asking, "Where are all the good men?" The answer is most men are Moderns.

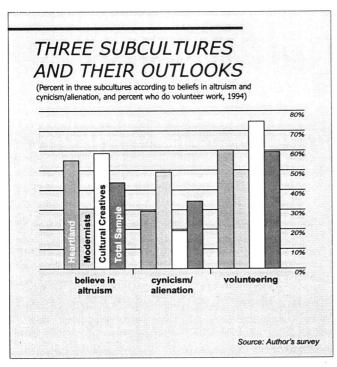

THREE SUBCULTURES AND THEIR OUTLOOKS

(Percent in three subcultures according to beliefs in altruism and cynicism/alienation, and percent who do volunteer work, 1994)

Source: Author's survey

Of the three major subcultures, Cultural Creatives are the least cynical and the most likely to do volunteer work.

THREE SUBCULTURES AND THEIR DEMOGRAPHICS

(Selected demographic characteristics of three subcultures and U.S. average for the total sample, 1994)

Demographics	Heartland	Moderns	Cultural Creatives	total sample
Males:Females	46:53	54:46	40:60	48:52
Average age	54	42	44	46
Median age	53	39	42	43
Average family income	$31,200	$60,000	$52,200	$45,883
Median family income	$23,750	$42,500	$47,500	$36,250
Income>$60,000	11%	30%	29%	25%
No college	60	39	32	44
College graduate	14	27	30	24
Managers/Professionals	9	26	23	20
Retired/Not in labor force	64	22	27	36
African Americans	11	8	6	9
Hispanics	8	9	4	8

Note: These summary measures on age, income, education, and occupation are used only to show the central tendency of each aspect of socio-economic status. In reality, it is important to remember that there are at least a few people at every age, income, education, and occupation level in each of the subcultures.

Source: Author's survey

Demographics don't predict values, but the three subcultures do have some broad demographic differences.

The second world view is Modernism. It holds sway over about 47 percent of Americans, or 88 million adults. Modernism emerged 450 years ago as the governing world view of the urban merchant classes and other creators of the modern economy. It defines modern politicians, military leaders, scientists, and intellectuals. Modernists place high value on personal success, consumerism, materialism, and technological rationality. It's not too far off to say that Moderns see the world through the same filters as *Time* magazine.

The third and newest world view goes beyond Modernism. Its current adherents are the Cultural Creatives, who claim 24 percent of U.S. adults (44 million). Trans-Modernism began with esoteric spiritual movements such as 19th-century American Transcendentalism. It gained strength as Western intellectuals discovered the diversity and coherence of other religions and philosophies. It caught fire in the 1960s, as millions of young people joined "movements" for human potential, civil rights, peace, jobs, social justice, ecology, and equal rights for women.

Conservative commentators often believe that each of the social movements listed above exists in isolation and is important only to a few. But from women's issues to environmentalism, the emblematic values of the 1960s are being embraced by more and more Americans. Few in the media recognize it, but these ideas are coalescing into a new and coherent world view. When Cultural Creatives look at Modernism, they see an antique system that is noisily shaking itself to pieces.

Cultural Creatives may be disenchanted with the idea of "owning more stuff," but they put a strong emphasis on having new and unique experiences. On the deepest level, they are powerfully attuned to global issues and whole systems. Their icon is a photograph taken by an astronaut that shows the earth as a blue pearl hanging in black space.

WHERE ARE ALL THE GOOD MEN?

Cultural Creatives are slightly more likely than average to live on the West Coast, but they are found in all regions of the country. They are altruistic and often less concerned with success or making a lot of money, although most live comfortably with middle to upper-middle incomes. They are far more likely than Modernists or Heartlanders to have graduated from college. Their median age (42 years) is close to the national average for adults, but they tend to cluster around their mid-age point with relatively few elderly and young adults.

Demographics don't predict values. But Cultural Creatives do have one outstanding demographic characteristic: six in ten are women. In Cultural Creative circles, it's common to meet women asking, "Where are all the good men?" The answer is that in the middle- and upper-class neighborhoods where Creatives live, most men are Moderns.

Despite their numbers, Cultural Creatives tend to believe that few people share their values. This is partly because their views are rarely represented in the mainstream media, which is mostly owned and operated according to the Modern world view. Yet little of what they read gives them any evidence of their huge numbers. It's a paradox, but Creatives are likely to be information junkies. They follow the news all the time and read a great deal, although they watch a lot less TV than the average American.

Cognitive style is a key to understanding the Cultural Creatives. While they take in a lot of information from a variety of sources, Creatives are good at synthesizing it into a "big picture." Their style is to scan an information source efficiently, seize upon something they are interested in, and explore that topic in depth.

Much of today's advertising and marketing does not appeal to the Creatives because it violates their preferred cognitive style. They are suspicious of bullet points that march to the bottom line. They want whole-process stories instead, and they are likely to want the stories behind the stories as well.

Cultural Creatives appear to fall into two subgroups. Core Cultural Creatives are a little less than 11 percent of adults, or 20 million people. They combine a serious concern with their inner lives with a strong penchant for social activism. They tend to be leading-edge thinkers who are in the upper-middle class, with 46 percent in the top one-fourth of the U.S. household income distribution. Their male-to-female ratio is 33 to 67, or twice as many women as men.

Greens are 13 percent of adults, or 24 million Americans. Their values are centered on the environment and social concerns from a more secular view, or from the view that nature itself is sacred. They show just an average interest in spirituality, psychology, and person-centered values, and they tend to have a conventional religious outlook. Their world views are less thought out than those of the Core group, and their values are often more pragmatic and less intensely held. Their male-to-female ratio is 47 to 53, close to the national adult ratio of 48 to 52. Greens are also more uniformly middle class.

VALUES OF THE CULTURAL CREATIVES

The distinctive values of Cultural Creatives separate them from the rest of American society. They tend to reject hedonism, materialism, and cynicism. For this reason, many are disdainful of modern media, consumer, and business culture. They also reject world views based on scarcity or fear, as well as the non-ecological orientation of ultra-conservatives and intolerance of the Religious Right.

The positive values of the Creatives suggest an outline for the "Trans-Modern" world view, or what is emerging beyond Modernism. They are:

Ecological Sustainability. If you can name an aspect of ecology and sustainability, Creatives are leading the way. They are eager to rebuild neighborhoods and communities, committed to ecological sustainability, and believe in limits to growth. They see nature as sacred, want to stop corporate polluters,

THREE SUBCULTURES AND THEIR VALUES

(percent in each subculture and total sample who agree with the stated value, 1994)

	Heart-land	Mod-erns	Cultural Creatives	Total sample
Heartlander Values				
Religious Right	70%	26%	31%	40%
Traditional relationships	55	25	26	34
Conservative religious beliefs	53	21	30	33
Conventional religious beliefs	47	36	15	34
Against feminism in work	46	35	20	35
Modernists Values				
Financial materialism	61%	82%	51%	68%
Not Religious Right	14	55	46	41
Not self-actualizing	43	51	26	43
Not altruistic	21	49	16	33
Cynicism about politics	29	48	19	35
Not idealistic	33	44	18	35
Secular/nature is sacred	15	42	29	31
Orthodox religion and beliefs	29	40	17	31
Success and high priority	11	36	12	23
Not relationship-oriented	14	32	8	21
Hedonism	5	12	4	8
Cultural Creative Values				
Want to rebuild neighborhoods/communities	86%	84%	92%	86%
Fear violence	84	75	87	80
Like foreign places and the exotic	69	63	85	70
Nature is sacred	65	72	85	73
General green values	58	59	83	64
Ecological sustainability	52	56	83	61
Voluntary simplicity	65	53	79	63
Relationships important	65	49	76	60
Success is not high priority	61	39	70	53
Pro-feminism in work	45	56	69	56
Not concerned about job	41	50	62	50
Altruism	55	32	58	45
Idealism	36	32	55	39
Religious mysteries exist	19	25	53	30
Self-actualization	29	32	52	36
Not financial materialism	34	17	48	29
Want to be activist	34	29	45	34
Not financial problems	33	31	44	35
Spiritual psychology	36	24	40	31
Not cynical on politics	24	21	40	27
Optimism about future	26	24	35	27
Want creative time	19	31	33	28

Source: Author's survey

Heartlanders, Modernists, and Cultural Creatives live in three different worlds of meaning.

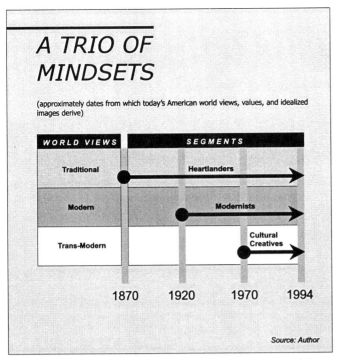

A TRIO OF MINDSETS

(approximately dates from which today's American world views, values, and idealized images derive)

WORLD VIEWS	SEGMENTS
Traditional	Heartlanders →
Modern	Modernists →
Trans-Modern	Cultural Creatives →

1870   1920   1970   1994

Source: Author

On the eve of the 21st century, American society contains three world views, compared with two a generation ago.

are suspicious of big business, are interested in voluntary simplicity, and are willing to pay to clean up the environment and stop global warming.

Globalism. If Sustainability is one of the top values for the Creatives, the other is Xenophilism, or love of foreigners and the exotic.

Women's Issues. The fact that six in ten Creatives are women is a major focus for understanding this subculture. Their focus on issues women claim as their own includes concerns about violence and abuse of women and children, the desire to rebuild neighborhoods and community, the desire to improve caring relationships, and concerns about family. Yet they are about as likely as other Americans to live in family households.

Altruism, Self-Actualization, and Spirituality. This is a complex of highly interrelated beliefs and values centered on the inner life. Creatives are forging a new sense of the sacred that incorporates personal growth psychology, the spiritual realm, and service to others. It also includes a stronger orientation to holistic health and alternative health care.

Social Conscience and Optimism. Their emphasis on the personal includes social concerns, for they believe that rebuilding and healing society is related to healing the self, physically and spiritually. With that goes a guarded social optimism.

Cultural Creatives tend to walk their talk. They are the most altruistic and least cynical of the three major subcultures, and they are particularly critical of the cynicism they see in the Modernist world view. Three-fourths of Creatives are involved in volunteer activities, compared with a national average of about six in ten adults. Creatives also spend a median of four hours a month volunteering, compared with a national average of one hour a month. Heartlanders have an average share of

volunteers and a median of two hours a month. Only about half of Modernists do volunteer work, and they volunteer a median of less than one hour each month.

CREATIVES AS CONSUMERS

Over the last decade, American LIVES has conducted dozens of surveys and hundreds of focus groups for clients. From these have come many insights into how the values of Cultural Creatives inform their consumer decisions. For example:

Print and radio, not TV. Creatives buy more books and magazines than average. They also listen to more radio, especially classical music and public radio, and watch less television than the other groups. They are literate and discriminating, and they dislike most of what is on TV.

Arts and culture. Creatives are aggressive consumers of cultural products. They also produce culture: they are more likely than average to be involved in the arts as amateurs or pros, to write books and articles, and to go to cultural meetings and workshops.

A good story. Creatives appreciate good stories. They demand a system-wide view of the "whole process" of whatever they are reading, from cereal boxes to product descriptions to magazine articles. They want to know where a product came from, how it was made, who made it, and what will happen to it when they are done with it. They hate reading materials that put on a specialist's blinders or refuse to deal with longer-term implications. For these reasons, they actively resent advertising on children's TV programs.

Careful consumers. Creatives are the kind of people who buy and use *Consumer Reports* for most of their purchase decisions on durable goods. For the most part, they read up on a purchase first and do not buy on impulse. All consumers are supposed to read labels, but the Creatives are practically the only ones who actually do it.

A different kind of car. Creatives are far more likely than average to want safety and fuel economy in a mid-priced car. They are also looking for an ecologically sound, high-mileage, recyclable car. In fact, American LIVES estimates that automakers pass up about 1 million new-car sales a year because they ignore those concerns. The Volvo speaks to many Creatives, but so do well-made Japanese cars. They express a greater dislike of car dealers than the average person does. The Saturn, with its fixed price and dealer service, is designed for Cultural Creatives.

Technology moderates. Although they're inquisitive, Creatives are not likely to be among the first to jump on a new technological product. Innovators are more likely to be technology specialists or impulse buyers who want techno-toys. The mantra of the 1980s, "He who dies with the most toys, wins," describes Modernist values.

The Foodies. Creatives do tend to be innovators and opinion leaders for knowledge-intensive products such as fine foods, wines, and boutique beers. They like to talk about food before and after consuming it. They also like to cook with

Modernists and Heartlanders

CULTURAL CREATIVES are on the leading edge of change. But more than three-fourths of American adults belong to the other two subcultures, according to the American LIVES typology. Six subgroups exist within these two subcultures.

MODERNISTS are 47 percent of adults (88 million). They are more likely to be men than women, but their age profile, educational attainment, and income fit neatly into national averages. A group this large is far from uniform and has within its broad confines four subgroups, largely determined by social status:

Economic Conservatives are the most affluent segment of Modernists, at about 6 percent of adults (almost 11 million). These are upper-middle to upper-class free-market conservatives, with 59 percent in the top one-fourth of household incomes. They believe in the American Way, with a materialist focus on success and a heavy dose of the work ethic. Though they are often interested in personal growth, they are likely to oppose those who preach ecological sustainability. The Modern world favors this group, who strongly believe the world should not change.

Conventional Moderns are 12 percent of adults (23 million). They dislike both Heartland and Cultural Creatives' values and beliefs. They stay strongly within mainstream opinion, seeing only Modernist beliefs as "correct." They are more cynical and less success-oriented than are other Moderns. Yet they are about as affluent as the previous group, with 61 percent in the top income quartile.

Striving Centers are 14 percent of adults, (26 million). Most in this group are lower-middle to middle class, and they are intensely interested in moving up the income ladder. They yearn for spiritual meaning, but upward mobility is their real creed. Many belong to ethnic minorities. Striving Centers mix cultural and religious conservatism with many of the same person-centered concerns of Cultural Creatives.

Alienated Modernists are 15 percent of adults, or 29 million Americans. Half of them hold blue-collar jobs. Many are "sliders" who have lost better-paying jobs, while others have poor job prospects. Clearly, America in the 1990s is not working for them. They are the most alienated and cynical group, but

are by no means the worst off. Their alienation stems more from dashed prospects than from poverty.

HEARTLANDERS are defined by their traditional and conservative values and beliefs. They are, on average, older

past. The higher they are in social class, the more they also take on big-business conservatism.

Lower-Status Heartlanders are 22 percent of adults, or 41 million Americans. They include many elderly people

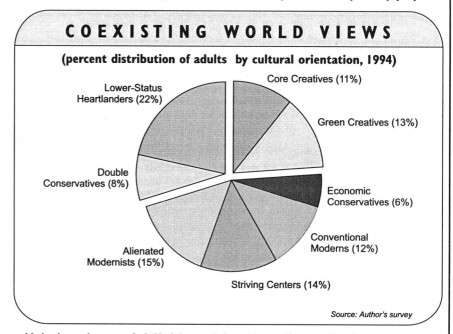

COEXISTING WORLD VIEWS

(percent distribution of adults by cultural orientation, 1994)

Lower-Status Heartlanders (22%)

Core Creatives (11%)

Green Creatives (13%)

Double Conservatives (8%)

Economic Conservatives (6%)

Alienated Modernists (15%)

Conventional Moderns (12%)

Striving Centers (14%)

Source: Author's survey

Modernists make up nearly half of the population, although their specific values and socioeconomic status divides them into four distinct subgroups.

and less-educated than Modernists or Cultural Creatives, but this group also includes upper-middle-class people who are conservative in both a cultural and economic sense. Heartlanders are 29 percent of the adult population (56 million). Retirees and the poor bring the median family income of this group down to $24,000.

Middle-class Heartlanders are more sympathetic to business interests, while lower-class members are more sympathetic to environmental protection. This family-centered group shares a low regard for civil liberties and is much more likely to trust the political teachings of religious leaders. A number of ethnic minorities are also in this subculture, as well as union supporters who may be more politically liberal.

Heartlanders include two subgroups:

Double Conservatives are 8 percent of adults, or 15 million Americans. This group forms the core of the religious right. This cultural conservatism draws on symbols and images of an idealized

with low incomes and education, for whom conservatism is rooted in longing for a simpler world. Surveys show that many in this group are pro-ecology and anti-big-business.

The other side of this group is younger people in the lower classes of American society. They tend to be traditional but have also absorbed much of modern culture. Many in this group are conflicted about values, for their traditional beliefs often do not fit well into their program for economic survival.

Heartlanders have difficulty handling complexity and the modern world, and they are suspicious of change. As time goes by, their numbers are likely to decline: their current median age is about 53, and Heartlanders are dying faster than they are being replaced by younger people.

—Paul H. Ray

Using Values to Study Customers

Values speak to what is most important in our lives. Values change on a time scale of generations, not months or years. Attitudes and opinions, on the other hand, change quickly because they grow out of attempts to reconcile long-held values with a constant stream of new information. If you want to use values instead of attitudes in a market segmentation, here are four things to consider.

First, **values usually don't follow demographics.** There are some broad correlations: Heartlanders do have more elderly and poor members than the other two groups, and Cultural Creatives have proportionately more women, college-educated people, and professionals. But on a more practical level, two households with identical demographics can live in entirely different worlds of meanings and values.

Second, **values do not predict all purchase behaviors.** They work best on prod-

ucts and services that are laden with meaning and symbolism; on large, complex purchases; or on goods and services that are status markers. Values segmentation usually aren't useful for predicting consumer behavior related to packaged goods and commodities. Its best use is for durable goods, like houses and cars; symbolic goods like food and clothing; and lifestyle-defining activities, such as vacation travel, books, and media use.

Third, **values are context-specific.** That is, the way people use values to buy a home is different than the way they use values to make a charitable donation. If you are used to predicting consumer behavior with multiple regression models, think of the meanings of each situation as intervening variables between values and the predicted behaviors. If you are comfortable with market segmentation, then think of values as providing a benefit segmentation that is elaborated by

the multiple meanings of each situation. You can crosstabulate that elaborated benefit segmentation with the values segmentation to show a matrix of behaviors. Each meaning-laden benefit segment works differently in the context of each values subculture.

Finally, **values subcultures are slow-changing.** The ideas in this article will still apply several years from now, with only slow changes in overall consumer preferences. Opinions and attitudes will shift; for example, consumers may adopt a radically different idea about the price of your product in a single year, as they regularly do for computers. The meanings that each segment uses to filter their reactions to products and services may change, too. But you can explain these alterations and predict further shifts, as long as you keep track of which values come to bear on particular purchase situations.

—*Paul H. Ray*

---

friends, eat out a lot, do gourmet and ethnic cooking, and try natural and health foods.

Desire for authenticity. Creatives invented the term "authenticity" as consumers understand it. They lead the rebellion against things that are fake, imitation, or poorly made. They eschew high fashion in favor of high integrity. If they buy something in a traditional style, they want it to be authentically traditional, with a story about its traditions. If it is to be in a modern style, then it must be an authentic Bauhaus or Herman Miller chair.

A different kind of new house, please. Creatives tend to buy fewer new houses than most people of their income level, because most new houses are not designed with Creatives in mind. So they buy existing houses and fix them up the way they want. They abhor status display homes that show off to the street. Instead, they prefer their homes to be hidden from the street by fences, trees, and shrubbery. They also prefer established neighborhoods. All of this militates against the kinds of new homes that builders are now making for the upper-middle class. Creatives rate builders down there with car dealers.

The home as nest. When Creatives buy homes, they like to buy "nests" with a lot of privacy inside and out. They like private spaces within, separating children's spaces from adult spaces, and with lots of interesting nooks and niches in each space. They are more prone to live out of the living room and not bother with a family room.

Creatives also like authentic styling in homes, but the style itself is less important. You can sell them an authentic New England salt box, authentic Georgian, authentic desert adobe, or an authentic contemporary Californian. Whatever fits into its proper place on the land is good. Creatives want access to natural and social ecosystems, so they go for walking and bik-

ing paths, ecological preserves, historic preservation sites, and master plans that show a way to recreate community.

Personalization of the home. Interior decoration for Creatives is typically eclectic, with a lot of original art on the walls and crafts pieces around the house. Many think that a home is not complete without walls of books. The same house that is invisible from the street should on the inside say a lot about its occupants. Cultural Creatives do not go in for a single decorator style that runs through the whole house, and they do not use interior decorators.

Experiential consumers. Core Cultural Creatives are the prototypical consumers of the experience industry, which sells intense, enlightening, enlivening experiences rather than things. Creatives buy psychotherapy, weekend workshops, spiritual gatherings, and personal growth experiences in all forms. Providers of these services have to be Cultural Creatives, too, or they fail the "authenticity" test.

The leading edge of vacation travel. Creatives define the leading edge of exotic vacation travel. They are looking for trips that are adventuresome (but not too dangerous), educational, genuine, altruistic, and spiritual. These include tours of temples in India, tours of the back country, tours where tourists don't go, eco-tourism, photo-safaris, fantasy baseball camps, vacations that involve rebuilding a Mayan village, and a Zen-Vipassana-Sufi-Yoga retreat instead of a vacation. They don't do package tours, fancy resorts, or cruises, and they resent having to take the kids to Disney World.

Holistic everything. Creatives are the core market for psychotherapy, alternative health care, and natural foods. What ties these together is the belief that body, mind, and spirit should be unified. Creatives may include a high proportion of people whom some physicians describe as "the worried well," those who monitor every twitch and pain and bowel movement in minutely detailed attention to the body. As a result, they spend more on all forms of health care, even though most are fairly healthy. This is a stark contrast to the Modernist pattern of treating the body like a machine that you feed, exercise, and otherwise ignore until it breaks down.

CREATIVE LIMITATIONS

The emergence of Cultural Creatives is the larger change that lies behind recent articles on the "Me Generation," the "New Age," the "Culture of Narcissism," "Inner Directeds," or even the views of baby boomers. All of these labels describe aspects of a cultural shift in shared values and beliefs.

People who disapprove of these labels are missing the point, because psychological development is not the issue. Selfishness and self-indulgence are as common among Modernists and Heartlanders as among Cultural Creatives, although they show up in different forms. Within any given subculture, people range from dumb to smart, from immoral to moral, and from unaware to enlightened.

The appearance of the Cultural Creatives in America is a very hopeful thing for our society, for it offers a chance to create a more positive new culture. Business can play a major role in that cultural development, and serve the leading edge of many consumer markets by catering to the new values.

Paul H. Ray Ph.D., is executive vice president of American LIVES in San Francisco, a market research firm specializing in the Lifestyles, Interests, Values, Expectations, and Symbols of Americans.

BEHIND THE NUMBERS

The author has written a longer description of the American LIVES typology and its historic context in a journal article, "The Rise of Integral Culture," in *The Noetic Sciences Review,* Spring 1996; and in book form as *The Integral Culture Survey: A Study of the Emergence of Transformational Values in America.* Both are available from The Institute of Noetic Sciences, 475 Gate Five Road, Suite 300, Sausalito, CA 94965. American LIVES is at 2512 Filbert Street, San Francisco, CA 94123; telephone (415) 921-1946.

Much of the information on Cultural Creatives was drawn from an American LIVES survey mailed to a representative national sample of the population by National Family Opinion in November and December 1994, using its panel of persons who have pre-agreed to be available for a mail survey. National averages cited in this article are drawn from the total sample and compared with the Census Bureau's 1994 Current Population Survey to ensure its comparability to the total U.S. population. This research was sponsored by the Fetzer Institute and the Institute of Noetic Sciences.

Marketing Mix Customization and Customizability

Marc Logman

We are sailing out of this century and into the next with our marketing methods in full-scale metamorphosis. Top-down marketing is becoming bottom-up. Transaction marketing is giving way to relationship marketing. One-way or broadcast marketing is moving to an interactive style to encourage a dialogue with the customer. And mass marketing is shifting to a customized, one-on-one method of reaching individual customers.

Because of fierce competition, long-term competitive advantages often are no longer sustainable. The policy to be followed, says d'Aveni (1994), is one of continuous market disturbance in order to create "temporary" competitive advantages. Hamel and Prahalad (1994) suggest that firms should look almost continuously for new opportunities. In the midst of such dizzying change, companies must be able to make "real-time" decisions, so their planning and tactics horizons often become shorter. To be flexible and highly responsive to market moves, a top-down approach in which business strategy decisions precede tactical and planning decisions often no longer works. Companies should be able to adapt their tactics immediately.

In the same context, a firm's communication approach becomes more and more bottom-up. Rather than determining target groups (who?) and communication aims (what?) before deciding on the instruments (how?), specific methods of communicating, such as via the Internet, are leading to the identification of *who* and *what*. Moreover, many writers claim that a paradigm shift is occurring from transaction marketing to relationship marketing. Firms are beginning to realize that keeping current customers may be more important than trying to attract new ones.*

Especially in business-to-business markets, many firms are starting to involve their customers in the product development process. Along with an increased concern about customers' real needs, wants, and demands, the information flow between customers and firms becomes more important. The Internet and other new communication media allow companies to interact with customers much more directly. Face-to-face or phone and fax contacts are no longer the only means of doing so.

Marketing strategies are also becoming more individually oriented. Businesses have begun to develop databases that allow them to approach customers on an individual basis. This in turn allows companies to customize their ways of introducing, providing, and delivering products and services to the customers.

> *Businesses looking for custom methods of designing, pricing, selling, and delivering their wares can do it themselves or leave it up to the customer.*

*Editor's Note: See [the] point/counterpoint articles by John V. Petrof and Thomas W. Gruen debating relationship marketing, Business Horizons, *November/December 1997.*

From *Business Horizons,* November/December 1997, pp. 39-44. © 1997 by the Foundation for the School of Business at Indiana University. Reprinted by permission.

Figure 1
Marketing Mix Customization and Customizability Options

Marketing Mix Elements	Customization	
	By Company	By Customer ("Customizability")
Product	• Offering enhanced and/or bundled products (to meet individual customer needs)	• Offering final products with different options • Offering a menu of product components (from which customers can select and design their final product)
Purchase Price	• Price discounting (dependent on sales volume, sales history, time of purchase) • As a result of product customization	• As a result of product customizability • As a result of customers' bargaining power • As a result of customers' decision timing
Communication	• Using one-to-one communication tools (direct mail, sales force)	• Offering a customizable interactive information network (such as the Internet)
Distribution and Logistics	• Offering multiple channel and logistics solutions (partly customizable)	• Offering a customizable interactive logistics and distribution network (such as EDI)
After-Sales Support and Costs	• Offering augmented product solutions (with single or bundled services) • Using remote control systems	• Offering do-it-yourself solutions • As a result of product customizability (such as the way the product is used)

A FRAMEWORK FOR MARKETING MIX CUSTOMIZATION

In light of all these transformations in the marketing field, particularly the trend toward "individualization" of the consumer, the focus here is on the impact of "customization" on the marketing mix. Five different instruments of the marketing mix–product, purchase price, communication, distribution and logistics, and after-sales support and costs–can be customized, either by the marketing firm or by consumers themselves. This is outlined in **Figure 1.**

Product

When discussing product as part of the marketing mix, three levels can be distinguished: (1) basic, or core; (2) enhanced; and (3) augmented. An enhanced product is a core product that has been differentiated by adding such tangible properties as features, styling, and quality. An augmented product combines the core or enhanced product with the intangible benefits customers reap from purchasing it, such as training, service, or logistics support. Augmented products will be discussed in more depth later. For now, we shall focus on the enhanced product.

Products can be customized by manipulating their enhanced properties. A business generally has the following options: (a) it can offer a customized product that meets the specific needs of the user; or (b) it

can offer a standard but customizable product that can be altered by users themselves. Lampel and Mintzberg (1996) maintain that different customizing strategies may be developed, depending on the levels of customization in the design, fabrication, assembly, and distribution stages.

Feitzinger and Lee (1997) argue that to offer customized products cost-effectively, the earlier stages of production should be standardized and the customizing should be postponed until the latest possible point in the production-supply network. The final step may be delegated to distributors, who have to integrate standard modules into a customized product. In this way, distributors may service different types of customers with the same stock (of standard modules), reducing inventory and shipping costs. No additional costs result from canceling an order because, again, the same standard modules can be used for different customers. The modules can be shipped from one region to another when a significant imbalance between supply and demand occurs. And the manufacturer may concentrate on production of the modules, which is an interesting option in view of economies of scale.

Hewlett-Packard experienced the advantages of customizing its local distribution centers when its total manufacturing, shipping, and inventory costs of the DeskJet printer for European and Asian markets dropped 25 percent. Taking such savings a step further, developing a flexible and responsive "customized" production-supply network may reduce not only costs but delivery times as well.

In many industries, different product models (with a different look or varied options) are derived from the same core product. Different car models, for instance, are often based on the same chassis. Offering products with different options may allow customers to upgrade or extend their product in a later stage, perhaps because of price considerations.

Companies should take care to time their product development process properly. At Daf Trucks, which are developed for the European market, dashboards are being renewed every four years. A truck owner has the choice of upgrading his dashboard with the latest options or waiting to replace the entire dashboard once the new one has been marketed.

Another popular way to customize is to bundle interrelated products into one specific product solution. This is what computer companies do when they offer a selection of software already installed in the PCs they sell. However, as more and more enhanced properties are integrated into one product, bundling as such may become less prevalent. Computers, for instance, are becoming their own communication instruments through integrated communication technology, while telephones are partly becoming computers through integrated computer technology.

Instead of customizing products, standard "customizable" products can be offered. These are appropriate when users want to be able to change product options from time to time, such as customizing software on their own by using the available setup modules built into it. Rather than offering final products with varied options, companies can introduce a menu system from which customers can select different components to use in designing the final products themselves.

In the computer industry, different hardware configurations may be developed by the customer. Menu options offer choices of disk capacity, processing speed, software drivers, and so on. Capacity can be expanded, new cards can be added. Software firms are also developing new tools that allow users to perform several operations more effectively. Powerquest recently introduced the package "Partitionmagic," which allows users to partition their hard disks more effectively.

Business-to-business markets, in which suppliers sell products to manufacturers, are using both customization options. Some manufacturers, such as auto makers, hold suppliers responsible for integrating their products into the final version. Others tend to prefer buying customizable products from the supplier and adapting them on their own. In the latter case, manufacturers often rely on competent integration-engineering departments. The Laboratory of Production Technologies of Siemens in Belgium transforms basic technology into integrated solutions that fit perfectly into the production lines of different Siemens divisions.

Purchase Price

Offering price discounts is one of the most popular ways to customize prices. Criteria for discounting often include a customer's sales volume, sales history (such as being loyal or not), and time of purchase. High-volume customers may get special discounts, users of old product versions may get discounts on new product versions, and so on. Another way to customize prices is by customizing the product, with additional product options leading to higher prices.

Product bundling allows firms to customize prices as well. A distinction should be made, however, between pure bundling, in which products can *only* be bought bundled, and mixed bundling, in which they can be bought separately or together. Various price policies can be pursued in the case of mixed bundling. One product might be discounted if another is bought; this is called mixed leader bundling. Or a favorable price might be set for a package of products, which is known as mixed joint bundling.

Purchase price may also be considered a customizable marketing mix instrument to be manipulated by the customers themselves—again, often as a result of customizing the product. Customers may design a final product, such as when they select components from a menu, so that the total price does not exceed their budget. Chrysler allows its potential customers to design their favorite car, selecting options through a special design section on the company's Web site that automatically calculates the price of the auto using those specifications. Self-checkout systems in supermarkets are letting customers monitor the total price of their purchases as they go along.

Of course, purchase price may be only partly customizable in some markets, especially in business-to-business sales, because of a dependence on customers' bargaining power. And to some extent customers may control purchase price over time by choosing the right moment to buy a new product or waiting until its price has dropped. When a manufacturer such as Chrysler provides product information on its Web site, customers may be more prepared and knowledgeable when they visit a dealer. And with new software being developed, such as Netscape's "Constellation," customers can obtain ever more customized information.

Communication

Logman (1996) points out that, especially in today's rapidly changing business environment, customers may have different information needs. Some may want to be informed about new product versions, whereas others are interested in information about possible upgrades of old product versions. Price-sensitive customers may be interested to some extent in promotional information, whereas quality-sensitive customers may be interested in product information.

To meet these individual information needs, a firm can either communicate directly to customers and adjust its information (such as through direct mail) or it can offer a customizable information network that allows customers to find the desired information easily. The World Wide Web is the most salient example of the latter framework, with customers selecting from corporate Web sites the information that is particularly relevant to them.

Distribution and Logistics

Customers now have much more latitude in choosing the logistics and methods of distribution to fit their specific requirements. They can determine where, when, and how they want goods to be delivered; they can even specify the manner in which they want goods to be handled before and after delivery. Gilmore and Pine (1997) refer to this as "representation" requirements.

Especially in industrial markets, where many firms are working in a just-in-time (JIT) environment, suppliers have to become more flexible in terms of distribution and logistics. Volvo Europe Truck (VET) in Belgium has moved to replace its push supply system with a pull system, which means supplies and raw materials are stocked and delivered only after a specific demand from a production division. Customized distribution and logistics solutions therefore have to be provided by VET's suppliers.

To attain distribution flexibility, companies may use multiple channels. Depending on the customer's product knowledge, service needs, and price sensitivity, one channel may be more appropriate than another. Customers who are looking for lower prices and are very knowledgeable about product features may prefer to buy from a direct mail catalogue. Less knowledgeable customers with bigger pocketbooks may prefer specialty stores that can provide the necessary information and support. Using a multiple channel system, companies can offer the best customized solution on the basis of each customer's needs. Then, as customers learn more over time, they may opt for another distribution channel.

When it comes to aspects of logistics, such as transportation and inventory, a firm has the same two op-

> "Customizable solutions may be appropriate for customers whose needs and expectations change from time to time."

tions as with distribution: customize or be customized. Using such modern technology as EDI (electronic data interchange), customers can continuously monitor and adjust orders, delivery schedules, places of delivery, and so on. To guarantee this flexibility, firms often work with multiple partners, some of whom may be specialized in logistics within the firm's industry. Faxion, for instance, offers complete logistics services, such as unpacking and storage labeling, to the fashion industry. Moreover, with choices such as electronic shopping, consumers too may become more powerful in determining where and how they want goods to be delivered.

After-Sales Support and Costs

As with many products, services may also be bundled into a customized service package. In many industries, customized "augmented" solutions that include both product and service are offered. In business-to-business markets, such as in the mainframe computer industry, sales contracts often cover agreements on product maintenance, replacement, and so on.

By using a remote-control system that allows diagnosis and possible remedy of product defects from a distance, customers' after-sales costs may be reduced. Nashuatec uses such a system in the fax industry. The Web provides another opportunity in this direction. By transferring video images of a product performance, product failures may be detected.

After-sales costs can, to some extent, be customized by end users. Someone who buys a new car may decide to opt for lower energy costs by driving at an economical rate of speed. A company may manufacture a copy machine that is easy for customers to maintain and repair themselves. Service costs are thereby reduced and the customers' after-sales cost perceptions may be positively influenced.

CUSTOMIZED OR CUSTOMIZABLE: A TRADE-OFF?

Businesses, then, clearly have two options when it comes to producing and marketing a product or service: either customize the marketing mix instruments themselves or let the customers do it. The choice depends on several considerations.

Customizable solutions may be appropriate for customers whose needs and expectations change from time to time. This is most obvious at the product level. A customizable lighting system with user-controlled light effects may be used in different ways, depending on the occasion: a business meeting, a romantic dinner, an hour of reading. Similarly, a customizable communication network such as the Web allows users to select which information they need at a certain time. People who are primarily looking for user guidelines in the beginning may become interested in new information topics–upgrading, new applications, and so on–as they gain more experience. Companies that develop well-structured Web sites, containing separate information sections for beginners and experienced users, stand to gain.

An important moderating factor, then, is the buyer's knowledge and experience. Customizable solutions are more suitable for savvy or experienced customers than for neophytes. People may lack the experience and skills for dealing with customizable solutions properly. They may not know how to design their own products from a component menu, or how to select the information they need from a company's Web site.

A firm should also evaluate the cost and profitability implications of the different customizing options. What are the inventory requirements in the case of product customization by the manufacturer rather than by the buyer? What is the cost of using an interactive logistics network such as EDI? Should different customization options be combined?

Security might also be a consideration. Can certain information be provided over the Internet for customers to use? Or is it so confidential that the company needs to customize the product itself?

Finally, a firm must consider the independencies and interdependencies of its marketing mix decisions. Can it offer customized final products while offering a customizable information network for after-sales communication? Does price customizability result from product customizability? Can experienced computer users design their own PCs from a menu of standard components at a price that seems acceptable to them? Will customizing methods of distribution affect price?

With marketing practices in such flux, companies are ever looking for new solutions to customize their ways of providing products and services. Using the framework provided here allows marketing practitioners to evaluate different customization options for their marketing mix instruments. But some caveats are in order.

When a firm chooses to customize the marketing mix on its own, it should take care to ensure that its marketing policy is transparent and unambiguous to customers. Offering inconsistent solutions to different people may be seen as giving special treatment to some while slighting or discriminating against others. And offering inexperienced customers a "do-it-yourself" customizable product or service could result in confusion, dissatisfaction, or even disaster. Along with advances in technology that facilitate both customization and customizability come a new array of challenges. But careful decisions based on a proper framework for evaluating the options can result in a marketing mix that comes close to providing everything to every customer.

References

Yoji Akao, *Quality Function Deployment: Integrating Customer Requirements Into Product Design,* trans. Glenn H. Mazur (Cambridge, MA: Productivity Press, 1990).

Antonio J. Bailetti and Paul F. Litva, "Integrating Customer Requirements Into Product Designs," *Journal of Product Innovation Management, 12,* 1 (1995): 3-15.

Barry L. Bayus, "Are Product Life Cycles Really Getting Shorter?" *Journal of Product Innovation Management,* September 1994, pp. 300-308.

Pierre Berthon, Leyland Pitt, and Richard T. Watson, "Marketing Communication and the World Wide Web," *Business Horizons,* September-October 1996, pp. 24-32.

John A. Courtney and Doris C. Van Doren, "Succeeding in the Communiputer Age: Technology and the Marketing Mix," *Industrial Marketing Management,* January 1996, pp. 1-10.

Bernard Cova, "The Postmodern Explained to Managers: Implications for Marketing," *Business Horizons,* November–December 1996, pp. 15-23.

D. W. Cravens, C. W. Holland, C. W. Lamb Jr., and W. C. Moncrief, "Marketing's Role in Product and Service Quality," *Industrial Marketing Management,* November 1988, pp. 285-304.

Richard A. d'Aveni, *Hypercompetition: Managing the Dynamics of Strategic Maneuvering* (New York: The Free Press, 1994).

Sally Dibb, Lyndon Simkin, William M. Pride, and O. C. Ferrell, *Marketing: Concepts and Strategies* (Boston: Houghton-Mifflin Company, 1994).

Robert J. Dolan, "How Do You Know When the Price Is Right?" *Harvard Business Review,* September–October 1995, pp. 174-183.

E. Feitzinger and H. L. Lee, "Mass Customization at Hewlett Packard: The Power of Postponement," *Harvard Business Review,* January–February 1997, pp. 117-121.

Jeffrey M. Ferguson, Lexis F. Higgins, and Gary R. Phillips, "How to Evaluate and Upgrade Technical Service," *Industrial Marketing Management,* August 1993, pp. 187-193.

Bradley T. Gale with Robert Chapman, *Managing Customer Value* (New York: The Free Press, 1994).

Els Gijsbrechts, "Prices and Pricing Research in Consumer Marketing: Some Recent Developments," *International Journal of Research in Marketing, 10,* 2 (1993): 115-151.

James H. Gilmore and B. Joseph Pine II, "The Four Faces of Mass Customization," *Harvard Business Review,* January-February 1997, pp. 91-101.

G. Gordon, R. Calantone, and C. A. diBenedetto, "How Electrical Contractors Choose Distributors," *Industrial Marketing Management,* February 1991, pp. 29-42.

Christian Grönroos, "From Marketing Mix to Relationship Marketing: Towards a Paradigm Shift in Marketing," *Management Decision,* March 1994, pp. 4-20.

J. Guiltinan, "The Price Bundling of Services: A Normative Framework," *Journal of Marketing,* April 1987, pp. 74-85.

G. Hamel and C. K. Prahalad, *Competing for the Future* (Boston: Harvard Business School Press, 1994).

Kee Young Kim, Jeffrey G. Miller, and Janelle Heineke, "Mastering the Quality Staircase, Step by Step," *Business Horizons*, January–February 1997, pp. 17-21.

Joseph Lampel and Henry Mintzberg, "Customizing Customization," *Sloan Management Review*, Fall 1996, pp. 21-30.

Marc Logman, "Information Needs in a Rapidly Changing Consumer Environment: A Survey Among PC Users," Working Paper 96-230, DBE-UFSIA, University of Antwerp, Belgium, June 1996.

Marc Logman, "Intrafirm Marketing-Mix Relationships: Analysis of Their Sources and Modeling Implications," unpublished Ph.D. dissertation, UFSIA, University of Antwerp, Belgium, 1995.

Laura Loro, "IBM Mends Marketing Using Customer Database," *Business Marketing*, February 1996, p. 24.

Min Hua Lu, Christian N. Madu, Chu-hua Kuei, and Dena Winokur, "Integrating QFD, AHP and Benchmarking in Strategic Marketing," *Journal of Business and Industrial Marketing, 9,* 1 (1994): 41-50.

David M. McCutcheon, Amitabh S. Raturi, and Jack R. Meredith, "The Customization-Responsiveness Squeeze," *Sloan Management Review,* Winter 1994, pp. 89-99.

Rudy K. Moenaert, William E. Souder, Arnoud De Meyer, and Dirk Deschoolmeester, "R and D–Marketing Integration Mechanisms, Communication Flows and Innovation Success," *Journal of Product Innovation Management,* January 1994, pp. 31-45.

A. Parasuraman, Valarie Zeithaml, and Leonard L. Berry, "SERVQUAL: A Multiple-Item Scale for Measuring Consumer Perceptions of Service Quality," *Journal of Retailing,* Spring 1988, pp. 12-40.

Adrian Payne, *Advances in Relationship Marketing* (London: Kogan Page, 1995).

Joseph Pine II, Don Peppers, and Martha Rogers, "Do You Want to Keep Your Customers Forever?" *Harvard Business Review,* March–April 1995, pp. 103-114.

V. Kasturi Rangan, "Reorienting Channels of Distribution," in V. K. Rangan et al. (eds.), *Business Marketing Strategy: Cases, Concepts and Applications* (Chicago: Irwin, 1995), pp. 586-598.

Robert R. Reeder, Edward G. Brierty, and Betty H. Reeder, *Industrial Marketing: Analysis, Planning and Control* (London: Prentice-Hall, 1991).

Al Ries and Jack Trout, *Bottom-Up Marketing* (New York: McGraw-Hill, 1989).

W. F. Van Raaij, "You Pick What You Want: New Marketing Communication for New Customers," in W. F. Van Raaij et al. (eds.), *Proceedings of the 2nd International Research Seminar on Marketing Communications and Consumer Behavior* (IAE, 1997), pp. 477-486.

J. T. Vesey, "The New Competitors Think in Terms of 'Speed-To-Market,'" *Advanced Management Journal,* Autumn 1991, pp. 26-33.

William G. Zikmund and Michael d'Amico, *Effective Marketing: Creating and Keeping Customers* (St. Paul, MN: West, 1995).

Marc Logman is a professor of marketing management and international marketing at EHSAL (Economische Hogeschool St. Aloysius) in Brussels, Belgium.

Marketing myopia

(With Retrospective Commentary)

*Shortsighted managements often
fail to recognize that in
fact there is no such
thing as a growth industry*

Theodore Levitt

*At the time of the article's publication,
Theodore Levitt was lecturer in business
administration at the Harvard
Business School. He is the author of
several books, including* The Third Sector: New Tactics for a Responsive Society *(1973) and* Marketing for Business
Growth *(1974).*

*How can a company ensure its continued growth? In 1960 "Marketing
Myopia" answered that question in a
new and challenging way by urging organizations to define their industries
broadly to take advantage of growth
opportunities. Using the archetype of
the railroads, Mr. Levitt showed how
they declined inevitably as technology
advanced because they defined themselves too narrowly. To continue growing, companies must ascertain and act
on their customers' needs and desires,
not bank on the presumptive longevity
of their products. The success of the article testifies to the validity of its message. It has been widely quoted and
anthologized, and HBR has sold more
than 265,000 reprints of it. The author
of 14 subsequent articles in HBR, Mr.
Levitt is one of the magazine's most
prolific contributors. In a retrospective
commentary, he considers the use and
misuse that have been made of "Marketing Myopia," describing its many interpretations and hypothesizing about
its success.*

Every major industry was once a
growth industry. But some that are
now riding a wave of growth enthusiasm are very much in the shadow of
decline. Others which are thought of
as seasoned growth industries have actually stopped growing. In every case
the reason growth is threatened,
slowed, or stopped is *not* because the
market is saturated. It is because
there has been a failure of management.

Fateful purposes: The failure is at
the top. The executives responsible for
it, in the last analysis, are those who
deal with broad aims and policies.
Thus:

• The railroads did not stop growing
because the need for passenger and
freight transportation declined. That
grew. The railroads are in trouble today not because the need was filled by
others (cars, trucks, airplanes, even
telephones), but because it was *not*
filled by the railroads themselves.
They let others take customers away
from them because they assumed
themselves to be in the railroad business rather than in the transportation
business. The reason they defined
their industry wrong was because they
were railroad-oriented instead of transportation-oriented; they were product-oriented instead of customer-oriented.

• Hollywood barely escaped being
totally ravished by television. Actually,
all the established film companies

went through drastic reorganizations.
Some simply disappeared. All of them
got into trouble not because of TV's inroads but because of their own myopia.
As with the railroads, Hollywood defined its business incorrectly. It
thought it was in the movie business
when it was actually in the entertainment business. "Movies" implied a specific, limited product. This produced a
fatuous contentment which from the
beginning led producers to view TV
as a threat. Hollywood scorned and rejected TV when it should have
welcomed it as an opportunity—an
opportunity to expand the entertainment business.

Today TV is a bigger business than
the old narrowly defined movie business ever was. Had Hollywood been
customer-oriented (providing entertainment), rather then product-oriented (making movies), would it have
gone through the fiscal purgatory that
it did? I doubt it. What ultimately
saved Hollywood and accounted for its
recent resurgence was the wave of new
young writers, producers, and directors
whose previous successes in television
had decimated the old movie companies and toppled the big movie moguls.

There are other less obvious examples of industries that have been and
are now endangering their futures by
improperly defining their purposes. I
shall discuss some in detail later and
analyze the kind of policies that lead

to trouble. Right now it may help to show what a thoroughly customer-oriented management can do to keep a growth industry growing, even after the obvious opportunities have been exhausted; and here there are two examples that have been around for a long time. They are nylon and glass—specifically, E. I. duPont de Nemours & Company and Corning Glass Works.

Both companies have great technical competence. Their product orientation is unquestioned. But this alone does not explain their success. After all, who was more pridefully product-oriented and product-conscious than the erstwhile New England textile companies that have been so thoroughly massacred? The DuPonts and the Cornings have succeeded not primarily because of their product or research orientation but because they have been thoroughly customer-oriented also. It is constant watchfulness for opportunities to apply their technical knowhow to the creation of customer-satisfying uses which accounts for their prodigious output of successful new products. Without a very sophisticated eye on the customer, most of their new products might have been wrong, their sales methods useless.

Aluminum has also continued to be a growth industry, thanks to the efforts of two wartime-created companies which deliberately set about creating new customer-satisfying uses. Without Kaiser Aluminum & Chemical Corporation and Reynolds Metals Company, the total demand for aluminum today would be vastly less.

Error of analysis: Some may argue that it is foolish to set the railroads off against aluminum or the movies off against glass. Are not aluminum and glass naturally so versatile that the industries are bound to have more growth opportunities than the railroads and movies? This view commits precisely the error I have been talking about. It defines an industry, or a product, or a cluster of know-how so narrowly as to guarantee its premature senescence. When we mention "railroads," we should make sure we mean "transportation." As transporters, the railroads still have a good chance for very considerable growth. They are not limited to the railroad business as such (though in my opinion rail transportation is potentially a much stronger transportation medium than is generally believed).

What the railroads lack is not opportunity, but some of the same managerial imaginativeness and audacity that made them great. Even an ama-

teur like Jacques Barzun can see what is lacking when he says:

"I grieve to see the most advanced physical and social organization of the last century go down in shabby disgrace for lack of the same comprehensive imagination that built it up. [What is lacking is] the will of the companies to survive and to satisfy the public by inventiveness and skill."[1]

Shadow of obsolescence

It is impossible to mention a single major industry that did not at one time qualify for the magic appellation of "growth industry." In each case its assumed strength lay in the apparently unchallenged superiority of its product. There appeared to be no effective substitute for it. It was itself a runaway substitute for the product it so triumphantly replaced. Yet one after another of these celebrated industries has come under a shadow. Let us look briefly at a few more of them, this time taking examples that have so far received a little less attention:

• *Dry cleaning*—This was once a growth industry with lavish prospects. In an age of wool garments, imagine being finally able to get them safely and easily clean. The boom was on.

Yet here we are 30 years after the boom started and the industry is in trouble. Where has the competition come from? From a better way of cleaning? No. It has come from synthetic fibers and chemical additives that have cut the need for dry cleaning. But this is only the beginning. Lurking in the wings and ready to make chemical dry cleaning totally obsolescent is that powerful magician, ultrasonics.

• *Electric utilities*—This is another one of those supposedly "no-substitute" products that has been enthroned on a pedestal of invincible growth. When the incandescent lamp came along, kerosene lights were finished. Later the water wheel and the steam engine were cut to ribbons by the flexibility, reliability, simplicity, and just plain easy availability of electric motors. The prosperity of electric utilities continues to wax extravagant as the home is converted into a museum of electric gadgetry. How can anybody miss by investing in utilities, with no competition, nothing but growth ahead?

But a second look is not quite so comforting. A score of nonutility com-

panies are well advanced toward developing a powerful chemical fuel cell which could sit in some hidden closet of every home silently ticking off electric power. The electric lines that vulgarize so many neighborhoods will be eliminated. So will the endless demolition of streets and service interruptions during storms. Also on the horizon is solar energy, again pioneered by nonutility companies.

Who says that the utilities have no competition? They may be natural monopolies now, but tomorrow they may be natural deaths. To avoid this prospect, they too will have to develop fuel cells, solar energy, and other power sources. To survive, they themselves will have to plot the obsolescence of what now produces their livelihood.

• *Grocery stores*—Many people find it hard to realize that there ever was a thriving establishment known as the "corner grocery store." The supermarket has taken over with a powerful effectiveness. Yet the big food chains of the 1930s narrowly escaped being completely wiped out by the aggressive expansion of independent supermarkets. The first genuine supermarket was opened in 1930, in Jamaica, Long Island. By 1933 supermarkets were thriving in California, Ohio, Pennsylvania, and elsewhere. Yet the established chains pompously ignored them. When they chose to notice them, it was with such derisive descriptions as "cheapy," "horse-and-buggy," "cracker-barrel storekeeping," and "unethical opportunists."

The executive of one big chain announced at the time that he found it "hard to believe that people will drive for miles to shop for foods and sacrifice the personal service chains have perfected and to which Mrs. Consumer is accustomed."[2] As late as 1936, the National Wholesale Grocers convention and the New Jersey Retail Grocers Association said there was nothing to fear. They said that the supers' narrow appeal to the price buyer limited the size of their market. They had to draw from miles around. When imitators came, there would be wholesale liquidations as volume fell. The current high sales of the supers was said to be partly due to their novelty. Basically people wanted convenient neighborhood grocers. If the neighborhood stores "cooperate with their suppliers, pay attention to their costs, and improve their service," they would be able

1. Jacques Barzun, "Trains and the Mind of Man," *Holiday*, February 1960, p. 21.

2. For more details see M. M. Zimmerman, *The Super Market: A Revolution in Distribution* (New York, McGraw-Hill Book Company, Inc., 1955), p. 48.

to weather the competition until it blew over.[3]

It never blew over. The chains discovered that survival required going into the supermarket business. This meant the wholesale destruction of their huge investments in corner store sites and in established distribution and merchandising methods. The companies with "the courage of their convictions" resolutely stuck to the corner store philosophy. They kept their pride but lost their shirts.

Self-deceiving cycle: But memories are short. For example, it is hard for people who today confidently hail the twin messiahs of electronics and chemicals to see how things could possibly go wrong with these galloping industries. They probably also cannot see how a reasonably sensible businessman could have been as myopic as the famous Boston millionaire who 50 years ago unintentionally sentenced his heirs to poverty by stipulating that his entire estate be forever invested exclusively in electric streetcar securities. His posthumous declaration, "There will always be a big demand for efficient urban transportation," is no consolation to his heirs who sustain life by pumping gasoline at automobile filling stations.

Yet, in a casual survey I recently took among a group of intelligent business executives, nearly half agreed that it would be hard to hurt their heirs by tying their estates forever to the electronics industry. When I then confronted them with the Boston streetcar example, they chorused unanimously, "That's different!" But is it? Is not the basic situation identical?

In truth, *there is no such thing* as a growth industry, I believe. There are only companies organized and operated to create and capitalize on growth opportunities. Industries that assume themselves to be riding some automatic growth escalator invariably descend into stagnation. The history of every dead and dying "growth" industry shows a self-deceiving cycle of bountiful expansion and undetected decay. There are four conditions which usually guarantee this cycle:

1. The belief that growth is assured by an expanding and more affluent population.
2. The belief that there is no competitive substitute for the industry's major product.
3. Too much faith in mass production and in the advantages of rapidly declining unit costs as output rises.
4. Preoccupation with a product that lends itself to carefully controlled scientific experimentation, improvement, and manufacturing cost reduction.

I should like now to begin examining each of these conditions in some detail. To build my case as boldly as possible, I shall illustrate the points with reference to three industries—petroleum, automobiles, and electronics—particularly petroleum, because it spans more years and more vicissitudes. Not only do these three have excellent reputations with the general public and also enjoy the confidence of sophisticated investors, but their managements have become known for progressive thinking in areas like financial control, product research, and management training. If obsolescence can cripple even these industries, it can happen anywhere.

Population myth

The belief that profits are assured by an expanding and more affluent population is dear to the heart of every industry. It takes the edge off the apprehensions everybody understandably feels about the future. If consumers are multiplying and also buying more of your product or service, you can face the future with considerably more comfort than if the market is shrinking. An expanding market keeps the manufacturer from having to think very hard or imaginatively. If thinking is an intellectual response to a problem, then the absence of a problem leads to the absence of thinking. If your product has an automatically expanding market, then you will not give much thought to how to expand it.

One of the most interesting examples of this is provided by the petroleum industry. Probably our oldest growth industry, it has an enviable record. While there are some current apprehensions about its growth rate, the industry itself tends to be optimistic.

But I believe it can be demonstrated that it is undergoing a fundamental yet typical change. It is not only ceasing to be a growth industry, but may actually be a declining one, relative to other business. Although there is widespread unawareness of it, I believe that within 25 years the oil industry may find itself in much the same position of retrospective glory that the railroads are now in. Despite its pioneering work in developing and

applying the present-value method of investment evaluation, in employee relations, and in working with backward countries, the petroleum business is a distressing example of how complacency and wrongheadedness can stubbornly convert opportunity into near disaster.

One of the characteristics of this and other industries that have believed very strongly in the beneficial consequences of an expanding population, while at the same time being industries with a generic product for which there has appeared to be no competitive substitute, is that the individual companies have sought to outdo their competitors by improving on what they are already doing. This makes sense, of course, if one assumes that sales are tied to the country's population strings, because the customer can compare products only on a feature-by-feature basis. I believe it is significant, for example, that not since John D. Rockefeller sent free kerosene lamps to China has the oil industry done anything really outstanding to create a demand for its product. Not even in product improvement has it showered itself with eminence. The greatest single improvement—namely, the development of tetraethyl lead—came from outside the industry, specifically from General Motors and DuPont. The big contributions made by the industry itself are confined to the technology of oil exploration, production, and refining.

Asking for trouble: In other words, the industry's efforts have focused on improving the *efficiency* of getting and making its product, not really on improving the generic product or its marketing. Moreover, its chief product has continuously been defined in the narrowest possible terms, namely, gasoline, not energy, fuel, or transportation. This attitude has helped assure that:

• Major improvements in gasoline quality tend not to originate in the oil industry. Also, the development of superior alternative fuels comes from outside the oil industry, as will be shown later.

• Major innovations in automobile fuel marketing are originated by small new oil companies that are not primarily preoccupied with production or refining. These are the companies that have been responsible for the rapidly expanding multipump gasoline stations, with their successful emphasis on large and clean layouts, rapid and efficient driveway service, and quality gasoline at low prices.

Thus, the oil industry is asking for trouble from outsiders. Sooner or later,

---

3. Ibid., pp. 45–47.

in this land of hungry inventors and entrepreneurs, a threat is sure to come. The possibilities of this will become more apparent when we turn to the next dangerous belief of many managements. For the sake of continuity, because this second belief is tied closely to the first, I shall continue with the same example.

Idea of indispensability: The petroleum industry is pretty much persuaded that there is no competitive substitute for its major product, gasoline—or if there is, that it will continue to be a derivative of crude oil, such as diesel fuel or kerosene jet fuel.

There is a lot of automatic wishful thinking in this assumption. The trouble is that most refining companies own huge amounts of crude oil reserves. These have value only if there is a market for products into which oil can be converted—hence the tenacious belief in the continuing competitive superiority of automobile fuels made from crude oil.

This idea persists despite all historic evidence against it. The evidence not only shows that oil has never been a superior product for any purpose for very long, but it also shows that the oil industry has never really been a growth industry. It has been a succession of different businesses that have gone through the usual historic cycles of growth, maturity, and decay. Its overall survival is owed to a series of miraculous escapes from total obsolescence, of last-minute and unexpected reprieves from total disaster reminiscent of the Perils of Pauline.

Perils of petroleum: I shall sketch in only the main episodes.

First, crude oil was largely a patent medicine. But even before that fad ran out, demand was greatly expanded by the use of oil in kerosene lamps. The prospect of lighting the world's lamps gave rise to an extravagant promise of growth. The prospects were similar to those the industry now holds for gasoline in other parts of the world. It can hardly wait for the underdeveloped nations to get a car in every garage.

In the days of the kerosene lamp, the oil companies competed with each other and against gaslight by trying to improve the illuminating characteristics of kerosene. Then suddenly the impossible happened. Edison invented a light which was totally nondependent on crude oil. Had it not been for the growing use of kerosene in space heaters, the incandescent lamp would have completely finished oil as a growth industry at that time. Oil would have been good for little else than axle grease.

Then disaster and reprieve struck again. Two great innovations occurred, neither originating in the oil industry. The successful development of coal-burning domestic central-heating systems made the space heater obsolescent. While the industry reeled, along came its most magnificent boost yet—the internal combustion engine, also invented by outsiders. Then when the prodigious expansion for gasoline finally began to level off in the 1920s, along came the miraculous escape of a central oil heater. Once again, the escape was provided by an outsider's invention and development. And when that market weakened, wartime demand for aviation fuel came to the rescue. After the war the expansion of civilian aviation, the dieselization of railroads, and the explosive demand for cars and trucks kept the industry's growth in high gear.

Meanwhile, centralized oil heating—whose boom potential had only recently been proclaimed—ran into severe competition from natural gas. While the oil companies themselves owned the gas that now competed with their oil, the industry did not originate the natural gas revolution, nor has it to this day greatly profited from its gas ownership. The gas revolution was made by newly formed transmission companies that marketed the product with an aggressive ardor. They started a magnificent new industry, first against the advice and then against the resistance of the oil companies.

By all the logic of the situation, the oil companies themselves should have made the gas revolution. They not only owned the gas; they also were the only people experienced in handling, scrubbing, and using it, the only people experienced in pipeline technology and transmission, and they understood heating problems. But, partly because they knew that natural gas would compete with their own sale of heating oil, the oil companies pooh-poohed the potentials of gas.

The revolution was finally started by oil pipeline executives who, unable to persuade their own companies to go into gas, quit and organized the spectacularly successful gas transmission companies. Even after their success became painfully evident to the oil companies, the latter did not go into gas transmission. The multibillion dollar business which should have been theirs went to others. As in the past, the industry was blinded by its narrow preoccupation with a specific product and the value of its reserves. It paid little or no attention to its customers' basic needs and preferences.

The postwar years have not witnessed any change. Immediately after World War II the oil industry was greatly encouraged about its future by the rapid expansion of demand for its traditional line of products. In 1950 most companies projected annual rates of domestic expansion of around 6% through at least 1975. Though the ratio of crude oil reserves to demand in the Free World was about 20 to 1, with 10 to 1 being usually considered a reasonable working ratio in the United States, booming demand sent oil men searching for more without sufficient regard to what the future really promised. In 1952 they "hit" in the Middle East; the ratio skyrocketed to 42 to 1. If gross additions to reserves continue at the average rate of the past five years (37 billion barrels annually), then by 1970 the reserve ratio will be up to 45 to 1. This abundance of oil has weakened crude and product prices all over the world.

Uncertain future: Management cannot find much consolation today in the rapidly expanding petrochemical industry, another oil-using idea that did not originate in the leading firms. The total United States production of petrochemicals is equivalent to about 2% (by volume) of the demand for all petroleum products. Although the petrochemical industry is now expected to grow by about 10% per year, this will not offset other drains on the growth of crude oil consumption. Furthermore, while petrochemical products are many and growing, it is well to remember that there are nonpetroleum sources of the basic raw material, such as coal. Besides, a lot of plastics can be produced with relatively little oil. A 5,000-barrel-per-day oil refinery is now considered the absolute minimum size for efficiency. But a 5,000-barrel-per-day chemical plant is a giant operation.

Oil has never been a continuously strong growth industry. It has grown by fits and starts, always miraculously saved by innovations and developments not of its own making. The reason it has not grown in a smooth progression is that each time it thought it had a superior product safe from the possibility of competitive substitutes, the product turned out to be inferior and notoriously subject to obsolescence. Until now, gasoline (for motor fuel, anyhow) has escaped this fate. But, as we shall see later, it too may be on its last legs.

The point of all this is that there is no guarantee against product obsolescence. If a company's own research does not make it obsolete, another's will. Unless an industry is especially lucky, as oil has been until now, it can easily go down in a sea of red figures—just as the railroads have, as the buggy whip manufacturers have, as the corner grocery chains have, as most of the big movie companies have, and indeed as many other industries have.

The best way for a firm to be lucky is to make its own luck. That requires knowing what makes a business successful. One of the greatest enemies of this knowledge is mass production.

Production pressures

Mass-production industries are impelled by a great drive to produce all they can. The prospect of steeply declining unit costs as output rises is more than most companies can usually resist. The profit possibilities look spectacular. All effort focuses on production. The result is that marketing gets neglected.

John Kenneth Galbraith contends that just the opposite occurs.[4] Output is so prodigious that all effort concentrates on trying to get rid of it. He says this accounts for singing commercials, desecration of the countryside with advertising signs, and other wasteful and vulgar practices. Galbraith has a finger on something real, but he misses the strategic point. Mass production does indeed generate great pressure to "move" the product. But what usually gets emphasized is selling, not marketing. Marketing, being a more sophisticated and complex process, gets ignored.

The difference between marketing and selling is more than semantic. Selling focuses on the needs of the seller, marketing on the needs of the buyer. Selling is preoccupied with the seller's need to convert his product into cash, marketing with the idea of satisfying the needs of the customer by means of the product and the whole cluster of things associated with creating, delivering, and finally consuming it.

In some industries the enticements of full mass production have been so powerful that for many years top management in effect has told the sales departments, "You get rid of it; we'll worry about profits." By contrast, a truly marketing-minded firm tries to create value-satisfying goods and services that consumers will want to buy. What it offers for sale includes not only the generic product or service, but also how it is made available to the customer, in what form, when, under

what conditions, and at what terms of trade. Most important, what it offers for sale is determined not by the seller but by the buyer. The seller takes his cues from the buyer in such a way that the product becomes a consequence of the marketing effort, not vice versa.

Lag in Detroit: This may sound like an elementary rule of business, but that does not keep it from being violated wholesale. It is certainly more violated than honored. Take the automobile industry.

Here mass production is most famous, most honored, and has the greatest impact on the entire society. The industry has hitched its fortune to the relentless requirements of the annual model change, a policy that makes customer orientation an especially urgent necessity. Consequently the auto companies annually spend millions of dollars on consumer research. But the fact that the new compact cars are selling so well in their first year indicates that Detroit's vast researches have for a long time failed to reveal what the customer really wanted. Detroit was not persuaded that he wanted anything different from what he had been getting until it lost millions of customers to other small car manufacturers.

How could this unbelievable lag behind consumer wants have been perpetuated so long? Why did not research reveal consumer preferences before consumers' buying decisions themselves revealed the facts? Is that not what consumer research is for—to find out before the fact what is going to happen? The answer is that Detroit never really researched the customer's wants. It only researched his preferences between the kinds of things which it had already decided to offer him. For Detroit is mainly product-oriented, not customer-oriented. To the extent that the customer is recognized as having needs that the manufacturer should try to satisfy, Detroit usually acts as if the job can be done entirely by product changes. Occasionally attention gets paid to financing, too, but that is done more in order to sell than to enable the customer to buy.

As for taking care of other customer needs, there is not enough being done to write about. The areas of the greatest unsatisfied needs are ignored, or at best get stepchild attention. These are at the point of sale and on the matter of automotive repair and maintenance. Detroit views these problem areas as being of secondary importance. That is underscored by the fact that the retailing and servicing ends of this industry are neither owned and operated nor

controlled by the manufacturers. Once the car is produced, things are pretty much in the dealer's inadequate hands. Illustrative of Detroit's arm's-length attitude is the fact that, while servicing holds enormous sales-stimulating, profit-building opportunities, only 57 of Chevrolet's 7,000 dealers provide night maintenance service.

Motorists repeatedly express their dissatisfaction with servicing and their apprehensions about buying cars under the present selling setup. The anxieties and problems they encounter during the auto buying and maintenance processes are probably more intense and widespread today than 30 years ago. Yet the automobile companies do not *seem* to listen to or take their cues from the anguished consumer. If they do listen, it must be through the filter of their own preoccupation with production. The marketing effort is still viewed as a necessary consequence of the product, not vice versa, as it should be. That is the legacy of mass production, with its parochial view that profit resides essentially in low-cost full production.

What Ford put first: The profit lure of mass production obviously has a place in the plans and strategy of business management, but it must always *follow* hard thinking about the customer. This is one of the most important lessons that we can learn from the contradictory behavior of Henry Ford. In a sense Ford was both the most brilliant and the most senseless marketer in American history. He was senseless because he refused to give the customer anything but a black car. He was brilliant because he fashioned a production system designed to fit market needs. We habitually celebrate him for the wrong reason, his production genius. His real genius was marketing. We think he was able to cut his selling price and therefore sell millions of $500 cars because his invention of the assembly line had reduced the costs. Actually he invented the assembly line because he had concluded that at $500 he could sell millions of cars. Mass production was the *result* not the cause of his low prices.

Ford repeatedly emphasized this point, but a nation of production-oriented business managers refuses to hear the great lesson he taught. Here is his operating philosophy as he expressed it succinctly:

"Our policy is to reduce the price, extend the operations, and improve the article. You will notice that the reduction of price comes first. We have never considered any costs as fixed. Therefore we first reduce the price to the

4. *The Affluent Society* (Boston, Houghton Mifflin Company, 1958), pp. 152–160.

point where we believe more sales will result. Then we go ahead and try to make the prices. We do not bother about the costs. The new price forces the costs down. The more usual way is to take the costs and then determine the price; and although that method may be scientific in the narrow sense, it is not scientific in the broad sense, because what earthly use is it to know the cost if it tells you that you cannot manufacture at a price at which the article can be sold? But more to the point is the fact that, although one may calculate what a cost is, and of course all of our costs are carefully calculated, no one knows what a cost ought to be. One of the ways of discovering . . . is to name a price so low as to force everybody in the place to the highest point of efficiency. The low price makes everybody dig for profits. We make more discoveries concerning manufacturing and selling under this forced method than by any method of leisurely investigation."[5]

Product provincialism: The tantalizing profit possibilities of low unit production costs may be the most seriously self-deceiving attitude that can afflict a company, particularly a "growth" company where an apparently assured expansion of demand already tends to undermine a proper concern for the importance of marketing and the customer.

The usual result of this narrow preoccupation with so-called concrete matters is that instead of growing, the industry declines. It usually means that the product fails to adapt to the constantly changing patterns of consumer needs and tastes, to new and modified marketing institutions and practices, or to product developments in competing or complementary industries. The industry has its eyes so firmly on its own specific product that it does not see how it is being made obsolete.

The classical example of this is the buggy whip industry. No amount of product improvement could stave off its death sentence. But had the industry defined itself as being in the transportation business rather than the buggy whip business, it might have survived. It would have done what survival always entails, that is, changing. Even if it had only defined its business as providing a stimulant or catalyst to an energy source, it might have survived by becoming a manufacturer of, say, fanbelts or air cleaners.

---

5. Henry Ford, *My Life and* Work (New York, Doubleday, Page & Company, 1923), pp. 146–147.

What may some day be a still more classical example is, again, the oil industry. Having let others steal marvelous opportunities from it (e.g., natural gas, as already mentioned, missile fuels, and jet engine lubricants), one would expect it to have taken steps never to let that happen again. But this is not the case. We are now getting extraordinary new developments in fuel systems specifically designed to power automobiles. Not only are these developments concentrated in firms outside the petroleum industry, but petroleum is almost systematically ignoring them, securely content in its wedded bliss to oil. It is the story of the kerosene lamp versus the incandescent lamp all over again. Oil is trying to improve hydrocarbon fuels rather than develop *any* fuels best suited to the needs of their users, whether or not made in different ways and with different raw materials from oil.

Here are some things which nonpetroleum companies are working on:

• Over a dozen such firms now have advanced working models of energy systems which, when perfected, will replace the internal combustion engine and eliminate the demand for gasoline. The superior merit of each of these systems is their elimination of frequent, time-consuming, and irritating refueling stops. Most of these systems are fuel cells designed to create electrical energy directly from chemicals without combustion. Most of them use chemicals that are not derived from oil, generally hydrogen and oxygen.

• Several other companies have advanced models of electric storage batteries designed to power automobiles. One of these is an aircraft producer that is working jointly with several electric utility companies. The latter hope to use off-peak generating capacity to supply overnight plug-in battery regeneration. Another company, also using the battery approach, is a medium-size electronics firm with extensive small-battery experience that it developed in connection with its work on hearing aids. It is collaborating with an automobile manufacturer. Recent improvements arising from the need for high-powered miniature power storage plants in rockets have put us within reach of a relatively small battery capable of withstanding great overloads or surges of power. Germanium diode applications and batteries using sintered-plate and nickel-cadmium techniques promise to make a revolution in our energy sources.

• Solar energy conversion systems are also getting increasing attention. One usually cautious Detroit auto executive recently ventured that solar-powered cars might be common by 1980.

As for the oil companies, they are more or less "watching developments," as one research director put it to me. A few are doing a bit of research on fuel cells, but almost always confined to developing cells powered by hydrocarbon chemicals. None of them are enthusiastically researching fuel cells, batteries, or solar power plants. None of them are spending a fraction as much on research in these profoundly important areas as they are on the usual run-of-the-mill things like reducing combustion chamber deposit in gasoline engines. One major integrated petroleum company recently took a tentative look at the fuel cell and concluded that although "the companies actively working on it indicate a belief in ultimate success . . . the timing and magnitude of its impact are too remote to warrant recognition in our forecasts."

One might, of course, ask: Why should the oil companies do anything different? Would not chemical fuel cells, batteries, or solar energy kill the present product lines? The answer is that they would indeed, and that is precisely the reason for the oil firms having to develop these power units before their competitors, so they will not be companies without an industry.

Management might be more likely to do what is needed for its own preservation if it thought of itself as being in the energy business. But even that would not be enough if it persists in imprisoning itself in the narrow grip of its tight product orientation. It has to think of itself as taking care of customer needs, not finding, refining, or even selling oil. Once it genuinely thinks of its business as taking care of people's transportation needs, nothing can stop it from creating its own extravagantly profitable growth.

'Creative destruction': Since words are cheap and deeds are dear, it may be appropriate to indicate what this kind of thinking involves and leads to. Let us start at the beginning—the customer. It can be shown that motorists strongly dislike the bother, delay, and experience of buying gasoline. People actually do not buy gasoline. They cannot see it, taste it, feel it, appreciate it, or really test it. What they buy is the right to continue driving their cars. The gas station is like a tax collector to whom people are compelled to pay a periodic toll as the price of using their cars. This makes the gas station

a basically unpopular institution. It can never be made popular or pleasant, only less unpopular, less unpleasant.

To reduce its unpopularity completely means eliminating it. Nobody likes a tax collector, not even a pleasantly cheerful one. Nobody likes to interrupt a trip to buy a phantom product, not even from a handsome Adonis or a seductive Venus. Hence, companies that are working on exotic fuel substitutes which will eliminate the need for frequent refueling are heading directly into the outstretched arms of the irritated motorist. They are riding a wave of inevitability, not because they are creating something which is technologically superior or more sophisticated, but because they are satisfying a powerful customer need. They are also eliminating noxious odors and air pollution.

Once the petroleum companies recognize the customer-satisfying logic of what another power system can do they will see that they have no more choice about working on an efficient, long-lasting fuel (or some way of delivering present fuels without bothering the motorist) than the big food chains had a choice about going into the supermarket business, or the vacuum tube companies had a choice about making semiconductors. For their own good the oil firms will have to destroy their own highly profitable assets. No amount of wishful thinking can save them from the necessity of engaging in this form of "creative destruction."

I phrase the need as strongly as this because I think management must make quite an effort to break itself loose from conventional ways. It is all too easy in this day and age for a company or industry to let its sense of purpose become dominated by the economies of full production and to develop a dangerously lopsided product orientation. In short, if management lets itself drift, it invariably drifts in the direction of thinking of itself as producing goods and services, not customer satisfactions. While it probably will not descend to the depths of telling its salesmen, "You get rid of it; we'll worry about profits," it can, without knowing it, be practicing precisely that formula for withering decay. The historic fate of one growth industry after another has been its suicidal product provincialism.

Dangers of R&D

Another big danger to a firm's continued growth arises when top management is wholly transfixed by the profit possibilities of technical research and development. To illustrate I shall turn first to a new industry—electronics—and then return once more to the oil companies. By comparing a fresh example with a familiar one, I hope to emphasize the prevalence and insidiousness of a hazardous way of thinking.

Marketing shortchanged: In the case of electronics, the greatest danger which faces the glamorous new companies in this field is not that they do not pay enough attention to research and development, but that they pay *too much* attention to it. And the fact that the fastest growing electronics firms owe their eminence to their heavy emphasis on technical research is completely beside the point. They have vaulted to affluence on a sudden crest of unusually strong general receptiveness to new technical ideas. Also, their success has been shaped in the virtually guaranteed market of military subsidies and by military orders that in many cases actually preceded the existence of facilities to make the products. Their expansion has, in other words, been almost totally devoid of marketing effort.

Thus, they are growing up under conditions that come dangerously close to creating the illusion that a superior product will sell itself. Having created a successful company by making a superior product, it is not surprising that management continues to be oriented toward the product rather than the people who consume it. It develops the philosophy that continued growth is a matter of continued product innovation and improvement.

A number of other factors tend to strengthen and sustain this belief:

1. Because electronic products are highly complex and sophisticated, managements become top-heavy with engineers and scientists. This creates a selective bias in favor of research and production at the expense of marketing. The organization tends to view itself as making things rather than satisfying customer needs. Marketing gets treated as a residual activity, "something else" that must be done once the vital job of product creation and production is completed.
2. To this bias in favor of product research, development, and production is added the bias in favor of dealing with controllable variables. Engineers and scientists are at home in the world of concrete things like machines, test tubes, production lines, and even balance

sheets. The abstractions to which they feel kindly are those which are testable or manipulatable in the laboratory, or, if not testable, then functional, such as Euclid's axioms. In short, the managements of the new glamour-growth companies tend to favor those business activities which lend themselves to careful study, experimentation, and control—the hard, practical realities of the lab, the shop, the books.

What gets shortchanged are the realities of the *market*. Consumers are unpredictable, varied, fickle, stupid, shortsighted, stubborn, and generally bothersome. This is not what the engineer-managers say, but deep down in their consciousness it is what they believe. And this accounts for their concentrating on what they know and what they can control, namely, product research, engineering, and production. The emphasis on production becomes particularly attractive when the product can be made at declining unit costs. There is no more inviting way of making money than by running the plant full blast.

Today the top-heavy science-engineering-production orientation of so many electronics companies works reasonably well because they are pushing into new frontiers in which the armed services have pioneered virtually assured markets. The companies are in the felicitous position of having to fill, not find markets; of not having to discover what the customer needs and wants, but of having the customer voluntarily come forward with specific new product demands. If a team of consultants had been assigned specifically to design a business situation calculated to prevent the emergence and development of a customer-oriented marketing viewpoint, it could not have produced anything better than the conditions just described.

Stepchild treatment: The oil industry is a stunning example of how science, technology, and mass production can divert an entire group of companies from their main task. To the extent the consumer is studied at all (which is not much), the focus is forever on getting information which is designed to help the oil companies improve what they are now doing. They try to discover more convincing advertising themes, more effective sales promotional drives, what the market shares of the various companies are, what people like or dislike about service station dealers and oil companies, and so forth. Nobody seems as interested in probing deeply into the basic human needs that the industry might be trying to satisfy as in probing into the basic properties of the raw material that the companies work with in trying to deliver customer satisfactions.

Basic questions about customers and markets seldom get asked. The latter occupy a stepchild status. They are recognized as existing, as having to be taken care of, but not worth very much real thought or dedicated attention. Nobody gets as excited about the customers in his own backyard as about the oil in the Sahara Desert. Nothing illustrates better the neglect of marketing than its treatment in the industry press.

The centennial issue of the *American Petroleum Institute Quarterly,* published in 1959 to celebrate the discovery of oil in Titusville, Pennsylvania, contained 21 feature articles proclaiming the industry's greatness. Only one of these talked about its achievements in marketing, and that was only a pictorial record of how service station architecture has changed. The issue also contained a special section on "New Horizons," which was devoted to showing the magnificent role oil would play in America's future. Every reference was ebulliently optimistic, never implying once that oil might have some hard competition. Even the reference to atomic energy was a cheerful catalogue of how oil would help make atomic energy a success. There was not a single apprehension that the oil industry's affluence might be threatened or a suggestion that one "new horizon" might include new and better ways of serving oil's present customers.

But the most revealing example of the stepchild treatment that marketing gets was still another special series of short articles on "The Revolutionary Potential of Electronics." Under that heading this list of articles appeared in the table of contents:

- "In the Search for Oil"
- "In Production Operations"
- "In Refinery Processes"
- "In Pipeline Operations"

Significantly, every one of the industry's major functional areas is listed, *except* marketing. Why? Either it is believed that electronics holds no revolutionary potential for petroleum marketing (which is palpably wrong), or the editors forgot to discuss marketing (which is more likely, and illustrates its stepchild status).

The order in which the four functional areas are listed also betrays the alienation of the oil industry from the consumer. The industry is implicitly defined as beginning with the search for oil and ending with its distribution from the refinery. But the truth is, it seems to me, that the industry begins with the needs of the customer for its products. From that primal position its definition moves steadily back-stream to areas of progressively lesser importance, until it finally comes to rest at the "search for oil."

Beginning & end: The view that an industry is a customer-satisfying process, not a goods-producing process, is vital for all businessmen to understand. An industry begins with the customer and his needs, not with a patent, a raw material, or a selling skill. Given the customer's needs, the industry develops backwards, first concerning itself with the physical *delivery* of customer satisfactions. Then it moves back further to *creating* the things by which these satisfactions are in part achieved. How these materials are created is a matter of indifference to the customer, hence the particular form of manufacturing, processing, or what-have-you cannot be considered as a vital aspect of the industry. Finally, the industry moves back still further to *finding* the raw materials necessary for making its products.

The irony of some industries oriented toward technical research and development is that the scientists who occupy the high executive positions are totally unscientific when it comes to defining their companies' overall needs and purposes. They violate the first two rules of the scientific method—being aware of and defining their companies' problems, and then developing testable hypotheses about solving them. They are scientific only about the convenient things, such as laboratory and product experiments.

The reason that the customer (and the satisfaction of his deepest needs) is not considered as being "the problem" is not because there is any certain belief that no such problem exists, but because an organizational lifetime has conditioned management to look in the opposite direction. Marketing is a stepchild.

I do not mean that selling is ignored. Far from it. But selling, again, is not marketing. As already pointed out, selling concerns itself with the tricks and techniques of getting people to exchange their cash for your product. It is not concerned with the values that the exchange is all about. And it does not, as marketing invariably does, view the entire business process as consisting of a tightly integrated effort to discover, create, arouse, and satisfy customer needs. The customer is somebody "out there" who, with proper cunning, can be separated from his loose change.

Actually, not even selling gets much attention in some technologically minded firms. Because there is a virtually guaranteed market for the abundant flow of their new products, they do not actually know what a real market is. It is as if they lived in a planned economy, moving their products routinely from factory to retail outlet. Their successful concentration on products tends to convince them of the soundness of what they have been doing, and they fail to see the gathering clouds over the market.

Conclusion

Less than 75 years ago American railroads enjoyed a fierce loyalty among astute Wall Streeters. European monarchs invested in them heavily. Eternal wealth was thought to be the benediction for anybody who could scrape a few thousand dollars together to put into rail stocks. No other form of transportation could compete with the railroads in speed, flexibility, durability, economy, and growth potentials.

As Jacques Barzun put it, "By the turn of the century it was an institution, an image of man, a tradition, a code of honor, a source of poetry, a nursery of boyhood desires, a sublimest of toys, and the most solemn machine—next to the funeral hearse—that marks the epochs in man's life."[6]

Even after the advent of automobiles, trucks, and airplanes, the railroad tycoons remained imperturbably self-confident. If you had told them 30 years ago that in 30 years they would be flat on their backs, broke, and pleading for government subsidies, they would have thought you totally demented. Such a future was simply not considered possible. It was not even a discussable subject, or an askable question, or a matter which any sane person would consider worth speculating about. The very thought was insane. Yet a lot of insane notions now have matter-of-fact acceptance—for example, the idea of 100-ton tubes of metal moving smoothly through the air 20,000 feet above the earth, loaded with 100 sane and solid citizens casually drinking martinis—and they have dealt cruel blows to the railroads.

---

6. Jacques Barzun, "Trains and the Mind of Man," *Holiday,* February 1960, p. 20.

What specifically must other companies do to avoid this fate? What does customer orientation involve? These questions have in part been answered by the preceding examples and analysis. It would take another article to show in detail what is required for specific industries. In any case, it should be obvious that building an effective customer-oriented company involves far more than good intentions or promotional tricks; it involves profound matters of human organization and leadership. For the present, let me merely suggest what appear to be some general requirements.

Visceral feel of greatness: Obviously the company has to do what survival demands. It has to adapt to the requirements of the market, and it has to do it sooner rather than later. But mere survival is a so-so aspiration. Anybody can survive in some way or other, even the skid-row bum. The trick is to survive gallantly, to feel the surging impulse of commercial mastery; not just to experience the sweet smell of success, but to have the visceral feel of entrepreneurial greatness.

No organization can achieve greatness without a vigorous leader who is driven onward by his own pulsating *will to succeed.* He has to have a vision of grandeur, a vision that can produce eager followers in vast numbers. In business, the followers are the customers.

In order to produce these customers, the entire corporation must be viewed as a customer-creating and customer-satisfying organism. Management must think of itself not as producing products but as providing customer-creating value satisfactions. It must push this idea (and everything it means and requires) into every nook and cranny of the organization. It has to do this continuously and with the kind of flair that excites and stimulates the people in it. Otherwise, the company will be merely a series of pigeonholed parts, with no consolidating sense of purpose or direction.

In short, the organization must learn to think of itself not as producing goods or services but as *buying customers,* as doing the things that will make people *want* to do business with it. And the chief executive himself has the inescapable responsibility for creating this environment, this viewpoint, this attitude, this aspiration. He himself must set the company's style, its direction, and its goals. This means he has to know precisely where he himself wants to go, and to make sure the whole organization is enthusiastically aware of where that is. This is a first requisite of leadership, for *unless he knows where he is going, any road will take him there.*

If any road is okay, the chief executive might as well pack his attaché case and go fishing. If an organization does not know or care where it is going, it does not need to advertise that fact with a ceremonial figurehead. Everybody will notice it soon enough.

Retrospective commentary

Amazed, finally, by his literary success, Isaac Bashevis Singer reconciled an attendant problem: "I think the moment you have published a book, it's not any more your private property.... If it has value, everybody can find in it what he finds, and I cannot tell the man I did not intend it to be so." Over the past 15 years, "Marketing Myopia" has become a case in point. Remarkably, the article spawned a legion of loyal partisans—not to mention a host of unlikely bedfellows.

Its most common and, I believe, most influential consequence is the way certain companies for the first time gave serious thought to the question of what businesses they are really in.

The strategic consequences of this have in many cases been dramatic. The best-known case, of course, is the shift in thinking of oneself as being in the "oil business" to being in the "energy business." In some instances the payoff has been spectacular (getting into coal, for example) and in others dreadful (in terms of the time and money spent so far on fuel cell research). Another successful example is a company with a large chain of retail shoe stores that redefined itself as a retailer of moderately priced, frequently purchased, widely assorted consumer specialty products. The result was a dramatic growth in volume, earnings, and return on assets.

Some companies, again for the first time, asked themselves whether they wished to be masters of certain technologies for which they would seek markets, or be masters of markets for which they would seek customer-satisfying products and services.

Choosing the former, one company has declared, in effect, "We are experts in glass technology. We intend to improve and expand that expertise with the object of creating products that will attract customers." This decision has forced the company into a much more systematic and customer-sensitive look at possible markets and users, even though its stated strategic object has been to capitalize on glass technology.

Deciding to concentrate on markets, another company has determined that "we want to help people (primarily women) enhance their beauty and sense of youthfulness." This company has expanded its line of cosmetic products, but has also entered the fields of proprietary drugs and vitamin supplements.

All these examples illustrate the "policy" results of "Marketing Myopia." On the operating level, there has been, I think, an extraordinary heightening of sensitivity to customers and consumers. R&D departments have cultivated a greater "external" orientation toward uses, users, and markets—balancing thereby the previously one-sided "internal" focus on materials and methods; upper management has realized that marketing and sales departments should be somewhat more willingly accommodated than before, finance departments have become more receptive to the legitimacy of budgets for market research and experimentation in marketing, and salesmen have been better trained to listen to and understand customer needs and problems, rather than merely to "push" the product.

A mirror, not a window

My impression is that the article has had more impact in industrial-products companies than in consumer-products companies—perhaps because the former had lagged most in customer orientation. There are at least two reasons for this lag: (1) industrial-products companies tend to be more capital intensive, and (2) in the past, at least, they have had to rely heavily on communicating face-to-face the technical character of what they made and sold. These points are worth explaining.

Capital-intensive businesses are understandably preoccupied with magnitudes, especially where the capital, once invested, cannot be easily moved, manipulated, or modified for the production of a variety of products—e.g., chemical plants, steel mills, airlines, and railroads. Understandably, they seek big volumes and operating efficiencies to pay off the equipment and meet the carrying costs.

At least one problem results: corporate power becomes disproportionately lodged with operating or financial executives. If you read the charter of one of the nation's largest companies, you will see that the chairman of the finance committee, not the chief executive officer, is the "chief." Executives with such backgrounds have an almost trained incapacity to see that getting "volume" may require understanding and serving many discrete and sometimes small market segments, rather than going after a perhaps mythical batch of big or homogeneous customers.

These executives also often fail to appreciate the competitive changes going on around them. They observe the changes, all right, but devalue their significance or underestimate their ability to nibble away at the company's markets.

Once dramatically alerted to the concept of segments, sectors, and customers, though, managers of capital-intensive businesses have become more responsive to the necessity of balancing their inescapable preoccupation with "paying the bills" or breaking even with the fact that the best way to accomplish this may be to pay more attention to segments, sectors, and customers.

The second reason industrial products companies have probably been more influenced by the article is that, in the case of the more technical industrial products or services, the necessity of clearly communicating product and service characteristics to prospects results in a lot of face-to-face "selling" effort. But precisely because the product is so complex, the situation produces salesmen who know the product more than they know the customer, who are more adept at explaining what they have and what it can do than learning what the customer's needs and problems are. The result has been a narrow product orientation rather than a liberating customer orientation, and "service" often suffered. To be sure, sellers said, "We have to provide service," but they tended to define service by looking into the mirror rather than out the window. They *thought* they were looking out the window at the customer, but it was actually a mirror—a reflection of their own product-oriented biases rather than a reflection of their customers' situations.

A manifesto, not a prescription

Not everything has been rosy. A lot of bizarre things have happened as a result of the article:

• Some companies have developed what I call "marketing mania"—they've become obsessively responsive to every fleeting whim of the customer. Mass production operations have been converted to approximations of job shops, with cost and price consequences far exceeding the willingness of customers to buy the product.

• Management has expanded product lines and added new lines of business without first establishing adequate control systems to run more complex operations.

• Marketing staffs have suddenly and rapidly expanded themselves and their research budgets without either getting sufficient prior organizational support or, thereafter, producing sufficient results.

• Companies that are functionally organized have converted to product, brand, or market-based organizations with the expectation of instant and miraculous results. The outcome has been ambiguity, frustration, confusion, corporate infighting, losses, and finally a reversion to functional arrangements that only worsened the situation.

• Companies have attempted to "serve" customers by creating complex and beautifully efficient products or services that buyers are either too risk-averse to adopt or incapable of learning how to employ—in effect, there are now steam shovels for people who haven't yet learned to use spades. This problem has happened repeatedly in the so-called service industries (financial services, insurance, computer-based services) and with American companies selling in less-developed economies.

"Marketing Myopia" was not intended as analysis or even prescription; it was intended as manifesto. It did not pretend to take a balanced position. Nor was it a new idea—Peter F. Drucker, J. B. McKitterick, Wroe Alderson, John Howard, and Neil Borden had each done more original and balanced work on "the marketing concept." My scheme, however, tied marketing more closely to the inner orbit of business policy. Drucker—especially in *The Concept of the Corporation* and *The Practice of Management*—originally provided me with a great deal of insight.

My contribution, therefore, appears merely to have been a simple, brief, and useful way of communicating an existing way of thinking. I tried to do it in a very direct, but responsible fashion, knowing that few readers (customers), especially managers and leaders, could stand much equivocation or hesitation. I also knew that the colorful and lightly documented affirmation works better than the tortuously reasoned explanation.

But why the enormous popularity of what was actually such a simple preexisting idea? Why its appeal throughout the world to resolutely restrained scholars, implacably temperate managers, and high government officials, all accustomed to balanced and thoughtful calculation? Is it that concrete examples, joined to illustrate a simple idea and presented with some attention to literacy, communicate better than massive analytical reasoning that reads as though it were translated from the German? Is it that provocative assertions are more memorable and persuasive than restrained and balanced explanations, no matter who the audience? Is it that the character of the message is as much the message as its content? Or was mine not simply a different tune, but a new symphony? I don't know.

Of course, I'd do it again and in the same way, given my purposes, even with what more I now know—the good and the bad, the power of facts and the limits of rhetoric. If your mission is the moon, you don't use a car. Don Marquis's cockroach, Archy, provides some final consolation: "an idea is not responsible for who believes in it."

Customer Loyalty: Going, Going . . .

Customer loyalty is an increasingly elusive but worthwhile creature. Here's why it's dropped out of sight, why it matters, what to do about it, and why it might make a comeback on its own.

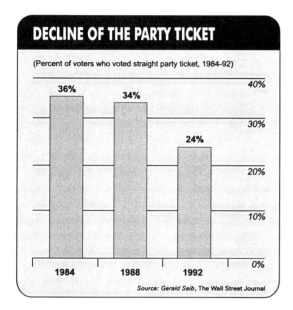

DECLINE OF THE PARTY TICKET

(Percent of voters who voted straight party ticket, 1984-92)

1984	1988	1992
36%	34%	24%

Source: *Gerald Seib*, The Wall Street Journal

Just one in four voters placed all their eggs in the same party's basket when President Clinton won his first term.

Loyalty, an all-American icon, was last seen heading south. Words like "fidelity" and "obligation" are almost quaint reminders of a past era, when people worked for the same company for a lifetime, regularly purchased the same make of automobile, and voted a straight party ticket. Now, the unwritten contract implying a two-way allegiance between employer and employee, sales and customer, government and citizen, is more likely perceived as null and void.

Take professional basketball, for example. It's a canary in a mine shaft, a microcosm of fidelity's general decline. In the last 20 years, Dr. Naismith's 1891 invention has mutated from "just a game" into a 4,600-square-foot stage upon which image, salary, exposure, squabbles, endorsements, and individual stardom are played out larger than life.

The rupturing of the bond between worker and employer has also come under scrutiny. Three in four senior corporate leaders note that loyalty from boss to worker, and vice versa, has declined, according to a recent Wirthlin Worldwide survey. These days, as Americans routinely expect to have five or six jobs during their working lives, both sides see employment fidelity as practically passé.

Customer loyalty has also fallen off. "Conclusive new panel data from MRCA Information Services show that declines in brand loyalty are both pervasive and substantial," writes Garth Hallberg in *All Consumers Are Not Created Equal*. The overall direction is clear: downward. And the degree is often unnerving.

Loyalty cannot be assumed as it was 50 years ago. No one is ready to pledge allegiance easily or forever–particularly not the legions of free agents, tactical consumers, and do-it-yourselfers springing up rapidly in postmodern America. In what Roper Starch Worldwide calls the Age of Autonomy, earning consumer loyalty becomes an increasingly iffy proposition.

"CONCLUSIVE NEW DATA SHOW THAT DECLINES IN BRAND LOYALTY ARE BOTH PERVASIVE AND SUBSTANTIAL."

WHY ARE CUSTOMERS LESS LOYAL?

Loyalty does not erode in a vacuum. Six major interconnected forces or causes act daily upon consumers to accelerate the general diminution of customer loyalty.

1. The first cause is **choice**, of which there is now overwhelming abundance. American consumers in the 1990s have more styles, options, services, products, accessories, and variations to choose among than ever before. As the field of choice grows too large, values blur, distinctions are lost, and people grow distracted.

2. The second contributor is the availability and easy application of **information**. Product information from in-store brochures, consumer publications, and the Internet empowers the buyer and raises buyer expectations. Well-developed systems of customer support encourage comparison shopping, creating the precise, "I know what I want and where to get it for the lowest cost" consumer.

3. A third factor could be called **entitlement**. Many Americans assume that rights, choice, and self-definition are automatically owed them. They are the "What have you done for me lately?" consumers. In this stony national soil of severe individualism, it is difficult for loyalty to take root and thrive.

4. The fourth cause, one that is centrally important yet receives scant notice, is **commoditization**. No one questions the triumph of the Industrial Revolution. But the ubiquity of quality, shortened product cycles, increased competition, and price discounts have a vanillizing effect: more and more offerings and messages look the same. Nothing stands out to be loyal to. "Pick any industry, and you find products, services, and prices all beginning to look alike, to blur together," writes Larry Wilson in his 1994 book, *Stop Selling*.

5. The fifth cause impacting customer loyalty is **insecurity**. Many Americans have one foot on an economic banana peel—slippery indeed. Personal bankruptcies topped 1 million in 1996, with many more projected in the near future. Folks work much harder and longer just to stay afloat; indeed, nearly 75 percent of all married couples headed by someone aged 20 to 55 have two full-time working spouses, up from 33 percent 30 years ago. The on-ramp to the American Dream has drastically steepened, and doubt plays hell with loyalty.

6. So, too, does **time scarcity**, the sixth cause. When it comes to time, there isn't enough to go around. There is too much to do and so little perceived time. With more activities, a longer work week, and longer commutes, Americans have become parallel processors, simultaneously juggling multiple tasks. Show loyalty to a store, community organization, or television miniseries? We just don't have the time.

The flip side to this trend is the fact that we buy many brands and patronize certain merchants because it's convenient. It's easier and faster to grab the same brand of toothpaste every time, to fill up at the same gas station every week. To the extent that loyalty is driven by ease of access, people's lack of time conveys an edge to the products and services that we're already in the habit of buying.

EFFECTS OF DECLINING LOYALTY

What happens when customers aren't loyal? All kinds of terrible things. Here are six of them:

1. The first, **defection**, is a killer. Look at the rise of consumer switching behavior. Within the telecommunications industry, consumers go first with one company and then another, avidly following the scent of price drops. AT&T has identified 1.7 million customers as "spinners": the ones who switch carriers at least three times a year, looking for the best deal.

2. Another effect is the rise of **complaints**. Not only are consumers harder to satisfy, they are also more willing to actively express themselves. Contrast this with the 1950s, say, when consumers would rather politely bite their tongues than complain. This is a critical behavioral shift.

3. The third effect, **cynicism**, is mortal poison to loyalty. It may be the easiest effect to understand: Corporate de-layering, star-system compensation, the vanishing American Dream, and grim awareness of rapidly dwindling resources are having a brutal impact on the national psyche. As a result, faith in institutions, along with loyalty, has plummeted.

4. Since the mid-1980s, **affiliation**, the fourth effect, has taken quite a beating. Allegiance to brand, credit card, and even fraternal order are all down. On the political front, guess which party is attracting new members? Not Republicans nor Democrats, but Independents—the quintessential unaffiliated.

CHOICE OR OVERLOAD?

	1960	1990
Products in U.S. supermarkets	6,000	30,000
Daily advertising message exposure	1,500	3,000

Source: Consumer Reports, 1992

The clutter level in our lives has skyrocketed in the past several decades.

5. In order to compete for a fussy, well-informed, independent, and financially sensitive consumer, businesses have turned to discounting. The result: consumers have become even more **price-sensitive**, the fifth effect. And businesses have learned that loyalty is difficult to earn when price is the competitive attribute.

6. The final effect is **litigiousness**. Between 1981 and 1991, tort-system expenditures increased 400 percent. This includes product liability, medical malpractice, and other personal-injury suits. America's eagerness to sue suggests a more mercenary mindset.

REBOUND ON THE HORIZON?

Eroding loyalty has frightening consequences. United States corporations now lose half of their customers in five years, half of their employees in four years, and half of their investors in a matter of months, according to Bain and Company, Inc. Profitability, as we now understand it, means retaining customers. "Companies can boost profits by almost 100 percent by retaining just 5 percent more of their customers," write Frederick E. Reichheld and W. Earl Sasser, Jr., in the *Harvard Business Review*.

How can an organization actively influence the consumer loyalty needle to lean in their direction? Effective strategies include frequent-buyer premiums, exclusive customer clubs that enhance the value of dollars spent, and cause-related marketing. These strategies work because they offer reciprocity up-front: immediate or long-term benefits in exchange for continued patronage.

As long as they don't make the customer work too hard, that is. Some relationship-building efforts have failed miserably because they were too complex and demanded too much from consumers. People have enough complexity to deal with in their personal lives; they don't want to "work at" their customer-provider relationships, too.

What's ahead for the business world? Americans seem to be grow-ing ever more comfortable as tactical consumers. Many have tried switching and found that the world didn't end; in fact, it improved. Each time they try something new, they gain a breadth of experience that will inevitably hasten the evolution of the new marketplace. The future promises faster and more zealous switching. Add this to the forces that continue to erode loyalty, and a monstrous challenge confronts American business: wooing the indifferent customer.

Tomorrow's consumers may well be too busy to focus, too worried to care, too skeptical to listen, too confused to connect, and too savvy to be sold. There is, however, a promising counter-trend. The very loss of loyalty is alerting and sensitizing people to its importance. This has helped to fuel a public conversation, a reevaluation of our national social fabric. As Americans openly examine their values, they are becoming more interested in the concept of loyalty.

You can see today the seeds of loyalty's possible rebound. Many consumers are opting for voluntary simplicity, where less is more, and a product's relevance to the community is taken into account along with its quality, usefulness, and price. Parental responsibility and other trends that strengthen family and community ties are gaining followers and media attention.

Businesses would do well to heed this wake-up call. Americans may be ready to act on pent-up yearnings to recivilize, remoralize, and respiritualize life on the new frontier. With these counter-trends in place, loyalty only stands to benefit.

—Steve Schriver

Steve Schriver is principal of S2 Intelligence in Eugene, Oregon, which provides specialized market research for health-care, utility, resort, and other industries; telephone (800) 515-9573.

by Robert S. Duboff and Lori Underhill Sherer

Customized Customer Loyalty

In the real world, all customers are not created equal.

It may sound like heresy, but the fact is that customer loyalty is not always a good thing. If, for example, you're losing money in serving a particular set of customers, the last thing you want to do is invest in forging long-term relationships with them. And, if your customers are loyal to old products and services, you might be lulled into a false sense of security that leaves you vulnerable to new competitive threats. A blind devotion to the concept of loyalty, like an addiction to chocolate cake or martinis, can be a dangerous thing.

That said, ignoring loyalty is even more dangerous. Companies that pay little or no attention to building loyalty among their customers (and, sad to say, most still fall into this category) are doomed to eventual decline. They will either succumb to terminal customer churn or, more likely, lose their best customers to a nimble new competitor with a more compelling value proposition. We see such fates played out again and again in the business world, as once-prosperous companies give in to the "sin of success" and begin taking their market positions and customers for granted. Many of the original 1955 *Fortune* 500 companies—once the largest and most powerful beasts on the business planet—no longer exist. Once they had loyal customers—lots of them—and now they have none.

Principles of Loyalty

Through our work, we have identified four "principles of loyalty" that are applicable to virtually every company (see Exhibit 1). Each flies in the face of conventional thinking about the topic.

The first principle—"focus on specific types of customers"—is controversial, as it forces a company to admit that some customers are more desirable than others. We have found that building loyalty among *all* customers is more often than not detrimental to the long-term health of an enterprise. After all, customers exhibit dramatic differences in their buying behavior and their cost to serve, leading to equally dramatic variations in the profitability they generate for a company. Building loyalty among nonprofitable customers can thus undermine a company's bottom line.

Moreover, trying to please the least profitable customers (who also tend to be the most demanding) can impede a company's ability to serve its most profitable customers. Designing business systems to meet the needs of all the diverse customer types, for example, keeps enterprises from tailoring their products and services to the needs of the most attractive customers. Many banks that try to provide top-notch electronic, ATM, telephone, and branch services, for instance, cannot compete effectively with more focused competitors who master only one of these channels. The marketing advantage will always lie with the specialist. We have certainly seen this in the credit card business, where innova-

EXECUTIVE BRIEFING

Many companies today strive to develop and keep loyal customers. But this overly simplistic strategy can lead to disaster in some cases. Four "principles of loyalty" should guide managers in forming relationships with customers. All of these principles defy conventional wisdom and can be applied in almost every company—even in so-called commodity markets.

...f loyalty

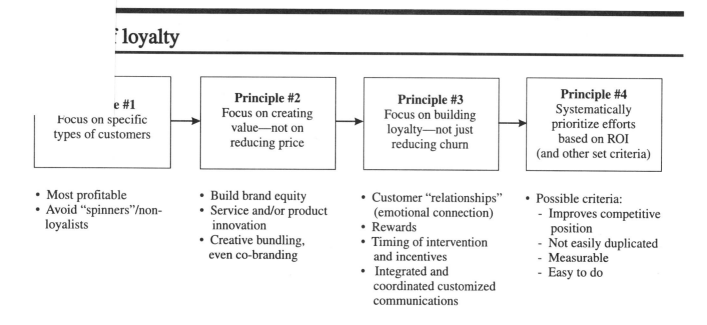

tive specialists like MBNA and Capital One have grabbed the most lucrative customers from traditional banks. Similarly, old-line department stores have found it extremely difficult to counter attacks from more narrowly focused specialty stores (see "Loyalty in a Commodity World").

While the criteria for selecting which customers to target may vary, a company should focus on those it will be able to profitably satisfy and those who are constitutionally willing to be loyal. The mistake most stock brokerage houses have made is to target those who are the most wealthy and the most active. They are all going after the same market, a market that is savvy enough to be loyal to none of them. Study after study pinpoints these "high rollers," "players," "big-ticket traders" as a segment that can provide high revenues. But the people in this segment are aware of their value and sophisticated in their ability to select investment opportunities. Furthermore, they enjoy the game–part of which is finding the best deal on every transaction. Loyalty carries little weight in their buying decisions.

That leads us to our second principle–"focus on creating value, not on reducing price." Though this may be counter-intuitive to some executives, who view discounting for one's best customers as a part of doing business, the fact is that cheap prices alone will not provide a stable base upon which to build loyalty.

The problem is that discounting, in isolation, has negative ramifications: It suggests that prices have been set higher than value (and that the company knows it); it also suggests that the only reason for loyalty is, in essence, a bribe. All of this diminishes the perceived quality of the brand and sets up an indus-

try dynamic wherein loyalty is bought and sold–as we see today in the telephone long distance markets. In the current world of long distance, only a person who cares little about money would choose to be loyal to any firm. By switching regularly between competing carriers, even a frequent caller can show a positive cash flow by accepting the highest offer each month for switching or staying. No other industry has yet paid up to $100 cash to keep or entice a customer with no barrier to exit when the next offer comes a day or two later.

We saw further proof of this several years ago working for a leading Big Six accounting firm. The issue was whether or not they should continue "buying business" in the audit practice. Clients wanted cheaper audits and the theory was that low-balling an account would get the firm into a relationship that would ultimately be profitable. Analysis showed that this strategy rarely paid off. Most of these clients continued to apply price pressure. Furthermore, client satisfaction studies for the same firm demonstrated that the more-satisfied clients were actually paying higher hourly fees on average than less-satisfied clients.

Far better, we have learned, is to provide other forms of value–perhaps in addition to pricing tactics. Innovations, particularly those offered only or first to valuable customers, are the best strategy. Bundling and cobranding can also enhance loyalty. There are many other routes to building value-based loyalty, including:

• Using databases to acknowledge key events in the customer's life (e.g., a child's birthday) or to track and accommodate personal preferences.

• Providing special previews of new offerings.

• Creating customized packages of services that meet specific needs.

In some instances, loyalty can be enhanced at little or no cost. Many marketers, for example, are seeking access to the high-end business market–a market that is held captive on planes and in hotels. These marketers could partner with hotels and airlines, allowing them to reward their best customers by giving them access to (perhaps even possession of) these new products. That's a loyalty win-win-win.

The importance of building a positive value perception underlies the third principle: "focus on building loyalty–not just reducing churn." One can reduce churn fairly simply (see "Early Response"). Focusing wholly on churn typically leads to a series of costly, last-ditch efforts to stop customers as they are about to walk out the door–efforts that typically amount to "too little, too late." The better approach is to understand the underlying drivers of loyalty and use that understanding to preempt churn by reinforcing loyalty at critical junctures throughout the customer's life cycle. Discounts, presents, timely interventions all work–but only until a competitor tries again. The best defense is to win both hearts and minds. This re-quires an emotional connection with customers through communications and a reward/thank you after behavior rather than an incentive at the front-end to induce it.

Finally, loyalty programs, like quality programs, are not free. Each program and initiative must be rigorously tested to ensure it is working and paying off. The fourth principle–"systematically set priorities for efforts based on ROI (and other set criteria)"–is the logical conclusion of our initial point. Loyalty is not a good idea if it means keeping unprofitable customers longer. It is a necessity if it means–as it should–developing and retaining a profitable group of customers.

Even though each enterprise is unique, the process of developing a loyalty program can be generalized (see Exhibit 2). The first step is diagnostic and contains two equally important interrelated elements:

• Identify the key drivers/causes of both customer retention and customer defection.

• Identify customer segments that can be served profitably.

Each of these diagnostics *must* be based on research–and, in the case of the drivers of defections, this must be blind research in which the sponsor/client is not identified. Relying on what customers

---

Loyalty in a Commodity World

Loyalty is most compelling in product areas that are considered to be commodities. Be it credit cards or long distance calls or audit services or airlines, most marketers excuse the churn of their company by complaining they are caught in a commodity.

Marketing guru Ted Levitt saw the truth a long time ago with his classic refrain that you can differentiate anything. That's what the winners do in these industries. Southwest Airlines and American outperform their rivals, so do Arthur Andersen, MBNA and, recently, Sprint.

The key is to follow a process that focuses on what keeps customers. For a cellular telephone company, this journey starts by segmenting its customers. Fresh research is needed to marry attitudinal and demographic information with the behavioral data about customers of the company. This allows the company to pursue traditional segmentation analyses (we like correspondence analysis) before determining the actual profitability of the customers in each segment.

Then we consider which segments to target for loyalty programs (e.g., which segments can we make more loyal and more profitable). Through the melding of attitudes (e.g., proclivity for loyalty and satisfaction with the company) and behaviors (e.g., the company can serve profitably), the company can isolate groups that become the magnet for building the future.

Usually this means avoiding trying to please the highest volume user–the one who always demands a discount and often is attitudinally incompatible with loyalty. Always, this means marketing to the target both through products and services and emotional connections (communications, icons, etc.) that are meaningful. The old AT&T "reach out and touch someone" is the classic emotional/right brain appeal that prompted incredible loyalty when the monopoly was ended and consumers could choose their carrier.

In the cellular arena, a potential connection is through understanding the pace of users' life. Bundling of "free" voice mail or a free extra unit for a spouse or child are value added concepts that bind customers while maintaining price premiums for the core product. Allowing (and understanding) busy customers to pay electronically and/or to register questions by e-mail or v-mail at night are other signals that build the relationship.

Most important, taking the time to put the customer in the best pricing plan for him or her is the winning move (among several tested) for this company. The "busy business" segment appreciates being treated fairly and develops trust for companies that don't take advantage of the fact that they could.

–Robert Duboff and
Lori Underhill Sherer

Exhibit 2

Loyalty program process

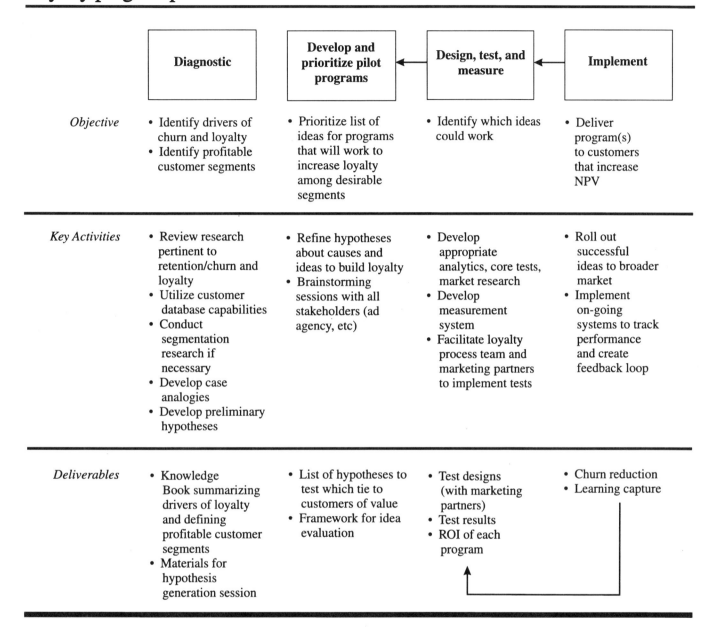

	Diagnostic	**Develop and prioritize pilot programs**	**Design, test, and measure**	**Implement**
Objective	• Identify drivers of churn and loyalty • Identify profitable customer segments	• Prioritize list of ideas for programs that will work to increase loyalty among desirable segments	• Identify which ideas could work	• Deliver program(s) to customers that increase NPV
Key Activities	• Review research pertinent to retention/churn and loyalty • Utilize customer database capabilities • Conduct segmentation research if necessary • Develop case analogies • Develop preliminary hypotheses	• Refine hypotheses about causes and ideas to build loyalty • Brainstorming sessions with all stakeholders (ad agency, etc)	• Develop appropriate analytics, core tests, market research • Develop measurement system • Facilitate loyalty process team and marketing partners to implement tests	• Roll out successful ideas to broader market • Implement on-going systems to track performance and create feedback loop
Deliverables	• Knowledge Book summarizing drivers of loyalty and defining profitable customer segments • Materials for hypothesis generation session	• List of hypotheses to test which tie to customers of value • Framework for idea evaluation	• Test designs (with marketing partners) • Test results • ROI of each program	• Churn reduction • Learning capture

told the sales force is not enough. Too often, companies believe what they want to believe about why customers don't return and have only the vaguest ideas about what truly motivates their most loyal customers.

The segmentation effort must encompass customer attitudes, behaviors, and demographics. It should also be tied to actual customer purchasing histories—assuming such data has been collected and stored. Only by looking at both rational factors and emotional factors can segments be constructed that both describe and (at least partially) explain behavior. The segments

must then be carefully analyzed from an economic perspective to determine reliable estimates of their profitability over time.

Key outputs for this step are a "Knowledge Book" which summarizes what has been learned historically (and from any fresh research) as well as a set of hypotheses about potential loyalty programs. Once segments and motivations have been identified, the enterprise must hypothesize how to combine the learning—that is, develop hypotheses about what program(s) will improve the loyalty of which profitable segments.

In the second step, these ideas are triaged and those deemed most promising are fully fleshed out and then refined. It is important in this stage to ensure that all the ideas are practical (i.e., can be implemented) and that the juice appears worth the squeeze (i.e., the potential impact is relatively large with incremental revenues exceeding program costs).

The next step is to test the potential programs. This requires careful design with explicit criteria and measurements, both of revenues and costs.

The final step is to implement the program(s) while continuing to rigorously measure the impact. It is vital that feedback mechanisms be built in with the flexibility to amend/enhance the program as it continues. It is also critical that marketing and communications to customers are part of what is tested and monitored over time.

Beyond the Hype

Now that loyalty has become a flavor-of-the-day management issue, many companies will inevitably launch new programs. As they do, managers should be aware of the pitfalls that can thwart success (see "Overcoming Common Barriers"). The major barrier is an inability to recognize that different customer seg-

ments have different values and therefore must be served differentially. As noted, these differences usually manifest themselves as diverse wants and needs both on the left-brain (e.g., product features) and the right-brain (e.g., emotional connection) sides. The key is to communicate appropriately to each valuable segment. Given today's sophisticated marketing tools (database modeling, interactivity, etc.), this is now technically feasible, which makes loyalty programs potentially far more powerful than before the days of database manipulation and mining and before the possibility of individualized messaging.

Even after a targeted approach is taken, marketers must avoid these potholes:

• Not focusing on the future–serving only today's needs instead of anticipating what key customer segments will want in the future.

• Failing to connect acquisition efforts with loyalty programs. A key sign of danger is if those involved in acquisition are organizationally distinct from the loyalty team.

• Failing to measure properly and comprehensively. A company shouldn't just look at customers' tenure or at their short-term revenues or even their profit-

Early Response

If one's goal is to stop churn, the most effective response is to cut costs–usually through the added expense of a personal intervention. The problem is what this communicates. As the long distance telephone industry has learned, their attempts to stop churn have boomeranged. Initially, customers don't leave–but then a month or two later a better offer comes along and they are gone. In fact, over a two- to three-year period, churn went up for all three major U.S. players—and so did costs of retaining customers. More important, as the saying goes, "Discount often enough and your customers will learn the value you place on your product." Customers started to believe long distance is a commodity because the providers acted that way, using price as the only important marketing and sales lever.

The alternative is to understand why people might want to stay loyal. This is what we emphasize. To make the work useful, a client team is required so that the thinking and the findings are ac-

cepted within the organizations that will have to implement them. This team (with or without new research) needs to reach consensus on (1) which customer segments the company wants to retain, (2) which, though potentially attractive, cannot easily be made loyal, and (3) which to serve well but not to target aggressively because they do not provide enough profits to yield a return on an incremental investment.

The next step is the most critical. Data are required to analyze the path of loyalty. First, the team must learn the danger spots: what events (e.g., the first bill, a change in residence) form the critical events that can create churn and/or those that can engender more loyalty. This latter point is often ignored. For instance, "the sign-up" is rarely a cause of churn, but is almost always an opportunity to enhance loyalty by engendering positive feelings and setting proper expectations.

A related inquiry is to map out a customer life cycle noting where points of churn typically arise and determining

(e.g., through fishbone and root cause analyses) the reasons.

Instead of thinking about reactions and last minute save efforts, we encourage thinking about how to solve the underlying problem. For example, if people leave after their first bill, that means the company did not set expectations properly and/or attracted the wrong customers in the first place. A more candid sign-up is a better solution than a massive telemarketing effort to re-convert someone after sticker shock.

The next step is to brainstorm for practical ideas to engender loyalty. This requires a true understanding of the target customers with regard to needs and value systems. Once you have a set of solid ideas that can be converted to programs, the company can progress to test alternatives, measure outcomes and capture learnings. Having the team continue to meet regularly with these three continuing topics ensures follow-through.

–*Robert Duboff and Lori Underhill Sherer*

Overcoming Common Barriers

Barrier: "We don't have a good database to study and then track loyalty."

This is a good excuse for inaction but not a rational one. The process can be followed to improve loyalty even if it will be more difficult than situations in which information is "perfect" or close to that. Any company can use sampling and market research techniques to learn what will work among customers who—to the extent possible—appear to be profitable.

Barrier: "We focus on customer satisfaction. If we can increase it, loyalty will follow."

This belief, though widespread, is not true. Satisfaction is necessary but not sufficient for loyalty. This has been proven

over and over again by looking at client data. Match satisfaction scores by customer from a year ago with behavior during the past 12 months. Typically, there will be correlations (i.e., more satisfied people will be more likely to remain customers), but the relationship is not perfect. Even satisfied customers leave. Furthermore, often the most satisfied customers are not the most profitable. Thus, companies must disaggregate their satisfaction scores to focus on the most powerful drivers of loyalty.

Finally, "satisfaction" measures vary dramatically. Many are very left-brain, focusing only on product or service attributes that might be fine (i.e., "very satisfactory") but still not meet needs or match competitively superior offers. At a minimum, satisfaction measures should be a combination of questions that the company has found statistically (e.g., with regression and/or time/series analyses) to contribute to profitable loyalty be-

havior. There should be probing on trust and perceptions that the company cares as well as comparisons with competition.

Barrier: "All our customers—our members—are equal. We want them all to be loyal."

This philosophy is quite positive and in many companies (such as USAA) forms an important driver of an internal culture that produces quality services. However, the point remains that no company can invest in developing aggressive efforts to satisfy all customers in the future. Thus, new initiatives must logically be designed—to the extent there are differing needs between segments—to meet the needs of those who will return the company's investment over time.

—Robert Duboff and
Lori Underhill Sherer

ability. In fact, each program should assess the proper weighting of at least four dimensions of loyalty: length (e.g., tenure), depth (e.g., amount of spending), breadth (e.g., number of accounts, services used), and width (e.g., other household members, referrals).

Making loyalty more than a fad requires doing it right from the start—in-depth analytics, followed by alignment and dedication. Like any initiative that requires major change to be effective, this requires, above all else, the continuing commitment of top management.

About the Authors

Robert S. Duboff is a Director of Mercer Management Consulting based in the firm's Boston office. He was one of the founders of Mercer's marketing practice and led its research arm for more than a decade. During that period, he developed methods of estimating the impact of alternative strategies on current and/or potential customers and then refocusing the enterprise to promote profitable growth. In addition, he instituted several of Mercer's proprietary tools (Strategic Choice Analysis®, correspondence analysis, "three-ring" Delphi panels, Knowledge Books, etc.).

Rob has taught numerous courses on marketing and research and written for such publications as The Journal of Business Strategy, Advertising Age, The New York Times, the American Bar Association's Bar Leader, and Across the Board. He has spoken before the Conference Board, the Marketing Science Institute, the American Marketing Association, Forbes' CEO Forum, and the Advertising Research Foundation, for which he has also developed and conducted many interactive symposia. He also serves on the Board of Directors of the Advertising Research Foundation and Mercer. Before working for Mercer, Rob con-

ducted political polls and served as an on-air commentator for several Boston-area television and radio stations.

Lori Underhill Sherer, a Principal in the Communications, Information & Entertainment Group in the San Francisco office of Mercer Management Consulting, consults to telecommunications companies on strategic and marketing issues. She develops and implements customer loyalty and retention strategies involving customer segmentation, valuation, competitive positioning, targeted offer development, channel management and database marketing. She also designs and conducts qualitative and quantitative research to support customer-focused strategies.

Lori has led teams that developed a competitive strategy for a major telecommunications provider based on the Telecommunications Act of 1996; designed and implemented customer loyalty and retention programs for the consumer services division of a wireline telecommunications company; conducted a segmented profitability analysis of the Centrex market for a local exchange company; and other projects. Before joining Mercer, Lori served as director of consulting at BIS Strategic Decisions.

Customer Intimacy

*You don't have the luxury of putting off customer intimacy, as customers
are becoming passionate about their service expectations.*

RON ZEMKE

THE FIRST COMMANDMENT of marketing and business is "Know thy customer!" Even in the throes of lightning-fast technological changes, you can obey the commandment to know your customers. You simply need the right research tool.

Customer research is the key to knowing your customers, whether they are flesh-and-blood people or a set of data in a computerized order-fulfillment database. And the better you know your customers, the more successful you are likely to be in meeting their needs—along with your own.

Four concepts capture what today's customers want: *faster, better, cheaper,* and *their way.* There is no mistaking the message. The company that can shave delivery and turnaround time, provide better quality, and tailor its products and service to the customer's precise needs is a company to be reckoned with.

If you want a company with an insurmountable edge on the competition, add one more dimension: *First-class customer care.* It pays to provide outstanding customer service as a part of the "package" you present to customers. In today's service-sensitive, service-focused, service-centered economy, companies that offer high-quality customer service: Keep customers 50 percent longer; have 30 percent lower sales and marketing costs; experience a 10 percent higher return on sales; and have about 12 percent better net profits.

But there's another economic dimension to good service. When customers are pleased, employees are frequently more satisfied with their jobs and more likely to stay with the organization. Why? Simple! Who wants to work for an organization that customers hate? And who isn't motivated by a customer's thanks and a manager's "well done!"?

In concept, delivering high-quality service is simple: Make sure you know what customers want and expect of you, be flexible in meeting these demands, treat customers like partners rather than adversaries or end-users, and make it easy for customers to do business with you.

This mission is easier to talk than walk. But you can make a go of it if you: Listen and understand your customers' wants and needs; respond effectively to customers' evaluations of their experiences with you; and discern what your customers will want in the future—an intimate knowledge of your customers' wants, needs and expectations.

Knowing your customers intimately means more than market research. It means listening to, understanding, and responding to—often in unique, creative ways—your customers' evolving needs and shifting expectations.

Knowing your customers intimately means knowing each other's businesses so well that you can anticipate each other's problems and opportunities, and work together on solutions and strategies.

Tom Peters writes: "Listening to customers must become everyone's business. With competitors moving ever faster, the race will go to those who listen (and respond) most intently."

How can you foster the kind of "intimacy" that creates long-term loyalty among customers? Start by seeing customer transactions not as a random collection of experiences, but as relationships built on knowledge, caring, and experience.

Customer Service Function

Customers are no longer shapeless, featureless, mass markets. They are specific, narrow groups with their own unique personalities and views of what constitutes high-quality service.

What customers want, how they want it, and how they do or don't get it add up to a service-satisfaction index that determines whether customers will continue doing business with you.

You need a rich, constant flow of fresh, timely information about your customers and how they view your products and services today.

In an era in which customers demand high-speed information, the role of the customer service function—and the customer service professional—is pivotal. Once considered a "backwater, mop-up-the-messes, out-of-sight, out-of-mind" operation, customer service has become "communication central" for day-to-day information on customer satisfaction, customer relations, and customer intentions.

The customer service frontline has become not only your first line of defense but, increasingly, your vital early-warning system. Today's customer service managers must be experts not only in customer relations, problem-solving, and their core products and services, but also experts in gathering, synthesizing, assessing, and distributing data. Every customer contact is a critical data point—a chance to learn something important about a valued customer.

Senior executives are beginning to view customer service as part of the profit chain and not as overhead, a drain on corporate resources. Today's customer service function is a profit center through its impact on customer retention and future plans. We all need to learn new ways to listen to customers and expand the parameters of what we listen for.

There is not a strong relationship between simple customer "satisfaction" and customer retention. Only by adding emotional words like "love" and "hate" to our surveys and focus group guidelines do we see what really bonds customers to us for the long term. Customers with strong feelings—positively or negatively—are the customers most likely and least likely to do business with us again.

You must broaden your perspective on your customers and their needs if you expect their repeat business. Service quality is recognized as the marketing edge that can differentiate one commodity from another. The service imperative means that we must pay increasing attention to whatever it takes, one-on-one and one-by-one, to earn the love and loyalty of our customers.

Ron Zemke is founder and president Performance Research Associates and author of Service America! *and* Delivering Knock Your Socks Off Service *612-338-8523.*

Wrap Your Organization Around Each Customer

The key to success today is to address each individual and his or her specific idiosyncrasies and problems. Solving them is the next step.

BY OREN HARARI

Over the past few issues of *Management Review,* I've been unveiling the results of research presented in my latest book, *Leapfrogging the Competition.* Now I want to talk about how superlative organizations—those that often do vault over existing competitors—deal with their customers.

Not surprisingly, I have found that what characterizes them, and what will increasingly define the winners in the emerging economy, is their capacity to go well beyond the empty "customer is king" lip service that accompanies everyday customer neglect in so many organizations today. In my research, I

The author is a professor at the University of San Francisco and a speaker to numerous business groups. His latest book is "Leapfrogging the Competition: Five Giant Steps to Market Leadership" (American Century Press, 1997). To order call 202-785-0990. He can be reached at oren@harari.com.

found that an increasing number of cutting-edge managers are coming to realize that each individual customer has unique desires, and that nowadays, the smart, knowledge-rich, technology-loaded organization can actually address the special needs of every one of them.

The 'Mass' Decline

This insight is the precursor to a giant step in leapfrogging the competition: The thriving organization of tomorrow is one that can literally wrap itself around *each individual customer.*

Competitive advantage in the emerging knowledge-based economy is no longer dependent on mass, as in mass production, mass marketing and mass distribution. Nor is it dependent on uniformity, standardization and scale. That's because the keys to business success lie in addressing each customer's individual needs and idiosyncrasies. It's a way to differentiate yourself from competitors, to forge long-term relationships and thus engen-

der customer loyalty, and to transform commodity products and services into genuine value-added.

Consider Dell Computer. My colleague Chip Bell, owner of four Dells, doesn't buy them because they "work" better than other computers. They work fine, but he buys them because, in his words, "they customize the product and personalize my experience in dealing with them. My specifications literally drive their production process. Once they know what I want, their systems can assemble it to my exact specifications with minimal turnaround time. They make *my* computer. By the way, I can send them my specs via fax or Web, but I like to place the order on the phone because they pull up my entire history with them and give me personal advice. It's my needs and expectations that drive the relationship. They remember stuff about me and my computers, and they treat me like I am their only customer."

Today, people like Chip Bell are slowly but inexorably driving a huge shift in customer expectations. In a world where they have myriad choices among products, services and competing vendors, they're assuming zero defects, timely delivery and contract compliance as givens. Increasingly, they're defining "quality" as the ability of the vendor to provide excitement and high-level personalized solutions. This means that in the emerging world order, the quality value of the vendor's output will be directly proportional to the extent to which it enhances the customer's overall experience, and alleviates the unique problems that that customer has. Quite a dramatic divergence from how most organizations function today! Certainly, it makes sense to capitalize on economies of scale whenever possible, as Dell does in its worldwide purchasing of parts and in maintaining its no-middleman distribution system. But Dell is the first to understand that scale per se is not salvation. As markets become more splintered, and customers more demanding, strategies that generate standardized products and services within uniform delivery systems will inevitably generate diminished margins and flat earnings—again, even if the output is efficiently produced and certifiably TQM defect-free.

Flexible Responses

Companies that grudgingly offer customers a few options in products and services still miss the point. The challenge today is to generate flexible, creative responses to each and every customer's needs. Thus, at Richmond, Calif.-based packaging distributor Conifer Crent, centralized truck routes are being eliminated in favor of decentralized routes run by self-managed, cross-disciplinary teams of truckers, accountants, sales and support people who electronically link with their assigned customer segment for two-way order and after-sale communication. Why? So that Conifer Crent can profitably deliver any value at any time to any customer.

As Conifer Crent President Jonathan Per-

"Everyone is used to the traditional structure and roles ... All of a sudden, we say we aren't selling just tools. That raises an identity crisis for many people in the company."
—Joe Costello, Cadence Design Systems

due points out, the new approach to the business means that "our customers determine our routes every day." At Conifer Crent, the integration of smart systems and smart people creates an organization that can quite literally wrap its resources around each customer. The payoffs? For

the past few years Conifer Crent has enjoyed a rabidly loyal customer base and has been the fastest-growing distributor in industrial and retail packaging in Northern California.

Already, companies as diverse as Houston-based Vallen (safety equipment), San Jose-based Cadence (electronic design tools), and multiproduct purveyor General Electric are determining that the products themselves are only one element of a total package they can offer, and that steep rises in both margins and earnings will come from selling the organization's expertise to resolve individual customer's specific problems. Thus, GE Chairman Jack Welch sees his company's future growth spurt not in selling, say, medical equipment in a mass hospital market, but rather by customizing products for individual hospitals, by servicing each hospital customer's medical equipment (including competitors' products) and by working consultatively with the people in that hospital to improve delivery of related services, like X-ray imaging.

This "wrap-around" customer obsession often has a literal physical dimension as well. The success of companies such as EDS and the architectural firm CRSS is in no small means due to their willingness to send small teams to actually camp out and "live" with customers at their businesses, working jointly on customer problems. Meanwhile, Cincinnati Milacron's chemical services division not only locates its personnel on customer General Motors' plant sites, but also manages the activities in the sites themselves. The fact that GM people actually report to Cincinnati Milacron managers is no longer a big deal; the only big deals are the awards and accolades that GM, a notoriously tough customer, has given Cincinnati Milacron for outstanding performance.

ILLUSTRATIONS: JENNIFER SKOPP

Made to Order

As Dell Computer has demonstrated, this trend applies to the manufacture and distribution of the products themselves. Levi Strauss is using a range of technologies, including EDI, CAD-CAM and computerized fabric cutting, to pilot the concept of custom-built jeans. The customer tries on a sample pair of jeans in a selected location, and the data needed to customize them is beamed to a facility where a robot makes the jeans to order. There's a three-week turnaround with a $10 to $20 price increment over a mass-produced, off-the-rack pair of jeans.

Similarly, Andersen Windows is leap-frogging the very notion of just-in-time inventory management because ultimately it will have no real finished product inventory to manage! The "inventory" will be listed in an electronic catalog that customers (contractors and homeowners) will use to customize their desired window products. Andersen provides each of its dealers with a PC, Oracle database and proprietary software. Once the customer delineates his or her specs, the computer checks them for engineering soundness and feasibility, and then generates a price. State-of-the-art flexible manufacturing and electronic linkages allow Andersen to respond to each request without having to keep countless variations of windows in stock. Last year, Andersen's pilot generated nearly 200,000 different products this way with minimum inventory.

This trend is applicable even in "soft" industries. At the 1996 Comdex convention in Las Vegas, Netscape CEO Jim Barksdale said: "We are entering the third wave of the Internet.... While the first waves focused on users being able to easily find information, the mark of this third wave is that information finds the user. Our new products will have the intelligence to help you focus on the information you care about."

Just Plain Good Marketing

Netscape is not alone. Sun Microsystems and several small startups are now using Java programming to deliver individualized software programs, Web pages, news updates and other specified data to each customer's personal computer. MCI allows customers to create a personalized search profile by selecting the kinds of news and information they desire; search matches are delivered to the customer via e-mail twice daily, with up to 10 news flashes per day. Dow Jones allows individual subscribers to create their own online *Wall Street Journal,* individually tailored to the reader's specifications. All this is just a beginning; each

> *The essence of leapfrogging the competition comes with the realization that the goal is to view the entire marketplace in terms of units of one, and to respond accordingly.*

company cited above is proceeding in fits and starts. But proceeding they are, and their efforts prepare them to leapfrog over competitor vendors who still offer products with limited features and service marked by uniform procedures at designated hours and locations—all convenient and smoothly efficient for the vendor.

This latter worldview made sense when competition was limited and customers' alternatives were few. Today, the organization that seeks to capture market leadership is building new organizational systems and cultures so as to wrap itself lovingly around each and every customer, for the purpose of providing a perpetual stream of innovative solutions to—and with—market units of one. (I use the word *with* because individual customers are huge potential sources of collaboration not only for customer loyalty, but for product development and cost reduction efforts as well; an issue I will address next month.)

I want to emphasize that this is much more than just a marketing issue. Certainly, it makes marketing sense to use data-mining technology to individually profile your customers, especially your more valuable customers. The Dorothy Lane grocery chain in Dayton, Ohio, has doubled its margins by tracking buying habits of frequent shoppers via questionnaires and electronic charge cards. Members of "Club DLM" receive customized direct mail and special promotions based on their individualized shopping history. This approach has allowed Dorothy Lane

to significantly boost its "favored-customer" loyalty while reducing its dependence on inefficient mass-promotion tactics such as newspaper ads and across-the-board price cuts. That's just plain good marketing.

Likewise, fast-growing Reno, Nev.-based Vending Supply Inc. (VSi), having recently attained big-player status in the vended children's sticker business, wanted to show its appreciation to its customers (vendors to retail outlets) by feting them to a gala Lake Tahoe celebration this fall. The problem was that little VSi could not afford to provide an all-expenses-paid junket to every one of its 160 major corporate customers, most of whom are larger than VSi itself. CEO Robert Winquist solved the problem by reviewing his records and determining that nine of those customers accounted for more than 50 percent of his revenues and profits. Guess where at least nine of the invitations went? Again, good marketing.

Dramatic Changes

But again, focusing on market units of one is much more than creative marketing. Dramatic changes in structure, systems, hiring and management thinking are necessary. The entire organization has to focus more on the customer than on its own product-service mix. Individuals on the payroll have to be motivated and equipped to have primary allegiance to the customer, not to their functions or job descriptions. Yes, to paraphrase George Orwell's *Animal Farm,* "some customers are more equal than other customers," as Dorothy Lane and VSi have learned. But the essence of leapfrogging the competition comes with the realization that the goal is to view the entire marketplace in terms of units of one, and to respond accordingly. The goal is to manage not in terms of the conventional "here's the rule, and then here are the exceptions to the rule," but rather in terms of "the rule is that exceptions rule." The trick—even as you focus special care on special customers—is to integrate systems, capital and people so that the organization can capitalize on the unique interaction with every single customer.

That's not easy to accomplish.

Joe Costello, the president of Cadence Design Systems, is on a personal mission to transform his company from a vendor of electronic design tools to one of customized services. Under his helm, the strategic shift at Cadence is already under way—from selling product and doing transactions to selling expertise and developing solutions—for individual corporate customers, of course. Yet even though Costello can document that the fastest growth is coming from this new way of addressing the business, he is still facing internal resistance.

"Everyone is used to the traditional structure and roles—marketing, R&D, application engineers and sales. All of a sudden, we say we aren't selling just tools. That raises an identity crisis for many people in the company. Costello has found that the new organizational persona requires engineers to think like consultants and spend time on the front lines. It requires people in sales to start thinking about after-sale relationships. It requires financial people to share data across the organization. In fact, it requires people in all functions and levels to share information openly, including with customers and suppliers, which means a lot of cross-disciplinary action and cross-pollination of ideas. It requires everyone to know the client's business, not merely Cadence's product line. All this, of course, demands radical changes in communications systems, information technology, training, employee development, performance expectations and compensation. This is a difficult transformation, to say the least. Costello reckons it will take at least two more years of constantly pounding away before the culture is completely changed.

The message in this column may sound far-fetched (I can already hear the "yeah, buts"), but I assure you that within a decade it'll be conventional wisdom. If you're truly committed to leapfrogging your competition today, let the message of this column begin to drive every capital-budgeting, personnel, product-development and after-sale decision. It won't be easy, because you and I are very adept in the old world but not particularly so in the new. But I can assure you of this: If you can really start moving your organization toward wrapping itself around each of your customers, they and your shareholders will thank you profusely.

Innovative Service

Innovative customer service is all about seeing what other people see but thinking about new applications.

CHIP R. BELL

INNOVATION STARTS WITH challenging assumptions about every aspect of the service experience and learning ways to better serve customers from service innovators.

Some people are naturally creative; most of us are not. And, our brains don't help us, given the way they work. Brains are basically information organizers. Brains look for patterns. Patterns, however, have their liability. Ideas which seem like a part of an old pattern get prematurely shelved. Patterns can make us rigid and self-righteous, arrogant and closed. "We've always done it that way" or "That's just the way it's done" are clues of a pattern that has become an idea-stopper.

Three Creative Techniques

Three creativ[e] techniques help to break the pattern, resulting in innovative applications.

1. Why, Why, Why, What if . . . Repeatedly asking "Why?" is an excellent way to start. Begin with some service aspect, such as the customer's initial contact.

2. Feelings benchmarking. Benchmarking involves selecting some business aspect you seek to improve, identifying the best at performing that aspect, and arranging to visit the "best of the best" to learn how they do what they do.

Benchmarking feelings involves looking at your service through the "eyes" of a service provider famous for making its customers feel the way you want your customers to feel.

First, identify a part of your customer's service experience that might benefit from a new approach. For example, you might choose the wait that customers experience during their initial encounter with your organization.

> *Innovation takes time, patience, and forgiveness—of your own false starts.*

Second, decide what you want your customer to feel at the end of that wait. Feelings or emotions are different from evaluations. FedEx, for example, works to make customers feel confident; Mary Kay Cosmetics works to make customers feel pampered.

Third, select some service provider you know is superb at making customers feel like you want your customers to feel.

Fourth, consider: How would the service hero you selected reinvent the service challenge you picked to make customers feel the particular emotion you chose? The goal of this technique is to use "new eyes" to review your service delivery.

3. Attribute triggers. Many great service breakthroughs come out of some innovative "What if" thinking. The goal is to identify some quality or attribute and apply it to your business. Domino's was by no means the first pizza company to deliver pizza. But, they perfected the thought about "let's make it faster . . . guaranteed." Southwest Airlines was the first to perfect "let's make it on time every time and . . . cheaper." Kinko's was the first to perfect "around the clock." And they've just added "free pick-up and delivery."

Ask yourself: What if we designed how we give great service so that it was . . .

• Faster • More fun • More inspirational • More inclusive • Done anywhere • More invisible • Done with something else • Larger • More elegant • Cheaper • More responsive • Bolder • More attractive • Done backwards • Funnier • More efficient • Done while you wait

Innovation comes with practice. Real innovation takes time, patience, perseverance, and forgiveness—of your own false starts. The urge to innovate—followed by action—will always be rewarded with a fresh view of your business and improvements your customers will love.

Chip R. Bell manages the Dallas, TX office of Performance Research Associates. He is the author or co-author of ten books including the best-selling books Customers As Partners *and (with Ron Zemke)* Managing Knock Your Socks Off Service *214–522–5777.*

HowYou CanHelp Them

BY ALAN M. WEBBER & HEATH ROW

EVERY COMPANY SAYS IT'S CUSTOMER-FOCUSED. EVERY mission statement *promises* great customer service. All executives claim they want close customer relationships. Don Peppers knows how to put the rhetoric to the test. "Do you know who your customers are?" he asks. "If a regular customer came into your store, would you recognize him? Are you tracking your regular customers on a regular basis? Do you have membership cards for your retail customers and email addresses for your business customers?"

According to Peppers, great service happens only when you relate to your customers "one to one." To do that, you have to identify your customers, differentiate them, interact with them, and finally, customize your products or services to meet their needs. It's a process that Peppers spells out with coauthor Martha Rogers in two best-selling books, *The One to One Future: Building Relationships One Customer at a Time* (Currency/Doubleday, 1993) and *Enterprise One to One: Tools for Competing in the Interactive Age* (Currency/Doubleday, 1997). As an evangelist for this new approach to customer service, Peppers maintains a full speaking schedule and, through his consulting firm Marketing 1:1, advises such blue-chip clients as AT&T, Paine Webber, Hewlett-Packard, Fujitsu, and EDS.

When FAST COMPANY asked Peppers how he would evaluate a company's customer service performance, he offered four simple questions: Do you treat different customers differently? Do you create a learning relationship with your customers? Do you keep your customers? Do you organize around customers?

To complement Peppers's answers to these questions, FAST COMPANY interviewed key innovators at four operations with cutting-edge approaches to customer service: the Willow Creek Community Church, Hitachi Data Systems, General Electric Medical Systems, and PeopleSoft. These profiles offer tools for delivering great service that you can apply today. Your own customers will benefit from these tools—after you customize them, of course.

MARKETING EXPERT DON PEPPERS ASKS— AND FOUR CUTTING-EDGE ORGANIZATIONS ANSWER—THE FOUR MOST IMPORTANT QUESTIONS TO HELP YOU DELIVER GREAT SERVICE TO YOUR CUSTOMERS.

Do you treat different customers differently?

Some customers are simply worth more to you than others are. And different customers also need different things from you. The rule is, treat different customers differently.

You should differentiate customers first by their value to you and then by their needs. It's simple: you don't want to waste time differentiating low-value customers by their needs, because you don't want to create a high-cost relationship with a low-value customer. Once you know who your highest-value customers are, you can differentiate them according to what they need.

You can even differentiate customers who seem to need the same thing. Simply expand your relationship into needs that aren't so uniform. For instance, if you're a phone company, you might think that all customers need the same thing from you: a clear, immediate connection. And in a way that's true: you can't do much to customize a phone call. *But you can customize the bundle of services that surround the phone call.*

Take invoicing. If I'm a business customer of a phone company, every month I get an inch-thick pile of paper—the phone company's invoice. What if the company gave me the invoice on a disk or if I could download it from a Web site? My accounting department could allocate the costs a lot faster and a lot more efficiently. Then we would return the information to the phone company with our own notations. Next month the invoice comes from the phone company with the costs predistributed the way we want them. Each cycle, the billing process gets faster, easier, more accurate, more *customized*.

That's the fundamental principle of the customer service relationship: the more each customer teaches you about what she wants, the more you can make it or deliver it that way, and the more difficult it is for her to take her business elsewhere.

Four Who Know How

Best-practice answers to the four key customer service questions

1. Do you treat different customers differently?

Company Willow Creek Community Church
Service Innovator Lee Strobel (leeps206@aol.com), teaching pastor and director of communications
Customer Service Program Seeker Services

WHEN BILL HYBELS STARTED THE WILLOW Creek Community Church in 1975, he was preaching to about 100 people in a converted theater in Palatine, Illinois. Today he attracts about 17,000 churchgoers every weekend to a 78,000-square-foot auditorium on a 145-acre campus in South Barrington, Illinois. Willow Creek is a superchurch that has tackled the peskiest customer service problem of all: How can you convince people to use your product or service without compromising the integrity of your mission? That's an even tougher challenge when your mission is to turn atheists into missionaries.

To meet that challenge, Willow Creek offers seeker services—church services geared toward people who don't usually go to church. Lee Strobel, a teaching pastor for Willow Creek, is one of the church's atheists-turned-missionaries. He converted to Christianity in 1981, after almost three decades as an atheist. "I don't think I would have converted had I set foot in a traditional church. I had a bad church experience early in life," says Strobel, who started examining Christianity after attending one of Willow Creek's seeker services.

Strobel has preached at Willow Creek's seeker services since 1987 and works as the organization's director of communications. He explained to FAST COMPANY how Willow Creek has grown by treating different "customers" differently.

In the beginning, church founder Bill Hybels understood the need to create two services—one for seekers and one for believers. The idea was to optimize what could be done at each of those services. It was an intuitive look at the situation. The problem he saw was, How can we worship God at a church service when lots of folks don't even know God? The answer he came up with was, Let's create a worship service that is purely a worship service. Let's also create a service for spiritual seekers to help them understand who God is.

We thought about the seeker service from the perspective of the unchurched person. If you're already a follower of Jesus and you're looking for a church, you're looking for brothers and sisters of Christ who are going to love you and invite you into their community. But seekers are almost the opposite: their biggest value is anonymity.

During our weekend seeker services, we provide anonymity; it's a nonparticipative experience. We use art, drama, multimedia, dance, and video to open up the issue of the day. It may be parenting, marriage, the workplace, or relationships—practical, everyday issues. The design of the auditorium is neutral. There are no crosses, no religious symbols. It's just a regular auditorium.

We also have a seeker service for Generation X, the Baby Busters. The question we ask is, How can we translate Christianity into a language and an art form that Generation X can relate to? They're a different generation with different experiences—so they need a different service. We have a Saturday night service designed for them, with their music and their drama. We address different topics and break the sermons up into smaller pieces.

Another innovation is a new ministry called "seeker small groups." Here we're addressing the epidemic of loneliness—people becoming alienated from one another, people not sharing their lives with one another at a profound level. We're seeking an increasing number of people who don't want the anonymity of our seeker services. Studies show that 23% of unchurched people have some interest in processing their spiritual journey with others. They want to investigate Christianity in the context of community.

As teaching pastor, I preach at our seeker services, where I look into the eyes of people who are like I was—people who are skeptics, confused about Christianity, or investigating. I can look them in the eye and say, "I know what you feel. I've thought what you've thought."

We're going to continue to innovate to keep our focus—turning atheists into missionaries. And we'll use whatever method is appropriate to the changing culture to accomplish that goal. New ways, but the same message.

Do you create a learning relationship with your customers?

Here's the underlying idea: the customer teaches the provider how to give him the service he wants, and that installed base of knowledge makes the bond extremely tight. That's a learning relationship—a relationship that gets smarter with every interaction. It's the linchpin of customer loyalty.

To make that happen, you have to find the most cost-efficient and effective ways of interacting with your customers. That's how you learn what they want and how valuable they are to you. The people at Dell excel at this. When you order a computer from Dell, they start by asking you what you need the computer to do. Is it your first computer? Are you going to use it only at home, or is it for home and work? Will kids use it? Do you want to do presentations on it? Do you have a printer? Do you need a printer? Will you be doing graphics? Are you ever going to be on the Internet? Then they recommend a particular configuration based on your answers.

They don't start out by saying, Do you want 133 MHz or 200 MHz? They start by asking what you need to do. That's fundamentally an interactive process.

You can create this interaction any number of ways. The trick is to find the one approach that works best for you. The phone, for example, is very effective. The bandwidth is high, you can read voice inflection, and data capture is good because a customer service agent punches everything in. But the phone is also a very expensive tool.

The Web offers an increasingly effective way to interact. When you interact on the Web, the cost to the supplier is zero. *Nothing.* Compare that with the phone: Every time you call Federal Express and ask them to track your package, your call costs them $2 to $3. They lose money on that package. But when you go to their Web site and track the package yourself, they make money. The more people use the Web site, the more cost-efficient the business becomes.

2. Do you create a learning relationship with your customers?

Company Hitachi Data Systems
Service Innovator Al Mascha (mascha@hdshq.com), vice president of service operations
Customer Service Program Customer Advisory Panel

IN THE WORLD OF NEW PRODUCT DEVELOPment, user groups and customer advisory panels are nothing new: car companies, software operations, even sneaker manufacturers have been using them for years. But the service business? For some reason, service companies have been slow to appreciate the insight—and foresight—that listening to customers can provide. One exception is Hitachi Data Systems (HDS), a $2 billion mainframe, storage devices, and service company headquartered in Santa Clara, California. Says Al Mascha, vice president of service operations at HDS, "Because we're in such a rapidly changing industry, we need first-hand information, directly from the customer."

To get as close to the customer as possible, Mascha developed and launched a customer advisory panel (CAP). In early 1993 he brought together about 20 of HDS's most significant customers for a three-day meeting to discuss service issues, new technological developments, and emerging strategic directions at their companies. FAST COMPANY talked with Mascha about the ideas behind the CAP, its implementation, and the lessons HDS has learned from it.

The CAP allows a small group of customers to get together to discuss service issues, problems, and new ideas. It's straight talk, direct to us—our customers talking about where they're going and what services they think they'll require. There's no pressure and there are no salespeople present. Even the agenda is developed with the participation of the customers.

We've learned a lot about what it takes to make a CAP work. The most important thing is to pick the right people. You have to select the members very carefully—which means that you need to know your customers very well before you even start this kind of program. We want people from companies using state-of-the-art information systems for critical applications—companies that are really stretching the technological envelope. Usually they're the ones who are under the gun and need leading-edge services. So our CAP has several large banks, an airline, a large shipping company, and other big information technology users.

Overall, we want no more than 20 companies to participate. And from each company, I'm not looking for a buyer; I'm looking for a technocrat. I want a technical recommender—someone who knows about the technology and how it's used within the company. Most important, all members of the CAP must be outspoken! We want strong opinions and heated debates, because that's how you get useful information.

We're looking for these people to give us clear signals on what state-of-the-art service means to them. They help us design different delivery structures, different training programs, different service offerings. For instance, we asked them to talk about product reliability and availability, and ended up redesigning the specifications for one of our products because of what they told us.

The full group meets every nine months at a different location, which we and the CAP members select jointly. Sometimes we bring in an outside speaker to stimulate their thinking. One thing we have learned: you cannot have a full agenda. These are people who want some freedom to decide what they will talk about. So we leave a lot of white space on the agenda.

Now that we've been doing this for four years, the customers are using the meetings to make presentations to each other. They share their own best practices or identify improvements they've made to their own operations.

The biggest benefit to us is clear: we get direct input from our customers on what they think we need to do—what services we should design and deliver. But there are also real benefits to our customers. When a product comes out, for example, they get it before anyone else. For three or four months, they're ahead of the rest of their industry because they have the product first and know it better than anyone else.

They also benefit from communicating with each other on a regular basis. They have ongoing conversations among themselves about technical and service issues. The CAP is a community of companies that not only help us improve service performance but also help themselves.

Do you keep your customers?

You never want to turn a customer loose. If you're a home builder and I come to you to build my house, you know that I'm also going to need an architect, a realtor, a lawyer, an insurance agent. You can't deliver those services. But it would pay you to have alliances with other high-quality companies and professionals who *could* deliver those services. That way you continue to own the relationship.

You have to be on top of what the customer wants. Customers are diverse and dynamic—their tastes and needs change from day to day and even hour to hour.

The more you customize your product or service, the more marketing becomes part of customer service—and the more customer service becomes part of marketing. You erase the distinction between getting a customer, keeping a customer, and growing a customer.

If you want to do a good job of acquiring new customers, you can hire a marketing director or an ad agency. *No problem.* But if you want to do a better job of keeping your customers longer and growing them into bigger customers, there's nobody you can hire to do that. It has to permeate your organization. It has to become a way of doing business.

3. Do you keep your customers?

Company General Electric Medical Systems
Service Innovator Jack Albertson, applications program manager
Customer Service Program TiP-TV

MOST PEOPLE LOOK AT GENERAL ELECTRIC Medical Systems (GEMS) and see a $4 billion global manufacturer of technologically advanced medical equipment. X-ray devices, magnetic resonance (MR) and computed tomography (CT) scanners, and other diagnostic imaging machines. Jack Albertson sees a company whose real business is service. "We need to be there for the entire life cycle of the product, to keep in touch with the customer on a regular basis," he says.

When Albertson became applications program manager at the Waukasha, Wisconsin-headquartered company in 1990, those customers—mostly large hospitals and clinics—told him that GEMS was out of touch. "They said, 'You don't touch us nearly enough. We like some of the training you do, but you're not communicating enough with us,'" says Albertson. In fact, when GEMS did customer surveys, it discovered that customer training was the highest "dis-satisfier."

Fast-forward to 1997. Thanks to a comprehensive program created by Albertson and dubbed Training in Partnership—or TiP (a trademarked name)—GEMS's customer education activities now rank as its highest customer "satisfier."

The most innovative and far-reaching element of the TiP program is a television network (TiP-TV) that carries live training broadcasts into subscribers' workplaces. TiP-TV now has 1,950 subscription commitments; for general interest programs, it has drawn as many as 18,000 viewers. FAST COMPANY asked Albertson to describe TiP-TV's unique role in helping GEMS solidify its contact with its customers.

If you go out and ask your customers, they'll tell you what you're doing wrong and how to make it right. In our case, they made it clear that they wanted more "touches." They wanted someone to hold their hand, to see them as often as possible, and to walk them through the use of every product. We knew we

couldn't do all that training in person—it simply wasn't cost-effective. But we had a lot of technology available to us. We had interested customers who wanted to get information from us. The question was, What kinds of high-tech training could we develop?

We created a series of Training in Partnership, or TiP, products. TiP-TV is one of our best-known programs. From the beginning, the primary purpose was to train radiologists and other technologists to use the equipment more effectively. All the broadcasts are live and interactive, using physicians or trained GE technologists to demonstrate the correct procedures. Our customers can call in and get real-time answers to their questions.

It's simple for the customer to use—and it provides us with a ready-made feedback loop. Every site that's going to watch a program signs up in advance, telling us roughly how many people will be watching at the site. Then, about three weeks before the program airs, we send a syllabus—one for each person at each site. It could be as long as 60 or 70 pages, and it previews all the material in the program. With the syllabus they also get pre- and post-program tests and a survey. Now the only way they get their continuing-education credits is by sending all that information back to us.

There are a number of direct benefits to our customers from TiP-TV. First, we deliver information to them that reduces the number of retakes—times when a physician decides that an image isn't right and orders that it be taken again. Those retakes are very expensive for hospitals. Second, we help our customers cut down on procedure time. Today procedures involving an MR or CT take an average of 20 minutes each. What if using the right protocols would let you cut that time down to 10 minutes? That would represent a huge savings to our customers. And third, we reduce the cost of continuing education for our customers.

Of course, it's also a win for us. We want to keep that ongoing "touch" with the customer. We estimate that the average number of "touches" per customer has gone from 9 days per year four years ago to 21 days per year today. That's how to develop loyal customers.

It turns out that, like any network, we're in the ratings business. We ask our customers to rate our service on a scale of 1 to 5, with 1 being very poor and 5 being excellent. When we started this program, we were in the mid-3's. Since then we've gotten better and better, and now we're about 4.4. It's hard to get a perfect score from our customers—they're very tough.

Do you organize around customers?
Most companies aren't organized for this new way of working and don't have anyone in charge of making it happen. But the firm of the future will be organized around individual customer relationships.

You may not be able to make that change overnight. But you can start by identifying your highest-value customers and putting somebody in charge of them. That's an incremental step, but it speaks to three issues: organization, time, and money. As long as no one is responsible, no one is going to have the money or find the time. But if you put someone in charge, you'll make more money, and suddenly you'll also find the time.

Some people ask, Do our customers really want this? That's really old thinking! The fact is, customers want different things. Some really want this kind of individualized service. Others don't. Some will always award contracts strictly according to bids: they don't want a relationship with you. Others will gladly off-load functions to you if you perform them competently—and will remain loyal to you forever.

You have to think of customers as individuals. Once you start to think that way, you realize that your business is your customer, not your product or service. A great customer relationship gives you long-term business. The simple truth is, any company that can't identify its customers *individually* is going to be history.

DON PEPPERS (PEPPERS@MARKETING1TO1. COM) STARTED MARKETING 1:1 IN 1992, AFTER A CAREER IN DIRECT MARKETING, FINANCE, AND BUSINESS DEVELOPMENT IN INDUSTRIES RANGING FROM OIL TO AIRLINES.

4. Do you organize around customers?

Company PeopleSoft Inc.
Service Innovator Sebastian Grady (seb_grady@peoplesoft.com), vice president of customer services
Customer Service Program Account Managers

SINCE ITS FOUNDING IN 1987, PEOPLESOFT INC. has organized its operations around customers. Not products. Not sales. Customers. The developer of enterprise-wide application software is on target to bring in $1 billion next year. To get there, it's relying on more than 300 account managers—employees within PeopleSoft's customer service and development division—to put the customer's interests first.

The account manager is a customer's primary point of contact, acting as a liaison between the customer and the company's other divisions. Unlike account managers in many organizations, however, those at PeopleSoft are not commissioned sales staff. Instead, their performance rating is based on how easy it is for customers to implement PeopleSoft's software and on whether customers remain happy.

The stakes are high: PeopleSoft's average software sale is $1 million. It's clients include such giants as Ford, Dow Chemical, Siemens, Wal-Mart, and PepsiCo—so far, they're all smiles. In PeopleSoft's 1997 customer community survey, customer retention and satisfaction consistently push 100%.

"The account manager is really our differentiator," says Sebastian Grady, vice president of customer services. "It's the glue that holds PeopleSoft and the customer together." Grady joined Pleasanton, California-based PeopleSoft in 1993 as an account manager and now manages customer services for the company. FAST COMPANY talked with him about the role of account managers, their relationships with client companies, and how they increase customer loyalty.

The account manager focuses on two things: helping customers get up and running with PeopleSoft products so they can see a quick return on their invest-

ment, and making sure that we've got referenceable customers—happy customers. Account managers aren't paid for selling additional products to their accounts. Their only job is to make sure the customer is completely happy with the product after it's bought.

Each account manager handles anywhere from 1 to 10 customers; the average is probably somewhere around 6. One customer would be too few—you'd lose the chance to leverage one customer's experience into another's. But 60 accounts would turn account managers into purely administrative people. The idea is that an account manager in the health care industry has 5 or 6 accounts—mostly hospitals or medical centers— and can become an expert in that industry.

Our customers know that any time they've got an issue that's not getting handled in another part of PeopleSoft, their account manager can help them cut through the red tape. Around here the account manager is like E.F. Hutton in that old ad: when the account manager speaks, people listen.

The account managers are on the hook to make the customer successful. They know the customer's business. They're a powerful reality check for the rest of the company. They can call foul when we're doing something we shouldn't be doing, and because they're out in the trenches with the customer every day, they can tell us what is and what isn't going to work.

The account manager and the contact person inside the customer company are extremely close—like Siamese twins. They count on each other. If the customer doesn't call the account manager, the account manager calls the customer—whether or not there's a reason to call. Customers get so dependent on their account manager that when one gets promoted or moves on, we have to make sure there's a smooth transition. It's up to the old account manager to introduce the new one.

Customers get so comfortable with these people that they think they're part of their company. And the account managers are such customer advocates inside PeopleSoft that sometimes we wonder which company they really work for.

In our latest implementation report, we asked our customers, "Would you select PeopleSoft again?" The answers are amazing: 99.6% of those using our human resources management systems, 98.6% of those using our financial systems, and 100% of those using our distribution systems all said they'd choose us again. Survey professionals tell us that a response between 85% and 90% would represent maximum customer loyalty. Account managers are the biggest reason our customer loyalty is so high.

SERVICE IS EVERYBODY'S BUSINESS

On the front line of the new economy, service—bold, fast, imaginative, and customized—is the ultimate strategic imperative.

Ronald Henkoff

THE CRASH scene at the intersection of 40th Street and 26th Avenue in Tampa is chaotic and tense. The two cars are bent and battered. Their drivers and passengers are not bleeding, but they are shaken up and scared. Just minutes after the collision, a young man dressed in a polo shirt, khakis, and wingtips arrives on the scene to assume command. Bearing a clipboard, a camera, a cassette recorder, and an air of competence, Lance Edgy, 26, calms the victims and advises them on medical care, repair shops, police reports, and legal procedures. Edgy is not a cop or a lawyer or a good samaritan. He is a senior claims representative for Progressive Corp., an insurance company that specializes in high-risk drivers, high-octane profits—and exceptional service.

Edgy invites William McAllister, Progressive's policyholder, into an air-conditioned van equipped with comfortable chairs, a desk, and two cellular phones. Even before the tow trucks have cleared away the wreckage, Edgy is offering his client a settlement for the market value of his totaled 1988 Mercury Topaz. McAllister, who does not appear to have been at fault in this accident, is amazed by Progressive's alacrity: "This is great—someone coming right out here and taking charge. I didn't expect it at all."

REPORTER ASSOCIATE *Ann Sample*

Welcome to the front line of the new American economy, where service—bold, fast, unexpected, innovative, and customized—is the ultimate strategic imperative, a business challenge that has profound implications for the way we manage companies, hire employees, develop careers, and craft policies.

It matters not whether a company creates something you can touch, such as a computer, a toaster, or a machine tool, or something you can only experience, such as insurance coverage, an airplane ride, or a telephone call. What counts most is the service built into that something—the way the product is designed and delivered, billed and bundled, explained and installed, repaired and renewed.

Product quality, once a competitive advantage, is now just the ante into the game. Says Eric Mittelstadt, 58, president and CEO of Fanuc Robotics North America: "Everyone has become better at developing products. In robotics, the robot itself has become sort of a commodity. The one place you can differentiate yourself is in the service you provide."

Companies that achieve distinctive service often have to redefine their very reason for doing business. Fanuc has transmuted itself from an assembler of robots into a designer and installer of customized manufacturing systems. Progressive no longer simply sells insurance policies; it sees itself as a mediator of human trauma. Toyota's Lexus division has invented not just a new luxury car but a whole new standard of luxury service.

Johnson Controls, a seemingly mature manufacturer of thermostats and energy systems, has discovered startup-style growth in the business of managing other companies' buildings. ServiceMaster, a company that fertilizes lawns, kills bugs, and scrubs floors, has prospered by, in effect, selling people back their own leisure time. Taco Bell has been ringing up juicy profits because it knows that its main business is not preparing food but delivering it—and not just in restaurants but in schools, hospitals, kiosks, and pushcarts.

As a result of epiphanies like these, entire companies are—literally—moving closer to their customers. At Progressive, claims adjusters who used to spend much of their time working phones and pushing papers are ambulatory. At Johnson Controls, design engineers who were once ensconced in cubicles and harnessed to their computers are out in their customers' buildings, managing the systems they helped create. Says Patrick Harker, director of the Wharton School's Fishman-Davidson Center, which studies the service sector: "Once you start thinking of service as a process instead of as a series of functions, the old distinction between the front office (the people who did the selling) and the back office (the people who pushed the paper but never saw the customer) disappears."

The changing nature of customer relationships demands a new breed of service worker, folks who are empathetic, flexible, informed, articulate, inventive, and able to work with minimal levels of supervision. "Rather than the service world being derided as having the dead-end jobs of our time, it will increasingly become an outlet for creativity, theatricality, and expressiveness," says Larry Keeley, president of Doblin Group, a Chicago management and design consulting firm. It's no coincidence that companies everywhere now profess an ardent desire to "delight" their customers.

For far longer than most of us realize—for most of this century, in fact—services have dominated the American economy. They now generate 74% of gross domestic product, account for 79% of all jobs, and produce a balance-of-trade surplus that hit $55.7 billion last year, vs. a deficit of $132.4 billion for goods.

The demand for services will remain strong. The Bureau of Labor Statistics expects service occupations to be responsible for *all* net job growth through the year 2005, spawning whole new legions of nurses, physical therapists, home health aides, and social workers to minister to the needs of an aging population, along with phalanxes of food servers, child-care providers, and cleaning ladies to cater to the wants of harried two-earner families. Also rising to the fore will be a swelling class of technical workers, including computer engineers, systems analysts, and paralegals.

THE SERVICE ECONOMY, despite its size and growth, remains extraordinarily misunderstood, mismeasured, and mismanaged. "We still have this perception that making a product is better than providing a service," says James Brian Quinn, professor of management at Dartmouth's Tuck School and author of the book *Intelligent Enterprise.* That notion, which Quinn traces back to prophets as diverse as Adam Smith and Karl Marx, is reinforced by present-day politicians, economists, trade union officials, and journalists—service workers all—who decry the demise of high-paying manufacturing jobs and rue the propagation of low-paying service positions like burger flippers, floor sweepers, and bedpan changers.

Well, it's not that simple. The service sector, whose cohorts include richly remunerated cardiac surgeons, tort lawyers, and movie stars, is as varied as the economy itself. The gap between manufacturing and service wages is narrowing. So, too, is the difference between productivity rates in goods and services industries. In 1992 the median goods-producing job paid only $19 per week more than the median service-pro-

ducing job, according to a recently published study by the Federal Reserve Bank of Cleveland. More telling: The distribution of low-paying and high-paying jobs in each sector is virtually identical. The real problem isn't the wage gap between workers who produce goods and those who provide services. It's the wage chasm between employees with higher education and those without.

Despite the steady expansion of the service economy, American management practices, accounting conventions, business school courses, and public policies continue to suffer from an acute Industrial Age hangover. "Most people still view the world through manufacturing goggles," complains Fred Reichheld, leader of the customer-loyalty practice at Bain & Co. "We use an accounting system that was designed to serve 19th-century textile and steel mills." That system tallies returns on equipment, inventories, and other physical assets, but what really matters in a service business is the return a company reaps from its human assets—the brainpower of its employees and the loyalty of its customers. Try reporting something like "return on intellect employed" on your next P&L statement, and see how the analysts and auditors react to that.

Service executives often behave much like belly dancers trying to march to a John Philip Sousa song, subjecting their companies to management theories—both traditional and trendy—that were invented in the factory. Says Leonard Schlesinger, a Harvard business school professor who has studied service companies for two decades: "Old legends die hard. Many service firms have aped the worst aspects of manufacturing management. They oversupervise; they overcontrol."

Even new managerial precepts like total quality management, statistical process control, reengineering, and benchmarking are rooted in manufacturing. "Senior management continues to focus on incremental improvements in quality, on redesigning internal processes, on restructuring, on taking people out of the equation," says a frustrated Craig Terrill, an innovation consultant at Kuczmarski & Associates in Chicago. "That's such a defeatist approach. They should be coming up with whole new ways to serve their customers."

The good news is that an increasing number of companies are inventing new ways to reach those customers. Forcing them to change is that fabled taskmaster—the marketplace. Progressive Corp. used to have a winning formula for coining money in auto insurance, a business with notoriously low margins. The company, headquartered in Cleveland, wrote policies for high-risk drivers that its competitors wouldn't touch, and charged high prices to match. The ride ended in 1988, when two things happened. Allstate outflanked Progressive in the high-risk

Employment

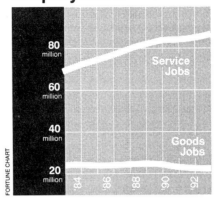

niche, and voters in California, where Progressive made 25% of its profits, passed Proposition 103, a law that sharply curtailed insurance rates.

Peter Lewis, 60, Progressive's plain-speaking chairman, CEO, and president, saw the double wake-up call as an opportunity both to revise his company's practices and to tame the public's hostility. Says he: "People get screwed seven ways from Sunday in auto insurance. They get dealt with adversarially, and they get dealt with slowly. I said, 'Why don't we just stop that? Why don't we start dealing with them nicely? It would be a revolution in the business.'"

With its round-the-clock Immediate Response program, introduced four years ago, Progressive representatives now make contact with 80% of accident victims less than nine hours after learning of the crash. Adjusters inspect 70% of damaged vehicles within one day and wrap up most collision damage claims within a week. By scurrying to the scene, adjusters obtain accurate information fast, which they feed into PACMan (Progressive automated claims management system). The streamlined process reduces costs, builds customers' good will, and keeps the liability lawyers at bay. At the crash scene in Tampa, even the driver of the other car, Xavia Culver, was impressed: "I think all insurance companies should come out and see what's going on, to help out with all the hassle and confusion."

Lance Edgy, Progressive's man on the scene in Tampa, is the very model of a modern service worker. The lead member of a six-person team of adjusters, Edgy joined progressive in 1990 after graduating from the University of Florida with a degree in finance. The company has invested heavily in his training, offering him courses not just in the arcana of insurance regulation but also in the art of negotiation and in grief counseling (part of his job involves dealing with the relatives of dead crash victims). Progressive's gain-sharing program, keyed to a formula based on revenues, profits, and costs, gives Edgy an opportunity to increase his base salary of $38,480 a year by as much as $5,400.

Says CEO Lewis: "To the extent that auto insurance is a commodity, our biggest differentiator is our people. We want the best people at every level of the company, and we pay at the top of the market." When a competitor recently tried to hire away three of Progressive's highly paid division claims managers by offering them large pay hikes, Lewis increased the pay scales not just for the three would-be defectors but for all 15 of their colleagues as well. Investing in people pays dividends. Progressive's net income, $267 million last year, has increased at an average annual compound rate of 20% since 1989.

For service companies, retaining good employees is essential to winning and keeping good customers. "It's impossible to build a loyal book of customers without a loyal employee base," says Fred Reichheld of Bain. "It's like trying to build a brick wall without mortar." As obvious as this connection seems, managers of service companies routinely disregard it. The annual rate of employee turnover in department stores and restaurants routinely tops 100%. Says Harvard's Schlesinger: "Most service companies operate with a cycle-of-failure mentality. They assume labor is an expendable, renewable resource, and they create a cadre of poor, unmotivated employees who couldn't care less if the customer is satisfied."

WHEN IT COMES to the link between employee turnover, customer loyalty, and profits, Lexus understands the nexus. Two-thirds of the people who buy a Lexus have bought one before, the highest repeat purchase rate in the luxury car market. 'That's an extraordinary statistic, considering that the first Lexus went on sale less than five years ago, and considering that the appreciation of the yen has sent the price of a top-of-the-line LS 400 sedan soaring above $54,000.

For three years running, customers surveyed by J.D. Power & Associates, the industry's leading pollster, have ranked Lexus No. 1 in product quality and dealer service among all cars sold in the U.S. "We try to make it very hard for you to leave us," says Lexus general manager George Borst. "When you buy a Lexus, you don't buy a product. You buy a luxury package."

Wrapped in the package is a style of service crafted with the same precision Toyota put into the design of the car itself. Says Borst: "Our challenge was to get people to buy a Japanese luxury car. The quality of the product wasn't the issue. Everybody knew that Toyota could make a top-quality product. The issue was creating a sense of prestige. And where we saw the hole in the market was in the way dealers treated their customers."

When you walk into the showroom at South Bay Lexus, not far from Toyota's Torrance, California, headquarters, the most striking thing is what doesn't happen. No salesmen—sales consultants, to use the proper title—approach. They don't hover, they don't pry, they don't solicit. Even though they're paid on commission, these guys stay totally out of sight until you tell the receptionist you're ready for a consultation. Says South Bay service manager John Lane: "Customers won't stand for the hustle effect."

Like all employees at Lexus dealerships (including receptionists), Lane regularly attends national and regional training courses to learn about cars, even those made by competitors, and customers. Lane figures he received more training in his first month at Lexus than he did in his entire 18-year career at Cadillac.

But back to the showroom. If you want to buy a car—and most customers make two or three visits before they're ready—your sales consultant will usher you into a product presentation room, an alcove with no doors, no clutter, a semicircular marble-topped table, and three leather chairs that are precisely the same height. The implicit message: There are no traps and no surprises.

The first two regularly scheduled maintenances of your car are free. While you're waiting for the work to be done, you can use an office with a desk and a phone. Or you can stand in the customer viewing room and watch the mechanic—sorry, the service technician—attend to your car in a brightly lit garage that seems devoid of grease. If you need to be someplace, the dealer will lend you a car or give you a ride. When you pick up your vehicle, you'll find that it has been washed and vacuumed by a "valet detail specialist," whose compensation, like everyone else's at South Bay, is pegged to customer satisfaction. The annual employee turnover rate since South Bay opened its doors in 1989 is a lowly 7%.

Okay, it's one thing to provide silky service when you're selling a silk-purse-type product. But how much innovation can you possibly bring to the preparation and delivery of a $1.39 chicken taco or a 99-cent bean burrito? Plenty.

Over the past decade Taco Bell, a subsidiary of PepsiCo, has evolved from a regional quick-service restaurant chain with $700 million in system-wide sales and 1,500 outlets into a multinational food delivery company with $3.9 billion in revenues and more than 15,000 "points of access" (POAs). What, you ask, is a POA? It is any place where people can meet to munch—an airport, a supermarket, a school cafeteria, a college campus, or a street corner. Says Charlie Rogers, Taco Bell's senior vice president for human resources: "We've changed the way we think about ourselves, moving from a company that prepares food to one that feeds hungry people."

Like many business insights, this one sounds insanely simple, almost like a Peter Sellers pronouncement in the movie *Being There*. But don't be fooled. Getting from Point A to Point B necessitated a revolution in the way Taco Bell manages people, information, and machines. The first step, unveiled by President and CEO John Martin in 1989, was called K-minus. (The "K" stands for kitchen.) Martin took the heavy-duty food preparation—crushing beans, dicing cheese, and preparing beef—out of the restaurants and centralized it in commissaries run by outside contractors. The cost savings allowed Taco Bell to slash its prices. More significantly, the company was able to shrink the average size of a restaurant kitchen by 40%, freeing up more space—and more employees—to serve customers. Says Rogers: "Most of the people in our restaurants really worked in manufacturing, not service."

Once Taco Bell got the manufacturing out of its restaurants, it began to get the manufacturing out of its management. Like most fast-food chains, Taco Bell used a command-and-control system of supervision that came straight out of Detroit, circa 1960. There was one manager for each restaurant, one area manager for every six restaurants, and one repetitious, mindnumbing job for each employee. Today many Taco Bell outlets operate with no manager on the premises. Self-directed teams, known as "crews," manage inventory, schedule work, order supplies, and train new employees—make that "crew members." Team-managed restaurants have lower employee turnover and higher customer satisfaction scores than conventionally run outlets.

Regional managers, formerly factory-style supervisors who earned about $25,000 a year, are now business school graduates who oversee as many as 30 POAs. Their pay, closely linked to sales results and customer-satisfaction scores, can top $100,000. "I see myself not just as a fast-food manager

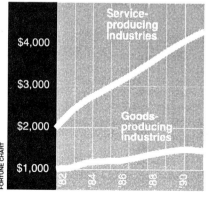

Share of GDP
In billions of dollars

FORTUNE CHART

$4,000

$3,000

$2,000

$1,000

Service-producing Industries

Goods-producing Industries

'82 '84 '86 '88 '90

but as an entrepreneur who manages a multi-million-dollar corporation with 250 employees," says Sueyoung Georgas, a forty-something native of South Korea, whose territory in the southern suburbs of Detroit includes five restaurants, five schools, three community colleges, and a catering service that provisions banquets and festivals. With people like Georgas on board, CEO Martin is aiming to increase Taco Bell's points of access to 200,000—a more than tenfold increase—by the year 2000.

SOME OF THE MOST exciting action in services is occurring behind the scenes, deep in the bowels of the economy—down in the boiler room, to be precise. Okay, a boiler room isn't an intrinsically thrilling place. But it is for Johnson Controls, an old-line Milwaukee manufacturing company, whose founder, Warren Johnson, invented the thermostat in 1883. Sales of Johnson's traditional products—heating controls, batteries, plastic bottles, and automobile seats—continue to expand at a steady pace. But "facilities management services," which Johnson entered in 1989, is running like a racehorse, with revenues growing at a triple-digit clip.

Controls Group vice president Terry Weaver waxes euphoric when he describes the opportunity in managing the heating, lighting, security, and cleaning operations of office buildings. "It's explosive. It's almost impossible to quantify, a market worth tens of billions of dollars in the U.S. alone. It's a wave. It's a megatrend."

Yep, it's exciting. And here's why: As companies restructure, they are paring costs and focusing on what they do best (their core competencies, in B-school jargon). At the same time, they are ditching the things that they do worst, like managing their computer networks, phone systems, and boiler rooms. Through the magic of outsourcing, one company's cost center becomes Johnson Controls' (or some other firm's) profit center.

Johnson Controls Chairman and Chief Executive James Keyes, 53, says service now drives his entire corporation. "Most of our growth has come from the fact that we do more for our customers." Strictly speaking, Tina Brueckner, 27, an engineer in the Controls Group's Milwaukee branch office, had always been a service worker. But she almost never met the people she was serving. Hunched in front of a computer, she designed heating, ventilation, and air-conditioning control systems to specifications drawn up by the customer or the customer's consultant.

Now, instead of basically filling orders, Brueckner finds solutions to her customers' problems. She spends at least half her time in the field as part of a four-person team that helps schools improve their energy efficiency. Says she: "Before I sat at a desk and engineered. Now I go out and talk to my customers. This makes the job a lot more satisfying."

THE OUTSOURCING phenomenon fueling growth at companies like Johnson Controls is also spreading to the consumer world. There the powerhouse is ServiceMaster, a company in Downers Grove, Illinois, that has made a mint by doing things for people that they don't want to do themselves: Dust their bookshelves, care for their lawns, and exterminate their roaches. The company, which also cleans and maintains hospitals, schools, and other buildings, reported net income of $145.9 million on revenues of $2.8 billion in 1993, its 23rd consecutive year of record top-and-bottom-line results.

Chairman William Pollard, 56, admits to being miffed that his colleagues in the business community don't always treat his enterprise with the greatest respect: "They say, 'Oh, you're just the mop-and-bucket guys.'

But then they look at our financial results and wonder, 'How did they do that?' " How indeed? By carefully selecting employees ("service partners" is what the company calls them), training them thoroughly, and giving them the right tools to do the job. Service-Master's R&D center, which is focusing this year on floor care, recently invented the Walk-Behind Scrubber, a self-propelled contraption that helped cut by 20% the amount of time it takes to clean a vinyl surface. Next year, incidentally, will be the Year of the Carpet.

ServiceMaster's real genius lies in the way it manages to instill a sense of dignity and importance in low-paid people doing menial jobs. The company's Merry Maids subsidiary rejects nine out of ten applicants for the entry-level position of "teammate." Every prospective teammate goes through a 45-question interview known as the Perceiver. Managers review the results, looking for WOO words—for Winning Others Over—such as "win," "commitment," "we," "yes," and "us."

Merry Maids' pickiness in hiring teammates stems from a new perception of why it's in business. Says President Mike Isakson: "We used to focus on the process of cleaning, making sure the home was free from dust. Now we understand that the ultimate benefits to the customer are peace of mind, security, and stress reduction." In other words, the customer wants to know not only that her home will be cleaned but that nothing will be stolen, broken, or rearranged. Says Cindy Luellen, 33, a Merry Maids office manager in Indianapolis who started out as a teammate: "This job is very rewarding emotionally, especially for a divorced, single mother with just a high school education. It's nice to have the respect of your fellow employees and your customers too."

Respect, loyalty, security, dignity—old-fashioned qualities for a new-fashioned economy. Earlier this century machines helped liberate our ancestors from the toil of the fields. In this generation, wondrous technology has freed us from the drudgery of the assembly line and enabled us to speed new products to far-off markets. As we approach a new millennium, it is people who will carry us forward. In an economy built on service, the extent to which we prosper will depend on our ability to educate, entertain, empower, and ennoble ourselves—and each other.

INSIGHTS

- **All net job creation through 2005 will come from services.**

- **Think of service as a process, not as a series of functions, then realign the organization.**

- **The changing nature of customer service demands a new breed of worker—one who is empathetic, flexible, inventive, and able to work with minimal levels of supervision.**

Whatever It Takes

In the battle to win sales in today's ferocious marketplace, ethical behavior is the first casualty

By Michele Marchetti

"Is there anything more you need from me?"

The owner of a Los Angeles promotion company sat in front of his customer, looked him directly in the eye, and repeated the question. "Is there anything more you need from me?" The innuendo was clear: If the customer, a Hollywood film executive, wanted something on the side—perhaps cash or a trip—he could make arrangements. In the past, no request had surprised him.

Until today.

The studio executive knew exactly what he wanted. A party. A private party. One that involved two prostitutes and a hotel room. On the morning after the meeting, the promotion company owner called his customer to confirm that a limousine would pick him up at his office. "Aren't you coming?" the client asked. He politely declined, saying his wife wouldn't appreciate such extracurricular activity. The client was offended, but not enough to cancel his little soirée—or his intended purchase. For the price of $3,500—a cost that ultimately would be "baked" into the final bid—the sales executive acquired another satisfied customer.

Since that afternoon last August, the owner has continued to conduct business with the film executive. Does it make him queasy? Is he insulted by the fact that sex, not the quality of his company's service, was the deciding factor in the deal? Not at all. "I want to be on a level playing field [with my competitors]. That means being open-minded enough to think somebody else may be on the take."

Such a story may alarm managers who'd like to believe the sales process has evolved beyond kickbacks and other serious acts of unethical conduct. But while this isolated case can't be used to indict all sales professionals, it shows that some salespeople and their bosses aren't above rationalizing shady behavior. Take note: Sleaze in sales is not a thing of the past—it's alive and well in 1997. And the culprits are not just used-car peddlers.

The results of an exclusive *Sales & Marketing Management* survey of 200 sales managers—from major corporations to privately held companies—reveal just how far salespeople will go to make a sale. Among the findings:

■ 49 percent of surveyed managers say their reps have lied on a sales call.

■ 34 percent say they've heard reps make unrealistic promises on a sales call.

■ 22 percent say their reps have sold products their customers didn't need.

30 percent say customers have demanded a kickback for buying their product or service.

54 percent say the drive to meet sales goals does a disservice to customers.

While the ethics of salespeople have always been called into question, these findings are so glaring because we're supposedly living in the age of client-centered organizations and win-win relationships. The results of our survey and interviews with dozens of sales executives show a marketplace sullied by unethical behavior. According to sales professionals and experts, the driving force behind this questionable activity is the pressure to do business in today's combative marketplace. The stress brought on by quotas, pay plans, and a selling environment that encourages fierce competition is, in too many cases, eroding morality.

Michael Daigneault, president of the Ethics Resource Center, a Washington, D.C.-based nonprofit educational organization dedicated to improving ethical practices in the workplace, says the issue has more to do with market conditions than with the integrity of salespeople. "The prevailing notion is that bad people do bad things," he says. "Our interest is finding out what makes good people do bad things."

Years of downsizing, reengineering, and cost-cutting have undermined any sense of loyalty that salespeople might feel toward their companies. Qualified salespeople hop from job to job at whim, with little regard for the long-term objectives set by their bosses. And for sales professionals in hypergrowth industries, the propensity for unethical behavior is even greater. The advent of technology has enabled upstarts to attack niche markets at breakneck speed, threatening both multinational companies and smaller organizations. For these sales forces, the burden to reach the market faster than the next company is staggering. "The biggest challenge we face is that the bar keeps going up," says one Silicon Valley sales executive. "Wall Street tends to crucify you if you don't prove your sales every quarter."

Companies in these competitive industries often use aggressive compensation plans to quickly boost sales. The chance to earn six-figure paychecks could tempt even the do-gooders of a sales force—especially in a society where it's common to live above one's means. As compensation gurus often point out, the likelihood of unethical behavior is directly proportionate to the size of the carrot.

Beyond the statistics and expert opinions, the number of recent scandals involving sales professionals demonstrates the extent of ethical violations:

Prudential Insurance Company of America recently agreed to pay a minimum of $425 million to settle a class-action suit. Its troubles began a few years ago when agents in search of fatter commissions convinced customers to purchase new policies, promising that they would virtually pay for themselves. Unbeknownst to customers, these agents were eating up the cash value in older policies to pay for the new ones.

Columbia/HCA Healthcare Corporation, the largest for-profit hospital—generating some $20 billion a year in revenues—has been accused of improperly inflating costs in reports to the government and pocketing more Medicare reimbursement than deserved. Industry sources predict that Columbia will pay a $1 billion fine.

Sears, Roebuck & Company recently admitted to having used flawed judgment after it collected debts from some of its credit-card holders who had sought bankruptcy. The retailer

Stretching the Truth to Make the Sale

S&MM EXCLUSIVE SURVEY

Reps frequently lie to clients, according to the results of an *S&MM*/Global Strategy Group phone survey of 200 sales managers. The survey, conducted between June 2 and June 18, has a margin of error of +/-6.9 percent.

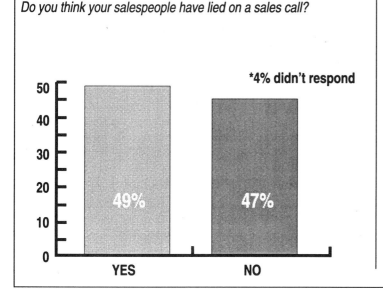

Do you think your salespeople have lied on a sales call?

*4% didn't respond

YES 49% NO 47%

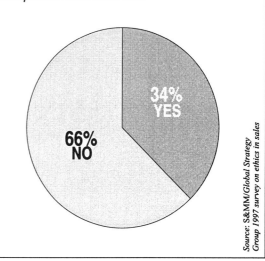

Have you ever heard one of your salespeople make an unrealistic promise on a sales call?

34% YES 66% NO

Source: S&MM/Global Strategy Group 1997 survey on ethics in sales

took a $475 million pretax write-off to cover the costs of the settlement.

▣ This past October a former Archer Daniels Midland executive, Mark Whitacre, pleaded guilty to 37 criminal charges, including theft, money laundering, conspiracy, and tax evasion. The plea bargain is the latest development in a corporate tale that began when Whitacre blew the whistle on a global price-fixing scandal involving Archer, the United States' largest miller of corn, soybeans, and wheat. Last year the company pleaded guilty and paid a $100 million fine.

▣ Wall Street has reported a boom in fraud. Last April two men were indicted in Federal District Court in Brooklyn on charges they solicited the murder of rivals who attempted to get a cut of the cash they received selling the stock of a fake company. "In a market like this, parasites crowd in to feast on the bull's success," said Arthur Levitt, chairman of the SEC, in a recent Senate subcommittee hearing.

These cases present a widespread pattern of unethical behavior and a clear picture of the type of deception rampant in the business world. They also demonstrate how compensation models, profit goals, and sales quotas influence both salespeople and managers to bend rules, cheat customers, and act in a questionable manner. For that sales executive who shrugs at or ignores the unethical activity of a rep—lying to customers, offering kickbacks, or trashing competitors—the consequences are grave: costly lawsuits, a deluge of negative press, and a weakened market position.

Case in point: Charges against Prudential have soured its sales. The company's share of the U.S. ordinary life insurance market fell from 7.78 percent in 1994 to 6.59 percent in 1996, according to rating agency A.M. Best Company. "The effect is already material," says Kevin Ceurvorst, senior analyst for the Duff & Phelps Credit Rating Company. "The repair period is a long-term proposition."

"The pressure was ungodly"

WITH A PLEASANT voice and an upbeat attitude, Deb Farrell sounds like a stress-free sales executive. Her primary concern these days is the launch of a new product for Lanyon Ltd., a privately held software company in London that develops products for the travel industry.

Things were much more intense a year ago. Prior to joining Lanyon, Farrell worked for a software maker that was preparing for an initial public offering. Under pressure to succeed in the marketplace, managers would brow-beat reps, shaming them for not reaching quotas, she says. To meet quarterly revenue objectives, salespeople pursued an overly aggressive sales approach, pushing products on customers before they were ready to buy. The atmosphere placed Farrell in a compromising position: Both her and her reps' actions did not always benefit their customers. "It's balancing what's best for the company and what's best for the customer," Farrell says. "You're the one that's always squarely in the middle."

Such a high-pressure atmosphere breeds unethical behavior. According to a recent survey of 1,300 workers by the Ameri-

can Society of Chartered Life Underwriters and Chartered Financial Consultants, nearly half of the respondents took part in unethical or illegal activity, such as deceiving customers, as a result of pressure. The largest offenders were those in the computer and software companies—high-growth, ultracompetitive organizations that have little time to weigh the consequences of their actions. "It's real easy to lose sight of [long-term objectives]," Farrell says.

This is especially true in industries like telecommunications, in which companies are scrapping for market share. Since deregulation in 1984, following the breakup of the AT&T Corporation, more than 800 companies have muscled into the $82 billion long-distance business. "It's probably the most competitive market there is," says one telecommunications sales manager. "It's a down-and-dirty business."

One company known for having a sullied image was ALC Communications Corporation. According to several former managers, salespeople routinely practiced underhanded sales techniques. Perhaps the most blatant deception involved several reps who cut the account number off of invoices and pasted them onto other invoices. They wanted to prove that an account was bringing in a certain level of revenue or had an acceptable credit history, says one former ALC sales manager. By the time the accounting department caught on, the reps, who were paid monthly commissions, had collected their paychecks and quit the company, the manager says.

Such acts, says one manager, were the results of audacious, and sometimes unrealistic, demands put upon reps that led to a 200 percent annual turnover in the company's sales force. As he recalls, a typical day at ALC started with a 7:30 a.m. meeting in which salespeople were grilled on their weekly progress, including the number of scheduled appointments and expected revenue. Managers then documented this information on a board, and referred to it the following day. And that's when the fun started. If a salesperson didn't produce, the punishment was a berating in front of the rep's peers. In one instance, a rep burst into tears.

"The pressure was ungodly," says another former ALC sales manager. "Some of the managers were complete idiots."

Since ALC was acquired by Frontier Corporation in 1995, much has changed for the sales force. Frontier's compensation plan has less pay at risk than ALC's, says Randal Simonetti, a spokesman for Frontier. And in the future, Frontier plans to shift that equation even more, toward a plan that offers an even higher base salary and lower incentive pay. "The higher the risk, the less the base, and the more aggressive the behavior," he says. "If you want your salespeople to own that [customer] relationship, you need to make sure there's a balance between the base and the risk."

Another difference between the two sales organizations is the goal-setting process. At Frontier, upper management conducts a "bottom-up review," in which sales managers meet with regional executives and the executive vice president of sales to ensure that goals are realistic, Simonetti says. "We still have to set stress objectives, but these targets are attainable."

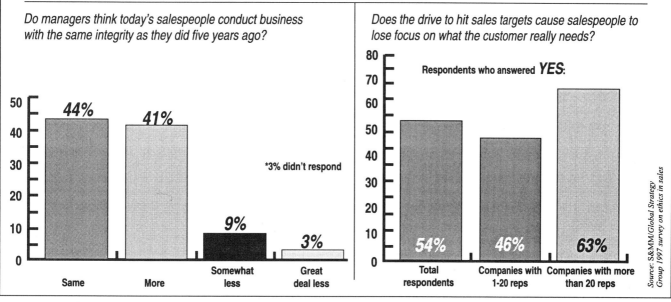

Even in 1997, Ethical Problems are Sullying Customer Relationships

Do managers think today's salespeople conduct business with the same integrity as they did five years ago?

44%
41%
9%
3%
*3% didn't respond

Same | More | Somewhat less | Great deal less

Does the drive to hit sales targets cause salespeople to lose focus on what the customer really needs?

Respondents who answered **YES**:

54% | 46% | 63%

Total respondents | Companies with 1-20 reps | Companies with more than 20 reps

Source: S&MM/Global Strategy Group 1997 survey on ethics in sales

"What's in it for me?"

CURBING UNETHICAL BEHAVIOR requires more than cooling an overly aggressive sales culture. Understand, salespeople are not the only culprits. Customers face ethical challenges, too. With fierce competition dominating the marketplace, salespeople are using anything—dinner at New York's Le Cirque or 18 holes at Pebble Beach—to gain an edge. The problem is, give customers a round of golf and sooner or later they'll want the country club membership.

"Customer expectations are way out of hand," says a sales executive for a manufacturer of sonogram machines. Adds Memo Diriker, a marketing professor at Salisbury State University in Salisbury, Maryland: "[Salespeople] are being asked very boldly, 'What's in it for me?'"

In the medical industry the buying power has shifted from doctors to business executives, says the sales executive at the sonogram manufacturer. The result? Customers are continually asking for more. Some clients are demanding that the sonogram manufacturer cover both their own and their spouses' expenses to attend medical trade shows.

But in extreme cases the requests are even more blatant than reimbursement for industry junkets. The fact is, kickbacks—a flat-out cash payment, or some other gift that enables reps to win business they otherwise wouldn't—are still part of the sales process. Apparently some executives believe that a win-win relationship amounts to receiving something under the table from reps. For the owner of the L.A.-based promotion agency, he will often set a price for customers that is slightly inflated. If, for example, they agree on a price of $900, the customer accepts the bid at $1,000, and the extra $100 is

kicked back to him. "[My customers] are stealing from their own companies," says the owner.

But kickbacks can also hurt the sales professional's company—by tarnishing its reputation and undermining its professionalism. Diriker, director of the Project Management Group, a consulting arm at Salisbury State, frequently receives requests from companies looking for ways to conduct successful business without kickbacks. "They see that as a marketing threat," he says, adding that the requests range from cash to country club memberships. "They want to get the order without losing to the next guy."

Contrary to conventional beliefs, Diriker says kickbacks are an inevitable part of business that should be managed, not ignored or written off as a taboo. If a rep is selling a sound product at a competitive price, and the buyer's only objection is that a competitor is offering him a trip to Tahiti, the rep should have options for handling the situation, he says. Perhaps the salesperson could find another way to personally reward the buyer. "Right now, there are no management tools to say these are ways of handling these things without quoting what's legal and what's not," he says. "We're failing by ignoring the problem. The idea of a universal black and white only seems to work in textbooks."

Yet according to the National Association of Purchasing Management, which represents about 40,000 buyers in a variety of industries, the problem is nonexistent. "I can't see a buyer risking a job for some incremental income," says Jack Wagner, a supply chain manager at BellSouth Telecommunications in Atlanta and chairman of the ethical standards committee of NAPM. Wagner says most companies have strict guidelines against kickbacks, and that some use NAPM's prin-

T & E: Trickery & Exploitation?

MANY SALES REPS cheat on their expense reports. How do managers rein them in without ruining trust?

It seems every sales manager has a legendary tale about a rep who tried to slip something by on an expense report. A publisher remembers, for instance, how an advertising salesman claimed to be entertaining clients once or twice a month at a restaurant called the Country Squire—until the company president discovered that the Country Squire was a men's clothing store.

Or there was the sales rep for an Orlando-based manufacturing company who went out to dinner by himself, and wrote on

Have you ever caught an employee cheating on an expense report?

27% YES

70% NO

*3% didn't respond

his expense report that he was entertaining clients. When his manager examined the receipt, he noticed "number of guests: one" written at the top.

But should managers have to examine the fine print on their reps' receipts and T&E forms? In many cases the answer is yes. An *S&MM* survey of 200 sales managers revealed that 27 percent of managers say they've caught employees cheating on expense reports. Not surprisingly, those numbers grow for managers who have been in the business 15 years or longer: 38 percent of those managers say they have caught reps in the act.

The challenge for managers is developing a system that prevents cheating, while avoiding an antagonistic environment. Jonathan Howe, a Chicago-based attorney who has worked extensively in the travel industry, says that strict corporate guidelines eliminate many problems: "The policy should set out specific situations. What is needed for support and verification? What can be included as a legitimate business expense? By what date do you have to produce the receipts?" There are tax issues as well, he says. If a company is audited by the IRS, it must furnish proof of all business expenses of more than $75.

Rolfe Shellenberger, a senior consultant in travel management at Runzheimer International, a travel consulting company in Milwaukee, offers several tips for eradicating

expense report abuses. First, sales managers have to set a policy and stick to it, and that means reps can't just assume every expense they incur on the road will be reimbursed. "Managers really have to look at travel reports seriously, and the traveler is responsible for the expense until they do." Shellenberger says.

In addition, managers should require reps to get a receipt for anything with a price of $10 or more. Mandate that travelers use the corporate credit card, he says, because a copy of the bill is sent to the company, giving managers an opportunity to review expenses. And Shellenberger advises against giving cash advances. "Travelers take more money than they need, and spend all of it."

But expense reports don't have to be a point of contention. "The sales manager should make sure to tell travelers that every justified expense will be covered," Shellenberger explains. "Reps shouldn't make the mistake of lying if they are caught in a situation where they have to exceed spending guidelines. Guidelines are just that—guidelines."

But if sales reps still don't follow the standards? Both Howe and Shellenberger believe they should be fired. "If you can't trust them with travel vouchers," Howe asks, "how can you trust them with anything else?"

—Sarah Lorge

Source: S&MM/Global Strategy Group 1997 Survey on ethics in sales

ciples, one of which reads: "Refrain from soliciting or accepting money, loans, credits, or prejudicial discounts, and the acceptance of gifts, entertainment, favors, or services from suppliers that might influence, or appear to influence, purchasing decisions."

Even so, at one $18 million packaging equipment company, kickbacks are viewed as a sales tool, not as a grounds for dismissal. The standard kickback is 5 percent of the total sale, somewhere between $10,000 and $25,000, and is sanctioned when a competitor has an airtight relationship with a client, says a salesperson at the company. The money may even be wired into a personal account in the Cayman Islands or Switzerland. "It's kind of James Bondish," he says.

Although he has never personally paid someone for closing a deal, he admits to a less blatant form of bribery—entertaining clients with lavish business dinners at four-star restaurants. In another instance, when a customer discovered that the salesperson was a wine connoisseur, the client dropped a few hints about a certain bottle. "It's simply knowing they got something out of you," he says. "Kind of like, 'I won and you didn't.' "

"People compete on fear, not merit"

NOT EVERY INCIDENT of unethical activity lends itself to a John Grisham novel. To many sales professionals, today's moral dilemmas are the mundane issues present in any competitive environment. But they've been compounded by a variety of supposed advances in the sales process—from working with competitors on client solutions to the advent of technology.

Mike Coker is familiar with the rigors of this high-pressure environment. Earlier this year, Coker, vice president of sales and marketing for SBE, Inc., a $26 million networking company in San Ramon, California, solicited the help of a competitor to seal a deal with a customer. The guidelines were clear: The competitor would complete one part of the solution and SBE would work on the other. But that didn't stop the competitor from creating its own rules. Three months after introducing the competitor to the customer, Coker discovered he had been quietly shut out of the sale.

So why are managers collaborating with the same company they trash in sales meetings? Because the total partnership is

Is Blowing the Whistle Worth It?

NICE GUYS REALLY do finish last.

At least that's the case for Ron Wells. Wells, a self-employed dealer in medical equipment for more than a decade, uncovered a fraudulent practice that was cheating the government and placing the profits in his competitors' pockets. But by refusing to participate in this practice, Wells committed business suicide.

This is Wells's version of the story: In 1991 a sales manager from Huntleigh Technology approached his company, PVD America Inc., with a new lymphedema pump, used by cancer patients to treat swelling of the limbs. Though the pump's price tag was $495, the manufacturer claimed the pump, known as a Flowplus, had design features that made it eligible for Medicare reimbursement of more than $4,000. Wells smelled a scandal. After examining the pump, he determined it had the same features as Huntleigh's low-grade pump—the only difference was its color. Instead of participating in the scam, Wells voiced his concerns to Medicare officials, competing suppliers, and attendees of trade shows.

In March 1993 Medicare responded to Well's accusations, downgrading the reimbursement for the Flowplus to $475. Wells wasn't satisfied. He believed Huntleigh's tactics had caused other manufacturers to come out with their own substandard pumps. So while Wells paid upward of $3,000 for a high-grade piece of equipment, his competitors ponied up a few hundred dollars for a pump purported to be of the same caliber, he claims. And by inflating the Medicare reimbursements, Wells says, they made profits of close to $4,000 on each sale.

Using these profits, his competitors sent reps to bribe doctors into writing prescriptions, Wells says. One doctor says reps offered him rent payments in exchange for the use of his office space to do vascular evaluations—a precautionary procedure performed before doctors can prescribe the pumps. The reps attempted to woo the doctor with dinners at four-star restaurants, and with a part-time employee, who would perform exams and any other services free of charge—all of which the doctor refused.

By abstaining from this bribery, Wells lost clients. "I had doctors saying X company gave me this. What are you going to offer?" And the doctors who didn't take the bribes decided to wash their hands of the equipment altogether. "I watched my business deteriorate, because of the bastardization of this product," he says.

With the help of federal legislation entitled the False Claims Act, also called the Whistle Blower Law, Wells retaliated. This regulation empowers citizens with evidence of fraudulent activity against the U.S. government to sue the offender. If the case is won, the whistle blower earns a percentage of the government's earnings. In 1997 the law is more critical than ever: Up to 10 percent of the entire federal budget is lost to fraud.

In July 1995 the federal government took another step in reclaiming some of its losses—Huntleigh Technology settled its suit for $4.9 million. Wells's share: $882,000. And this past May the medical supply company called Jalopy Shoppe agreed to pay the U.S. government $1.35 million—the second major settlement from Wells's original complaint—for participating in the fraudulent activity. This time Wells took home $243,000. But the retribution still isn't enough.

Since 1995 his company's revenues have decreased by $1 million. That spring Medicare rewrote the guidelines detailing the medical conditions that necessitate the pump's use. The new standards, Wells say, have made it virtually impossible for patients to qualify for reimbursement. As one doctor says: "My geriatric patients would pass a Marine Corps physical first." The Health Care Finance Association (HCFA) refused to comment.

While Wells hasn't given up hope—he recently wrote a letter to the HCFA detailing his complaints—the prognosis for his business is bleak. "I went from doing business in five states with more than twenty employees to one state and two employees," Wells says. "You can be the honest businessman, do the right thing, and lose." —*M.M.*

---

more valuable than what each company can bring to the table alone. It's called coopetition, and the protocol for these alliances is still unclear. "Because there's a lot of business today conducted by multiple companies, there's certainly a greater chance for things to get twisted," says Rick Carbone, director of business development for Unisys Corporation, a computer maker that partners with other technology providers.

In the situation involving SBE, the competitor was a larger, more well-known player in the industry. Coker believes it used what's referred to as the FUD factor: planting fear, uncertainty, and doubt in the buyer's mind. In other words, while the competitor's product may not be the best solution, the purchaser may choose it anyway, because the company is a safer bet. And how many purchasing agents welcome a risk?

"People tend to compete on fear, not merit," Coker says.

Another technology-industry buzzword these days is vaporware, a term that goes hand-in-hand with the FUD factor. Vaporware refers to a product that is not available to the buying public, yet has been publicized with fanfare in order to create demand and prevent customers from buying a competitor's product. This kind of manipulation can drive smaller companies out of business, causing customers to delay their buying decision until the hyped product hits the market. Some people may call this a savvy business practice, but it has left managers in smaller companies snarling.

"It's completely unethical," says Paul Basson, the newly appointed CEO of Point Information Systems, a maker of sales and customer service software, and the former vice president of worldwide sales and marketing for Avid Technology. While working at Avid, which sells digital video-editing systems, a major competitor in the analog side of the business attempted to stop its customers from switching to a digital version, which Avid provided, Basson says. In a strong show of resistance, the competitor announced its version of the system three years before even a prototype was released, he claims. As a result, some of Avid's largest clients delayed their buying decisions. "If you're a small start-up and half the market decides to wait for six months, you're in trouble," he says. "You're in a very weak position."

"The toughest job in the sales force"

AS BASSON'S COMMENTS indicate, the ethical conundrums that surface in today's marketplace don't invite easy solutions. Fur-

Putting Reps to the Test

EVEN THE SLEAZIEST rep can look like a saint in an interview. So how can you tell if a rep is ethical before you make the job offer?

There's no foolproof method, but human resources experts say sales and marketing executives need to probe candidates for important characteristics—self-discipline, honesty, openness, self-respect, level-headedness, and a mix of aggressiveness and empathy. One way to uncover these qualities is by posing hypothetical dilemmas to potential hires. Timothy Hansen, a consultant with Personnel Decisions International, a global management and human resources consulting firm based in Minneapolis, explains how the combined responses from the following questions present an overall pattern of ethics, or the lack thereof, in job candidates.

THE QUESTIONS:

■ A few months after joining the company your colleagues tell you about a diner's club card that gives 20 percent cash refunds at certain restaurants. Easy money—especially if you're just beginning to establish a territory. Since the company encourages entertaining, the salespeople reason, why not take clients to those restaurants and pocket the refunds? It won't cost the company any money. Do you join in?

■ While speaking with a sales manager at a competitor's trade show booth, you spot hard copy from the competitor's database listing 100 qualified leads from the show. You can slip it into your briefcase easily, and no one will see. What do you do?

■ After meeting with a customer you discover a competitor has lowballed your offer by 15 percent. This competitor has a reputation for offering products at the lowest possible price, but failing to provide an acceptable level of service. Do you warn the customer, attempting to push him toward your offer, or walk away from the business, hoping he'll find out for himself and choose your company in the future?

■ The standard rate for your product is $15,000. After negotiations with an important customer you discover the company can realistically only afford $13,000. A few weeks later you receive the purchasing order with the original $15,000 price. You receive a 5 percent commission on the total dollar value of the deal. Do you correct the customer's mistake, or allow the company to be billed for $15,000, hoping the error is never discovered?

■ You're on a sales call and a key customer from a Fortune 500 company says she won't buy from you unless you match a competitor's offer. The competitor's offer includes a 10-day trip to Hawaii for the customer and her husband. What do you do?

HANSEN'S RESPONSE:

Salespeople represent two "opposing" constituencies: their organization and their clients. As intermediaries, they must balance the needs of both groups, because they're critical to their professional success.

So how can sales managers spot unethical reps? Beware of a salesperson who will do anything to make a sale—especially in ways that jeopardize the company's reputation. For example, he would not hesitate to steal the competitor's list of qualified leads during a trade show. Or, when faced with the situation of the competitor who wooed the client with a trip to Hawaii for the customer and her husband, the unethical salesperson would match the offer.

Know the behaviors of ethical salespeople. Recognize that successful salespeople are persistent, persuasive, and dominant enough to change their clients' minds. However, these characteristics are balanced with an understanding of their clients' needs. For example, the ethical rep is dedicated to helping customers make informed decisions. Therefore, the ethical rep would warn a customer about the competitor who offers products at a low price, but provides substandard service.

In addition, the moral salesperson asks, "What is best for my company?", not "What is best for me?" If tempted to pocket the 20 percent cash refund from the diner's club, the ethical salesperson would consider how the action would affect the company and would raise the issue with management. Finally, keep in mind that even ethical salespeople enjoy collecting commissions. However, these commissions are most appreciated when the customer—and the company—are satisfied. In the instance of the "$15,000" mistake, the ethical rep would correct the error immediately, because she is most interested in preserving relationships based on trust, and less interested in collecting extra cash on the side.

ther complicating matters, sales executives must continually make decisions that please three parties: their customers, their salespeople, and their bosses.

"The middle manager is probably the toughest job in the sales force," says Gary Lawrence, a managing consultant with Towers Perrin, a compensation consulting firm in New York. "You have to be the coach, teacher, and disciplinarian all at once. At the same time your pay is linked with [your reps'] performance. If you have a high performer, you don't want to discourage him or hinder him too much, but you want to keep his behavior in ethical boundaries."

So what can be done? Will salespeople always be compelled to lie to win a deal? Will compensation plans and quotas work at cross-purposes with customers' needs? And is there any way to reduce the number of customers asking for kickbacks? Implementing a code of conduct statement will communicate to salespeople—and their customers—that companies have high moral standards. The findings of a 1997 survey conducted by the Ethics Resource Center and the Society for Human Resources Management show widespread usage of ethics statements: 84 percent of surveyed companies have codes of conduct. And 45 percent have ethics offices.

If reps violate the company's principles, managers shouldn't be afraid to fire them. "If you allow [unethical behavior] to continue, other people feel they need to do it to be successful," says Daigneault of the Ethics Resource Center. But these guidelines can only be effective if sales managers are reinforcing them on a daily basis—traveling with reps, guiding them through the sales process, and engaging them in open, honest dialogue.

When designing sales compensation plans, managers should pay particular attention to the amount of pay at risk—a common driver of unethical behavior, Lawrence says. While high-growth organizations use aggressive incentive plans to quickly approach a market, many managers forget to alter their plans once their products mature. Tying incentive pay to factors other than revenue, such as account retention, is one way to realign the plan, he says.

At Bell & Howell's information management product group, salespeople are paid against what the reseller sells, as opposed to what the reps sell into the channel. "This promotes cooperation and long-term thinking throughout the entire channel and through to the end user," says Bruce Moeller, president of the group. "If long-term customer satisfaction and retention are the end goals, you can make your quantitative measures geared to that instead of traditional sales dollar numbers."

But Moeller's beliefs don't fly in all companies. Many industries are so entrenched in unethical activity that executives believe the only way to survive is to play along. Questionable judgment, such as paying someone under the table, has become a routine, and necessary, part of the sales process. The alternative—taking a stand against an industrywide phenomenon—isn't so attractive. The owner of the L.A.-based promotion agency who paid two prostitutes to entertain his customer justified the kickback with a simple rationale: If he didn't fulfill the request, maybe his competitor would. "When it comes right down to it, we haven't done anything wrong," he says. "We've done what it took to get an account."

This isn't to say that managers have become desensitized to ethical violations. Basson, who earlier in his career founded a software consulting firm in the United Kingdom, says the U.S. is the most difficult place to implement long-term objectives because of its obsession with quarterly performance. The incessant drive to grow profits and displace the market leaders forces salespeople into situations that compromise their ethical integrity, he says.

But the new CEO isn't foolish. Despite his frustration with the quarterly demands of the marketplace, he isn't about to risk the success of his company by attempting a new approach to the software market, one that focuses on more altruistic objectives. In fact, when asked whether he would subject his own sales force to the pressures of the numbers game, he gave this telling response: "Absolutely. We're a growing company in search of capital. I'll indoctrinate the entire sales force to focus on quarterly goals just because of that."

THE NEW HUCKSTERISM

Stealth ads creep into a culture saturated with logos and pitches

Parents and teachers across the country notice a surge in teenagers sporting electronic beepers this summer. Foot soldiers in a drug cartel? Not quite. Just participants in a PepsiCo Inc. sales promotion. The cut-rate pagers beep weekly messages from sports figures and pop stars flogging soda and other teen-targeted brand-name goods.

TV viewers, used to channel-surfing past the commercials, encounter a strange phenomenon on CBS. On a winter evening, every show during a two-hour period features screen-legend-cum-perfume-vendor Elizabeth Taylor. She wanders in and out of everything from The Nanny *to* High Society, *searching for a missing string of black pearls—and shamelessly flogging her about-to-be-launched perfume of the same name. No actual commercial airs. In each case, Taylor is part of the story line.*

Smokers around the country looking for an alternative to Big Tobacco are confronted with an array of brands with funky names from Moonlight Tobacco Co. Hidden in the fine print on the sides of the distinctive packaging is the name of the real corporate parent, RJR Nabisco Inc.

What happened to the days when logos from America's biggest makers meant quality and integrity and were displayed with pride? When an ad was something that ran in 30-second slots on TV or on a page in a magazine? When commercials actually talked about the products they were trying to sell? Meet the New Hucksters: Part P. T. Barnum-style impresario, part MBA-toting tactician, they reflect the zeitgeist of a generation skeptical of any sales pitch and insatiable in its hunger for nonstop entertainment. In this postmodern advertising, sales messages, once clearly labeled, have now been woven subtly into the culture. Stealth pitches are embedded in movies, TV shows, or made into their own tiny entertainments, complete with fictional histories.

These New Age advertisers are redefining the notion of what an ad is and where it runs. Ads and even products are packaged to hide the big-bucks marketing machines that created them and to obliterate the line between advertising and entertainment and—in some cases—ad-vertising and real life. How? Some marketers aim for an ad that looks as much like an expression of the popular will, and as little like a paid sales message, as possible.

Rejecting the familiar "and now for a word from our sponsor" segue, these advertisers salt the content of a TV show, a movie, or even a video game with product mentions—or better yet, have their brands become part of the story. On the Internet, an online soap opera called *The Spot* builds its plot around the latest advertisers. Other marketers create music-and-celebrity-laced commercials that mimic popular entertainment. That's what Diet Coke did when it got the cast of *Friends* to pitch the brand—while remaining in character. Perhaps most insidious, ads have migrated from their traditional nesting grounds to invade spaces and institutions once deemed off limits.

Popular culture reflects the pervasive commercialism. TV serials, once oddly devoid of recognizable brands on the set, are now chock-full. The characters on *Seinfeld* shop at Price Club and chew Junior Mints. Over

A NEW GILDED AGE

The History Channel was all set to run a series of company profiles that would have been vetted—and to an extent, produced—by the sponsoring companies. But the concept created such a brouhaha that it ended up on the ash heap.

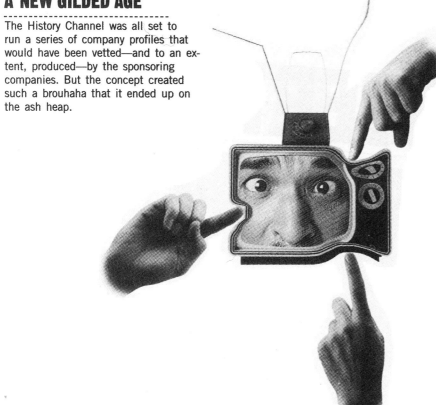

places are innocent of advertising. With total U.S. ad spending up almost 8%, to $162 billion last year, according to McCann-Erickson USA Inc., the new ad permutations aren't replacing the traditional television, magazine, and billboard messages. Rather, advertisers are adding new weapons to their arsenals because the traditional venues are packed full.

Even fresh fruit isn't immune. Quaker Oats' Snapple Beverage Div. slapped ad stickers on kiwis and mangoes this spring. It also bought ad space in bowling alleys on the arms that sweep away toppled pins. Lingerie maker Bamboo Inc. stenciled messages on Manhattan sidewalks two years ago that said: "From here, it looks like you could use some new underwear." Regina Kelley, director of strategic planning at Saatchi & Saatchi Advertising New York, warns that "any space you can take in visually, anything you hear, in the future will be branded, I believe. It's not going to be the Washington Monument. It's going to be the Washington Post Monument." That may not be such a stretch when cities across the continent have mothballed the venerable names that once graced their sports arenas in favor of the brand names of the highest-bidding advertiser, replacing Brendan Byrne Arena and Boston Garden with Continental Airlines Arena and Fleet Center.

Consumers may loathe the nonstop sellathon, but advertisers are only giving us what we want, or at least what we'll tolerate. The least-zapped commercials on TV are the fast-paced, lavishly produced soft drink spots that lean heavily on entertainment and little on product attributes. But the true postmodern advertising goes even further: It tries to morph into the very entertainment it sponsors. To that end, advertisers have taken up the role of filmmaker, gamemaker, and even novelist in a bid to create messages so entertaining, so compelling—and maybe so disguised—that rapt audi-

on prime-time sitcom *Ellen*, they watch marketer *extraordinaire* Martha Stewart, in a guest-starring role, sign copies of her real-life cookbook. One of the most talked-about novels of the past season, *Infinite Jest: A Novel* by David Foster Wallace, envisions a time when years are named for their sponsors; most of the story is set in the Year of the Depend Adult Undergarment.

SNEAK ATTACKS. Advertisers, of course, have always been willing to stretch a point. And the steady volume of complaints at the Federal Trade Commission attests that there's still plenty of old-fashioned misrepresentation going on. But the new deceptions have less to do with puffery than with disguise. And while advertisers have long scouted out new territory ripe for slapping on a logo, now many are more interested in subterfuge than ubiquity.

Why are marketers going to such trouble to hide their sales pitches? It's because the buying public has been virtually buried alive in ads.

Consumers are bombarded with hundreds of ads and thousands of billboards, packages, and other logo sightings every day. Old ad venues are packed to the point of impenetrability as more and more sales messages are jammed in. Supermarkets carry 30,000 different packages, each of which acts as a minibillboard, up from 17,500 a decade ago, according to the Food Marketing Institute. Networks air 6,000 commercials a week, up 50% since 1983, according to Pretesting Co., a market research company. Prime-time TV carries more than 10 minutes of paid advertising every hour, roughly a minute more than at the start of the decade. Add in the promos, and almost 15 minutes of every prime-time hour are given over to ads. No wonder viewers zap so many commercials.

To circumvent that clutter, marketers are stamping their messages on everything that stands still. From popcorn bags in movie theaters to airsickness bags on planes to toilet stalls, shopping carts, and gas pumps, few

MOCK 'ZINES

If sponsoring the content is good, controlling it is even better. *Guess Journal* runs upbeat stories about the jeansmaker. Benetton's *Colors* runs the same kind of controversial art that helped build the retailer's image around the world.

ences will swallow them whole, oblivious to the sales component.

Guess? Inc. and Benetton Group both publish imitations of cutting-edge 'zines, with their jarring graphics and jumbled typefaces. Benetton's *Colors*, with a cover price of $4.50, springs from the same aesthetic—and ad budget—as the retailer's controversial high-shock ads. *Guess Journal*, which has a table of contents, masthead, and bylines, just like a real magazine, features the Guess? brand in most stories. There's either no advertising or nothing but, depending on your point of view.

BEEPER ADS. Knowing that consumers, especially young consumers, have learned to tune out conventional ads, marketers try to infiltrate their favorite entertainment. In Britain, Unilever's Van den Bergh Foods Ltd. is putting the finishing touches on a video game that will star its snack sausage, Peperami. (If you have to know, Peperami does battle with evil snack-food foes Carlos the Carrot and the Terminutter.) "This isn't a one-off cheap promotion," says Peperami Marketing Manager Paul Tidmarsh. "We are trying to produce a top-selling game. It is a new way of reaching our target audience."

Van den Bergh is not the first. In 1994, M&M/Mars bought a prominent role for its Snickers bar in Nintendo Co.'s *Biker Mice from Mars* video game.

Camouflaging a sales message in a teen's natural environment was what Pepsi was trying to do, too, when it came up with its beeper promotion. For $35 and a bunch of Mountain Dew box tops, kids can get a Motorola Inc. pager and six months of free service. The catch? Once a week for six months, they get beeped with an ad. By dialing the toll-free number, they'll hear messages from the likes of Lou Piniella and Ken Griffey Jr. of the Seattle Mariners alerting them to promotional offers and prizes from companies including MTV, Sony Music, and Specialized Mountain Bikes. The promotion has drawn criticism. For some adults, the combination of teens and beepers has only one association: drug dealing, which is why beepers are banned in some schools. Pepsi says the program advocates responsible beeper use. But the controversy isn't all bad for the soft-drink maker. Criticism from grownups could add to the brand's cachet with the young.

Even real life has been co-opted. To help revive Hennessy cognac two years ago, ad agency Kirshenbaum Bond & Partners hired models and actors to sit in trendy clubs and order martinis made with Hennessy. Co-chairman Jonathan Bond, whose company also dreamed up the Snapple Beverage ads, says this "word of mouth" technique was not deceptive, even though the buyers didn't identify their employer. "We were just trying to give people a chance to evaluate it," he says. "People are so cynical that you have to be more inventive just to get considered."

Meanwhile, commercials in conventional formats, such as the 15- and 30-second slots in prime time, work hard to blur the distinction between ad and program. MCI Communications Corp. had such a strong response to its Gramercy Press campaign that it extended it to addi-

FAKE REAL LIFE

Beware of a spontaneous product endorsement, especially for something you've never heard of from people you don't know. Hiram Walker & Sons hired cool-looking actors to hang out in bars and talk up a new drink made with an aging brand, Hennessy cognac.

tional media. The soap opera-like TV commercials centered on a fictional publishing house at which all problems were solved and plots furthered with the help of MCI technology. First, a Gramercy Web site appeared. Then came a real novel purportedly written by the campaign's fictional celebrity author Marcus Belfrey and published by the fictional Gramercy Press. The real author, Barbara Cartland, and real publisher, Random House Inc., were revealed only inside the dust jacket. MCI even commissioned a two-hour pilot script for a TV series based on the story, but found no takers.

SURPRISE ENDING. The Gramercy Press commercials, though long on intrigue, did at least talk about MCI products. Other advertisers have expanded the format and toned down the pitch to produce far more subtle commercials. Guess? jeans' newest spot, which aired alongside previews in movie theaters this spring, was a 90-second black-and-white drama starring Juliette Lewis, Harry Dean Stanton, Traci Lords, and Peter Horton. It had virtually no connection to the sponsor's casual clothing, and only when the triangular Guess? logo flashed at the end did audiences find out they had been watching a commercial. "A lot of companies go for a degree of entertainment," says Guess? President Paul Marciano. "We try to be more entertaining, with a twist of intrigue, mystery." Whether audiences find it intriguing or manipulative, Marciano is committed to the minifilm format and hopes to extend his next effort to four or five minutes.

But marketers who too aggressively blur the line between ad and entertainment risk a backlash. Last month, A&E Television Networks' History Channel was forced to scrap plans for a series of one-hour specials that would profile companies. The highly regarded channel drew heavy criticism for its plan to allow subject companies to sponsor the series, help prepare the segments, cover some of the production costs, and have veto power over the final

JUST LITTLE OLD US

Having a giant marketer behind a product used to be an advantage—but not when consumers are searching for something less mass-produced. Companies from Miller to GM to RJR/Nabisco have tried hiding the corporate logo behind a made-up company with a more homespun image.

cut. A similar uproar over at CNBC hasn't quashed plans for *Scan*, a series that will examine the impact of technology on different cultures. IBM, Scan's sole worldwide sponsor, will own the shows once they air and will sit on an advisory panel, though CNBC says it will retain editorial control. Making things even murkier: Two of the early segments show how priests at the Vatican use computers to digitize ancient religious texts and how commuters in traffic-clogged Bangkok use technology to work as they travel—both subjects of IBM ads in the computer giant's "Solutions for a Small Planet" ad campaign.

Other marketers spin fictions not to disguise their ads but to hide their corporate provenance. The idea is to fake an aura of colorful entrepreneurship as a way to connect with younger consumers who yearn for products that are handmade, quirky, and authentic. The seeds of the genre were planted in the 1980s when E&J Gallo Winery set up a dummy corporation to avoid using its own name in the ads or on the labels of its new Bartles & Jaymes wine coolers. A campaign revolving around a couple of faux-bumpkin entrepreneurs named Frank and Ed

inspired a generation of imitators. "A lot of people seemed to believe they were real, and we never intended that," says Hal P. Riney, head of San Francisco ad agency Hal Riney & Partners Inc., which created the ads.

INSTANT TRADITION. There is a direct line from Gallo's Bartles & Jaymes to Miller Brewing Co.'s Red Dog, which masquerades as a microbrew under the name Plank Road Brewery, and to RJR's Moonlight Tobacco Co. Moonlight markets cigarette brands with such quirky names as Politix, City, and North Star in selected markets. The cigarettes come in packages with eye-catching graphics and only the barest mention of their Big Tobacco parent. "People are looking for more personal products. They are looking for uniqueness, for things that are not the typical, average, familiar, mass-produced product that we've had around for so long," says Riney. "People are responding by creating these sort of fictional histories and fictional traditions."

Sometimes, too, companies adopt a new identity for the same reason people go into the witness protection program: The original ID has become bad news. That's what drove

NO LAUGHING MATTER

The dancing taco is part of a song-and-dance number spoofing Taco Bell, the first title sponsor on the *Dana Carvey Show*. Carvey built each week's sponsor into the gags. But the jokes were too raw for Taco's parent, PepsiCo. Despite the exposure, it bailed out of the show.

size cutouts of the cast, *Melrose* trivia, and plenty of Kahlúa knick-knacks.

Other advertisers seek out chances for noncommercial commercials on TV and in the movies. Owning a piece of the show is one way to sneak aboard. Anheuser-Busch Co. owns a small stake in *Second Noah*, a syndicated series. The payoff? Exposure for Busch Gardens Tampa Bay, where the show is shot. Increasingly, networks are happy to cater to advertisers who want a bigger role. Witness Capital Cities/ABC Inc.'s short-lived *Dana Carvey Show*, which tried selling title sponsorships each week. The ex-*Saturday Night Live* comic lampooned sponsors' products as part of the night's entertainment. The strategy backfired in Week One, when Pepsi's Taco Bell found it didn't have the stomach for Carvey-style humor, which included calling himself a "whore" for the sponsor. Although Carvey seemed to tone down the gags after the first week, there were only three other sponsors, all Pepsi beverages, before the gimmick was abandoned. The show was canceled in April.

CAMEO HEAVEN. Sometimes, telling the show from the commercial is even harder. Elizabeth Arden Co. didn't pay for Elizabeth Taylor's appearances on four CBS sitcoms earlier this year. But the exposure for the star's new Black Pearls perfume

General Motors Corp. to dissociate itself from its innovative offspring, the Saturn. Because Detroit in general has suffered from a reputation for shoddy cars, sleazy dealers, and lousy service, GM set up a Saturn plant in Tennessee and hired Riney to package it as a small-town enterprise, run by folks not terribly unlike Frank and Ed. Whether Saturn customers are buying into better service and cars or buying into Riney's vision of small-town values, their cult-like devotion is the envy of other marketers. Two years ago, 44,000 of them trekked to Tennessee for a "reunion." Last year, Saturn was the nation's fifth-best-selling car.

Knowing that consumers are increasingly cynical about the claims in traditional ads, other advertisers have tried to ignite, appropriate, or imitate grassroots trends and fads. "When you're looking at younger consumers, you can't tell them what's cool," says Ric Militi, head of integrated communications at ad agency Lois/EJL in Los Angeles. "Generally, if it's advertised, it's immediately uncool."

That's why marketers work hard to make promotions look as unplanned as possible. Militi spotted an opportunity last fall when Spell-

ing Entertainment Group Inc., alleging trademark infringement, forced bar owners to stop hosting *Melrose Place* parties. The parties were springing up spontaneously at bars around the country on Monday nights when the prime-time soap opera aired. Militi quickly bought a license from Spelling on behalf of Hiram Walker & Sons' Kahlúa Royale Cream. He followed up each cease-and-desist letter the producer sent to bar owners with a marketing kit for a Spelling-sanctioned Kahlúa-sponsored party, complete with life-

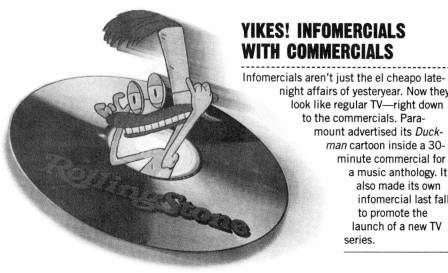

YIKES! INFOMERCIALS WITH COMMERCIALS

Infomercials aren't just the el cheapo late-night affairs of yesteryear. Now they look like regular TV—right down to the commercials. Paramount advertised its *Duckman* cartoon inside a 30-minute commercial for a music anthology. It also made its own infomercial last fall to promote the launch of a new TV series.

from Arden was a marketing coup. The plot of each show was written around Taylor, playing herself, and her perfume brand. Was this marketing? Entertainment? Who cares? Arden got better exposure than ad-budget money could buy, and CBS's ratings for the heavily hyped evening were way up. "From a marketing standpoint, it was brilliant," says Betsy Frank, executive vice-president of Zenith Media. "It was as seamless as you can get."

While shows have started looking more like commercials, commercials have started looking more like shows. Take the new breed of infomercials, those 30-or 60-minute ads that once were the domain of the purely schlocky. Now, solid-gold marketers from Microsoft to Ford to Eastman Kodak are airing them. Gone are the tacky sets and lousy production values. These slick segments now mimic talk shows or even newscasts. Time Inc.'s infomercial for its *Rolling Stone* "Sounds of the '80s" music collection even managed to sell time to yet another advertiser. Halfway through the 30-minute pitch, a cartoon character breaks into the program. In essence, the appearance of Paramount Television Group's Duckman is a paid message inside another paid message.

Even Broadway producers are getting into the sponsorship act. When *Big, the Musical*, opened on Broadway in April, toy seller F.A.O. Schwarz got co-producer billing—

and marketing mileage that extends far beyond the credits. The play's sets recreated the Fifth Avenue store for a crucial scene. Meanwhile, the store recreated the sets. Visitors at either location could buy plenty of Schwarz-marketed *Big* merchandise. "This has not been an attempt to overtly aggrandize F.A.O. Schwarz," says John H. Eyler, president of Schwarz. At least one critic at the Detroit tryout disagreed, lambasting the show for blatantly plugging the toy store. Some of the most adulatory bits were cut before the New York opening, but the producers said the changes had nothing to do with downplaying Schwarz.

As movie screens and other venues become infested with brand-name goods, such glorified product placements may start to lose their punch. "The problem with marketing that doesn't identify itself as marketing is that consumers catch on and it loses its impact," says adman Bond. "It's not in the movie because it's such a cultural icon, but because someone paid for it."

That's why marketers work so hard to make the graft between ad and entertainment as smooth as possible. When it comes to truly smooth melding of the two, no one matches Martha Stewart, queen of the domestic arts, who combines a potent promise that housework can be glamorous with unparalleled media savvy. Her empire, which includes magazines, books, TV shows, and a

nascent mail-order business, perfectly merges the Martha editorial message with the Martha marketing message. When Martha shows us how to make puff pastry on television or how to tend lilacs in her magazine, that's information, but it's also an extended look at a living, breathing logo. Stewart so completely embodies her brand that virtually everything she does, whether it's a commercial for American Express Co. or a guest spot on *Ellen*, brings in new customers for Brand Martha.

Stewart may be the best indicator of where advertising is headed as it converges with the editorial content on our TV screens, in our magazines, and on our computers. Clearly, Stewart's fans, who are legion, want what she is selling. But what if all entertainment and information came entwined with a brand name and every human encounter were mediated by a commercial sponsor? Advertisers say they only run the commercials that bring in customers. Stop buying, and they'll rethink their campaigns. Maybe.

But in a world weary of the incessant sales pitch, you have to wonder if there's anything that's not for sale. If you find it, enjoy it while it lasts—before somebody decides to sponsor it.

· *By Mary Kuntz in New York and Joseph Weber in Philadelphia, with Heidi Dawley in London*

Unit 2

Key Points to Consider

❖ As marketing research techniques become more and more advanced through the use of automation and the computer, and as psychographic analysis leads to more and more sophisticated models of consumer behavior, do you believe marketing will become more capable of predicting consumer behavior? If not, why not? If so, what ethical considerations must confront the marketing profession?

❖ Where the population lives, its age, and its ethnicity are demographic factors of importance to marketers. What other demographic factors must be taken into account in long-range market planning? What industries do you think are most concerned with these factors?

❖ In the essay "Tapping the Three Kids' Markets," James McNeal describes how children constitute three distinct consumer markets: primary, influence, and future. What are some examples of ways (e.g., advertisement, displays, selection of retailers) in which marketers have effectively addressed these three distinct markets?

❖ Psychographic segmentation is the process whereby consumer markets are divided up into segments based upon similarities in lifestyles, attitudes, personality type, social class, and buying behavior. In what specific ways do you envision that psychographic research and its findings will help marketing planning and strategy in the next decade?

 **Links** **www.dushkin.com/online/**

11. **CyberAtlas Demographics**
   http://www.cyberatlas.com/market/demographics/index.html
12. **General Social Survey**
   http://www.icpsr.umich.edu/GSS/
13. **"Identifying Your Appropriate Market Opportunity"**
   http://www.cba.neu.edu/alumni/m-article21.html
14. **"Market Research Essential in Determining Firm's Viability"**
   http://www.cba.neu.edu/alumni/m-article3.html
15. **Marketing Tools Directory**
   http://www.marketingtools.com/directory/
16. **U.S. Census Bureau Home Page**
   http://www.census.gov/
17. **USADATA**
   http://www.usadata.com/usadata/index.htm
18. **WWW Virtual Library: Demography & Population Studies**
   http://coombs.anu.edu.au/ResFacilities/DemographyPage.html

These sites are annotated on pages 4 and 5.

If marketing activities were all we knew about an individual, we would know a great deal. By tracing these daily activities over only a short period of time, we could probably guess rather accurately that person's tastes, understand much of his or her system of personal values, and learn quite a bit about how he or she deals with the world.

In a sense, this is a key to successful marketing management: tracing a market's activities and understanding its behavior. However, in spite of the increasing sophistication of market research techniques, this task is not easy. Today a new society is evolving out of the changing lifestyles of Americans, and these divergent lifestyles have put great pressure on the marketer who hopes to identify and profitably reach a target market. At the same time, however, each change in consumer behavior leads to new marketing opportunities.

The writings in this unit were selected to provide information and insight into the effect that lifestyle changes and demographic trends are having on American industry.

The first unit article, "Metaphor Marketing," by Daniel Pink, provides an enlightening look at the way pictures can be used to reveal consumers' deepest feelings and favorite brands. The next two articles in this subsection "Finding Unspoken Reasons for Consumers' Choices" by Jerry Thomas and "The New Market Research" by Joshua Macht discuss some new marketing research techniques and suggest ways to make marketing research more effective.

The three articles in the "Markets and Demographics" subsection examine the importance of demographic data, geographic settings, economic forces, and age considerations in making marketing decisions. In the first article "A Beginner's Guide to Demographics," Berna Miller provides a helpful background for understanding demographics. Then, James McNeal, in "Tapping the Three Kids' Markets," conveys how savvy marketers use knowledge about three distinct childrens' markets to sell to kids simultaneously in more than one market. Finally, "Culture Shock" by Shelly Reese suggests the importance of becoming cognizant of marketing to different cultures.

Two articles in the final subsection, "What Your Customers Can't Say" by David Wolfe and "The Joy of Shopping" by Mimi Avins examine how consumer behavior, social attitudes, cues, and quality considerations impact the evaluation and purchase of various products and services for different consumers.

Research, Markets, and Consumer Behavior

METAPHOR MARKETING

Harvard Business School professor **Jerry Zaltman** makes pictures that reveal your deepest feelings about your favorite brands. Can he scan your brain and unlock the images that lie within?

ARTICLE BY DANIEL H. PINK

JERRY ZALTMAN'S BRAIN IS ALL OVER THE PLACE. ONE LOBE has spilled onto a bookshelf, another has plopped onto a fallen picture frame, and the stem is buried beneath the edge of a half-read manuscript. It's not a pretty sight.

But there's hope. Zaltman eases himself from his chair and begins retrieving the pieces—plastic sections of a life-sized model of the human brain. He glances at each brain chunk and then, in a blur, effortlessly reassembles the whole. In an instant, he's got the brain back together again.

He pauses. And for a moment, he grasps it. Tenderly, Jerry Zaltman grasps the human brain. Which is why some of the biggest, richest companies on the planet have journeyed to his cluttered Harvard Business School office to rethink everything they know about marketing.

Marketing is a luxury of progress. It is necessary only in cultures that have largely satisfied basic human needs. The homeless and the hungry are still among us, but today most Americans have little trouble obtaining the basics: Their world is marked by oversupply in almost every category, from cars to candy bars. The average American supermarket is stuffed with 30,000 different items. Since 1980, the number of products launched each year has tripled; in 1996 alone, companies introduced some 17,000 new products. For sellers, this reality is daunting: How do I stand out? For buyers, it's confusing: How do I get what I want, when I want it? For Zaltman, a few

disciples, and a handful of forward-thinking companies, its an opportunity to reinvent marketing.

The problem, Zaltman says, is that our knowledge of what we need lies so deeply embedded in our brains that it rarely surfaces. Our native tongue is powerless to call it out of hiding; a second, more obscure language is needed. But few who speak to us in the marketplace even know that this second language exists—let alone how to speak it.

"A lot goes on in our minds that we're not aware of," says Zaltman. "Most of what influences what we say and do occurs below the level of awareness. That's why we need new techniques: to get at hidden knowledge—to get at what people don't know they know."

Zaltman invented perhaps the most powerful of these methods. He calls it the Zaltman Metaphor Elicitation Technique—this self-effacing man's only discernible act of ego. But to most, U.S. Patent Number 5,436,830 ("a technique for eliciting interconnected constructs that influence thought and behavior") is known simply as ZMET. The method combines neurobiology, psychoanalysis, linguistics, and art theory to try to uncover the mental models that guide consumer behavior—to illuminate the dark shadows of the customer brain. It is a bilingual phrase book that can narrow the linguistic gap between the marketer and the marketed-to. In other words, in the effort to decode the hieroglyphics etched on the walls of our minds—our emotions, feelings, and fears—ZMET may be the new economy's Rosetta Stone.

The Truth About Panty Hose

YOU DON'T HAVE TO BE A NEUROSCIENTIST TO GET YOUR MIND around panty hose. Women's stockings are often a form of nylon-based cruelty: They're hot, uncomfortable, and prone to run at the worst possible moment.

"Conventional research told us that women mostly hated wearing panty hose," says Glenda Green, a market-research manager at DuPont, which manufactures fibers for women's hosiery. "We did tremendous research—telephone interviews, mall-intercept interviews, everything you can think of." But she wasn't convinced that the company really understood what lurked deep in women's minds: "We thought there was a dimension of this that we were missing."

To test Green's suspicions, Zaltman selected 20 panty-hose-wearing women to be "Z-metted." The process began, as always, with a question: "What are your thoughts and feelings about buying and wearing panty hose?"

To answer the question, the women enacted ZMET's crucial next step: They collected a dozen pictures from magazines, catalogs, and family photo albums that captured their thoughts and feelings about the product. The women found images of steel bands strangling trees, of twisted telephone cords, and of fence posts encased in a tight plastic wrap—not too hard to figure out. But they also chose pictures of two African masks hanging on a bare wall, of an ice-cream sundae spilled on the ground, of a luxury car, and of flowers resting peacefully in a vase. Hmmmm.

A week later, after those images had simmered in each woman's subconscious, the subjects discussed each picture during an intense two-hour session with one of Zaltman's specially trained interviewer-cum-therapists. Then, with the aid of a technician using Adobe Photoshop, participants created collages of their thoughts and feelings about panty hose—works of art that doubled as windows into their minds.

The discovery: Yes, women do hate wearing panty hose. *But it's more complicated than that.* It's not that women have a love-hate relationship with nylons. Rather, they have a "*like*-hate" relationship.

"We got intensity, texture, and depth that we'd never gotten from other studies," Green recalls. "This was the first time we heard positive things that we could act on." For instance, the woman who chose the image of the fence posts encased in plastic wrap also selected the photo of the vase of flowers: Wearing the product made her feel thin and tall. The ice-cream sundae represented the embarrassment caused by stocking runs; the expensive car, the feeling of luxury. One woman's final collage pictured a cookie cutter wrapped in a garden hose, and set against the backdrop of a silk dress—conformity and discomfort on a field of elegance.

> ## "The [ZMET] images also brought out subtleties related to sexual issues," says DuPont's Glenda Green. "Eventually women would say they wanted to feel sexy to men."

"The images also brought out subtleties related to sexual issues," Green recalls. "Women would say, 'They make my legs feel longer.' Why is it important to have long legs? 'Men like long legs.' Why do men like long legs? 'They're sexy.' And eventually women would say they wanted to feel sexy to men. You don't get that in a straight interview."

These findings led hosiery manufacturers and retailers to alter their advertising to include not only images of supercompetent career women but also images of sexiness and allure—even when pitching the product to supercompetent career women. Inspired by Green's findings, one hosiery maker began including in each package a small card decorated with a yin-yang symbol on one side (to emphasize the like-hate duality) and a personalized quotation on the other (to send a message of understanding and caring). "It was a little card of female affirmation," says Green.

Market Research by the Book

IF THE $3.9 BILLION MARKET-RESEARCH INDUSTRY WERE A BOOK, ZMET would open chapter three. Chapter one began in the 1930s, when newspapers and magazines launched public-opinion polls—first to predict elections, then to gauge sentiment on other topics. As statisticians and demographers refined their techniques, companies began to build much of their marketing on survey research. Ask people what they think, catalog their responses, tally them up, slice the data this way and that, and—voilá!—you're inside the customer's head.

But numbers have their limitations, marketers discovered. Begin chapter two: qualitative research—whose impact on market research traces back to 1941, when Columbia University sociologist Robert Merton conducted the first focus group. Since then, a range of new qualitative techniques have burst onto the scene: in-depth interviews, participant observation (watch Billy play with a new toy from behind a one-way mirror), ethnographic research (move in with the Jones family and record their diurnal habits, like Margaret Mead in New Guinea), and projective techniques ("If this shampoo were a dog, what kind of dog would it be?").

But with more products filling store shelves, and with the Internet creating an entirely new way to reach customers, companies have grown restive with even the most

THIS IS MY BRAIN ON COFFEE

Call me Mr. Coffee. I don't just enjoy the stuff. I *need* the stuff. But why? Simply because of the happy dance that my brain cells perform whenever they meet caffeine molecules? Or is the need lodged somewhere deep in my subconscious? I turned to ZMET to find out.

The question: "What are your thoughts and feelings about coffee as a morning wake-up beverage?"

ZMET Act One: The Pictures

I spend about six hours paging through magazines and catalogs for images that capture my state of mind, adding a few photos of my own. I imagine what I feel like in the morning, both before and after my coffee, and look for pictures that portray my daily transformation. The big struggle: If I don't find 12 images, I'm in trouble.

ZMET Act Two: The Interview

At about noon in the Seeing the Voice of the Customer Lab, Randi Cohen, Z-metter extraordinaire, fastens a small microphone to my shirt. For the next two hours, she interviews me with the ferocity of Sam Donaldson and the subtlety of Sigmund Freud.

We begin with the image of a sport-utility vehicle. I explain: "I'm not really on a smooth path until I've had my coffee." "What is this path?" Cohen asks. "Where is this path going?" I mumble something about the path leading to the rest of my day.

Next picture: the newspaper from the day that Cal Ripken played in his 2,131st straight game. Because I drink coffee every morning, I'm "the Cal Ripken of coffee." She probes: "When Cal Ripken is playing, there are lots of people watching who appreciate his play." I backtrack: My coffee-drinking isn't a spectator sport. "It'd be like if Cal Ripken every day took batting practice in his backyard," I offer.

We go to a magazine photo of a man and a woman canoeing along a tranquil stream—which brings together the feeling of smoothness that I get from coffee and the fact that I always have morning coffee with my wife. "Why is it important to do that with your wife?" Cohen asks. "I

guess it's a sign that we're in it together," I speculate. "It's sort of a shared addiction."

Jerry Zaltman enters the interview room. He listens a bit, and then poses the next question: "If you could walk up to coffee and say, 'Hey, how ya doin' today? How do you feel today?' what would its answer be?" My response: "I think its answer would be 'I feel sharp. I feel acute.'" "Why sharp or acute?" Zaltman wonders. That's my idea of the personality of a cup of coffee: "It's serious, but serious in a very penetrating way." After letting that sink in, Zaltman softly continues his inquiry: "Now that we've anthropomorphized this cup of coffee, let's say that it's thinking. What's it thinking about *you*?" I reply, "What's it thinking about me? Well, this is my first thought, so I'll just go with it, even though it might be somewhat unflattering to me: The coffee's saying, 'Why are you trying to be like me?'"

ZMET Act Three: The Collage

The interrogation over, I walk—a little drained, a little perplexed—into another room at the lab. Graphic artist Marion Finkle helps me design the collage that will summarize all the ideas that have been percolating in my head. First we create a backdrop composed of several dozen small images of the Cal Ripken newspaper. Then I pick my way through the other images—water cascading into a body cast, a man kick-starting the sport-utility vehicle, the shot of the canoe.

Finkle asks me to summarize the story that the picture is telling. "The overall story is about preparation the night before because of the expectation of morning immobility, then the release of power and the start of the day, then the fact that this goes on every morning." "Anything else to add?" she asks. I look at my collage again. Then, for reasons I'd rather not subject to ZMET scrutiny, I begin to gush like Sally Field at the Oscars: "I like my image," I cry. "I really like it!"

The lesson for coffee-sellers: Market your product to me using images of movement and achievement. The lesson for myself: Maybe I'm drinking too much java.—*D.H.P.*

---

innovative qualitative techniques. Zaltman thought he knew why: Market researchers didn't understand the human brain, and they were speaking the wrong language.

Cognitive scientists have learned that human beings think in images, not in words. But most market research uses words, not images: It relies on surveys, questionnaires, and focus groups. Sociolinguists know that most communication is nonverbal. But most research tools are, as Zaltman puts it, "verbocentric."

Poets and psychiatrists understand that metaphor—viewing one thing in terms of another—is central to

thought and crucial to uncovering latent needs and emotions. But most marketers are so caught up in the literal, they neglect the metaphoric.

"People can give us only what we give them the opportunity to provide," Zaltman says. "To the extent that we structure the stimulus—whether it's a discussion guide in a focus group or a question in a survey—all people can do is respond. And there's value in that. But I see those as strip-mining techniques," Zaltman says, deploying—what else?—a metaphor. "Sometimes the valuable ore is on the surface. But often it's not. Strip-mining tech-

"The Nestlé Crunch bar turns out to be a very powerful icon of time," says Zaltman. The candy bar evoked powerful memories of childhood, of simpler times.

niques are inappropriate when there's a great deal more depth to be had. Typically, the deeper you go, the more value there is."

Chocolate Clocks & Security Dogs

BITE INTO A NESTLÉ CRUNCH BAR, AND YOU IMMEDIATELY SAVOR THE milk chocolate and crisped rice. It takes a more sophisticated palate to taste the metaphor.

When he used ZMET to probe the attitudes of 10 Nestlé Crunch fans, Zaltman first uncovered what you might expect. Through their pictures and Photoshop collages, subjects revealed that they saw the candy bar as a small indulgence in a busy world, a source of quick energy, and something that just tasted good.

But as Zaltman probed more deeply, he unearthed a surprise. "The Nestlé Crunch bar turns out to be a very powerful icon of *time*," Zaltman says. "The company had never noticed that before." Subjects brought in pictures of old pickup trucks, of children playing on picket-fenced suburban lawns, of grandfather clocks, of snowmen, and of American flags. The candy bar evoked powerful memories of childhood, of simpler times. It was less a workday pick-me-up than a time machine back to childhood. At the very least, Zaltman says, Nestlé found out that "a cue about time could be especially engaging—whether it's an hourglass or a clock or a sepia drawing on the wall. It can be a very small item, but you know that the eye is going to be directed toward it."

While Nestlé learned something new about a product that was old, Motorola learned something unexpected about a product not yet born. Late last year, the company was studying how to market a new security system. Hoping to understand the metaphorical side of the product, a few managers used ZMET to ask, How do potential customers feel when they're secure and when they're insecure? Then, same drill as always: pictures, interviews, artwork.

"I was struck by how very profound and fascinating the pictures were," says Wini Schaeffer, a Motorola manager involved in the project. What images did subjects select? Dogs. Lots of them. Interviewees revealed that canines represented comfort and security: the feeling of protection that comes from knowing that a loyal animal is looking out for them. This finding could have enormous implications for how the product is positioned—less as a techno-

logical gizmo, more as a companion—and for how it is named: Don't call it "The Talkatron." Call it, say, "The Watchdog."

"I can't imagine that a survey would uncover that," says Schaeffer. "In this method, there are *aha's*. You get answers to questions that you never thought to ask."

Thinking Across Boundaries

IN THE LAND OF THE METAPHOR, JERRY ZALTMAN IS AN EVANGELIST, loping across the country to spread the ZMET gospel. In recent months, he's traveled to Atlanta to advise Coca-Cola and to Cincinnati to consult with Proctor & Gamble. But the mother church is on the Harvard Business School campus, in a suite that resembles a doctor's office: a place called the "Seeing the Voice of the Customer Lab."

After luring Zaltman away from the University of Pittsburgh in 1991, Harvard agreed to help finance this site and to fill it with a small staff. One of Zaltman's most seasoned interviewers is consultant Randi Cohen, a lean and stylish 30-year-old Stanford PhD, who also teaches marketing at Boston University. For what she calls her "guided conversations," she stations herself in a windowless room not much different from the kind that police use to interrogate suspects. In one of the lab's other two rooms sits Marion Finkle, a 31-year-old graphic artist who helps subjects use the bleeding-edge software necessary to create beguiling digital images. And in the third room is Trevor Messersmith, a hip twentysomething who, like Finkle, designs the multimedia presentations that the lab delivers to clients at the end of a project. In this setting, the Z-Team members more resemble the staff of a Silicon Alley startup than the employees of North America's most venerable university.

But Zaltman isn't your typical business-school professor: He resists absolute pronouncements—often responding to a question with another question, or by admitting that he doesn't know the answer. Asked why he moved to Pittsburgh from a tenured position on the renowned marketing faculty at Northwestern University's Kellogg School, he says, "To tell you the truth, I don't have a good answer." Asked why he accepted Harvard's invitation to leave Pitt, he says, "Sometimes we do things for more complicated reasons than we'll allow ourselves to see."

And like the plastic models in his office, Zaltman's brain is all over the place. He studies neuroscience, art,

"Sometimes the valuable ore is on the surface," says Zaltman. "But often it's not. Typically, the deeper you go, the more value there is."

"I don't buy the notion that the world is organized the way universities and companies are," Zaltman says. "Ideas don't know what discipline they're in."

semiotics, computers, and, yes, even business. At Pitt, he held positions in the School of Public Health, the Department of Sociology, the Graduate School of Public and International Affairs, and the Business School. At Harvard, he's a fellow at the Mind, Brain, Behavior Initiative, one of the nation's most ambitious interdisciplinary undergraduate majors.

This ability to think across disciplines is the secret of ZMET, Zaltman says. And it's a skill that's becoming critical in the new world of business: "I don't buy the notion that the world is organized the way universities and companies are. Ideas don't know what discipline they're in," he explains. "We might kidnap them and say, 'That's a marketing idea' or 'That's an anthropology idea.' But if you walked up to an idea on the street, it wouldn't know about that."

Nepal Meets Magritte

THE TRAIL TO ZMET BEGINS IN NEPAL. IN 1990, PROPELLED BY THREE divergent interests (photography, cognitive neuroscience, and Third World anthropology) Zaltman traveled to Nepal to photograph periodic markets, commercial conclaves that meet in rural areas every few months.

While he was there, Zaltman says, "I started thinking about the issue of bias. I can take all the pictures in the world, and they'll still be my photographs of someone else. The idea occurred to me: Maybe I should give film and cameras to people who had never looked through a lens before."

He contacted Eastman Kodak, which provided him with plastic cameras and 650 rolls of film. Accompanied by his wife and another couple, Zaltman returned to Nepal. "We'd visit a place, give people cameras, ask them to take pictures. We'd say, 'If you were to leave this village, what pictures would you take with you to show others what your life is like?'"

The villagers snapped their photos. Then the Zaltmans developed them and showed them to the "photographers." Then, Zaltman explains, "We had people talk to us through an interpreter about what these photographs meant. We think of these people as unsophisticated, but it was exciting to discover how effective they were in telling stories. In every strip of negatives, there was a story—one full of paradox, contrast, and contradiction."

For instance, most of the photos cut off people's feet. "At first, I thought the villagers had just aimed wrong," Zaltman says. "But it turns out that being barefoot is a sign of poverty. Even though everyone was barefoot, people wanted to hide that—which is another important message."

Zaltman knew he was onto something. He just wasn't sure what. So when he returned to Pitt, he began experimenting with a new methodology, often with the help of Robin Coulter, one of his star PhD students. At first, the researchers gave participants cameras and told them to shoot images that captured their thoughts and feelings about a particular product or service. But subjects often had difficulty taking exactly the pictures they desired, so Zaltman and Coulter allowed them to select images from magazines and newspapers. Around this time, Zaltman says, "I also got interested in digital imaging." And in his spare moments, he studied some of the breakthrough research in neuroscience. Crossing the borders of many disciplines, Zaltman began to map a new approach to marketing.

In its final form, the approach recalls the surrealist movement in literature and art, which reached its zenith in the 1920s and 1930s. Rather than depict our conscious perception of the physical world, the surrealists sought to portray the subconscious, particularly as it was revealed in dreams. Visual art of the period often depicted melting clocks and liquid trees, incongruously positioned against hallucinatory landscapes. Zaltman has brought that sensibility to the world of market research. Goodbye, Gallup. Hello, Dalì.

In fact, Zaltman's approach stretches from those barefoot villagers in Nepal to the quote, taken from surrealist painter René Magritte, that opens his course syllabus: "Everything we see hides something else we want to see."

Brain-Scan Marketing

ON A BED IN MASSACHUSETTS GENERAL HOSPITAL, A WOMAN LIES ON her back, her head held motionless beneath a specially molded face mask. She breathes slowly and a bit tentatively. With each breath, she inhales a few radioactive particles—invisible messengers that enter her bloodstream, where they can easily be tracked. Her head rests in a small chamber that looks like a giant frosted donut. Then the experiment begins. A scientist slips a cassette into a tape player, and a voice describes the car dealership from hell—cigarette-stained linoleum floors, garish lights, an overbearing salesforce. In another room, a computer paints a picture of what's happening inside her brain.

This is one of ZMET's next frontiers. With Stephen Kosslyn, a Mind, Brain, Behavior faculty member, Zaltman has begun using positron emission tomography (brain scans) to see how—or more precisely, *where*—consumers think. In the pair's first and only study, subjects were read descriptions of three car dealerships—one good, one bad,

"If managers don't know their own minds," Zaltman says, "they're not going to understand the mind of the customer."

one humdrum—while researchers monitored blood flow through their brains.

"Sure enough," Zaltman says, "we found that when we played the audiotape of negative experiences, the area in the right brain associated with negative thoughts lit up." In particular, Kosslyn says, descriptions of the sleazy car dealership excited the subjects' right frontal lobe—the area of the brain associated with the primitive instinct of withdrawal. When they heard descriptions of the more welcoming dealerships—nice carpeting, gleaming computers, helpful staff—parts of the brain associated with positive emotions lit up instead. Tinker a little more with the description, and you could design the car dealership of people's dreams, a retail setting that you know will tickle their brains and move their feet.

Refine the process further, says Kosslyn, and "the potential is revolutionary." For instance, you could segment the market along entirely new lines—not only according to how big people's wallets are but also according to how people think. Some customers are visual; others are auditory. Use brain scans to classify your customer base, and then target the first group with a newspaper display ad and the second with a radio spot.

At the moment, however, Zaltman has taken only a few tentative steps into this new territory. The car-dealership study was of just six subjects—a half-dozen right-handed women. Zaltman and Kosslyn are hustling up funds for more such experiments. Meantime, Zaltman is pushing into new frontiers. Recently, for example, he used ZMET to study 24 executives enrolled in Harvard Business School's executive-education program. The question: What are your thoughts and feelings about being customer-focused? Part of the answer: It means collecting information, analyzing data, anticipating customer needs—all exactly what customer-service gurus advise. But ZMET revealed another part of the answer: Being customer-focused means having integrity, caring about customers in an authentic way, being a company worthy of trust. "The executives were surprised by how much of their individual thinking was shared by others, although they had never discussed these things with anyone," says Zaltman.

In another study of Harvard executives, researchers asked what it means to develop a marketing strategy. Again, ZMET surfaced unexpected meanings. Developing a marketing strategy meant having passion, demonstrating integrity, having fun. "This is not in the marketing textbooks," Zaltman says.

The Mind of the Manager

ULTIMATELY, EVEN A GREAT METAPHOR HAS TO DELIVER RESULTS— which is why Zaltman treats each project as a test. So far, ZMET has not only delivered the same kinds of findings as more conventional research methods; it has also generated its own metaphor-based insights. "The fact that we came up with what other techniques have also found provided a validation. You couldn't dismiss the special results without dismissing the other results," he says. "But in every case, we've come up with additional insights."

But even those who use and endorse Zaltman's approach are mindful of its limitations. "ZMET is not a replacement. It's a complement," says Jennifer Barron, head of strategic market research at Monitor Co., who has used the technique. "It's more helpful in a category that's not 100% rational. With something like financial services, where there's an emotional element—how you provide for your family—it makes sense. But I don't know if I'd use ZMET on industrial salt." For some purposes, a survey or a focus group does just fine.

Zaltman himself always makes clear that his technique doesn't offer neat solutions to any company's problems. "Research can never tell you what to do," he says. "It can only give you the basis for being creative in what you do. Ultimately, it's the mind of the manager that matters. If managers don't know their own minds, they're not going to understand the mind of the customer."

DANIEL H. PINK (DHPINK@IX.NETCOM.COM) IS A *FAST COMPANY* CONTRIBUTING EDITOR. HIS ARTICLE, "FREE AGENT NATION," APPEARED IN THE DECEMBER:JANUARY 1998 ISSUE. FIND OUT MORE ABOUT **JERRY ZALTMAN**'S WORK ON THE WEB (WWW.HBS.EDU/UNITS/MARKETING/ZMET).

Finding unspoken reasons for consumers' choices

By Jerry W. Thomas

As the type of marketing research that attempts to explain why consumers behave as they do, motivational research seeks to discover and comprehend what consumers do not fully understand about themselves.

Implicitly, motivational research assumes the existence of underlying or unconscious motives that influence consumer behavior. It attempts to identify influences that consumers may not be aware of—such as cultural factors and sociological forces. Typically, these unconscious motives (or beyond-awareness reasons) are intertwined with and complicated by conscious motives, cultural biases, economic variables and fashion trends.

Motivational researchers attempt to sift through all of these influences and factors to unravel the mystery of consumer behavior as it relates to a specific product or service, so that the marketer better understands the target audience and how to influence it.

Motivational research is most valuable when powerful underlying motives are suspected of exerting influence upon consumer behavior. Products and services that relate, or might relate, to attraction of the opposite sex, personal adornment, status, self-esteem, power, death, fears or social taboos all are likely candidates for motivational research.

For example, why is it that woman tend to increase their expenditures on clothing and personal adornment products as they approach ages 50 to 55? The reasons relate to the loss of youth's beauty and fertility, and perhaps to related fears of losing their husband's love. It also is a time when discretionary incomes are rising, often because the children are leaving the nest. Other motives are at work as well, but a standard marketing research survey never would reveal these motives because most women are not really aware of why their interest in expensive adornments increases at this point in their lives.

Even benign, or low-involvement, product categories often can benefit from the insights provided by motivational research. Typically, in low-involvement product categories, perception variables and cultural influences are most important.

Our culture is a system of rules and regulations that simplify and optimize our existence. Cultural rules govern how we squeeze a tube of toothpaste, how we open packages, how we use a bath towel, who does what work, and so on. Most of us are relatively unaware of these cultural rules, but understanding how they influence a particular product can be extremely valuable information for the marketer.

The major techniques

The three major motivational research techniques are observation, focus groups and depth interviews. Observation can be a fruitful method of making hypotheses about human motives. Anthropologists pioneered the development of this technique: we're all familiar with anthropologists living with natives to understand their behavior. This same systematic observation can produce equally insightful results about consumer behavior. Observation can be accomplished in person or, sometimes, through video. Usually, personal observation is simply too expensive a method.

Most consumers don't want an observer living in their household for a month or two. It is easier to observe consumers in buying situations, either in person or through video cameras. In-store observers can be used as long as they have some "cover" that makes their presence less obvious. Generally, video cameras are less intrusive than an in-person observer. Finding a representative set of cooperative stores, however, is not easy, nor is installing and maintaining video cameras.

Observation, whether by video or the human eye, cannot answer every question. Generally, it must be supplemented by focus groups or depth interviews to fully understand why consumers do what they do.

The focus group

In the hands of a skilled moderator, focus groups can be a valuable motivational research technique. To reach its full potential, the group interview must be largely nondirective in style and achieve spontaneous interaction. It is the

> **❝ Most of us are relatively unaware of these cultural rules, but understanding how they influence a particular product can be extremely valuable information for the marketer. ❞**

mutual reinforcement within the group (the group excitement and spontaneity) that produces the revelations and behaviors that reveal underlying motives.

However, a focus group discussion dominated by the moderator will rarely produce any motivational insights. Likewise, a focus group actively led by the moderator with much direct questioning of respondents will seldom yield motivational understanding.

The depth interview

The heart and soul of motivational research is the depth interview, a one- to two-hour, one-on-one interview, conducted by the researcher. Much of the power of the depth interview depends upon the researcher's insight, sensitivity and skill. This interviewing cannot be delegated to traditional marketing research interviewers, because they lack training in motivational techniques.

The emotional empathy between the motivational researcher and respondent is the single most important determinant of an effective interview. During the personal interview, the motivational researcher strives to create a feeling of rapport, mutual trust and understanding. The researcher creates a climate in which the respondent feels free to express feelings and thoughts without fear of embarrassment or rejection. The researcher conveys a feeling that the respondent and his opinions are worthwhile, no matter what those opinions are. The motivational researcher is accepting, nonthreatening and supportive.

The motivational researcher relies heavily upon nondirective interviewing techniques. The goal is to get the respondent to talk and keep talking. The researcher tends to introduce general topics, rather than ask direct questions, and probes with raised eyebrows or a questioning look, by paraphrasing what the respondent has said, or repeating the respondent's words in a questioning tone. Nondirective techniques are the least threatening and the least biasing to respondents.

Projective techniques can play an important role in motivational research. Sometimes, a respondent recognizes in others what he cannot—or will not—see in himself. The motivational researcher often asks the respondent to tell a story, play a role, draw a picture, complete a sentence, or associate words with a stimulus. Photographs, product samples,

packages and advertisements can also be used as stimuli to evoke additional feelings, imagery and comment.

During the interview, the researcher watches for cues that might indicate that a sensitive nerve has been touched. Long pauses by the respondent, slips-of-the-tongue, fidgeting, variations in voice pitch, strong emotions, facial expressions, eye movements, avoidance of a question, fixation on an issue and body language are some of the clues the motivational researcher looks for. Sensitive topics and issues are then the focus of additional inquiry and exploration later in the interview.

Each interview is tape-recorded and transcribed. A typical motivational study, consisting of 30 to 50 depth interviews, yields 1,000 to 2,000 pages of typed, verbatim dialogue. During the interview, the motivational researcher makes notes about the respondent's behavior, mannerisms, physical appearance, personality characteristics and nonverbal communications. These notes become a road map to help the researcher understand and interpret the verbatim transcript of the interview.

The analysis

The motivational researcher reads and rereads the pages of dialogue, looking for systematic patterns of response. The researcher identifies logical inconsistencies or apparent contradictions, compares direct responses against projective responses, notes the consistent use of unusual words or phrases, studies the explicit content of the interview and contemplates its meaning in relation to the implicit content and searches for what is not said. Like a detective, the researcher sifts through the clues and the evidence to deduce the forces and motives influencing consumer behavior. No one clue or piece of evidence is treated as being very important—it is the convergence of evidence and facts that leads to significant conclusions. In the scientific tradition, empiricism and logic must come together and make sense.

The analysis begins at the cultural level. Cultural values and influences are the ocean in which we all swim, and of which most of us are completely unaware. What we eat, the way we eat, how we dress, what we think and feel, the language we speak, are dimensions of our culture, and the basic building blocks that begin the motivational researcher's analysis. The culture is the

context that must be understood before the behavior of individuals within the context can be understood. Every product has cultural values and rules that influence its perception and its use.

The next analytic step is the exploration of the unique motivations that relate to the product category. For example: What psychological needs does the product fulfill? Does the product have any social overtones or anthropological significance? Does the product relate to one's status aspirations, to competitive drive, to feelings of self-esteem, to security needs? Are masochistic motives involved? Does the product have deep symbolic significance?

Some of these motives must be inferred since respondents often are unaware of why they do what they do.

Finally, the business environment, including competitive forces, brand perceptions and images, relative market shares, the role of advertising in the category, and trends in the marketplace must be understood. Only part of this business environment knowledge can come from the respondent, of course, but understanding the business context is crucial to the interpretation of consumer motives in a way that will lead to useful results. Understanding the consumer's motives is worthless unless somehow that knowledge can be translated into actionable marketing and advertising recommendations.

Sometimes, a motivational study is followed by quantitative surveys to confirm the motivational hypotheses as well as to measure the relative extent of those motives in the general population. But, many times motivational studies cannot be proved or disproved by survey research, especially when completely unconscious motives are involved. In these cases, the final evaluation of the hypothesized motives is by the testing of concepts (or advertising alternatives) that address the different motives, or by other types of contrived experiments.

Strongly held hypotheses, or rigid adherence to theory, will doom a motivational study to failure. Too often we see what we set out to see, or find that for which we search, whether it exists or not. An objective, open, unfettered mind is the motivational researcher's greatest asset.

Jerry W. Thomas is president of Decision Analyst Inc. in Arlington, Texas.

THE NEW MARKET RESEARCH

Anything worth knowing about your customers, traditional market research can't tell you anymore

By Joshua Macht

When Peter Shamir returned to New York City, in 1995, he slipped back into a lifestyle long forgotten. For the previous 25 years Shamir had lived in Jerusalem, where, in spite of political tumult, brutal wars, and chronic terrorism, life's pace seemed manageable—even serene. "Jerusalem is still a small city, very different from what I was entering," says Shamir. In Manhattan, everything was a blur: the cabs, the meals, the phone conversations. Each day Shamir was pummeled with raw insight into how Americans live. But he was more concerned with how they shop.

Shamir, age 47, had journeyed to the States as a scout for Sky Is The Ltd., a four-person Israeli-based start-up that distributes a wafer-thin cracker called Bible Bread. The company owners, Zack Shavin, Moshe Shuster, and Shuster's brother, Danny Yassor, had dispatched Shamir, their vice-president of marketing, to launch Galilee Splendor Inc., a U.S.-based subsidiary that would sell the product throughout North America. But the Israeli contingent lacked critical knowledge: the group hadn't a clue about why the average American grabbed one cracker versus an-

VIRTUAL SHOPPING

Have you seen a game like Quake?" Raymond R. Burke, professor of business administration at Indiana University, asks, referring to the video game that features eye-popping graphics of a quake-devastated city. "My idea is to harness that same 3-D horsepower for 3-D market research."

Today, Burke's lab in Bloomington, Ind., with its 20-inch touch-screen monitors and $20,000 PC workstations, is creating a virtual world to determine exactly how products catch a consumer's eye in a store. Computer graphics simulate the feeling of walking past shelves of soap and shampoo, just as a video game might simulate a violent encounter with a kickboxer. And this virtual world is similarly interactive—consumers can pick items off the shelves to examine them more closely and can indicate which items they would buy if this were real-life shopping.

Burke believes that virtual reality is less contrived than a focus group because it offers shoppers product choices in a natural, "cluttered" environment. Companies using his program can instantly change variables like packaging or price and get immediate feedback. Burke's software tracks, records, and tabulates a shopper's moves and hesitations. Not every product can be tested this way, however. Burke doesn't test clothing, for example, because the shopper can't feel the fabric or try on the items.

Burke's technique has already attracted big-name clients like Goodyear Tire and General Mills, but he believes that virtual market research will prove itself increasingly relevant to small companies. "As the price of computers comes down and as 3-D graphics become easier to do on the low end," he says, "we'll see these types of simulations used much more frequently."

—Mike Hofman

other. Shamir came to the States searching for answers.

For those who rank food shopping a notch above root-canal work, a season in hell might seem more appealing than Shamir's life in the United States. During his first six months he schlepped from family-owned convenience stores in Harlem to Von's supermarkets in Los Angeles. He met with dozens of distributors and brokers and peddled the product as he bobbed in and out of food stores in Detroit, Atlanta, and Nashville—to name just a few of his stops.

For the most part, Shamir was following a well-trodden path into American food stores. But the company needed more than just solid distributors to become successful. Driven by his own craving to understanding the American consumer, Shamir would often cruise the cracker aisles to observe unknowing consumers. That casual research provided pertinent feedback.

"The average consumer took about 10 seconds to find the cracker they wanted," says Shamir. "Bible Bread would clearly not get noticed in the cracker aisle of one of the big markets." But gourmet, health-food, and kosher stores seemed to be a better match. Even the deli section of the larger markets held more promise. At least there, consumers were more likely to linger in search of new products. "We already knew we had a good

cracker," says Shamir, "but the research let us know where to put it."

Since that time, Bible Bread has popped up in specialty and gourmet stores in 30 states. The number of stores has jumped by 50% in the past year, and U.S. revenues are projected to reach $1 million by the end of 1998. Although Galilee Splendor now has a better grip on its typical cracker customer, research efforts haven't slowed. Shamir, now based in Miami, continues to quietly stalk shoppers and gauge their reaction to Bible Bread.

But Galilee Splendor is a rare bird among small companies in its attitude toward market research. Most just assume that a market exists for their product or service. As Kathleen Seiders, assistant professor of marketing and entrepreneurship at Babson College, in Wellesley, Mass., puts it. "Entrepreneurs think they have divine intuition, which is fine if you're part of the audience you are trying to reach. But when you move outside that market, your gut instinct can let you down."

Shamir knew better than to trust his instincts alone when he arrived in the States. And by following his curiosity about shoppers, he unwittingly caught the latest wave in market research: a trend that shuns survey statistics in favor of passive observation of consumers and open-ended questioning. Increasingly, corporate behemoths and top-notch market-research firms have become

disenchanted with traditional research methods and have opted for more creative avenues into consumer thinking. Experts may charge heavily for the cutting-edge services, but many of the new methods can be easily adapted by companies with even the tightest of budgets.

Consumer behavior has long been a preoccupation for corporate America. But in spite of the millions of dollars poured into the traditional survey-based approach, untold numbers of new products die on the vine each year. The ever-widening chasm between survey results and reality has emboldened marketers to question the old-style methods. One problem with surveys is that respondents can be less than forthright. They fudge replies to avoid seeming foolish or ignorant. Some experts claim that consumers don't always recognize the need for product improvement. "Consumers will sometimes create what we call 'work-arounds' to compensate for a product's deficiencies," says Dorothy Leonard, professor of business administration at the Harvard Business School. "Those consumers often aren't even aware that they want something better."

More to the point for small-company owners, surveys and focus groups are tremendously costly and time-consuming. A single focus group can run as high as $20,000, and it can take months—even a year—to collect data and crunch numbers from a massive survey. "By the time you 'know the market,' the market has already changed," says Raymond R. Burke, a market-research expert and a professor of business at the Kelley School of Business at Indiana University. "We are in the midst of watching a real shift away from survey-based research."

The shift is toward a vastly different breed of innovative—and sometimes outlandish—approaches that seek to unveil the consumer's hidden thoughts. Today's methods borrow liberally from anthropology, cognitive psychology, and—through role-playing—even the performing arts. Rather than invite consumers into artificial testing situations, marketers now charge out into the field to observe and examine consumers at work, in stores, and even at home. And then they analyze their observations.

Taken at their highest level, those methods demand the skills of a thoroughly trained professional marketer. But company owners can appropriate many of the new techniques to uncover an enormous amount of market information on the cheap. Best of all, unlike survey-based studies, that research doesn't require massive numbers of people. The object is to uncover an array of ideas that might help you improve your product. "You don't necessarily care if 20% feel one way and 80% think another," says consumer-behavior specialist Roger D. Blackwell, a professor of marketing at Ohio State University, in Columbus, Ohio. "You want a range of views."

But don't expect your discoveries to dictate your company's direction. Rather, that sort of research should gently guide product-development and marketing efforts. Oh, there's another catch: to gain a new perspective on your product or service, you must cast aside your own biases—and your divine intuition—about your product or service. If the consumer is to teach you anything, you must be open to the lesson. "Entrepreneurs often mistakenly try to 'fix' the consumer's faulty point of view," explains Blackwell. "But that's not research, that's selling."

For Shamir, it was a breeze. Having been away so long, he couldn't assume much about the American shopper. And that's precisely how the curious entrepreneur must approach market research: detach yourself from the intimate knowledge you have of your product or service. Although it might sound like heresy, try to forget what makes your product irresistible.

Of course, that's far easier to say than do, as Julia Knight, founder of Growing Healthy Inc., a Minneapolis maker of frozen baby food, discovered. Knight had worked as a vice-president of marketing for Minnetonka, a fragrance and cosmetics designer in Minneapolis. When she held her baby-food package in her hands, she couldn't help recalling the hours of toil spent on the most minute design elements. "As a marketer you can spend hours on something that consum-

ers barely even see," she says. "The hardest thing is to become an innocent consumer again."

When Knight began her foray into frozen baby food, in 1989, she was a newly married 31-year-old. To capture the consumer's perspective, Knight would dress in a blue-jeans shirt and leg warmers (it was Minnesota, after all) and then roll through the aisles of local supermarkets. "The dress was critical because you feel much different in casual clothes than if you're wearing high heels and carrying a clipboard," says Knight. "I was literally trying to shake off my marketing self."

But initially, her in-store vigilance led to frustration—even agony. "It's painful to watch consumers pick up your product and then not buy it," warns Knight. It wasn't always easy for her to listen to dissenting consumers. The tendency was to explain to each customer why her baby food should be a best-seller. But she soon learned that "you can't convince customers one at a time to buy your product."

Instead, she immersed herself further in the role of the consumer. Not yet a parent herself, Knight enlisted friends who would go with her on shopping runs, taking their children along. With kids in tow, she began to see why so many parents dread the supermarket: one child screams while the other lurches for the chocolate bars. The research

also revealed a potentially fatal flaw: kids don't like the frozen-food section; it's too cold, and parents are under pressure to move speedily through the icy aisles. So Knight sought a warmer climate for her product. She lobbied supermarket managers to place cutaway freezers in the baby-food section.

By 1996, when Growing Healthy was sold, the company had climbed to $2.8 million in revenues. But it had been a constant struggle, and one that reaffirmed the breach between the customer's words and their actions. Now it all makes sense to Knight. "What mother, especially in front of other mothers, would really tell you that she spent more on cat food than on baby food?" she asks. But her observations had shown her otherwise.

Lurking behind shoppers is one way to get the skinny on the habits of the average Joe. Another is to watch potential customers actually use your product. That's why many companies pay a high price for behind-the-glass focus groups. The trouble is, consumers rarely act in real life the way they do in a "laboratory" setting.

So some clever entrepreneurs have replaced focus groups with small gatherings in more lifelike surroundings. There they combine anthropological observation with the sort of open-ended questioning you might hear in a therapist's office. The bonus is that real-world focus groups often don't cost

WHY THE NEW MARKET RESEARCH?

We asked Roger D. Blackwell to help make sense of the impact that accelerating product cycles has had on market research. In his role as professor of marketing at Ohio State University and as an independent consultant to companies such as Victoria's Secret and J.C. Penney, Blackwell spends his time studying consumer behavior and the retail sector.

INC.: Why is it more important than ever for companies to speed up their market research?

BLACKWELL: Fierce competition. There are too many companies chasing too few consumers, and the survivors are getting better and better at providing what consumers want. In the past, many companies faced competition from great, average, and bad companies. But the bad and the average are being eliminated rapidly, and we are left with only top-notch companies that are more likely to strive to have what the consumer wants. That puts pressure on all the surviving corporations, whatever their size, to conduct precise and speedy market research so they can offer products that match consumers' desires sooner than the competition.

Product cycles have shortened in part because new products and product improvements have come from country-wide chains. A good idea in one part of the country quickly

rolls out across the landscape. Local companies no longer have the luxury of waiting years before their competitors come up with better ideas. Now new products that have been tested elsewhere—including in other countries—quickly become competitive with local products. Honda, for example, has cut conception-to-production time from years to a matter of months. Technological advances in product design and development also have greatly sped up the pace of new-product offerings.

INC.: Does consumer opinion change more rapidly today?

BLACKWELL: For sure. Information now travels so quickly that consumers learn about new products and competitive improvements almost immediately. If Intel has a problem with a new chip, the information flies over the Internet in nanoseconds.

INC.: Does information that flies around so quickly force the company owner to make faster decisions?

BLACKWELL: It increases the penalty for making wrong decisions. In the past, you might have corrected a problem long before very many people knew about it. But that era is history. Today there's real pressure to have dead-on market research. You've got to get it right because the whole world will know instantly if you've got it wrong. And they may never forgive you for a major mistake.   —J.M.

HOCUS-POCUS FOCUS

David Feld, founder of Today's Man, a $204-million retailer based in Moorestown, N.J., guessed that many men equated buying clothes with going to the dentist, but he didn't know why. Feld paid for focus groups and phone surveys to uncover the truth. But he never met a focus group he trusted.

Finally, Feld's advertising agency recommended he talk to a company of professional hypnotists based in New York. Feld was skeptical, but he was desperate and curious enough to commission a study focused on why men feel uncomfortable in clothing stores. "The results really shook us up," Feld reports. The comments the men made under hypnosis had the ring of authenticity he had been searching for.

Hypnotized men revealed that they often hated the way their clothes fit but didn't know how to complain. "One guy told us that the last time he bought a suit, it didn't fit right—but he didn't say anything," Feld says. "He then told the hypnotist how insecure and dopey he felt when he wore that suit." Further, some of the groggy men admitted to a sense of powerlessness—they felt ganged up on by both their wives and pushy salespeople. "We had never gotten that answer before," Feld says.

Feld changed his business based on the responses. "We show the tapes of the hypnosis as part of our training," he says. "We now understand how important it is to become an advocate for men—to create more of a comfort zone in our stores and to get rid of that dentist's office feeling."

Two years after the study was conducted, Feld concedes, "I don't know that I totally believe in hypnosis to begin with. But I tell you, those people were out of it. They were in another world." A world, it seems, where people want their pants to fit.   —M.H.

"Then at the end, when we give them something for Johnny or Suzie, they all clamor for the purple one or the blue one."

Sometimes the information has a direct impact on product development. Boyle might discover that a prototype is simply too unwieldy for small children or is not particularly enticing. But more often the information provides only hints into a child's sensibility. "You never know where the next blockbuster will come from," says Mandelbaum. "There's no formula, but if you work with the kids long enough, you start to develop a kid sense."

The focus play groups have another distinct advantage over traditional focus groups: payment. Whereas most companies must offer focus-group participants some incentive, Boyle and Mandelbaum reverse the charges. The play group is a valuable service for which parents pay $30 per child. "In the beginning it was actually a line of revenue on our P&L," says Mandelbaum.

The play groups have had a positive effect. In an industry in which designers come as fast as they go, Skyline has licensed 70 products and grown to eight employees. The company expects revenues of $5.7 million over the next two years. Today the duo isn't as dependent on the play-group cash to make payroll. Last January the $50-million product-development company IDEO, based in Palo Also, acquired Skyline as an independent subsidiary.

For other entrepreneurs, though, the action can't be caught in a passing glimpse. When the shopping is hectic and consumers are in and out of a store in minutes, critical experiences can be lost forever. Here's where a video camera has value beyond your child's birthday party.

Consider Judy George, the CEO and founder of Domain Stores, a fast-growing $50-

much. In fact, if you're smart, they may just earn you some extra cash.

In 1991, Brendan Boyle and Fern Mandelbaum created Skyline Products Inc. to invent and license new children's toys. The twosome knew little about toys and even less about children. Boyle had been a product designer for David Kelley Design, in Palo Alto, Calif., developing items such as water bottles and other sports accessories, while Mandelbaum prospered as a marketing guru for Giro, makers of bike helmets. To get a boost up the learning curve, the two cleared a path straight to their target audience and created a focus play group.

Silicon Valley's harried parents are all too willing to enroll their children in Skyline's six-week play-group sessions. Six to eight kids get an hour with the latest games and toys on the market, and Mom or Dad gets an hour off. The groups typically meet at local parks or schools; Boyle and Mandelbaum appear as the Santas of summer, carrying a slew of toys.

Boyle admits that as an adult, it can be pretty easy to lose touch with a child's perspective. "You learn so much just by getting down on the ground with the kids," he says. "You can really forget how small their hands are or how much bigger your wingspan is."

Throughout the hour, the two owners probe the children, asking why certain toys are more appealing than others. "We're searching for a range of opinions," says Boyle. "Many kids will give that to you. They'll say, 'This sucks,' or 'This is awesome.'" On the other hand, some children hide their true likes and dislikes with strangers but reveal all in the car ride home. That's why Mandelbaum and Boyle frequently follow up with parents.

The parents themselves provide a trove of information. Just watching their facial expressions as their child gallops around with a newfangled toy can indicate whether they'd be likely to buy, says Boyle. Occasionally, Mandelbaum gathers parents into informal groups for brief grilling sessions. There, once again, the striking contrast between the consumers' words and actions becomes apparent. "We ask them in the beginning if color matters, and they all say a resounding no," recalls Mandelbaum.

'WHAT MOTHER WOULD TELL YOU SHE SPENDS MORE ON CAT FOOD THAN ON BABY FOOD?'

million chain of 23 furniture stores headquartered in Norwood, Mass. George has been a presence in her local stores for more than 10 years. But on the bustling floors, she can overlook the subtle nuances of the shoppers' experience. "People know me here, and I can get very easily distracted," she says.

Although she had previously operated video cameras in the stores on her own, George recently hired Grid II, a market-research firm based in New York City, to place

RESOURCES

From Mind to Market: Reinventing the Retail Supply Chain, by Roger D. Blackwell (HarperBusiness, 800–242–7737, 1997, $25). Blackwell's treatise can be scattered at times, covering everything from market research to logistics. But chapters three through five offer a good introduction to the new thinking in market research.

Do-It-Yourself Marketing Research, by George Edward Breen and Albert B. Blankenship (McGraw-Hill, 1989), is out of print but worth a trip to your library. It is a classic for those just beginning their market-research efforts, but it's concerned mostly with surveys and focus groups. You'll find little on the latest techniques.

"The Science of Shopping," by Malcolm Gladwell (The New Yorker, November 4, 1996). If you've ever wondered why fast-food restaurants are on the left and gift shops are on the right as you walk toward the gate in a newly constructed airport, track down a copy of this article for the answer. Gladwell profiles Paco Underhill, a man who devotes his life to studying shoppers. Underhill is the man responsible for the "buttbrush" theory, which Gladwell sums up: "Touch—or brush or bump or jostle—a woman on the behind when she has stopped to look at an item, and she will bolt."

Rocking the Ages, by J. Walker Smith and Ann Clurman (HarperBusiness, 800–242–7737, $15). Demographics aren't enough, according to Smith and Clurman. The authors claim that you must understand the values of the generation you're targeting if you want to have the right product for the right age group. Members of each generation—defined by the authors as matures, boomers, and X-ers—behave differently in different stages of their lives. The worst mistake a marketer can make is to assume one generation is just like the next.

In "Spark Innovation Through Empathic Design" (Harvard Business Review, November–December 1997), Harvard Business School's Dorothy Leonard, professor of business administration, and Jeffrey F. Rayport, associate professor of business administration, examine the latest techniques in product innovation and market research. Leonard's 1995 book, Wellsprings of Knowledge, has just been released in paperback (Harvard Business School Press, 800–262–7429, 1998, $16.95).

ON-LINE RESOURCES: There are lots of market-research resources on-line, but most of them aren't very good. You might try EASI Demographic Reports (www.easidemographics.com), from Easy Analytic Software, for numbers and facts. The Small Business Advisor (www.ec2.edu/sba) provides a few reports on marketing and market research. And if you want to chat with others, check out this newsgroup: misc.business.marketing.moderated.

---

one camera in her Short Hills, N.J., location for just six hours. The Short Hills location attracted picky customers, and it was far afield from George's home turf in Massachusetts, where customers were bound to know her. Later, in the privacy of her home, George pored over the tape. And suddenly, she saw something that more than 10 years of experience had not revealed: people shop for furniture in twos. Of the 1,034 customers who entered the store, 954 came in pairs.

Upon further examination, George recognized that many male customers were visibly ill at ease amid fluffed pillows and floral duvets. "The typical customer needs to be in the store for at least nine minutes to feel comfortable enough to buy," says George. "But if the spouse or boyfriend pulls her away too soon, we lose out on the sale." In the coming months, George will retrofit her 23 stores with entertainment centers where sports fans can watch live events via cable. Now, however, she might face a new problem: who would take her spouse or significant other to a place where he can watch the very thing she's been trying all afternoon to pry him away from?

But in-store observation offers only half the story. For the rest of the picture, entrepreneurs must be willing to take the cameras into the kitchens, the living rooms, and even the bedrooms and bathrooms of their potential customers. But you've gotta have the guts to enter.

When Kelly Franznick asks end users of his product if he can place a tripod-mounted video camera in their homes, they raise their eyebrows. "Customers typically agree once they learn about my purpose," says Franznick, who is the user-research manager for Lexant, a Seattle-based start-up with projected 1998 revenues of $5 million. The company sells health information, such as stress-management and smoking-cessation tips, to large employers and insurance corporations. The companies then pass the information along to their employees or agents. Lexant offers the product, called Do-Health, via the World Wide Web, in print, or by telephone counseling.

Franznick's in-home footage shows him not just how customers use the product but also how they live. In a recent study of customers using the DoHealth Web site, Franznick placed video cameras in the computer areas of five homes. With just a small number of participants and only about 36 hours' worth of taping in each house, Franznick began to answer a number of nagging research questions. What time of day did people access DoHealth? What other computer activities were completed before or after users accessed the on-line service? What else was happening in the room when they were on-line? What pulled them away from the computer?

And perhaps most important, the tape uncovered problems that might have otherwise gone unnoticed. For example, Franznick saw that on-line users became frustrated when they couldn't click from the bottom of the page to move forward or backward within the site, but he also saw that they had invented their own solutions, or work-arounds, for the problem. They simply scrolled to the top of the page and then clicked onward. "That's the sort of thing that might never have been revealed in a survey," says Franznick. It wasn't a tough problem to solve. Lexant's Web master simply added electronic links to the bottom of the page.

That was just one of several ideas the videos revealed. Franznick has developed a method for moving from idea to reality: After he's identified patterns among users from viewing the videos, he sketches out potential solutions or new products. The Web-site study yielded more than 25 penciled drawings. Franznick then presents the roughs to the designers and developers, who quickly estimate the costs in time, money, and resources. The objective is to pick the ideas that will give the greatest bang for the buck.

Even if you gain entry into the consumer's home, you still might find that you're cordoned off from touchy subjects. When Lexant began to develop an on-line area to address weight-management issues, Franznick quickly recognized that the company had stumbled into one of those sensitive zones. "It's very hard to get people to talk about their weight," says Franznick.

"You need to use methods that allow them to reveal what they want on their own terms."

So Franznick mailed logbooks and disposable cameras to 30 potential customers from the Chicago and Seattle areas. They were asked to snap photos whenever they became "conscious of a weight-management issue." They were also told to scribble down a caption for the photo in the logbook.

The study lasted just five weeks. In the end, it revealed some intensely personal moments. All of the photos and captions were first sorted according to similar themes and ideas. "Here's where you start to see patterns," says Franznick. For example, a couple of participants took photos of the bathroom mirror still fogged over from the morning shower. One caption read, "This is the mirror where 'I size myself up' every day." There were a few photos of bridal magazines with comments such as, "Someday, after I lose weight, I'll get married." The information gathered from the study will help Lexant design the new Web site, and many of the issues raised will become on-line discussion topics.

NOT ALL MARKET-RESEARCH OPPORTUNITIES must be so contrived. Life often provides windows to view a consumer's lifestyle, if you're alert to the possibilities. Blackwell suggests that attending real estate open houses in your town may give you ideas for products or services. "Look for problems that don't have solutions and for innovative consumer-made solutions," says Blackwell. "Here's where you might find ideas to commercialize or ways to improve an existing product."

Long before Bible Bread made the voyage to the United States, Zack Shavin and his crew had seized an opportunity to expose Americans to their product. Shavin moonlights as a tour guide in Jerusalem, and he tested the cracker, the packaging, and various slogans on the herds of Americans who make the pilgrimage to the Holy Land each year. "By the time we went to America, we were quite sure that our product and message would be accepted," says co-owner Moshe Shuster. He says that the company resisted more formalized focus group because they were too costly and too risky. "We could have spent everything just to find out that people didn't like the product," says Shuster, "and then we would have been sunk."

The lesson for other bootstrappers is straightforward. Explore natural settings. Observe. Listen. *Really* listen. Put aside biases. Analyze. Those are the ingredients of the new market research that blue-chip companies and market-research firms are leaning toward. The beauty, of course, is that unlike market surveys of fancy focus groups, these new methods are, quick and can be adapted by any company.

Joshua Macht (josh.macht@inc.com) is an associate editor at Inc.

A BEGINNER'S GUIDE TO
Demographics

Who are your customers?
Where do they live?
How many are there?

Answering these and similar questions can help you
sharpen your marketing strategy.

BERNA MILLER
WITH AN INTRODUCTION BY PETER FRANCESE

*Whatever you sell, customer demographics are important to
your business. Demographics can tell you who your current
and potential customers are, where they are, and how many
are likely to buy what you are selling. Demographic analysis
helps you serve your customers better by adjusting to their
changing needs. This article provides a review of the basic
concepts used in such analysis.*

*The most successful use of demographic analysis identifies
those population or household characteristics that most accurately differentiate potential customers from those not likely to
buy. The second part of using demographics is finding those
geographic areas with the highest concentrations of potential
customers. Once potential customers are described and located,
and their purchase behavior analyzed, the next step is to determine their media preferences in order to find the most efficient
way to reach them with an advertising message.*

*It wasn't always this complicated. Until fairly recently eve-
ryone practiced mass marketing, dispersing one message via
media—newspapers, radio, broadcast television—that pre-
sumably reached everyone. No special effort was made to
ensure that the message would appeal to (or even reach) the
most likely customers.*

*The result: A great deal of money was spent pitching prod-
ucts and services to sections of the audience who didn't want
or need them. In buying a prime-time spot for its television
ads, a motorcycle company would be paying to reach the*

(continued)

The most important marketing question a business
faces is: "Who are my customers?" And the first
demographic* question a business must ask about
its product or service is whether it is to be sold to an
individual or a **household.** Refrigerators, for example, are
household products; and most households have only one
or two refrigerators. On the other hand, everyone within
the household has their own toothbrush and dozens of
other personal-care products.

There are more than 261 million individuals in the
United States and nearly 100 million households. Those
classified as "**family** households" include married couples
with **children** (26 percent), married couples without children (29 percent), single parents living with their children
(9 percent), and brothers and sisters or other related family
members who live together (7 percent). "**Nonfamily** households" include people who live alone (24 percent) and
cohabiting couples and other unrelated roommates (5
percent).

Different types of households are more prevalent
among certain age groups. For instance, the majority of
women who live alone are over age 65, while the majority

For definitions for this and other terms in **bold-faced type, see the
[article] glossary.*

housebound elderly as well as the young adults for whom their product was designed. A swimsuit manufacturer that ran an ad in a national magazine would pay a premium to reach the inhabitants of Nome, Alaska, as well as Floridians. Gradually it was recognized that the "shotgun" approach is not an efficient use of marketing dollars.

Mass marketing has since given way to target marketing, whose guiding principle is Know Thy Customers. How old are they? Where do they live? What are their interests, concerns, and aspirations? Knowing the answers to questions like these gives you insight into the marketing approaches most likely to appeal to your customers—and whether you're even shooting for the right customers in the first place! (Sometimes there is more than one set of customers: for example, research shows that low-fat frozen dinners are purchased by young women wishing to stay slim and by much older retired people who just want a light meal.)

Let's say that you find out that your customers are predominantly college graduates, and that you know in which zip codes your existing customers reside. How do you use this information?

The first step is to obtain a tabulation of the number of college graduates by zip code, which is available through an information provider (see the American Demographics Directory of Marketing Information Companies for names and numbers) or the Census Bureau. Then, for any metropolitan area that you serve, establish the percent of all college graduates in the metropolitan area who reside in each zip code. Calculate the percent of existing customers who reside in each zip code. By dividing the percent of college graduates in zip 12345 by percent of customers (and multiplying by 100), we get an index of penetration for each zip code. If the index of penetration is 100 or above, the market is being adequately served. If it is below 100, there is more potential, which can be realized through direct mail to those specific zip codes.

This analysis can be done using any group of geographic areas that sum to a total market area, such as counties within a state or metropolitan areas within a region. The object is to compare the percent of customers who should be coming from each sub-market area against the percent who are actually coming from there. The resulting indexes essentially measure marketing performance zip by zip or county by county.

Not so long ago, demographic information came printed on reams of paper or rolls of computer tape. With the tremendous advances in technology in recent years, it is now readily available on your personal computer. Demographic statistics can be obtained on CD-ROM or via the Internet, complete with software for accessing the data.

Information providers can analyze these data for you, as well as provide customized data, such as how many pairs of shoes people own and how often they shop for new ones. Census demographics can't tell you how many times a week people use floor cleaners, but it does have basic demographic characteristics that will help determine who your market is, how many of them there are, and where they live. Information providers can help you take these data and merge them with customer data to form a clearer picture of your market and its potential.

—Peter Francese

Peter Francese is founding president of American Demographics Inc., and publisher of American Demographics *and* Marketing Tools *magazines.*

of men who live alone are under age 45. Household types differ between **generations** as well. Younger people today are much more likely to live in the other type of nonfamily household because they are moving out of their parents' homes before marriage and living with friends or lovers; such living arrangements being more acceptable today, younger people are much more likely than earlier generations to do so.

The U.S. can no longer be effectively treated as a mass market, because Americans and their lifestyles have changed dramatically.

Everyone in the United States except for the homeless lives in either a household or **group quarters.** Many businesses ignore group-quarter populations, reasoning that nursing-home patients and prison inmates probably are not doing much shopping. However, if your market is computers, beer, pizza, or any number of products that appeal to young adults or military personnel, you cannot afford to overlook these populations. This is especially important when marketing a product in a smaller area where a college or military base is present. People who live in these situations may have different wants and needs from those who live in households; in addition, the area may have a much higher rate of population turnover than other **places** do.

Refining Your Customer's Profile

Once you have determined whether you want to market to households or people, the next step is to find out which segment of households or of the population would be most likely to want your product or service. Demographics allow you to refine your conception of who your market is, who it can or should be, and how it is likely to change over time. People have different needs at different ages and lifestages, and you need to factor that into your customer profile. In addition, there are both primary and secondary markets. For instance, if you were marketing baby food, you would first target married couples with young children and single parents, and then possibly grandparents.

This level of refinement was made necessary by the massive social, economic, and technological changes of the past three decades. The United States can no longer be effectively treated as a mass market, because the people who live here and their lifestyles have changed dramatically. Due to increasing divorce rates, increasing cohabitation, rising number of nonmarital births, and increased female participation in the labor force, married couples with one earner make up only 15 percent of all households. Dual-earner households have become much more common—the additional income is often necessary for the family to pay their bills. Thus, the stereotypical family of the 1950s has been replaced by two harried, working parents with much less time available.

At the same time, there has been an explosion in the number of products available to the American public, each of which, either by design or default, tends to appeal to the very different segments of the population.

Another important trend is the increasing diversity of that population. The United States has always been an immigrant nation. However, large numbers of immigrants from Latin America and Asia have increased the proportion of minorities in the country to one in four, up from one in five in 1980.

This increasing diversity is particularly noticeable in the children's market. Minorities are overrepresented in the younger age brackets due to the higher fertility and the younger population structure of these recent immigrants. The result: one in three children in the United States is black, **Hispanic**, or Asian. Nearly all of today's children grow up in a world of divorce and working mothers. Many are doing the family shopping and have tremendous influence over household purchases. In addition, they may simply know more than their elders about products involving new technology, such as computers.

The recent influx of Hispanics, who may be of any **race**, has important implications for understanding the demographic data you have on your customers. "Hispanic" is an ethnicity, not a race; a person who describes himself as Hispanic must also choose a racial designation: white, black, Asian/Pacific Islander, American Indian/Eskimo/Aleut, or "other." Confusion on this score . . . can result in accidentally counting Hispanics twice, in which case the numbers won't add up.

Income and education are two other important demographic factors to consider when refining your customer profile. As a general rule, income increases with age, as people get promoted and reach their peak earning years. Married couples today often have the higher incomes because they may have two earners. Married couples may also have greater need for products and services, because they are most likely to have children and be homeowners.

Income is reported in several different ways, and each method means something very different in terms of consumer behavior. Earnings, interest, dividends, royalties, social security payments, and public assistance dollars received before taxes and union dues are subtracted are defined in the **census** as money income. **Personal** income, as reported by the Bureau of Economic Analysis, is money income plus certain noncash benefits (such as food stamps

and subsidized housing). **Disposable** income is the money available after taxes, while **discretionary** income is the money available after taxes and necessities (food, shelter, clothing) have been paid for.

All of these are useful measures as long as their differences are fully understood. For example, discretionary income of $30,000 has much more potential for businesses than does a personal income of $30,000. But none of these statistics measures wealth, which includes property owned. Ignoring wealth may provide a skewed picture: a 70-year-old woman with a personal income of $15,000 who must pay rent is much less able to afford additional items than a woman of the same age and income who owns a fully paid-for house, which she could sell if she needed to.

Income can be reported for people or households; household income is the most commonly used measure in business demographics since it provides the best picture of the overall situation of everyone in the household. Income is often reported as **mean income.** But mean income can be distorted by very large or small incomes, called "outliers," which are very different from most of the other values. Thus multimillionaires skew the mean income upward, overestimating the income of the population in question. Using a measure called **median income** can avoid this bias and is more widely used as a measure of income in demographics. The mean income of all United States households is $41,000. The median income is $31,200—almost $10,000 lower than the mean.

Education is another very important and commonly used demographic characteristic—in today's increasingly technological and highly skilled economy, education makes a big difference in occupation and thus in earning power. Education is most often measured as number of years of schooling or in terms of level of education completed. Today's adults are better educated than ever before; however, only one in four adults older than age 24 has a college degree or higher. Another 23 percent have attended college. Eight in ten American adults have a high school diploma. One reason for the low percentages of college graduates is that many older people did not attend college. Therefore, we should expect to see the percentage of college graduates and attendees increase substantially in the future.

College-educated people are one of the most lucrative markets, but you may have to work extra hard to get and keep them as customers. They are more open to technology and innovation, but they are also less brand loyal, since they are more able financially to take risks. They are more likely to read and less likely to watch television than those without any college education. They like to make informed decisions about purchases; hence, they are the most likely group to request product information.

Segmenting the Market

All of these demographic data are available in easy-to-understand packages called **cluster systems** (also knows as geodemographic segmentation systems), which are available from information providers. Cluster systems take many demographic variables and create profiles of different individual or household characteristics, purchase behaviors, and media preferences. Most cluster systems have catchy, descriptive names, such as "Town and Gown" or "Blue Blood Estates," making it easier to identify the groups most likely to be interested in what you have to sell.

Cluster systems are especially powerful when used in conjunction with business mapping. Sophisticated mapping software programs easily link demographics to any level of geography (a process called geocoding). Some software can pinpoint specific households within neighborhoods from your customer data and then create schematic maps of neighborhoods by cluster concentrations. Geocoding can be done for block group, counties, zip codes, or any other market area. Businesses can integrate knowledge of customer addresses and purchase decisions with basic demographic data based on geography and come up with a clearer, more informative picture of customers—and where they can be found.

Cluster analysis is sometimes confused with psychographics, but the two are very different. Cluster systems are based on purchase decisions and demographics that cover physical characteristics like age, sex, income, and education. Psychographics measure motivations, attitudes, lifestyles, and feelings, such as openness to technology or reluctance to try new products. Both demographics and psychographics need to be taken into account.

Looking to the Future

It is not only important to identify who your customers are and how many of them there are today, but how many of them there will be in five or ten years, and whether their wants and needs will change.

Projections of population or households by marital status, age, or income can be very useful in determining the potential of a market a few years down the road. All projections start with the assumption that the projected population will equal the current population plus births minus deaths and plus net migration. For example, let's take projections at the household level. New household configurations occur through in-migration of residents or through the formation of a household due to the separation of an already existing household (such as when a child moves out of a parent's home or a divorce occurs). Household losses occur when existing households are combined due to marriage, when a child moves back home, etc., or when the residents in a household move away from the area (out-migration).

Projections can vary greatly, so it is important to ask about the methodology and assumptions behind them and make sure you fully understand why these assumptions were made. Accurate demographic data can be very valu-

able, but data that are flawed or biased can be seriously misleading.

In general, the future population of a larger area of geography, such as the United States or a particular state, is much easier to estimate accurately than populations for small areas, such as neighborhoods, which often experi-

---

It is important to not only identify today's customers, but to predict how their wants and needs will change tomorrow.

---

ence greater population fluctuations. In addition, the shorter the time period involved, the more accurate the projections are likely to be, because there's less time for dramatic changes to take place. There will be factors in 15 years that we cannot begin to include in our assumptions, because they do not exist yet.

You can have more confidence in your educated guesses about the future if you know a little about past population trends in the United States, especially the baby boom and baby bust cycle. It is also important to understand the difference between a generation and a cohort.

The events for which generations are named occur when their members are too young to remember much about them (i.e., the Depression generation includes people born during the 1930s). That's why cohort is often the more useful classification for marketers; it provides insight into events that occurred during the entire lifetimes of the people in question.

To illustrate, let's look at the baby boomers, who were born between 1946 and 1965. In their youth, they experienced a growing economy, but they also dealt with competition and crowding in schools and jobs due to the sheer number of cohort members. Their lives were shaped by events like the civil rights movement, the Vietnam conflict, the women's movement, and Watergate. Baby boomers have seen increasing diversity and technology. They're living longer, healthier lives than the cohorts that came before them.

All these factors make baby boomers very different from 32-to-51-year-olds of 20 years ago. Traditional ideas concerning the preferences of 50-year-olds versus 30-year-olds are no longer accurate; age-old adages such as "coffee consumption increases with age, and young people drink cola" are no longer as valid as they once were—people who grew up on cola often continue to drink it. The same is true for ethnic foods and a host of other products.

The received wisdom will have to change constantly to reflect new sets of preferences and life experiences. For example, baby boomers remember when the idea of careers for women was considered pretty radical. Not so for younger Generation X women; most of them work as a matter of course, just like their own mothers. As a result, ideas about marriage, family, and jobs are changing and will continue to do so.

If you are marketing a product to a certain age range, be aware that the people who will be in that range in five or ten years will not be the same as the ones who are there now. A strategy that has worked for years may need to be rethought as one cohort leaves an age range and another takes its place.

Therein lies the challenge in contemporary marketing: the fact that it is no longer advisable to treat a market as an undifferentiated mass of people with similar fixed tastes, interest, and needs. In the age of target marketing, it is imperative to know who the customers are and how to reach them. When the customer's needs change, it's essential to know that, too, so you can adjust your marketing efforts accordingly. A working knowledge of demographics will keep you on top of the situation. It's a piece of marketing know-how that no one can afford to ignore.

Berna Miller is a contributor to American Demographics magazine.

Define Your Terms

A GLOSSARY OF DEMOGRAPHIC WORDS AND PHRASES

Demographic terms consist of fairly common words and phrases, but each one has a highly specific meaning. Study them carefully to ensure that when you discuss demographics with someone, you're both talking about the same thing.

demography: derived from two Greek words meaning "description of" and "people," coined by the French political economist Achille Guillard in 1855. Sometimes a distinction is drawn between "pure" demography (the study of vital statistics and population change) and "social" demography, which gets into socioeconomic characteristics. Business demography is also often understood to include consumer attitudes and behavior.

POPULATION COMPONENTS

The three things that add to or subtract from population are:
• **fertility:** having to do with births. There are several measures of fertility, mostly different kinds of annual rates using different base populations.
• **mortality:** otherwise known as death. There are different death rates, as there are for births.
• **migration:** the movement of people into or out of a defined region, like a state. It typically refers only to moves that cross county lines. A related term is **mobility,** meaning change of residence. This usually refers to how many people move any distance in a given period of time, even if they just move across town.

HOUSEHOLDS/FAMILIES/MARITAL STATUS

household: one or more people who occupy a housing unit, as opposed to group quarters (dorms, hospitals, prisons, military barracks, etc.). The vast majority of Americans live in households.

householder: formerly called "head of household," the householder is the one adult per household designated as the reference person for a variety of characteristics. An important thing to check when looking at demographics of households (such as age or income) is to see whether the information pertains to the householder or to the entire household. *Household composition is determined by the relationship of the other people in the household to the householder.*

family: a household consisting of two or more people in which at least one person is related to the householder by blood, marriage, or adoption. The major types of families are **married couples** (these may be male- or female-headed and with or without children), and **families without a spouse present,** which may also be headed by a man or a woman. The latter category includes single parents as well as other combinations of relatives, such as siblings living together or grandparents and grandchildren. Note that seemingly single parents

may live with a partner or other adult outside of marriage.

nonfamily: households consisting of persons living alone, or multiple-person households in which no one is related to the householder, although they may be related to each other. This includes unmarried and gay couples, as well as roommates, boarders, etc.

children: The United States Census Bureau makes a distinction between the householder's own children under age 18 (including adopted and stepchildren), and other related children, such as grandchildren or children aged 18 and older. Other surveys may define children differently.

marital status: this is an individual characteristic, usually measured for people aged 15 and older. The four main categories are never married; married; divorced; and widowed. The term "single" usually refers to a person who has never married, but may include others not currently married. Likewise, the term "ever-married" also includes widowed and divorced people. "Married" includes spouse present and spouse absent. "Spouse absent" includes couples who are separated or not living together because of military service.

RACE/ETHNICITY

race: white, black, Asian and Pacific Islander, and native American (includes American Indians, Eskimos, and Aleutian Islanders). That's it. The government does not use the term African American, but many others do.

Hispanics: the only ethnic origin category in current use. NOT A RACE. Most Hispanics are actually white. Used to be called Spanish Origin. The term Latino is becoming popular, but is currently not used by the government. It is becoming more common to separate out Hispanics from race categories and talk about non-Hispanic whites, blacks, etc. This way, the numbers add up to 100 percent.

Note: The Office of Management and Budget is considering revamping the racial categories used in federal data collection, including the addition of a mixed-race group. This may happen in time for use in the 2000 census.

GENERATIONS/COHORTS

cohort: a group of people who share an event, such as being born in the same year, and therefore share a common culture and history. The most commonly used cohorts are birth cohorts, although there are also marriage cohorts, etc.
generations: more loosely defined than cohorts, typically refers to people born during a certain period of time. These examples are not definitive:
• **GI Generation:** born in the 1910s and 1920s, served in WWII. Today's elderly.
• **Depression:** born in the 1930s. Boomers' parents. Now aged 56 to 65.
• **War Babies:** born during WWII, now aged 50 to 55. Sometimes lumped with the Depression group as the "silent generation."
• **Baby Boom:** born between 1946 and 1964, now aged 31 to 49. Further introductions are probably unnecessary.
• **Baby Bust:** born 1965 to 1976. Today's twentysomethings, although the

oldest turned 30 this year. Also called **Generation X**
• **Baby Boomlet:** or Echo Boom. Born 1977 to 1994. Today's children and teens.

EDUCATION

attainment: completed education level, typically measured for adults aged 25 and older because it used to be the case that virtually everyone was finished with school by then. This is less true today, with one-third of all college students over age 25. Until 1990, attainment was measured by years completed rather than actual degrees earned. The new categories include no high school, some high school but no diploma, high school graduate, some college but no degree, associate's degree, and other types of college degrees.

INCOME

Income can be measured for households, persons, or even geographic areas. When you look at income figures, make sure you know which kind is being referred to!

disposable: after-tax (net) income. In other words, all the money people have at their disposal to spend, even if most of it goes for things we have little choice about, like food, electric bills, and kids' braces.

discretionary: income left over after necessities are covered. This is extremely tough to measure: Who's to say what's necessary for someone else? It's generally accepted that very few of the poorest households have any discretionary income at all, but also that the level of necessary expenses rises with income.

personal and **per capita:** aggregate measures for geographic areas such as states and counties. Personal income is total income for all people in an area, and per capita divides it equally by total population, regardless of age or labor force status.

mean income: the average of all income in the population being studied.

median income: the midway point, at which half of the people being studied have higher incomes and half have lower incomes.

ESTIMATES/PROJECTIONS

census: complete count of a population.

survey: the process of collecting data from a sample, hopefully representative of the general population or the population of interest.

estimate: calculation of current or historic number for which no census or survey data are available. Usually based on what's known to have happened.

projection: calculation of future population or characteristic, based on assumptions of what might happen—a "what if" scenario. Two related terms are **prediction** and **forecast.** Both refer to a "most likely" projection—what the forecaster feels may actually happen.

MEDIA/MARKETING TERMS

The following are not defined by the government, so there are no real standards.
mature: an age segment, usually defined as those 50- or 55-plus, although some go so far as to include those in their late 40s. This is often seen as an affluent and active group, but it actually consists of several age segments with vastly diverse economic and health status. Related terms include:
• **elderly:** usually 65 and older, although sometimes narrowed down to very old (85 and older).
• **retired:** not necessarily defined by age; although most retirees are older people, not all older people are retired.

middle class: This is one of the most widely used demographic terms. it is also perhaps one of the most statistically elusive: If you ask the general public, the vast majority will claim to be middle class. It might be most sensible to start with the midpoint—that is, median income ($31,200 for households in 1993)—and create a range surrounding it (e.g., within $10,000 of the median) until you come up with a group of households that says "middle class" to you.

affluent: most researchers used to consider households with annual incomes of $50,000 or more as affluent, although $60,000 and $75,000 thresholds are becoming more popular. Upper-income households are sometimes defined more broadly as those with incomes of $35,000 or more. As of the mid-1990s, this merely means they are not lower income, suggesting that there is no middle class.

lifestyles/psychographics: these terms are somewhat interchangeable, but **psychographics** usually refers to a formal classification system such as SRI's VALS (Values and Lifestyles) that categorizes people into specific types (Achievers, Belongers, etc.). **Lifestyle** is a vaguer term, and many 'lifestyle' types or segments have been defined in various market studies. Generally speaking, these systems organize people according to their attitudes or consumer behavior, such as their involvement with and spending on golf. These data may seem soft, but they often use statistical measures such as factor analysis to derive the segments.

cluster systems/geodemographic segmentation: developed by data companies to create meaningful segments based on residence, and the assumption that people will live in areas where there are a lot of other people just like them. This geographic element is one thing that distinguishes clusters from psychographic segments. Another difference is that cluster categories are virtually always based on socioeconomic and consumer data rather than attitudinal information. Each system has at least several dozen clusters. The four major cluster systems are: Claritas's PRIZM, National Decision Systems' MicroVision, CACI's ACORN, and Strategic Mapping's ClusterPlus 2000.

GEOGRAPHIC TERMS

Census geography: areas defined by the government.
- **regions:** Northeast, Midwest, South, and West.
- **divisions:** there are nine Census Statistical Areas: Pacific, Mountain, West North Central, East North Central, West South Central, East South Central, New England, Middle Atlantic, and South Atlantic.
- **states:** note: data about states often include the District of Columbia for a total of 51.
- **Congressional district:** subdivision of a state created solely for Congressional representation; not considered a governmental area by the Census Bureau.
- **enumeration district:** census area with an average of 500 inhabitants, used in nonmetropolitan areas.
- **counties:** the U.S. had over 3,000 counties as of 1990.
- **places:** these include cities, towns, villages, and other municipal areas.
- **tracts:** these are subcounty areas designed to contain a roughly homogeneous population ranging from 2,500 to 8,000.
- **blocks** and **block groups:** blocks are what they sound like: an administrative area generally equivalent to a city block and the smallest unit of geography for which census data are published. Block groups are groups of blocks with average populations of 1,000 to 1,200 people; they are approximately equal to a neighborhood.
- **metropolitan areas:** these are defined by the Office of Management and Budget, and are built at the county level. Each consists of at least one central city of the appropriate size (usually at least 50,000), its surrounding "suburban" territory within the same county, and any adjacent counties with strong economic ties to the city. Metros may have one or more central cities and/or counties. Standalone metros are called **MSA**s (Metropolitan Statisical Areas). Metros that are right next to each other are called **PMSA**s (Primary MSAs), and the larger areas that they make up are called **CMSA**s (Consolidated MSAs). The U.S. currently has over 300 metros (depending on how you count PMSAs and CMSAs) that include about three-fourths of the nation's population.
- **NECMA**s are New England Metropolitan Areas and are similar to MSAs.
- **central city:** largest city in the MSA and other cities of central character to an MSA.

zip code: subdivision of an area for purposes of delivering mail; not a census area.

Two related terms are **urban** and **rural** The essential difference between "metropolitan" and "urban" is that metros are defined at the county level, while urbanized areas are more narrowly defined by density. An **urban area** has 25,000 or more inhabitants, with urbanized zones around the central city comprising 50,000 or more inhabitants. This means that the outlying portions of counties in many metropolitan areas are considered rural. Oddly enough, suburbs are commonly defined as the portions of metro areas outside of central cities and have nothing to do with the urban/rural classification system.

—Diane Crispell

Diane Crispell is executive editor of American Demographics *magazine, and author of* The Insider's Guide to Demographic Know-How.

(continued)

More Info

Recommended reading

The Insider's Guide to Demographic Know-how, by Diane Crispell (1993, American Demographics Books)*

The Official Guide to the American Marketplace, by Cheryl Russell (2nd edition, 1995, New Strategist Books)*

The Official Guide to American Incomes, by Cheryl Russell and Margaret Ambry (1993, New Strategist Books)*

Targeting Families: Marketing To and Through the New Family, by Robert Boutilier (1993, American Demographics Books)*

Targeting Transitions: Marketing to Consumers During Life Changes, by Paula Mergenhagen (1994, American Demographics Books)*

Multicultural Marketing: Selling to a Diverse America. by Marlene L. Rossman (1994, AMACOM Books)*

Marketing to Generation X: Strategies for a New Era, by Karen Ritchie (1995, Lexington MacMillan Free Press)*}

American Demographics magazine*
The 1995 American Demographics *Di-rectory of Marketing Information Companies* provides contact information for data sources.*

*Available through American Demographics, Inc.: to order, call (800) 828-1133.

Resources on the Internet

There are four different ways to reach the Census Bureau online:
1. The FTP site. At your Internet prompt, type "ftp.ftp.census.gov," then log in as "anonymous" or "ftp." Use your e-mail address as your password. Then change the /pub directory to "ftp>cd/pub."

2. The gopher server. Telnet to the server with the command "telnetgopher.censu.gov." At the login, type "gopher." By selecting "Access Our Other Information Services" at the initial menu and then selecting "Census Bureau Anonymous FTP," you can also reach the ftp site.

3. The World Wide Web site. Using a World Wide Web browser, type in the URL "http://www.census.gov" or "http://www.census.gov/index.html." You can also reach the ftp site through World Wide Web by connecting to URL "ftp://ftp.census.gov/pub."

4. The FTP site on the World Wide Web. The URL for the FTP site is "ftp://ftp.census.gov/." You can also send an email message to "ftpmail@census.gov." Leave the subject field blank and type "help" in the message body. You will then receive instructions via e-mail.

Marketing Tools on the World Wide Web: http://www.marketingtools.com

As the Marketing Tools Web site develops, we will be creating hypertext links (which are like doorways that take you to other sites with lightning speed) to the Census Bureau and private information providers. In the meantime, the site already offers searchable, full-text versions of all past issues of *Marketing Tools* magazine, and all issues of *American Demographics* magazine and *The Numbers News* newsletter back to 1993. The 1995 *Directory of Marketing Information Companies* is also available at the Marketing Tools site.

TAPPING THE THREE
KIDS'
MARKETS

Children constitute three distinct consumer markets: primary, influence, and future.
Savvy companies know the differences in the three. And the most skilled use that knowledge
to sell to kids simultaneously in more than one market.

BY JAMES U. McNEAL

With all their purchases ahead of them, and with their ability to pull their parents along, children are the brightest star in the consumer constellation. Virtually every consumer-goods industry, from airlines to zinnia-seed sellers, targets kids.

Just look at the thousands of products designed primarily for children. Toys, candy, soft drinks, sweetened cereals—traditional kids' products that have been around forever—have expanded their sales and offerings greatly in recent years. Supermarket candy racks are bigger than ever, and they display a broad range of candies with playful brand names such as Amazin' Fruit, Gummi Watch, and Goody Bag.

But companies aren't just expanding traditional kids' products. They're creating new ones. Computer technology is now designed or adapted for kids, from computers to software to online programs. Nickelodeon, the TV network for children, sells a computer accessory kit that transforms any personal computer into one that's kid friendly. Packaged-goods companies have created prepared kids' meals that come frozen, chilled, and shelf stable, along with an array of cosmetics and toiletries for boys and girls. In virtually every product category, entertainment-based licensed characters, such as the Flintstones and Batman, are selling products—an estimated $17 billion in 1996.

Many products for adults now have a kids' version. These include Dial for Kids (liquid and bar soap), Pert Plus for Kids

James U. McNeal is a professor of marketing at Texas A&M University, and author of the book Kids as Customers: A Handbook of Marketing to Children. *This article is adapted from his upcoming book* Myths and Realities of the Kids Market.

(shampoo), Kid Fresh (flushable wipes), and Ozarka Spring Water for Kids. Adult services have also been adapted for children. Banks offer banking and investment services for kids, including investment camps. We now see hair-and eye-care services; studios for studying dance, music, and karate; and day-care centers that may more appropriately be called "play-care centers."

In the past five or six years, retailing has really awakened to the clout of the children's market, and has done something about it. In the mid-1980s, perhaps one-third of major retail chains made some effort to target kids. Today, that figure is close to two-thirds and still growing. This trend includes retailers who have little or nothing to sell to children, such as auto dealers and stockbrokers. Companies like these recognize that there's more to the kids' market than securing a purchase today. Children constitute not one, but three distinct markets: the primary, influence, and future markets.

THE PRIMARY MARKET

The money kids aged 4 to 12 spend on their own wants and needs comes from five main sources: allowances (an unrestricted periodic distribution of money from parents); household chores; gifts from parents; gifts from others, such as grandparents; and work outside the home, such as baby sitting. About seven in ten children this age get an allowance. But on average, it constitutes only 45 percent of their income, down from 60 percent in the mid-1980s.

This is largely because total income has gone up, not that allowances have declined. In 1991, the typical allowance of a 10-year-old was $4.20 week. In 1997, it was $6.13, a 46 percent increase in unadjusted dollars. Over the same seven-year period, the average 10-year-old's weekly income rose 76 percent, from $7.90 to $13.93.

The rise in total income is largely due to children earning more from household chores. This is a barometer of change in family relationships. Less income from allowances and more from work in the home suggests that recession-scarred, dual-working parents are saying, "no more free lunch, kid; you've got to work for it and share responsibility for this household."

Kids are also enjoying more money from relatives, particularly grandparents. This kind of gift money is now 10 percent of their income, up from 5 percent a decade ago. Over the same period, parental gifts declined from 21 percent to 15 percent.

Kids save about one-third of their income on a week-to-week basis, with around half going into bank accounts. But they delve into their savings from time to time, particularly when school is out in the summer and during the Christmas season. On an annual basis, their net savings rate is about 15 percent, a rate higher than most of their parents can claim. Yet if you ask school-aged kids why they save, they're likely to answer, "Because I want to buy _____." They save to buy, not to secure a future guarantee of education or to compete with their pals.

Estimates show that children's aggregate spending roughly doubled during each decade of the 1960s, 1970s, and 1980s, and has tripled so far in the 1990s. And that's not because the number of children has increased dramatically. In the 1980s, there were around 35 million children in the U.S. aged 4 to 12, compared with an estimated 36 million in 1997. Yet in 1997, the estimated $24.4 billion spent by kids was about three times the value of the ready-to-eat cereal market. By 2001, their spending may reach $35 billion.

When children spent their money in the 1960s, it was mainly on confections. Today, only one-third of their money goes to food and beverages of all kinds, while the balance is spent on playthings, apparel, movies, pay-for-play games, and other items such as toiletries for themselves and gifts for their parents. Apparel spending was the fastest-growing category for kids during the past decade, possibly because children are assuming more responsibility for their own necessities.

Kids' power over their own money is precisely what induced Ty Inc. to introduce Beanie Babies, the fabulously successful line of about 100 different small stuffed creatures. They sell for $5 each—just right for a kid's weekly allowance. Some retailers have also realized that if children have a good shopping experience, they are likely to persuade their parents to bring them to that store to buy more items and more expensive merchandise.

What's more, children tend to make as many forays into the consumer market as their parents. A typical 10-year-old goes shopping with parents two or three times a week, somewhat more frequently than a decade ago. But he or she goes shopping alone much less frequently, at around once a week, compared with 2.3 times a week in the late 1980s.

One reason is parents' perceptions of the dangers of crime. They are increasingly asking their kids to wait until weekends when parents and children can shop together. Both alone and

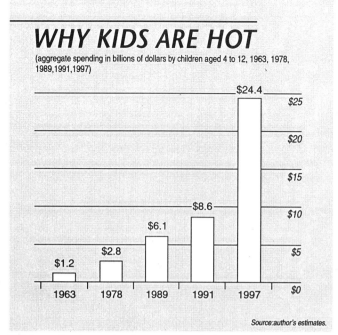

WHY KIDS ARE HOT

(aggregate spending in billions of dollars by children aged 4 to 12, 1963, 1978, 1989, 1991, 1997)

Source: author's estimates.

Kids' spending is growing fast, even though the population of children hasn't mushroomed.

with parents, kids still average more than 200 store visits a year. That's enough to form good relationships with retailers and to develop store preferences and dislikes.

In general, young children like convenience stores best because they are accessible, they have a lot of merchandise that appeals to young children, and they are probably the first store in which a child makes an independent purchase. As kids reach the teen years of 8 to 12, they transfer their preferences to mass merchandisers, because of these stores' breadth: toys, clothes, school supplies, and snack items. Children this age also favor specialty stores due to their depth of merchandise, such as extensive selections of toys, music, or shoes. As a rule, kids of all ages pick one supermarket as their favorite, and often recommend it to mom. Drugstores and department stores are often viewed by kids in the same way as they see banks—very adult, cold, and dull.

And remember, not all kids' purchases are made in stores. Who do you think made M&Ms candy one of the top-selling brands in vending machines? Kids, but not until machine makers acknowledged that children are three feet tall and lowered coin slots accordingly.

THE INFLUENCE MARKET

Children's influence on their parents' spending has grown at least as robustly as spending of their own money. Of course, kids can't influence parental spending unless their parents let them. They always do, although during the late 1980s and early 1990s, parents started ceding unprecedented decision-making power to their kids. This created "filiarchies" in many households where matriarchies would ordinarily exist. Parents no longer worried that their kids would have it as good as

> *Children usually have one brand they prefer, and one or two that they are willing to substitute in dire circumstances.*

them—they knew they wouldn't. Parents wanted their kids to have it at least as good as other kids. So they gave them more money, more things, and more power over household spending.

There are two ways children determine parental spending. Direct influence describes children's requests, demands, and hints, such as "I want some french fries." It also refers to joint decision making, where children actively participate with other family members in a purchase. This is different from indirect influence, or what is sometimes called passive influence. In the case of indirect influence, parents know the products and brands that their children prefer and buy them without being asked or told. Indirect influence may account for as much as $300 billion of the nearly $500 billion in 1997 household spending determined by children.

"Whenever I go to the store, Jenny always asks me to get some Cheerios," reports one mother. This is an example of direct influence. About 90 percent of product requests made by children to a parent are by brand name. Children usually have one brand they prefer, and one or two that they are willing to substitute in dire circumstances. These two or three salient brands are called a child's "evoked set" for a particular product line. If a marketer's brand is not in the kid's evoked set, the child will not buy it or ask for it.

Yet moms are intimately acquainted with their children's wants and the brands they like. Parents often buy these brands without being asked. "My kid won't eat any cereal except Cap'n Crunch, so I try to catch it on sale if I can," says one mother. This parental awareness of kids' brand preferences is what I call an "evokked set" to distinguish it from a parent's own evoked set of brand preferences. The evokked set is how children indirectly influence parental purchases.

Children also exert substantial indirect influence on parental purchases when they suggest a retail outlet, such as "Let's go to McDonald's." In a study of after-school behavior, we found another indirect influence. Many children adjust the central air-conditioning to make the house cooler when they get home from school. This action results in increased expenditures by parents, even though the child never directly asked for something.

The dollar value of the "kidfluence" market is more difficult to track than spending by children themselves. Here are my best guesses in unadjusted figures, based on estimates from several sources. In the 1960s, children aged 2 to 14 directly influenced about $5 billion in parental purchases. In the mid-1970s, the figure was $20 billion, and it rose to $50 billion by 1984. By 1990, kids' direct influence had reached $132 billion, and in 1997, it may have peaked at around $188 billion.

These increases aren't due solely to growing influence by children. It's also because of a growing number of products that interest children. I estimate the product categories that kids influence increased from 65 to 75 in the past decade.

Some of these categories are ones children have only recently begun to influence, such as isotonic drinks and home computers.

In addition, some kids' power is due to changes in family lifestyle. Children's direct participation in new-car selection is partly a result of families traveling more together for leisure and recreation. This in turn is part of a greater emphasis on an active lifestyle for families with children. Other underlying forces in the growing influence of children include parents being less willing to leave children alone, and parents' concerns about their kids' sedentary patterns.

Marketers of minivans and sport-utility vehicles have acknowledged children as a new influence on auto purchases with major advertising campaigns in magazines for kids. (Take a look at any issue of Crayola Kids.) Automakers also target kids at the point of purchase. This is smart, since kids influenced an estimated $17.7 billion in automobile purchases in 1997.

THE FUTURE MARKET

As a future market, kids have more market potential than their primary and influence purchases combined. Children usually begin performing as independent consumers in the first grade. They may not buy soft drinks for themselves at that point, but they are certainly exposed to messages about soft drinks and a multitude of other products. Children will eventually hit the prime purchase years for just about any product or service.

When companies successfully nurture kids as customers before children actually have the power to buy their products, they often create loyal future customers. Customers cultivated as children may be critical of changes in products, both those they love and hate. But they will probably be less resistant to price increases and size reductions.

In the late 1980s, Delta Air Lines started its Fantastic Flyer program for kids as a way of generating future customers. It targets kids aged 7 to 14 with *Fantastic Flyer* magazine, birthday greetings, special foods and gifts during flights, and bar-

MOM, BUY A JEEP

(aggregate spending in millions of dollars influenced by children aged 4 to 12 on selected items, and per-child spending, 1997)

	aggregate spending	per-child spending
Food and beverages	$110,320	$3,131
Entertainment	25,620	727
Apparel	17,540	498
Automobiles	17,740	503
Electronics	6,400	182
Health and beauty	3,550	101
Other	5,570	158
Total	$187,740	$5,328

Source:author's estimates and Census Bureau.

Children wield an enormous amount of influence on their parents' spending, even on big-ticket items like cars.

PIZZA, PEPSI, AND POWER RANGERS

(aggregate spending in millions of dollars by children aged 4 to 12 on selected items, and per-child spending, 1997)

	aggregate spending	per-child spending
Food and beverages	$7,745	$220
Play items	6,471	184
Apparel	3,595	102
Movies/sports	1,989	56
Video arcades	1,326	38
Other	2,302	65
Total	$23,429	$665

Source: author's estimates and Census Bureau.

The average U.S. child aged 4 to 12 personally spends more than $600 a year. Over half goes for food and toys.

gain airfares for their parents. Delta knows that there are only two sources of new customers: those who switch from competitors, and those Delta grows from childhood. The former is short-term and the most common; the latter is long-term and requires a commitment from top management.

How can firms such as Delta Air Lines justify courting kids as future customers if there is little or no return on market-development expenditures until kids reach their teens or adult years? A company can virtually guarantee itself customers tomorrow if it invests in them as children, so many insightful executives do so. With relatively small expenditures on public relations, promotion, and advertising, firms can build equity in their brand names among today's youth, making the companies acceptable and desirable tomorrow.

A firm may not know what products it will sell 10 or 20 years from now. But it does know that its name will be on them. So it tries to build a following for its name. That's called cradle-to-grave marketing, and it can be learned by observing the masters, like McDonald's and the Coca-Cola Company.

Many firms are in the enviable position of subsidizing their kids-as-a-future-market programs with revenue from selling in the primary and influence markets. Delta Air Lines targets kids as future and influence markets; M&M Mars as future and primary markets; and Target Stores as future, primary, and influence markets. Selling T-shirts, snacks, and toiletries directly to kids would help Target pay for programs to cultivate children as future customers. It could also appeal to kids as influencers of parental spending on back-to-school clothing and school supplies.

THE COMING DECADE

The market potential of kids will probably grow over the next decade at the double-digit annual rate that characterized the

past ten years. Within a couple of years, kids will be spending $35 billion of their own money and $300 billion of their parents'. The marketers' motto in the next decade will be, "If you don't have a kid's product, get one."

Yet the ongoing rush to youth is quickly reaching excess. It's providing children with many new products, but also producing plenty of bad ones that end up in their makers' loss columns. These errors appear randomly distributed among companies large and small, old and new. We might expect mistakes among the many adult products that have been scaled down and funned up for kids. But there are probably just as many in traditional kid products, such as toys and sweets.

Mistakes result from a lack of skill in marketing to children that's not buffered by good research. Many executives involved in kids' marketing are what I call "marents"—marketers who are also parents. Because they occupy these two roles, they believe they possess special insights into targeting children. You often hear parents saying things like, "The one thing I know is kids. I have three of my own." What happens all too often is a parent's company ends up experiencing millions in losses demonstrating just how unique those three kids are.

Another group of decision-makers is also causing errors in products for children. A "wiwak" can be recognized by the way he or she starts a marketing strategy statement with, "When I Was A Kid." A wiwak might say, "When I was a kid, our socks always had holes in them, and I bet the idea would sell to kids today, just as fast as jeans with holes."

The problem with the approaches of both parents and wiwaks is a lack of underlying research on the kids' market. There is probably much less marketing research per kids' product than for adult products, in spite of the high risks in selling to kids. The reasons may range from "I can't afford it," to "I don't need to do it." to "I don't want to give away my idea to the competition." But it mainly boils down to decision-makers believing that kids are mini adults who are easy to reach with a modified adult product.

This will change as mistakes and failures reach a critical mass, and weak players fall out of the market. Many of those scaled down, funned-up adult products, like shampoos and toothpastes with no distinctions from adult versions other than cartoon characters on the packages, will go away and not return. Good products in awful packages will be killed off by better products in packages that serve kids. How much longer will value-oriented parents buy Oreo cookies or Frito-Lay potato chips in packages their kids can't open or close sufficiently to preserve product freshness?

Advertising that encourages children to defy their parents, make fun of authority, or talk unintelligibly will be replaced with informative ads describing the benefits of products. Surely, too, most of those movie-hawking premiums that fast-food restaurants give away will be replaced with premiums that promote the restaurants themselves, instead of serving as distribution channels for entertainment companies. The net result of all these changes will be better products and services for kids and their parents, and more profits for the firms that demonstrate excellence in kids' marketing.

Culture SHOCK

When it comes to marketing to ethnic populations, what you don't know *can* hurt you

by Shelly Reese

Coors translated its slogan, "Turn it loose," into Spanish, where it was read as "Suffer from diarrhea."

Clairol introduced the "Mist Stick" curling iron to Germany, only to find out that "mist" is German slang for manure.

The American slogan for Salem cigarettes, "Salem—Feeling Free," was translated into the Japanese market as "When smoking Salem, you will feel so refreshed that your mind seems to be free and empty."

When Gerber started selling baby food in Africa, it used the same packaging as in the U.S., with the beautiful baby on the label. Later, Gerber learned that since most Africans can't read English, companies there routinely put pictures on the label of what's inside.

Colgate introduced a toothpaste in France called Cue, which is also the name of a notorious French porn magazine.

An American T-shirt maker in Miami printed shirts for the Spanish market that promoted the Pope's visit. Instead of "I saw the Pope" (el Papa), the shirts read "I saw the potato" (la papa).

In Italy, a campaign for Schweppes Tonic Water translated the name into "Schweppes Toilet Water."

Pepsi's "Come alive with the Pepsi Generation" translated into "Pepsi brings your ancestors back from the grave," in Chinese.

When Parker marketed a ball-point pen in Mexico, its ads were supposed to have read, "It won't leak in your pocket and embarrass you." The company assumed that the word "embarazar" meant "to embarrass." "Embarazar" actually means "to impregnate," so the resulting ad read: "It won't leak in your pocket and make you pregnant."

—*Internet posting adapted from "When Slogans Go Wrong,"* American Demographics, *February 1992*

Marketing blunders are hilarious when they happen to somebody else. But seriously, folks: imagine that you are the one who has to tell the executives at a paper-goods company that the brand name for its facial tissue (Puffs) is a colloquial expression for "whorehouses" in German—and that you only discovered the problem after the company had launched the product, at considerable expense, in Germany. Wipes the smile right off your face, doesn't it?

Words, images, gestures, and other forms of communication that seem forthright enough to the communicator can be loaded with nuance and unexpected associations for the communicated-to. There is also the simple, usually unconscious cultural arrogance of the type that "embarazared" Parker Pen. If it looks like the English word, and it sounds like the English word, it must be the equivalent of the English word, no?

Nien!

If your goal is to reach consumers whose culture differs from your own, it is essential to thoroughly acquaint yourself with their language, customs, prejudices, and tastes, or seek the assistance of someone who knows it well. Failure to do so can cost you dearly in unproductive advertising, forfeited sales, and—perhaps most importantly—lost goodwill.

This is not just a mandate for global marketing. As the U.S. population becomes increasingly diverse, the consequences of cultural ignorance will become more severe. By the year 2050, ethnic minorities are expected to comprise 50 percent of the U.S. population. That's a significant change from the current population distribution, which is 75 percent Anglo, 12 percent African American, 10 percent Hispanic, and 3 percent Asian American. What's more, roughly 60 percent of that growth will come from immigration, according to the U.S. Bureau of the Census. That means an increasing num-

I saw the potato

ber of U.S. consumers will be coming from regions with markedly different cultures and heritages.

Even the Anglo population, which tends to be treated as if it were homogeneous, is becoming more diverse. Since the fall of the Iron Curtain and the breakup of the former Soviet Union, immigration from Europe has been on the rise. Between 1985 and 1995, more than 1.2 million European migrants settled in the U.S., according to the Immigration and Naturalization Service. That represents 14 percent of total immigration, and it highlights the population's increasingly eclectic makeup, and the need to craft marketing messages that are relevant to specific groups within the total population.

There Are No Safe Assumptions

While the "dos" and "don'ts" of ethnic marketing are dependent upon the product being marketed and the intended audience, there are a handful of "nevers" and "alwayses" that should form the platform of any campaign.

Topping the "never" list is the inevitable injunction against assuming you know who the audience is and what it wants. The danger is that those assumptions may be based on inaccurate and even offensive stereotypes. There's a tendency to dismiss this warning as self-evident or, since few people recognize the limits of their own knowledge about other cultures, unnecessary (especially when you reckon the cost of research or hiring a consultant). It's possible to get by on empathy and guesswork some of the time, but it's risky.

A less obvious but even more common error is to assume that what works for one market will work for all. If there was a Golden Rule in ethnic marketing, it would read something like this: "Thou shalt not assume your general market campaign is appropriate for the ethnic consumer."

"Don't take your general market brochure, or whatever it is you've created, and assume that by translating it you'll be able to reach the ethnic markets," warns Cristina Benitez Turner, senior vice president and director of ethnic

marketing for Draft Worldwide in Chicago. That's particularly true when trying to reach the Hispanic- and Asian-American markets, Turner says, because they are composed largely of immigrants whose cultural reference points are neither white nor Madison-Avenue American.

Likewise, companies that substitute ethnic performers for white actors in a half-hearted attempt to reach minority consumers are making a flagrant error. "That's just balanced casting," says Ron Sampson, executive vice president of corporate development for Burrell Communications Group, a Chicago advertising firm that specializes in the African-American market. "Integrated advertising is not target marketing."

Real target marketing demands the creation of messages that appeal to the specific sensitivities of an audience. It means understanding the significance of minute details that might be meaningless to Anglo audiences. For example, Eliot Kang, president of Kang & Lee Advertising in New York City, cautions clients to avoid using the number four when addressing Chinese, Korean, and Japanese consumers. Although "four times the savings" might be a carrot for the general audience, four is the number for death in Asian numerology.

The colors you use can also have special significance for some consumers. "If you use red and gold, Korean and Japanese consumers will recognize the promotion as one created for Chinese consumers," says Kang. Not only are they less likely to respond to the ad, they may well feel snubbed by the oversight.

Kang's examples demonstrate the need for a level of familiarity with different cultures that the average marketer would be hard-pressed to match. But looking for an "inside" perspective also presents certain hazards. That leads us to the first corollary of the Golden Rule: make sure your creative resource replicates your target audience.

"That doesn't mean designing an ad and then running it by a Spanish-speaking person in your MIS department or the guy who fixes the copy machine," says Turner. "You need

native speakers who understand the psyche of the ethnic consumer."

AT&T: the Voice of Pravda?

Delving into an audience's collective psyche means finding out what's important to them and playing to their interests. It requires full acceptance of the fact that quintessentially American icons, holidays, and heroes are often meaningless to consumers from other cultures—even if doing so means tweaking a general market campaign or revamping it entirely.

A classic example, says Turner, is the case of the "cover girl." While Cindy Crawford's dazzling smile may be etched in white America's consciousness, in many Hispanic countries, a super model is just another pretty face.

"The whole idea of a 'cover girl' is unknown in that culture because there aren't that many beauty magazines there," says Turner. Beauty pageants, however, are common. Consequently, when Cover Girl cosmetics entered the Latin-American market, it employed a former Miss Universe from Venezuela to tout its products.

"It was the same strategy used in the U.S., but we made the concept relevant," explains Turner, who worked on the campaign.

Sometimes a highly effective general market campaign must be scrapped entirely. Several years ago AT&T used singer/actress Whitney Houston in a number of "true voice" spots touting the clarity of its phone connections. While the ads were popular in the general market, they would have been meaningless to the growing number of Russian immigrants in the United States. Not only did Houston lack cachet with this group, but the idea of fiberoptic clarity was irrelevant to people accustomed to unreliable, static-filled phone connections. Even more damning: the tag line, "your true voice" loosely translated to "the voice of Pravda," a Soviet newspaper notorious for ignoring inconvenient facts and pushing the Communist party line.

So refreshing that your mind will be empty

Won't leak and make you pregnant

Brings your ancestors back from the grave

Given the irrelevance of the spokesperson and the negative connotations of the message, AT&T, with the help of YAR Communications Inc., created a Russian-language ad featuring a popular Russian comedian. Russian consumers loved the new ads, says YAR president and CEO Yuri Radzievsky, because they appealed to their sense of humor and were created specifically for them. The attention to detail sent a message that AT&T really wanted their business and wanted to communicate with them in their own language.

When Anheuser-Busch Inc. of St. Louis, Missouri, was searching for a spokesperson for a responsible drinking spot for Spanish-language media, it turned to boxer and Olympic gold medal winner Oscar de la Hoya. Alejandro Ruelas, the brewer's director of ethnic marketing, says de la Hoya was the ideal choice, not only because he is easily recognizable but because he is handsome, well spoken, bilingual, and "his achievements show what hard work and perseverance can achieve." Even better, de la Hoya was already loyal to the brewer, which had employed him while he was training for the Olympics. In a similar vein, Anheuser-Busch designed spots featuring former Lakers basketball star James Worthy for the African-American audience.

The selection of sports promotions is equally important, Ruelas says. Understanding the importance of soccer to the Hispanic culture, Budweiser has for years sponsored Major League Soccer, the U.S. and Mexican national soccer teams, the U.S. women's national team, Olympic soccer, and three World Cups. Today, as soccer gains nationwide popularity among all groups, that early investment is paying off.

"There are two types of corporate identities," Ruelas says. "There are those that get involved at the building stage and those that get in at the height of a trend's popularity to capitalize on it. The role of soccer in the U.S. landscape has changed. There was a time when no one was out asking for the Hispanic order except us. Now it's not just us out there asking for the order. All of our competitors are doing the same thing, but we have credibility with the customer."

Cultural Relevance vs. Pandering

Cultural relevance also means presenting a product in light of positive, real-world experiences. A family reunion may be a great image for a long-distance carrier to conjure when marketing to African Americans, says Burrell's Ron Sampson, because the image ties in easily with the product. But he warns that cultural relevance is no substitute for product relevance, and marketers should avoid campaigns that might appear pandering.

"There's a difference between cultural relevance and cultural opportunism," Sampson cautions. For example, it might be culturally relevant for a soft-drink manufacturer to depict urban youths playing basketball (although Sampson says the image has become so hackneyed it verges dangerously on becoming stereotypical). But it would be offensive to advertise a cake mix in the same fashion.

Above all, cultural relevance means understanding a group's values and customs. Consequently, while target marketers may be wise to forgo generic "happy holidays" messages in favor of a greeting tailored to Kwaanza, or Cinco de Mayo, they'd better understand which observances are of the greatest significance and why. To illustrate: Hanukkah, while an important festival for the Jewish community, does not carry the same religious weight as Christmas does in the Christian calendar. Marketers who draw a direct correlation between the two are betraying their ignorance of the Jewish culture.

MoneyGram, a Lakewood, Colorado, money transfer service, derives more than half its revenues from customers wiring money to their families in Mexico and Latin America. Each May, executives noted a triple-digit increase in activity during the two weeks prior to Mother's Day. Understanding consumers' desire to care for their families and the important role of the mother in Hispanic culture, three years ago MoneyGram created "A Home for Mom," an annual sweepstakes with a $100,000 grand prize linked to Mother's Day.

"The majority of our customers send money to their countries to help their families, which is why we suggest in our promotion to use the prize money for the ultimate Mother's Day gift: a home," says Isaac Lasky, vice president of Hispanic market development. Not only does the promotion (which MoneyGram supports with Spanish-language television, radio, and outdoor advertising) propel sales, it generates a lot of media exposure and helps cement MoneyGram's good name in the Hispanic community.

Although MoneyGram had previously advertised competitive rates during the peak wire transfer season, Lasky says the sweepstakes is a much more effective way of reaching the market.

"Anybody can scream price," he says. "This is a dream: to own a home and give it to Mom. It's very attuned to the sensitivity of the target audience."

Watch for Unintentional Insults

It goes without saying that anyone marketing to another culture must steer clear of stereotyping and avoid condescending to the audience. This is not as easy as it might seem.

Most of us have come to recognize explicitly insulting words and images when we see them. But stereotypes needn't be blatant or ill-intentioned to be offensive. For example, an advertisement aimed at Cuban Americans that includes a Mexican colloquialism may backfire, because it suggests that the advertiser tends to lump all Hispanics together, says Turner.

What's more, a message that might be benign if voiced by a Caucasian speaker can be insulting coming from an ethnic actor. Kang cites an AT&T commercial for the general market emphasizing how competitors' claims can be misleading. The spot, as originally conceived, featured an elderly Korean woman who was upset about being deceived by a competitors's claims. Because the speaker spoke with a heavy accent, the ad seemed to imply she was gullible and ignorant about doing business in the United States.

"It showed her as weak and foolish," says Kang, whose firm suggested reworking the spot. "We said, Let's make her smart and aggressive, and let's throw in a Korean idiom: 'To really see which one is longer you have to put them side by side.' The change showed a very smart bilingual Korean American woman and it also shows AT&T represents value, which is important to the consumer."

It's Not Just a Pitch—It's a Process

As with marketing in general, understanding what's important to the ethnic consumer requires listening to the audience. What is the product? Why will it be purchased? How will it be used? Under what circumstances?

"You really need to do your research and take your product to the customer," says Turner. Too often, she says, companies mistakenly assume that their brand name carries clout and that the services they tout are meaningful to their target audiences. But that's not always the case. Marketers need to understand what's important to the client and only then determine what the message will be.

Consider banks, says Turner. Direct deposit and CD rates aren't important to someone who is new to the United States and who may never have used a bank before. Financial institutions "need to introduce their customers to their services," she explains. "Emphasize the relationship. They need to be more educational. Then, when the customer is comfortable and trusts them, they can explain more specific services."

In other words, ethnic marketing is a process that demands commitment: not just to a specific advertising campaign, but to the community itself, Sampson says.

"You can't substitute a creative approach and a good spot for an ongoing conversation with consumers," he says.

The dialogue shouldn't always be about the product either, says Ruelas. He recalls the situation at the time of California's Proposition 187, when Budweiser's sales started to decline slightly among Hispanics. At the same time Bud was losing ground, Mexican brands—which are generally more expensive and by default aren't very involved with the U.S. Hispanic community—began to gain share. As the brewer began to delve into the situation, it realized that convenience stores and other "Anglo" companies were reporting similar defections.

"When we went to the consumer, we heard, 'I like hamburgers, but I don't eat hamburgers anymore, now I buy tacos'," says Ruelas. "People were being very, very conscious about staying away from anything 'American,' because they felt that was the only way they had to respond to what they felt was a hostile, anti-Hispanic climate."

To combat the backlash, Budweiser created a 30-minute, Spanish-language "documercial" highlighting its support of Hispanic arts and education initiatives and its long-term support for the National Hispanic Scholarship Foundation. The program featured notable Hispanic figures, such as Archbishop Patrick Flores of San Antonio and de la Hoya, as well as ordinary people Anheuser-Busch has helped to succeed. In addition, Budweiser launched a voter registration drive among Hispanics in California. The message was clear: we are a team, and we support you.

"People's reaction was, 'Wow, here's a company that cares enough that they are coming out here to tell me what I need to do to be successful in this country'," recalls Ruelas.

Anheuser-Busch certainly would never have understood the market erosion without an ongoing conversation with its consumers, says Ruelas. Unfortunately, many marketers fail to see ethnic marketing as a long-term deal. They try to measure the success or failure of a campaign from the results of a commercial aired over a period of months.

"You can't just come in and expect instant returns," Sampson says. "The successful marketers are the ones that have been at this over a long period of time: companies like Coca-Cola, McDonald's, Procter & Gamble, and some of the phone companies. Their audiences understand that. They see that marketer as a supporter of their community who is asking for their sale. The marketer has to be there over time and do things beyond advertising. They have to be involved with the community and be a good place for minorities to work, and be a good corporate citizen."

None of this is meant to imply that the traditional rules of marketing don't apply to the ethnic consumer. Quite the opposite.

While Kang recommends that direct marketers take a more conversational approach to Asian Americans and introduce their offers with several paragraphs of pleasantries, lest they sound "too pushy or rude," he emphasizes that the offer itself must be the same. "You don't want people to think they're getting a different product if they don't speak English," says Kang.

And no matter what the message may be, the product remains the critical point. "You don't want to make something so ethnic it loses the marketing message," he says.

That's a point that marketers, in their efforts to explore new markets, should never forget, says Sampson.

"In an attempt to be cutting edge and win awards, you can't get away from what advertising is," he says. "Advertising is selling. It's what you do when you can't knock on somebody's door and show them your product."

Shelly Reese is a freelance writer living in Cincinnati, Ohio, and a regular contributor to Marketing Tools.

Eliot Kang
Kang & Lee Advertising
(212) 889-4509

Isaac Lasky
MoneyGram
(303) 716-6710

Yuri Radzievsky
YAR Communications Inc.
(212) 726-4000

Alejandro Ruelas
Anheuser-Bush Inc.
alejandro.ruelas@anheuser-busch.com

Ron Sampson
Burrell Communications Group
(312) 443-8600

Cristina Benitez Turner
Draft Worldwide
(312) 944-3500

What Your Customers Can't Say

by David B. Wolfe

Breakthroughs in brain science are challenging basic assumptions about consumer behavior. It's time to rewrite the rules of market research.

If your job depends on market research, prepare for a shock. New discoveries in brain science are radically revising our understanding of how human beings think and make decisions, and these new models of cognition are rewriting the conventional wisdom about consumer behavior.

Conventional marketing research depends on the assumption that people can accurately report their values, needs, and motivations. But many scientists no longer believe this. "We have reason to doubt that full awareness of our motives, drives, and other mental activities may be possible," says neurologist Richard Restak. "Our inability to accurately report intentions and expectations may simply reflect the fact that they are not qualitatively conscious" adds Bernard J. Baars, author of *In the Theater of Consciousness.*

The idea that consumers have limited knowledge of their motives is shocking on both a professional and personal level. Everyone wants to believe they know why they do what they do. It wounds one's sense of personal autonomy to think otherwise. Also, evidence that average people cannot accurately describe their motivations is a direct challenge to established methods of conducting research. It calls for radical changes in the status quo of research.

"CONSUMERS DON'T CHOOSE RATIONALLY, [SO] ANY RESEARCH THAT FORCES RATIONAL ANSWERS HAS TO BE FLAWED."

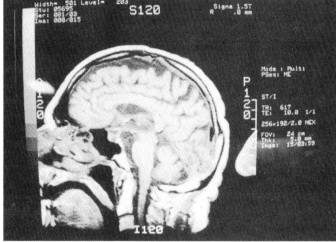

©1998 PHOTODISC

The natural tendency to resist change explains why many otherwise skilled researchers are trying to block out this truth. But it's also true that more accurate research produces better business decisions. That is why cutting-edge researchers are searching for new ways to reveal the subconscious roots of consumer behavior.

BEHIND MARKETING'S WOES

Marketing is ripe for a revolution because its failures are so apparent. "Everybody—stockholders, directors, CEOs, customers, the government—is angry because marketing, which should be driving business, doesn't work" write marketing executives Kevin Clancy and Robert Shulman. One of the most important reasons for this breakdown is that research is not working because of flaws in its basic premises.

Even academics, the primary source of research theory, see major flaws in mainstream research methods. Multivariate statistics that describe personality traits can account for no more than 7 percent of purchasing behavior, according to a paper published by William Massy, Ronald Frank, and Thomas Lodahl of Stanford, the University of Pennsylvania, and Cornell, respectively.

Consumer research's problems originate in psychology, a field that has long struggled to define human behavior with the same precision physicists use to describe the movement of bodies from atoms to stars. But human behavior is too unpredictable to describe with such precision, because it depends on an almost infinite number of relationships. An increasingly desperate search for cause-and-effect explanations leads many psychologists to "retreat to abstract ideas that ignore contexts completely," writes Harvard psychologist Jerome Kagan. Consumer research reflects similar tendencies.

CONSUMERS ARE NOT PATHOLOGICAL LIARS. THEY ARE MORE LIKE SPLIT PERSONALITIES.

Kagan is bothered by psychology's excessive dependence on behavioral models that conform better to statistical theory than to behavioral realities. Models of consumer behavior tend to extract their subjects from the complex, often unpredictable, but completely natural contexts in which people live and make purchasing decisions. The result is often an interesting manipulation of a hypothetical situation that leads to a marketing failure.

One of the most famous marketing busts was the reformulation of Coca-Cola. Extensive consumer research predicted success for "New Coke" because people said it tasted better. But the research failed to disclose that people also saw "Old Coke" as an important cultural icon, that would lose value by changing the original recipe. This subtle value proved to be far more influential than taste in determining consumer response.

Kodak's "Advanta" camera was an even costlier bust. Its research failed to warn executives of Advanta's biggest challenge: persuading a marketplace dominated by middle-aged baby boomers to buy what was proudly touted as a high-tech product. In mid-life, the bells and whistles of new technology generally begin to lose their appeal. Simplicity begins to edge out complexity in consumers' preferences.

Mainstream consumer research generally fails to take into account developmental changes in values and world views that happen across a person's life span. Research also tends to ignore the major changes in cognition, or how the mind processes information, that happen with age. The subliminal origins of these changes prevent consumers from adequately reporting them to researchers, but the changes are decisive in marketplace behavior.

Another assumption that leads consumer research astray is borrowed from classic economics. Researchers assume that people make buying decisions to satisfy their self-interest, and that they use reason to determine which product best serves that end. Brain researchers see reason playing a much weaker role in personal decisions, however. In their book *Marketing Revolution,* Clancy and Shulman state the problem this way: "Because consumers don't choose rationally, any research that forces rational answers has to be flawed."

RESEARCH IS TOO RATIONAL

For years marketers have complained that consumers often indicate one thing in research, yet behave differently in the marketplace. But consumers are not pathological liars. They are split personalities, according to University of Iowa neurologist Antonio Damasio. To be more specific, their decisions are split by the functions of reason and emotion.

Damasio's research shows that different brain sites and different mental processes are involved with different kinds of decision-making. We use one set of mental tools when we consider hypothetical matters, and another when

we make personal decisions. Emotions are triggered by changes in body states, according to Damasio. For example, when someone makes you angry, your face flushes while your heart pounds and stomach muscles tighten. Bodily functions also change when you see an old friend, enjoy a brilliant sunset, hear moving music, or sit down to an appetizing meal. According to Damasio, these changes in body states are essential to the production of emotions. And without emotions, we cannot make what Damasio calls "personally advantageous decisions." Emotions tell us how relevant a matter is to our needs. Reason alone cannot do this, says Damasio.

INSTEAD OF FINDING THE REAL REASON PEOPLE BUY SOMETHING, MAINSTREAM MARKET RESEARCH MAKES A RATIONALIZATION.

Damasio studies people who suffer from a condition that makes them similar to "Star Trek's" Mr. Spock. Brain lesions have wiped out their secondary emotions, which are critical to socially adaptable behavior. Reason is the only tool they have when they need to figure something out. One might think that this kind of brain damage would lead a person to make better decisions. After all, we are taught early in life that the best decisions are usually free of emotional taint. But Damasio's research indicates otherwise.

When presented with hypothetical issues, Damasio's patients experience no unusual difficulties. But when a matter directly involves them, problem-solving becomes difficult. Even deciding what to wear or when to make a doctor's appointment becomes a challenging act of mind.

Reason is qualitatively value free, according to Damasio. It does not operate to make decisions, but to analyze choices, assist in perceiving reality, and construct possibilities. Reason may help you recognize the tree you are looking at in a nursery and determine if it will fit in your garden, but you need emotions to understand the personal benefits that will accrue if you take the tree home. You also need emotion to decide whether or not the price is fair.

Emotions have a powerful effect on our consumer choices, because they push us toward decisions we think are best for us. We often bypass reason when making these decisions because experience endows us with what Damasio calls "somatic markers." Somatic markers are like computer shortcuts that incorporate many keystrokes into one or two. They exist in inherited behavior traits or are formed by experience. They are prerecorded behavior guides that can be instantly accessed and played back to assist in making new decisions. They often make reason irrelevant to decision-making.

Somatic markers are the most likely biological basis of intuition; they are the equivalent of what marketers call "hot buttons." They also serve as "safety buttons" that produce quick responses when reason operates too slowly to avoid calamity. Somatic markers take control when a errant car suddenly appears in your path, requiring quick action to avoid a collision. Only later, when you begin shaking, are you aware of the emotional buildup it took to quickly avert danger. Preset responses in somatic markers have kept you from serious harm.

Many research questions fail to deeply stimulate consumers' somatic markers or "hot buttons." Instead, they invite respondents to develop a reason-based explanation that often distorts reality. Instead of the real reason for buying or not buying something, researchers get a rationalization based on the respondent's idealized self-image. If they do not account for this bias, researchers are left with a model based on how people think they ought to be motivated, instead of a model based on their actual motivations. Applying these flawed models in the marketplace magnifies their

errors. It's like the errant path of a bullet whose course is only a hair's width off at the gun's muzzle, but well wide when it misses its target.

Even at their best, consumers give researchers mere approximations of reality. The human mind lacks the cold unambiguous precision of computers, which is why humans can be creative while computers cannot. Yet consumer research relies heavily on mathematical protocols that originated in the hard sciences. Tools that are designed to describe the black-and-white predictability of matter and energy are unsuited to the more uncertain world of human behavior. Until recently, these flawed tools are almost the only ones businesses have had at their disposal.

THE FUTURE DIRECTION OF RESEARCH

Brain science has come so far that researchers are now able to routinely eavesdrop on brains while they think. This gives scientists the ability to create more accurate models of how the mind/brain complex receives and processes information. Their work indicates that current market research methods tend to follow a backwards course. Market research is primarily focused on the workings of the conscious mind; it gives scant attention to the unconscious mind, and pays no attention [to] the brain. The reverse should be the rule.

Most of a marketer's message is processed outside a consumer's conscious mind. That is because the conscious mind is not capable of handling all the information the senses pick up. Our conscious mind only knows the things our brain and unconscious mind select for us to think about and take action on. Thus, when consumers talk to researchers about themselves, researchers are getting a much edited picture of the consumers' motivations and behavior.

Future research models will be based more faithfully on how consumers' decisions are really made. These models will reflect developmental changes in needs, motivations,

and behavior that happen across the lifespan, thus decreasing researchers' dependence on consumers' self-reports. Additionally, these models will incorporate new discoveries about how we perceive, think about, and make decisions on matters. Only then will research experience major improvement in uncovering consumers' root motivations.

Root motivations—the key to knowing how to press consumers' hot buttons—are innate behavioral dispositions, or personality at its most basic level. They give little direct evidence of their presence, even as they cue our behavior like offstage prompters. It is not the job of the conscious mind to originate motivations. Its job is more executive in nature. Brain scientists sometimes refer to the conscious mind as an "executive officer" who makes decisions based on information brought to it from the subliminal regions of the mind/brain complex. In this subliminal world are the origins of values, needs, and motivations.

The new insights we are gaining about the human brain and mind are astonishing. They are setting the stage for major changes in the way consumer research is conducted. Now that we are finding out why people cannot tell the whole truth about themselves, we have good reasons to start making these changes.

TAKING IT FURTHER

Overviews of recent advances in brain research can be found in Richard Restak's most recent book, *Brainscapes: An Introduction to What Neuroscience Has Learned About the Structure, Function, and Abilities of the Brain* (1996), published by Hyperion; Bernard J. Baar's *In the Theater of Consciousness* (1997), published by Oxford University Press; and Antonio Damasio's *Descartes' Error: Emotion, Reason, and the Human Brain* (1994), published by Avon Books. The crisis in marketing is described in *Marketing Revolution: A Radical Manifesto for Dominating the Marketplace* by Kevin J. Clancy and Robert S. Shulman (1993), published by Harperbusiness. To contact David Wolfe, telephone (703) 758-0759 or e-mail dbwolfe1@ix.netcom.com.

The Joy of Shopping

Whether it's cruising for casual wear at the Gap or mining for garb in malls or designer shops, women are drawn to clothes. Some to a fault. And L.A.'s a mecca for them.

By **MIMI AVINS**
TIMES FASHION WRITER

By definition, a great city offers superlative shopping. Welcome to Los Angeles, where fashionable stores are diverse and plentiful, and everything anyone needs can be had at the flash of a credit card.

The variety of stores in L.A. is the shopping equivalent of cross training. When sprawling department stores seem overwhelming, tiny boutiques beckon. When the financial muscles strained by those large and small retail shrines are exhausted, discount malls, resale and vintage stores can satisfy in a low-impact way.

To examine why and how many of us indulge in this shopper's paradise, it is essential to eliminate need as a motivator. A man who has gained 20 pounds since he bought a suit five years ago and must attend his mother's funeral really needs a new suit. But for most recreational shoppers, need is beside the point.

Michael Sharkey, who, as director of personal shopping for Barneys New York in Beverly Hills, shops with people for a living, said, "No one needs clothes. However, many people want clothes."

So if we don't need to shop, why do we do it? Because it's fun, it's legal, it isn't fattening and the mirrors in stores alter reality, making us look as tall and thin as borzois. New clothes are ripe with promise. You've never had a bad time in them, been stopped for speeding in them, had your picture taken wearing them only to discover that the woman in the snapshot looks frumpy in that dress.

Shopping is free, at least until the bills come. Sometimes they never do materialize, at least when a bright, shiny store, staffed by unctuous salespeople who have been schooled in the art of equal opportunity flattery is visited like a museum by a shopper more intent on educating her eye than depleting her wallet. Browsing in such aesthetically pleasing places is like smoking controlled substances without inhaling. It delivers some of the excitement and few of the consequences.

Shopping has never been easier, or less revered. Societal shifts have con-

The Looky-Loo

This sport shopper likes to try on clothes but seldom makes a purchase. If she does, she returns it.

The Hysteric

This frantic shopper is in search of something to wear for an occasion. But she starts looking at the last minute.

The Cinderella Shopper

She needs something for a special event or trip. And she has to see every dress in town before choosing one.

The Thrill Seeker

She is passionate in her pursuit of clothes and accessories. And she will buy whatever strikes her fancy.

The Blitzkrieg Shopper

She doesn't like shopping much, so a few times a year, she surveys the stores and stocks up on everything.

spired to cast a politically correct pall over conspicuous consuming. Before the numbers of women joining the work force swelled, Mom was the chief purchasing agent for her family, and shopping was something women were supposed to be good at. Then feminism spoiled the sport. A woman who loved to shop acquired all the social cache of a Hanson fan who indulges a taste for chicken fried steak when no one is looking.

The anti-shopping stance reeks of hypocrisy. Americans are incessantly subjected to marketing designed to entice them to shop and buy. Then those who do are ridiculed. (Imelda Marcos could have been pilloried for sins far more venal than an itch for shoes.) Dr. Donald Black, professor of psychiatry at the University of Iowa College of Medicine and a specialist in treating shopaholics, said, "The purpose of advertising, which is mostly geared toward women, is to get them to buy things that they don't need, and to convince them that they need them. There are constant stimuli urging people to shop. I work with people who can't control their responses to those stimuli, and I don't see any advertising agencies lining up to give me research grants."

Catalogs, the Internet and cable shopping channels were supposed to replace driving to the mall, hunting for a parking space and the other annoyances and indignities of three-dimensional shopping. But the dirty little secret of the home shopping channels is that most of the clothes they hawk are awful, homely little wallflowers you wouldn't dance into a dressing room if you encountered them in a store. If catalogs are so great, why are J. Crew and J. Peterman opening more and more stores? The Internet is lonely and sterile, the opposite of the sensual, communal experience shopping has been since big-city department stores became destinations for people bent on seeing and being seen.

Stores are still the best places for hunters and gatherers to do what they do in distinctive ways. Experienced salespeople can size up a shopper in seconds, deciding which of the following types she is:

■ The Blitzkrieg Shopper. Not an impulsive spree killer, the blitzkrieg shopper is an organized person who plans her attack. She doesn't like shopping much, but she likes less being without what she needs or what's current. So a few times a year, she surveys the stores and stocks up, on work clothes, play clothes, special occasion gowns, even underwear and socks. In between her big buying trips, she only needs to fill in with basics like turtlenecks if the temperature drops.

"That kind of shopper almost wants to get it over with," said Roberta Ross, manager of the Shauna Stein boutique in the Beverly Center. Men, if they shop at all, tend to fall into this category.

■ The Cinderella Shopper: She needs—yes, really needs—a dress for the ball, or to wear to a college reunion, or a wardrobe for an extended business trip to New York. The more emotionally significant the event, the more likely she is to feel she has to see every dress in town before choosing one. Of course sometimes Cinderella's need is more perceived than real.

"We cater to a very small percentage of the city," Ross said, "but our customer doesn't want to show up in something from last season. We know that everyone who comes in here does have something to wear, even to that special party, but they don't want to repeat."

■ The Hysteric. Like Cinderella, the frantic shopper is in search of something to wear for an occasion. But she doesn't reserve any time to find it. Instead, she barrels into a store the afternoon of an event or the day before an interview, toting more anxiety than a jumbo Bloomindale's shopping bag could contain.

"You wouldn't believe how many time an actress comes in the store two hours before an audition, picks out something to wear, waits while we do the alterations, and goes straight to the interview," Ross said.

■ The Looky-Loo. This sport shopper looks, tries on, but seldom makes a purchase. If she does buy something, she'll probably return the merchandise soon. Sometimes, she is driven by a love for beautiful things that compels her to be around them.

"I was that person," Shauna Stein said. "I would just visit clothes that I couldn't afford because I wanted to look at them and touch them."

Stein and her store manager seem to have unusual patience for "museum" shoppers, perhaps because some of them graduate to become actual customers.

"I can understand having a passion for clothes that you can't own. I have passion for things I can't afford that I still appreciate," Ross said. "But the woman who really never buys has a deeper psychological problem than I can analyze. She likes the attention we give her. She needs to fill up her time because she's lonely or bored. Or shopping is what she does instead of exercising. When she comes in the store we keep her company and we chat and she learns about fashion. It's a pleasant way to spend a few hours."

Enthusiastic salespeople can greatly enhance a looky-loo's shopping trip.

"We know the woman who can't wait to see the new Voyage collection as soon as we get it in," said Barneys' Sharkey. "She likes the idea of being the first to try it so she comes in, buys 15 pieces of it, spends $25,000 and then returns everything but one sweater five days later. The problem is that while she's in the store, trying everything on is very exhilarating, and the salesperson gets into the spirit of fun and makes her feel special. Then, when the woman gets home, she's alone, and all the pieces that were so exciting in the store are just a pile of clothes."

■ The Thrill Seeker. Merchants should genuflect in the presence of this rarefied species, the true, passionate shopper. For the thrill seeker, the urge to shop consumes the body with the furor of flesh-eating bacteria. She ventures into a store hoping to be seduced and delighted. What is she looking for? Whatever sings to her. Any garment, shoe, bauble or dainty lingerie masterpiece that, once she has seen it, invades her thoughts, lingering like a catchy tune.

"Certain clothes create that feeling that you just have to have them," said designer Anna Sui, a black belt shopper. "Even if it costs a fortune and you don't need it, the feeling that you must own it just takes hold of you."

Somewhere, there is a confessional where passionate shoppers cleanse their souls. Forgive me, mother, for I have sinned. I bought a Richard Tyler suit at Neiman Marcus, then hung it next to the eight black jackets I already had at home. I pretended to listen to details of my best friend's marital crisis while visions of cashmere cardigans I'd seen at Madison danced in my head. "Should

I leave him?" she asked, interrupting my internal debate over whether to drop by the store on my next lunch hour to pick up a yellow or a purple one. "Well, sure," I said, oblivious to her question, but resolute in my preference for purple.

"Shopping doesn't make our customers happy," Stein said. "It makes them ecstatic. The biggest reason women shop is to have a total emotional experience. To get dressed in something new that you like gives you a rush."

The thrill seeker often worries that she has a shopping problem, especially when bills mount and closet rods creak under the weight of her treasures. Black, the Iowa psychiatrist who has been testing a serotonin re-uptake inhibitor similar to the anti-depressant Prozac as a treatment for shopaholics said, "In most compulsive buyers or shopaholics, shopping and spending habits are so far out of the norm that the fact that they have a serious problem is very obvious," he said. "Most of the cases I've seen are so extreme even the housekeeper would be able to make a diagnosis. It doesn't take a psychiatrist."

■ The Shopaholic. Shopaholics represent between 2% and 8% of the population, Black said, and "the problem is relatively uncommon among men. It's a woman's disease, so to speak." These loonies, people who have rooms so stuffed with merchandise they'll never use that they have to sleep in the garage, are in a different class than the shopper who gets a buzz when she finds the perfect pair of white jeans, even if she decides to buy three pairs in case they shrink when they're washed.

Dr. Drew Pinsky, a specialist in addiction medicine, program medical director of chemical dependency at Las Encinas Hospital in Pasadena and co-host of MTV's and KROQ-FM's nightly "Loveline" advice show said, "The consequences define the problem. If you're filing for bankruptcy, or having things is so compelling that you start stealing, them you have a problem. The pharmacology of drug dependency isn't present in shopping, but the similarity is there because, in general, people use drugs and activities like shopping, which is rewarding, as a way of managing unpleasant feelings. Shopping can be a coping strategy that makes people feel better temporarily, just as food does. It is effective, because we are literally rewarding ourselves. But it isn't necessarily dysfunctional. When you have to shop to feel good about yourself, that's when you know that things are out of balance."

Enter shopper's guilt. Director Henry Jaglom, whose film "Eating" examined women's relationship with food, is so convinced that shopping is the other major female obsession that he's preparing a film about it, to be called, "Shopping."

"For women, shopping is the other source of comfort and guilt," he said. "Men don't know how deeply connected it is to the darkest and most pleasurable sides of the female psyche. They have no idea how intense it can be for women. They think it's some kind of cute diversion. It has so much to do with a woman's sense of vanity and sexuality and her concerns about whether she's attractive. Their vulnerability and insecurity about how they look are all wrapped up in it."

One way to alleviate guilt is to rationalize. That T-shirt isn't expensive. A nice lunch would cost the same.

"We hear it all the time," Ross said. "A woman will say, 'My husband spends $300 on a bottle of wine with dinner. So what's $300 for a pair of shoes?' " And then, of course, everyone practices creative financing when they pay. Like, 'Put half of the bill on my husband's American Express, and here's some cash, and put the rest on my Visa.' It's hilarious."

Adultery and bathroom habits are the only human activities cloaked in greater secrecy. Women develop elaborate rituals to cover their shopping tracks. Packages stay in the trunk of the car till the coast is clear, then they're hidden in the guest room closet. Jaglom's wife, actress Victoria Foyt, said, "If I've bought a lot of stuff, I'll show it to him in stages. It's not because he'd have a fit if I spent a lot of money, because he wouldn't. But I like just showing up one day in something new, as if the dress just miraculously materialized out of nowhere. It's more goddess-like to do it that way."

Exactly. Women who love to shop are goddesses, and not just to the stores they enrich.

"By shopping, we're participating in the way media promotes fashion and glamour," Pinsky said. "We need to nurture ourselves and treat ourselves regularly, to certain kinds of foods and shopping expeditions, as long as it's appropriate and realistic. Self-denial that is chronic is unhealthy."

The only real problem is that shopping isn't a finite pastime. It gives rise to ancillary activities—trips to the tailor, laundry and cleaners. New clothes require new shoes, hosiery and underwear. At times, clothes are as demanding as pets. The long jersey dresses must be lopped over a padded hangar so they don't stretch and grow. Delicate knits are subject to pulled threads; they must be gently hand washed, then laid out, just so. And some garments, even with careful tending and training, remain like wild animals who refuse to be tamed. They willfully crease and shrink, lose their shape and discolor. So the hunt continues, for a garment both transforming and obedient, flattering and docile. There's always a reason to shop.

Unit 3

Unit Selections

Key Points to Consider

❖In general, the marketing concept states that the key to business success is the satisfaction of customer needs. Some critics believe that too strict an adherence to this principle has damaged U.S. industry by leading to a dearth of true innovation, particularly in the area of product development. What emphasis do you think should be put on the product in relationship to the other elements of the marketing mix?

❖Most ethical questions seem to arise in regard to the promotional component of the marketing mix. How fair is the general public's criticism of some forms of personal selling and advertising? Give some examples of this type of personal selling and advertising.

❖What role, if any, do you think the quality of a product plays in making a business competitive in consumer markets? What role does price play? Would you rather market a higher-priced, better-quality product or one that was the lowest priced? Why?

❖What do you envision will be the major problems or challenges retailers will face in the next decade? How should retailers deal with them?

❖Given the rapidly increasing costs of personal selling, what role do you think it will play as a strategy in the marketing mix in the future? What other promotional strategies will play roles in the next decade?

 **Links** | **www.dushkin.com/online/**

These sites are annotated on pages 4 and 5.

Marketing management objectives, the late Wroe Alderson once wrote, "are very simple in essence. The firm wants to expand its volume of sales, or it wants to handle the volume it has more efficiently." Although the essential objectives of marketing might be stated this simply, the development and implementation of strategies to accomplish them is considerably more complex. Many of these complexities are due to changes in the environment within which managers must operate. Strategies that fail to heed the social, political, and economic forces of society have little chance of success over the long run. The lead article in this section provides helpful insight suggesting a framework for developing a comprehensive marketing plan.

The selections in this section provide a wide-ranging discussion of how marketing professionals and U.S. companies interpret and employ various marketing strategies today. The readings also include specific examples from industry to illustrate their points. The articles are grouped in four subsections, each dealing with one of the main strategy areas: product, price, distribution (place), and promotion. Since each selection discusses more than one of these areas, it is important that you read them broadly. For example, many of the articles covered in the distribution section discuss important aspects of personal selling and advertising.

Product Strategy. The essence of the marketing concept is to begin with what consumers want and need. After determining a need, an enterprise must respond by providing the product or service demanded. Successful marketing managers recognize the need for continuous product improvement and/or new product introduction.

The articles in this subsection focus on various facets of product strategy. The first one, "Discovering New Points of Differentiation," advocates the importance of companies' opening up their creative thinking to encompass their customers' entire experience with a product or service. The next two articles investigate the importance of companies' nurturing the significant link between consumers and brands. "Built to Last" ends this subsection by reflecting on the low success rate of new products and by suggesting some ideas for a successful product launch.

Pricing Strategy. Few elements of the total strategy of the "marketing mix" demand so much managerial and social attention as pricing. There is a good deal of public misunderstanding about the ability of marketing managers to control prices and even greater misunderstanding about how pricing policies are determined. New products present especially difficult problems in terms of both costs and pricing. The costs for developing a new product are usually very high, and if a product is truly new, it cannot be priced competitively, for it has no competitors.

The two articles in this subsection scrutinize the tremendous pricing pressures that companies face and suggest some ways to make better pricing decisions.

Distribution Strategy. For many enterprises, the largest marketing costs result from closing the gap in space and time between producer and consumer. In no other area of marketing is efficiency so eagerly sought after. Physical distribution seems to be the one area where significant cost savings can be achieved. The costs of physical distribution are tied closely with decisions made about the number, the size, and the diversity of marketing intermediaries between producer and consumer.

The first subsection article, "The Stores That Cross Class Lines," shows why Target is seen as the epitome of retail cross-shopping. The next two articles delineate how, despite considerable hypercompetition, some retailers are performing well.

Promotion Strategy. The basic objectives of promotion are to inform, persuade, or remind the consumer to buy a firm's product or pay for the firm's service. Advertising is the most obvious promotional activity. However, in total dollars spent and in cost per person reached, advertising takes second place to personal selling. Sales promotion supports either personal selling and advertising, or both. Such media as point-of-purchase displays, catalogs, and direct mail place the sales promotion specialist closer to the advertising agency than to the salesperson.

The four articles in this final unit subsection cover such topics as a critical look at the best use of advertising, personal selling, sales promotions, and the effective use of the World Wide Web.

THE VERY MODEL OF A
MODERN MARKETING PLAN

SUCCESSFUL COMPANIES ARE REWRITING THEIR STRATEGIES TO REFLECT CUSTOMER INPUT AND INTERNAL COORDINATION

SHELLY REESE

Shelly Reese is a freelance writer based in Cincinnati.

IT'S 1996. DO YOU KNOW WHERE YOUR MARKETING PLAN IS? *In a world where competitors can observe and rapidly imitate each other's advancements in product development, pricing, packaging, and distribution, communication is more important than ever as a way of differentiating your business from those of your competitors.*

The most successful companies are the ones that understand that, and are revamping their marketing plans to emphasize two points:

1. Marketing is a dialog between customer and supplier.

2. Companies have to prove they're listening to their customers by acting on their input.

WHAT IS A MARKETING PLAN?

At its most basic level, a marketing plan defines a business's niche, summarizes its objectives, and presents its strategies for attaining and monitoring those goals. It's a road map for getting from point A to point B.

But road maps need constant updating to reflect the addition of new routes. Likewise, in a decade in which technology, international relations, and the competitive landscape are constantly changing, the concept of a static marketing plan has to be reassessed.

Two of the hottest buzz words for the 1990s are "interactive" and "integrated." A successful marketing plan has to be both.

"Interactive" means your marketing plan should be a conversation between your business and your customers by acting on their input. It's your chance to tell customers about your business and to listen and act on their responses.

"Integrated" means the message in your marketing is consistently reinforced by every department within your company. Marketing is as much a function of the finance and manufacturing divisions as it is the advertising and public relations departments.

Integrated also means each time a company reaches out to its customers through an advertisement, direct mailing, or promotion, it is sending the same message and encouraging customers to learn more about the product.

WHY IS IT IMPORTANT?

The interaction between a company and its customers is a relationship. Relationships can't be reproduced. They can, however, be replaced. That's where a good marketing plan comes into play.

Think of your business as a suitor, your customers as the object of your affection, and your competitors as rivals.

ILLUSTRATED BY KELLY KENNEDY

GETTING STARTED

A NINE-STEP PLAN THAT WILL MAKE THE DIFFERENCE BETWEEN WRITING A USEFUL PLAN AND A DOCUMENT THAT GATHERS DUST ON A SHELF

by Carole R. Hedden and the *Marketing Tools* editorial staff

In his 1986 book, *The Goal,* Eliyahu M. Goldratt writes that most of us forget the one true goal of our business. It's not to deliver products on time. It isn't even to manufacture the best widget in the world. The goal is to make money.

In the past, making money depended on selling a product or service. Today, that's changed as customers are, at times, willing to pay for what we stand for: better service, better support, more innovation, more partnership in developing new products.

This section of this article assumes that you believe a plan is needed, and that this plan should weave together your desires with those of your customers. We've reviewed a number of marketing plans and come up with a nine-step model. It is perhaps more than what your organization needs today, but none of the steps are unimportant.

Our model combines some of the basics of a conventional plan with some new threads that we believe will push your plan over the edge, from being satisfactory to being necessary. These include:

• Using and improving the former domain of public relations, image, as a marketing tool.

• Integrating all the business functions that touch your customers into a single, customer-focused strategic marketing plan.

• Borrowing from Total Quality theories to establish performance measures beyond the financial report to help you note customer trends.

• Making sure that the people needed to deliver your marketing objectives are part of your plan.

• "Selling" your plan to the people whose support is essential to its success.

Taking the Plan Off the Shelf

First, let's look at the model itself. Remember that one of the primary criticisms of any plan is that it becomes a binder on a shelf, never to be seen again until budget time next year. Planning should be an iterative process, feeding off itself and used to guide and measure.

Whether you're asked to create a marketing plan or write the marketing section of the strategic plan for your business, your document is going to include what the business is trying to achieve, a careful analysis of your market, the products and services you offer to that market, and how you will market and sell products or services to your customer.

1. Describe the Business

You are probably in one of two situations: either you need to write a description of your business or you can rely on an existing document found in your annual report, the strategic plan, or a capabilities brochure. The description should include, at minimum:

• Your company's purpose;

• Who you deliver products or services to; and

• What you deliver to those customers.

Too often, such descriptions omit a discussion about what you want your business to stand for—your image. This is increasingly important as customers report they are looking for more than the product or service; they're in search of a partner. The only way to address image is to know who you want to be, who your customers think you are, and how you can bridge the gap between the two.

Part of defining your image is knowing where you are strong and where you are weak. For instance, if your current yield rate is 99.997 percent and customers rate you as the preferred supplier, then you might identify operations as a key to your company's image. Most companies tend to be their own worst critic, so start by listing all your strengths. Then identify weaknesses or the threats you face, either due to your own limitations or from the increased competency of a competitor.

The description also includes what your business delivers to its owners, be they shareholders, private owners, or employees. Usually this is stated in financial terms: revenue, return on investment or equity, economic value added, cash generated, operating margin or earnings per share. The other measures your organization uses to monitor its performance may be of interest to outsiders, but save them for the

A marketing plan is your strategy for wooing customers. It's based on listening and reacting to what they say.

Because customer's priorities are constantly changing, a marketing plan should change with them. For years, conventional wisdom was 'prepare a five year marketing plan and review it every year.' But change happens a lot faster than it did 20 or even 10 years ago.

For that reason, Bob Dawson of The Business Group, a consulting firm in Freemont, California, recommends that his clients prepare a three year plan and review it every quarter. Frequent reviews enable companies to identify potential problems and opportunities before their competition, he explains.

"Preventative maintenance for your company is as important as putting oil in your car," Dawson says. "You don't wait a whole year to do it. You can't change history but you can anticipate what's going to happen."

ESSENTIAL COMPONENTS

Most marketing plans consist of three sections. The first section should identify the organization's goals. The second section should establish a method for attaining them. The third section focuses on creating a system for implementing the strategy.

Although some plans identify as many as six or eight goals, many experts suggest a company whittle its list to one or two key objectives and focus on them.

"One of the toughest things is sticking to one message," observes Mark Bilfield, account director for integrated

measurement section of your plan.

The result of all this describing and listing is that you should have a fairly good idea of where you are and where you want to be, which naturally leads to objectives for the coming 6, 12, or 18 months, if not longer.

2. Analyze the Market

This is the section you probably believe you own. *Marketing Tools* challenges you to look at this as a section jointly owned by most everyone working with you. In a smaller company, the lead managers may own various pieces of this section. In a larger organization, you may need to pull in the ideas and data available from other departments, such as logistics, competitor intelligence, research and development, and the function responsible for quality control or quality assurance. All have two things in common: delivering value to customers, and beating the competition. Together, you can thoroughly cover the following areas:

• **Your target markets.** What markets do you currently compete in? What do you know about them in terms of potential, dollars available, and your share of the market? Something frequently prepared

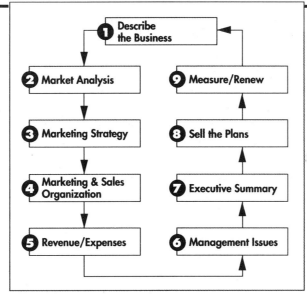

1. Describe the Business
2. Market Analysis
3. Marketing Strategy
4. Marketing & Sales Organization
5. Revenue/Expenses
6. Management Issues
7. Executive Summary
8. Sell the Plans
9. Measure/Renew

for products is a life cycle chart; you might want to do the same for your market. Is it embryonic, developing, mature or in decline? Are there new markets to exploit?

• **Customer Knowledge.** Your colleagues in Quality, Distribution, Engineering, or other organizations can be helpful in finding what you need.

The customer's objectives. What threats does your customer face? What goals does the customer have? Work with your customer to define these so you can become a partner instead of a variable component.

How is the customer addressing her or his markets? Do you know as much about your cus-

tomer's position as you know about your own? If not, find out.

How big is each customer, really? You may find you're spending more time on a less important customer than on the customers who can break you. Is your customer growing or in decline? What plans does the customer have to expand or acquire growth? What innovations are in development?

What does your customer value? Price, product quality, service, innovation, delivery? The better you know what's driving your customer's purchasing decision, the better you'll be able to respond.

• **Clearly identify the alternatives your customer has.**

As one customer told employees at a major supplier, "While you've been figuring out how to get by, we've been figuring out how to get by without you." Is backward integration—a situation in which the customer develops the capability in-house—possible? Is there an abundance of other suppliers? What is your business doing to avoid having your customers looking for alternatives?

• **Know your competition.** Your competitors are the obvious alternative for your customer, and thus represent your biggest threat. You can find what you need to know about your competitors through newspaper reports, public records, at trade shows, and from your customers: the size of expansions, the strengths that competitor has, its latest innovations. Do you know how your competition approaches your customers?

• **Describe the Environment.** What changes have occurred in the last 18 months? In the past year? What could change in the near future and over a longer period of time? This should include any kinds of laws or regulations that might affect you, the entry or deletion of competitors, and shifts in technology. Also, keep in mind that internal change does affect

---

marketing of Nissan and Infiniti cars at TBWA Chiat/Day in Los Angeles, which handles national advertising, direct marketing, public relations, and promotions for the automaker. Bilfield argues that a focused, consistent message is easier to communicate to the market place and to different disciplines within the corporation than a broad, encompassing one. Therefore, he advises, "unless there is something drastically wrong with the idea, stick with it."

SECTION I: GOALS

The goals component of your plan is the most fundamental. Consider it a kind of thinking out loud: Why are you writing this plan? What do you want to accomplish? What

do you want to achieve in the next quarter? The next year? The next three years?

Like taping your New Year's resolution to the refrigerator, the goals section is a constant reminder of what you want to achieve. The key difference between a New Year's resolution and your marketing goals, however, is you can't achieve the latter alone.

To achieve your marketing goals you've got to convince your customers to behave in a certain way. If you're a soft drink manufacturer you may want them to try your company's latest wild berry flavor. If you're a new bank in town, you need to familiarize people with your name and convince them to give your institution a try. Or perhaps you're a family-owned retailer who needs to remind your customers. For instance, is a key leader in your business planning to retire? If so, decision-making, operations or management style may change—and your customer may have obvious concerns. You can add some depth to this section, too, by portraying several different scenarios:

• What happens if we do nothing beyond last year?
• What happens if we capitalize on our strengths?
• What might happen if our image slips?
• What happens if we do less this year than last?

• 3. The Marketing Strategy
The marketing strategy consists of what you offer customers and the price you charge. Start by providing a complete description of each product or service and what it provides to your customers. Life cycle, again, is an important part of this. Is your technology or product developing, mature or in decline? Depending on how your company is organized, a variety of people are responsible for this information, right down to whoever is figuring out how to package the product and how it will be delivered. Find out who needs to be included and make sure their knowledge is used.
The marketing strategy is driven by everything

you've done up to this point. Strategies define the approaches you will use to market the company. For instance, if you are competing on the basis of service and support rather than price, your strategy may consist of emphasizing relationships. You will then develop tactics that support that strategy: market the company vs. the product;

increase sales per client; assure customer responsiveness. Now, what action or programs will you use to make sure that happens?
Note: strategy leads. No program, regardless of how good it is, should make the cut if it doesn't link to your business strategies and your customer.

The messages you must craft to support the strategies often are overlooked. Messages are the consistent themes you want your customer to know, to remember, to feel when he or she hears, reads, or views anything about your company or products. The method by which you deliver your messages comes under the heading of actions or programs.

Finally, you need to determine how you'll mea-

sure your own success, beyond meeting the sales forecast. How will you know if your image takes a beating? How will you know whether the customer is satisfied, or has just given up complaining? If you don't know, you'll be caught reacting to events, instead of planning for them.

Remember, your customer's measure of your

success may be quite different from what you may think. Your proposed measures must be defined by what your customer values, and they have to be quantifiable. You may be surprised at how willing the customer is to cooperate with you in completing surveys, participating in third-party interviews, or taking part in a full-scale analysis of your company as a supplier. Use caution in assuming that winning awards means you have a measurable indicator. Your measures should be stated in terms of strategies, not plaques or trophies.

4. The Marketing and Sales Organization

The most frequently overlooked element in business is something we usu-

ally relegate to the Personnel or Human Resources Office—people. They're what makes everything possible. Include them. Begin with a chart that shows the organization for both Marketing and Sales. You may wish to indicate any interdependent relationships that exist (for instance, with Quality).

Note which of the roles are critical, particularly in terms of customer contact. Just as important, include positions, capabilities, and numbers of people needed in the future. How will you gain these skills without impacting your cost per sale? Again, it's time to be creative and provide options.

5. Revenue and Expense

In this section, you're going to project the revenue your plan will produce. This is usually calculated by evaluating the value of your market(s) and determining the dollar value of your share of that market. You need to factor in any changes you believe will occur, and you'll need to identify the sources of revenue, by product or service. Use text to tell the story; use graphs to show the story.

After you've noted where the money is coming from, explain what money you need to deliver

---

customers of the importance of reliability and a proven track record in the face of new competition.

The goals in each of these cases differ with the audiences. The soft drink manufacturer is asking an existing customer to try something new; the bank is trying to attract new customers; the retailer wants to retain existing customers.

Each company wants to influence its customers' behavior. The company that is most likely to succeed is the one that understands its customers the best.

There's no substitute for knowledge. You need to understand the demographic and psychographic makeup of the customers you are trying to reach, as well as the best methods for getting their attention.

Do your research. Learn as much as possible about your audience. Trade associations, trade journals and government statistics and surveys are excellent resources, but chances are you have a lot of data within your own business that you haven't tapped. Look at what you know about your customer already and find ways to bolster that information. Companies should constantly be asking clients what they want and how they would use a new product.

"If you're not asking people that use your end product, then everything you're doing is an assumption," argues Dawson.

In addition, firms should ask customers how they perceive the products and services they receive. Too often, companies have an image of themselves that they broad-

the projected return. This will include staff wages and benefits for your organization, as well as the cost for specific programs you plan to implement.

During this era of budget cuts, do yourself a favor by prioritizing these programs. For instance, if one of your key strategies is to expand to a new market via new technologies, products, or services, you will need to allocate appropriate dollars. What is the payback on the investment in marketing, and when will revenues fully pay back the investment? Also, provide an explanation of programs that will be deleted should a cut in funding be required. Again, combine text and spreadsheets to tell and to show.

6. Management Issues

This section represents your chance to let management know what keeps you awake at night. What might or could go wrong? What are the problems your company faces in customer relations? Are there technology needs that are going unattended? Again, this can be a collaborative effort that identifies your concerns. In addition, you may want to identify long-term issues, as well as those that are of immediate significance.

To keep this section as objective as possible, list

the concerns and the business strategy or strategies they affect. What are the short-term and long-term risks? For instance, it is here that you might want to go into further detail about a customer's actions that look like the beginnings of backward integration.

7. Executive Summary

Since most senior leaders want a quick-look reference, it's best to include a one-page Executive Summary that covers these points:
- Your organization's objectives
- Budget requirements
- Revenue projections
- Critical management issues

When you're publishing the final plan document, you'll want the executive summary to be Page One.

8. Sell the Plan

This is one of the steps that often is overlooked. Selling your plan is as important as writing it. Otherwise, no one owns it, except you. The idea is to turn it into a rallying point that helps your company move forward. And to do that, you need to turn as many people as possible into ambassadors for your marketing efforts.

First, set up a time to present the plan to everyone who helped you with information and data. Make sure that they feel

some sense of ownership, but that they also see how their piece ties into the whole. This is one of those instances where you need to say your plan, show your plan, discuss your plan. Only after all three steps are completed will they *hear* the plan.

After you've shared the information across the organization, reserve some time on the executive calendar. Have a couple of leaders review the plan first, giving you feedback on the parts where they have particular expertise. Then, present the plan at a staff meeting.

Is It Working?

You may think your job is finished. It's not. You need to convey the key parts of this plan to co-workers throughout the business. They need to know what the business is trying to achieve. Their livelihood, not just that of the owners, is at stake. From their phone-answering technique to the way they process an order, every step has meaning to the customer.

9. Measure/Renew

Once you've presented your plan and people understand it, you have to continuously work the plan and share information about it. The best way to help people see trends and respond appropriately is to have meaningful measures.

In the language of Total Quality, these are the Key Result Indicators—the things that have importance to your customers and that are signals to your performance.

For instance, measure your ability to deliver on a customer request; the amount of time it takes to respond to a customer inquiry; your productivity per employee; cash flow; cycle time; yield rates. The idea is to identify a way to measure those things that are critical to you and to your customer.

Review those measurements. Share the information with the entire business and begin the process all over again. Seek new ideas and input to improve your performance. Go after more data and facts. And then renew your plan and share it with everyone—all over again.

It's an extensive process, but it's one that spreads the word—and spreads the ownership. It's the step that ensures that your plan will be constantly in use, and constantly at work for your business.

Carole Hedden is a writer and communication/planning consultant living in Elmira, New York.

---

cast but fail to live up to. That frustrates consumers and makes them feel deceived.

Companies that claim to offer superior service often appear to renege on their promises because their definition of 'service' doesn't mesh with their customers', says Bilfield.

"Airlines and banks are prime offenders," says Bilfield. "They tout service, and when the customers go into the airport or the bank, they have to wait in long lines."

The problem often lies in the company's assumptions about what customers really want. While an airline may feel it is living up to its claim of superior service because it distributes warm towels and mints after a meal, a business traveler will probably place a higher value on its

competitor's on-time record and policy for returning lost luggage.

SECTION II: THE STRATEGY

Unfortunately, after taking the time and conducting the research to determine who their audience is and what their message should be, companies often fail by zooming ahead with a plan. An attitude of, "OK, we know who we're after and we know what we want to say, so let's go!" seems to take over.

More often than not, that gung-ho way of thinking leads to disaster because companies have skipped a critical step: they haven't established and communicated an internal strategy for attaining their goals. They want to take their

HELP IS ON THE WAY

THREE SOFTWARE PACKAGES THAT WILL HELP YOU GET STARTED

Writing a marketing plan may be daunting, but there is a variety of software tools out there to help you get started. Found in electronics and book stores, the tools are in many ways like a Marketing 101 textbook. The difference lies in how they help.

Software tools have a distinct advantage: They actually force you to write, and that's the toughest part of any marketing plan. Sometimes called "MBA In a Box," these systems guide you through a planning process. Some even provide wording that you can copy into your own document and edit to fit your own business. Presto! A boiler plate plan! Others provide a system of interviewing and questioning that creates a custom plan for your operation. The more complex tools demand an integrated approach to planning, one that brings together the full force of your organization, not just Sales or Advertising.

1. Crush

Crush, a modestly named new product from a modestly named new company, HOT, takes a multimedia approach. (HOT stands for Hands-On Technology; *Crush* apparently stands for *Crushing the Competition*)

Just introduced a few months ago, *Crush* is a multimedia application for Macintosh or Windows PCs. It features the competitive analysis methods of Flegis McKenna, marketing guru to Apple, Intel and Genentech; and it features Mr. McKenna himself as your mentor, offering guidance via on-screen video. As you work through each section of a complete market analysis, McKenna provides germane comments; in addition, you can see video case studies of marketing success stories like Intuit software.

Crush provides worksheets and guidance for analyzing your products, customers, market trends and competitors, and helps you generate an action plan. The "mentor" approach makes it a useful tool for self-education; as you work through the examples and develop your company's marketing plan, you build your own expertise.

2. Marketing Plan Pro

Palo Alto's *Marketing Plan Pro* is a basic guide, useful for smaller businesses or ones in which the company leader wears a number of different hats, including marketing. It includes the standard spreadsheet capability, as well as the ability to chart numerical data. *Marketing Plan Pro* uses a pyramid process.

I liked the pyramid for a simple reason: It asks you to define messages for your business as part of your tactics. Without a message, it's easy to jump around, reacting to the marketplace instead of anticipating, leaving customers wondering what really is significant about your company or your product.

The step-by-step process is simple, and a sample plan shows how all the information works together. The customer-focus aspect of the plan seemed a little weak, demanding only sales potential and buying capacity of the customers. Targeted marketing is increasingly important, and the user may want to really expand how this section is used beyond what the software requires.

The package displays, at a glance, your strategy, the tactics you develop for each strategy, and the action plan or programs you choose to support the strategy. That could help when you're trying to prioritize creative ideas, eliminating those that really don't deliver what the strategy demands. Within

message to the public without pausing to get feedback from inside the company.

For a marketing plan to work, everyone within the company must understand the company's message and work cooperatively to establish a method for taking that message to the public.

For example, if you decide the goal of your plan is to promote the superior service your company offers, you'd better make sure all aspects of your business are on board. Your manufacturing process should meet the highest standards. Your financial department should develop credit and leasing programs that make it easier for customers to use your product. Finally, your customer relations personnel should be trained to respond to problems quickly and efficiently, and to use the contact as an opportunity to find out more about what customers want.

"I'm always amazed when I go into the shipping department of some company and say, 'What is your mission? What's the message you want to give to your end user?' and they say, 'I don't know. I just know I've got to get these shipments out on time,' " says Dawson.

Because the success of integrated marketing depends on a consistent, cohesive message, employees throughout the company need to understand the firm's marketing goals and their role in helping to fulfill them.

"It's very important to bring employees in on the process," says James Lowry, chairman of the marketing department at Ball State University. "Employees today are better than any we've had before. They want to know what's going on in the organization. They don't want to be left out."

Employees are ambassadors for your company. Every time they interact with a customer or vendor, they're marketing your company. The more knowledgeable and helpful they are, the better they reflect on your firm.

At Nordstrom, a Seattle-based retailer, sales associates are empowered to use their best judgment in all situations to make a customer happy.

"We think our sales associates are the best marketing department," said spokeswoman Amy Jones. "We think word of mouth is the best advertising you can have." As a result, although Nordstrom has stores in only 15 states, it has forged a national reputation.

each of three columns, you can click on a word and get help. Click on the heading program: a list of sample actions is displayed. They may not be what you're looking for, but if this is your first plan, they're lifesavers.

I also really liked *Marketing Plan Pro's* user's manual. It not only explains how the software works with your computer, it helps with business terms and provides a guide to planning, walking you through step-by-step.

3. Plan Write

Plan Write, created by Business Resource Software, Inc., is exponentially more powerful than *Marketing Plan Pro. Plan Write* brings together the breadth of the business, integrating information as far flung as distribution systems and image. And this software places your marketing strategy within the broader context of a business plan, the approach that tends to prove most effective.

As with *Marketing Plan Pro, Plan Write* provides a sample plan. The approach is traditional, incorporating a look at the business environ-

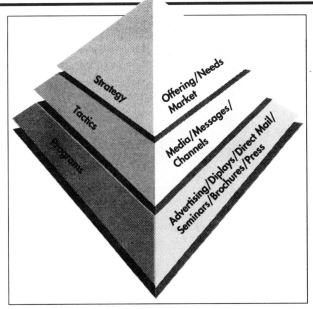

Pyramid Power: *Plan Write's pyramid approach asks the user to define the messages for a business as part of the tactics.*

ment, the competition, the product or service mix you are offering, the way you will tell customers about that mix, pricing, delivery, and support.

Among the sections that were particularly strong was one on customer alternatives and people planning. Under the heading of customer alternatives, you're required to incorporate competitive information with customer information. If you don't meet the customer's needs, where could he or she go? Most often we look only at the competition, without trying to imagine how the customer is thinking. This exercise is particularly valuable to the company who leads the market.

The people part of planning too often is dumped on the personnel guy instead of being seen as a critical component of your organization's capabilities. *Plan Write* requires that you include how marketing is being handled, and how sales will be accomplished. In addition, it pushes you to define what skills will be needed in the future and where the gaps are between today and the future. People, in this plan, are viewed as a strategic component.

Plan Write offers a fully integrated spreadsheet that can import from or export to most of the popular spreadsheet programs you may already be using. Another neat feature allows you to enter numerical data and select from among 14 different graphing styles to display your information. You just click on the style you want to view, and the data is reconfigured.

Probably the biggest danger in dealing with software packages such as *Marketing Plan Pro* and *Plan Write* is to think the software is the answer. It's merely a guide.

—*Carole Hedden*

If companies regard marketing as the exclusive province of the marketing department, they're destined to fail.

"Accounting and sales and other departments have to work together hand in hand," says Dawson. "If they don't, you're going to have a problem in the end."

For example, in devising an integrated marketing campaign for the Nissan 200SX, Chiat/Day marketers worked in strategic business units that included a variety of disciplines such as engineers, representatives from the parts and service department, and creative people. By taking a broad view of the business and building inter-related activities to support its goals, Chiat/Day was able to create a seamless campaign for the 200SX that weaves advertising, in-store displays, and direct marketing together seamlessly.

"When everybody understands what the mission is, it's easier," asserts Bilfield. "It's easier to go upstream in the same direction than to go in different directions."

After bringing the different disciplines within your company on board, you're ready to design the external marketing program needed to support your goals. Again, the principle of integrated marketing comes into play: The message should be focused and consistent, and each step of the process should bring the consumer one step closer to buying your product.

In the case of Chiat/Day's campaign for the Nissan 200SX, the company used the same theme, graphics, type faces, and message to broadcast a consistent statement.

Introduced about the same time as the latest Batman movie, the campaign incorporates music and graphics from the television series. Magazine ads include an 800 number potential customers can call if they want to receive an information kit. Kits are personalized and include the name of a local Nissan dealer, a certificate for a test drive, and a voucher entitling test drivers to a free gift.

By linking each step of the process, Chiat/Day can chart the number of calls, test drives, and sales a particular ad elicits. Like a good one-two punch, the direct marketing picks up where the national advertising leaves off, leveraging the broad exposure and targeting it at the most likely buyers.

While the elaborate 200SX campaign may seem foolproof, a failure to integrate the process at any step along the way could result in a lost sale.

For example, if a potential client were to test drive the car and encounter a dealer who knew nothing about the free gift accompanying the test drive, the customer would feel justifiably annoyed. Conversely, a well-informed sales associate who can explain the gift will be mailed to the test driver in a few weeks will engender a positive response.

SECTION III EXECUTION

The final component of an integrated marketing plan is the implementation phase. This is where the budget comes in.

How much you'll need to spend depends on your goals. If a company wants to expand its market share or promote its products in a new region, it will probably have to spend more than it would to maintain its position in an existing market.

Again, you'll need to create a system for keeping your employees informed. You might consider adding an element to your company newsletter that features people from different departments talking about the marketing problems they encounter and how they overcome them. Or you might schedule a regular meeting for department heads to discuss marketing ideas so they can report back to their employees with news from around the company.

Finally, you'll need to devise a system for monitoring your marketing program. A database, similar to the one created from calls to the 200SX's 800 number, can be an invaluable tool for determining if your message is being well received.

It's important to establish time frames for achieving your goals early in the process. If you want to increase your market share, for instance, you should determine the rate at which you intend to add new customers. Failing to achieve that rate could signal a flaw in your plan or its execution, or an unrealistic goal.

"Remember, integrated marketing is a long-range way of thinking," warns Dawson. "Results are not going to be immediate."

Like any investment, marketing requires patience, perseverance, and commitment if it is to bear fruit. While not all companies are forward thinking enough to understand the manifold gains of integrated marketing, the ones that don't embrace it will ultimately pay a tremendous price.

MORE INFO

Software for writing marketing plans:
Crush, Hands-On Technology; for more information, call (800) 772-2580 ext. 14 or (415) 579-7755; e-mail info@HOT.sf.ca.us; or visit the Web site at http://www.HOT.sf.ca.us.
Marketing Plan Pro, Palo Alto Software: for more information, call (800) 229-7526 or (503) 683-6162.
Plan Write for Marketing, Business Resource Software, Inc.: for more information, call (800) 423-1228 or (512) 251-7541.

Books about marketing plans:
Twelve Simple Steps to a Winning Marketing Plan, Geraldine A. Larkin (1992, Probus Publishing Co.)*
Preparing the Marketing Plan, by David Parmerlee (1993, NTC Business Books)*
Your Marketing Plan: A Workbook for Effective Business Promotion (Second Edition), by Chris Pryor (1995, Oregon Small Business Development Center Network)*
Your Business Plan: A Workbook for Owners of Small Businesses, by Dennis J. Sargent, Maynard N. Chambers, and Chris Pryor (1995, Oregon Small Business Development Center Network)*

Recommended reading:
Managing for Results, Peter Drucker
The One to One Future: Building Relationships One Customer at a Time, by Don Peppers and Martha Rogers, Ph.D. (1993, Currency/Doubleday)*
"Real World Results," by Don Schultz (*Marketing Tools* magazine, April/May 1994)*

Open up your thinking to your customer's entire experience with your product or service.

Discovering New Points of Differentiation

Drawings by Paul Meisel

by Ian C. MacMillan and Rita Gunther McGrath

Most profitable strategies are built on differentiation: offering customers something they value that competitors don't have. But most companies, in seeking to differentiate themselves, focus their energy only on their products or services. In fact, a company has the opportunity to differentiate itself at every point where it comes in contact with its customers—from the moment customers realize that they need a product or service to the time when they no longer want it and decide to dispose of it. We believe that if companies open up their creative thinking to their customers' entire experience with a product or service—what we call the *consumption chain*—they can uncover opportunities to position their offerings in ways that they, and their competitors, would never have thought possible.

Take the case of Blyth Industries, a candle manufacturer. By differentiating and redifferentiating its products, Blyth has been able to grow from a $2 million U.S. producer of candles used for religious purposes to a global candle and accessory business with nearly $500 million in sales and a market value of $1.2 billion. Not bad for a company in an industry that, as CEO Robert B. Goergen says, "has been in decline for 300 years." Blyth's story is, quite simply, a manifestation of the power of strategic differentiation.

Business history is full of stories of entrepreneurs who stumbled upon a great idea that then became the cornerstone of a successful company. But finding ways to differentiate one's company doesn't have to be an act of genius or intuition. It is a skill that can be developed and nurtured. We have designed a two-part approach that can help companies continually identify new points of differentiation and develop the ability to generate successful differentiation strategies. The first part, "Mapping the Consumption Chain," captures the customer's total experience with a product or service. The second, "Analyzing Your Customer's Experience," shows managers how directed brainstorming about each step in the consumption chain can elicit numerous ways to differentiate even the most mundane product or service.

Ian C. MacMillan is the George W. Taylor Professor of Entrepreneurial Studies and a professor of management at the University of Pennsylvania's Wharton School in Philadelphia. Rita Gunther McGrath is an assistant professor in the Management of Organizations Division of Columbia University's Graduate School of Business in New York City. MacMillan and McGrath are coauthors of "Discovery-Driven Planning" (HBR July–August 1995) and "Discover Your Products' Hidden Potential" (HBR May–June 1996).

Mapping the Consumption Chain

As we've said, the first step toward strategic differentiation is to map your customer's entire experience with your product or service. We recommend that companies perform this exercise for each important customer segment.

To begin, assemble groups from all

The first step is to map your customer's entire experience with a product.

areas of your company—in particular, those employees who use marketing data and those who have face-to-face or phone contact with customers. Charge the groups with identifying, for each major market segment, all the steps through which customers pass from the time they first become aware of your product to the time when they finally have to dispose of it or discontinue using it.

Naturally, every product or service will have a somewhat different consumption chain. However, a few activities are common to most chains. Consider the following questions, each of which illustrates one of those activities. Then, as the group begins to get a feel for the special relationship between your customers and your products, ask questions about more complex activities that pertain to your business.

How do people become aware of their need for your product or service? Are consumers aware that you can satisfy their need? Are they aware that they even have a need that can be satisfied? Your company can create a powerful source of differentiation if it can make consumers aware of a need in a way that is unique and subtle.

Consider the problem of differentiating an everyday consumer product, such as a toothbrush. For many people, brushing is a ritual to which they pay relatively little attention. As a consequence, many brushes are used well past the point when their bristles are worn and are no longer effective. Toothbrush maker Oral-B discovered a way to capitalize on this widespread habit. The company, by introducing a patented blue dye in the center bristles of its toothbrushes, found a way to have the brush itself communicate to the customer. As the brush is used, the dye gradually fades. When the dye

is gone, the brush is no longer effective and should be replaced. Customers are thus made aware of a need that previously had gone unrecognized. So far, the idea sounds like something out of Marketing 101. What gives it particular value is that the need can be filled *only* by Oral-B's patented process. The company turned differentiation into a competitive advantage.

How do consumers find your offering? Opportunities for differentiating on the basis of the search process include making your product available when others are not (24-hour telephone-order lines), offering your product in places where competitors do not offer theirs (the mini McDonald's outlets in Wal-Mart stores), and making your product ubiquitous (Coca-Cola). Making the search process less complicated, more convenient, less expensive, and more habitual are all ways in which companies can differentiate themselves. And when competitors can't or won't do the same—at least, not right away—you have the potential for a strategic advantage.

One example is the rapid growth of catalog sales in channels formerly dominated by retail chains. Consumers now can obtain detailed, up-to-the-minute information about a breathtaking range of products over the telephone or through the Internet, without enduring the inconvenience of visiting a showroom and the often inadequate knowledge of the floor sales staff. The PC Connection & Mac Connection, a company that sells computers through its catalog, operates a 24-hour-a-day, seven-day-a-week toll-free phone number for people wanting information about computers, software, and related products. When a caller expresses an interest in buying a computer system, a company representative asks a set of questions to narrow down the possibilities to a few good candidates. The rep and the consumer then can discuss each option in detail. What is remarkable about this approach is that, in effect, it allows consumers to tailor the search experience to their own needs.

How do consumers make their final selections? After a consumer has narrowed down the possibilities, he or she must make a choice. Can you make the selection process more comfortable, less irritating, or more convenient? Look for the ideal situation, in which competitors' procedures actu-

ally discourage people from selecting their products, while your procedures encourage people to come to you. Citibank for years captured a significant share of the college student market for credit cards simply by making it easy for students to obtain a card while competitors made it difficult.

Another example of this dynamic is playing out right now in the used-car business. For many potential customers, the experience of choosing a used car is an ordeal—to the point where one CEO of a major automaker observed that some people would rather have a root canal. But a new method of selecting cars is transforming the industry. Companies such as CarMax Auto Superstore and AutoNation USA have targeted the selection experience as their competitive focus. At a CarMax showroom, customers sit in front of a computer and specify what features they are looking for in an automobile. They can then, in private, scroll through detailed descriptions of cars that might meet their needs. The final (and only) price for each vehicle is listed. A sales assistant then lets the customers inspect the autos that interest them and handles all the paperwork if they decide to buy one. The "selling" is done not by the salespeople but by the selection process the customers create for themselves.

How do customers order and purchase your product or service? This question is particularly important for relatively low-cost, high-volume items. Can a company differentiate itself by making the process of ordering and purchasing more convenient?

Can you make the buying process more convenient and less irritating?

American Hospital Supply revolutionized its industry by radically simplifying the ordering and restocking process for such products as bandages, tongue depressors, syringes, and disinfectants. The company installed computer terminals at each hospital and medical supply store with which it did business. The terminals connected those customers directly to the company's system, allowing direct drop shipment and automatic restocking whenever supplies fell below a certain level. Hallmark uses a similar approach for its greeting cards.

Many companies, including ice-cream makers and pet-food manufacturers, are also using this method to stock supermarket shelves, reaping the benefits of preferred access to these crucial outlets as well as of superior displays. Another, more subtle benefit of this form of differentiation is that it imposes a switching cost on customers that might be tempted to try another supplier. Once customers have signed on, it is expensive for them to switch; this deterrent creates a barrier to competition and, once again, a potential strategic advantage for the supplier.

CarMax and AutoNation "sell" cars by letting customers create their own selection process.

How is your product or service delivered? Delivery affords many opportunities for differentiation, especially if the product is an impulse purchase or if the customer needs it immediately. Let's return to our catalog computer dealer, the PC Connection. Customers can call its toll-free number as late as 3 A.M. to receive "next-day" shipments of items in stock. How does the company do it? The amazing turnaround times are possible because the warehousing and distribution facilities are conveniently located near an Airborne Express hub. Packages can be picked up at the warehouse, transferred to Airborne, and shipped to the customer in a matter of hours. Not only does this delivery strategy constitute a real benefit for customers, but, because there are a limited number of opportunities for such a warehouse-hub connection, competitors will find it hard to adopt the same strategy.

What happens when your product or service is delivered? An often overlooked opportunity for differentiation lies in considering what has to happen from the time a company delivers a product to the time the customer actually uses it. Opening, inspecting, transporting, and assembling products are frequently major issues for customers.

That applies even to the delivery of services. Consider how difficult it can be to get an auto accident claim processed and paid by an insurance company. Now consider how Progressive Insurance of Cleveland, Ohio, tackled the problem. The company has a fleet of claims adjusters on the road every day, ready to rush to the scene of any auto accident in their territory. There they can record all the information they need and often settle claims on the spot for policyholders. The process has greatly increased customer satisfaction by eliminating the hassle and delay that so often accompany conventional reporting, inspection, and assessment methods. A side benefit for the company is that its approach also has decreased the incidence of fraud by reducing the opportunity to file false claims and inflate repair bills.

How is your product installed? This step in the consumption chain is particularly relevant for companies with complex products. For example, installation has presented an enormous barrier for computer manufacturers trying to break into the novice-PC-user market. Computer beginners are notoriously intolerant of such on-screen messages as "Disk Error 23."

Compaq Computer, with its Presario line, was among the first to target installation as a source of differentiation. Instead of providing an instruction book filled with technical terminology, Compaq offers its customers a poster that clearly illustrates the ten installation steps. The company uses color-coded cords, cables, and outlets to simplify installation further and also has rigged its computers so that a cheerful video and audio presentation leads new users through the setup and registration process when they first turn on the machine.

How is your product or service paid for? Many companies unwittingly cause their customers major difficulties with their payment policies. Here's a test to see whether payment might be such an issue for your customers: Take a walk over to your accounts-receivable department and ask to see a copy of a recent invoice. If your company is anything like about 80% of those we have worked with, the invoice will be virtually incomprehensible. Why? Because invoices are generally designed by systems people for systems, not customers. Given the prevalence of this situation, your company may find opportunities to set itself apart by making the whole payment process easier for customers to understand.

You may discover even greater opportunities by rethinking why your company uses its current payment policy in the first place. We once worked with a company in the energy control business that was having a hard time selling its services to residential co-op owners. At every co-op, the company ran into opposition from a hard core of owners who resisted the capital outlay involved in installing an energy management system. The company eventually won a huge share of the co-op market by altering its policy. Customers no longer pay an up-front installation fee; instead, they pay over time, out of the energy savings.

How is your product stored? When it is expensive, inconvenient, or downright dangerous for customers to have a product simply sitting around, the opportunities for differentiation abound. Air Products and Chemicals, a producer of industrial gases, grew to dominate its market segments by addressing the problem of storage. Realizing that most of its customers—chemical companies—would rather avoid the burden of having to store vast quantities of dangerous high-pressure gases, Air Products built small industrial-gas plants next to customers' sites. The move pleased customers; it also generated switching costs. Best of all, once an Air Products plant was in place, competitors had little opportunity to move in.

How is your product moved around? What difficulties do customers encounter when they must transport a product from one location to another? Whether the journey is across a room or across a state, this step in the consumption chain is another often-overlooked opportunity for differentiation. Ask yourself the following questions: Does the customer find the product fragile? Difficult to package? Awkward to move?

Consider how John Sculley's marketing team at Pepsi-Cola used packaging as a way to differentiate Pepsi from Coke. Sculley's team created a distinct—if temporary—advantage for Pepsi in the early 1970s by designing plastic bottles that were lighter, and thus easier for customers to carry, than the heavy glass bottles of the time. The beauty of the move was that it not only made carrying soda easier, but it also reduced the advantage of Coke's well-known contoured glass bottle. At the time, it was difficult to produce plastic bottles in that shape.

What is the customer really using your product for? Finding better ways for customers to use a product or service is a powerful differentiator. And such opportunities abound, especially for companies whose products are expensive and used relatively infrequently. General Electric's Transportation Systems division, which manufactures diesel-electric locomo-

Is There a Way to Differentiate Selling Gas?

Consider the "purchase link" of the consumption chain.

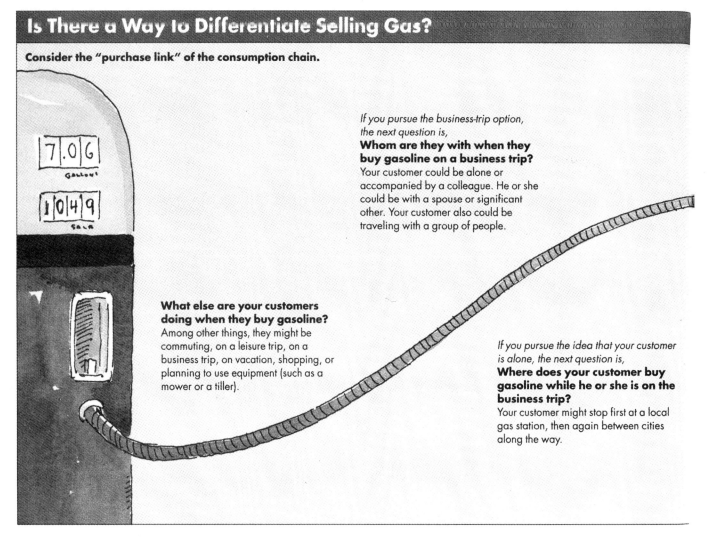

If you pursue the business-trip option, the next question is,
Whom are they with when they buy gasoline on a business trip?
Your customer could be alone or accompanied by a colleague. He or she could be with a spouse or significant other. Your customer also could be traveling with a group of people.

What else are your customers doing when they buy gasoline?
Among other things, they might be commuting, on a leisure trip, on a business trip, on vacation, shopping, or planning to use equipment (such as a mower or a tiller).

If you pursue the idea that your customer is alone, the next question is,
Where does your customer buy gasoline while he or she is on the business trip?
Your customer might stop first at a local gas station, then again between cities along the way.

---

tives, used this step in the consumption chain as the basis for rethinking its business.

With few exceptions, the railroads that are the customers for GE's locomotives are not all that attached to a particular unit. What they really want to know is, if they have freight to ship, will a locomotive be there to haul it? GE is working on an arrangement through which the company will guarantee that a locomotive will be available on demand. Under that arrangement, GE will take over the management of all the engines in the customer's system. It will relieve the customer of repair and maintenance concerns, and also will gain economies of scale by managing an entire network. What's more, the entry barrier created by such a system can be formidable.

What do customers need help with when they use your product?
The company with the most helpful response has a significant advantage here. GE, for instance, has an enormously popular 800 number that is available 24 hours a day to help people

who have difficulty using any of the company's consumer products. Similarly, Butterball Turkey's 24-hour hot line fields cooking questions from hundreds of customers every Thanksgiving. Butterball has recently supplemented its hot line with an Internet home page and a turkey-cooking guide that its customers can download.

What about returns or exchanges? Too many companies put all their efforts into the selling side of the product life cycle, forgetting that long-term loyalty requires attention to customers' needs throughout their experience with a product. Handling things well when the product doesn't work out can be as powerful as meeting the need that motivated the initial purchase.

Nordstrom is an excellent example of a company that has taken this issue to heart. The clothing retailer captured

national publicity in the 1970s when one of its store managers "took back" a set of tires from a customer despite the fact that Nordstrom did not sell tires. By focusing on and aggressively promoting its no-questions-asked return policy, Nordstrom has enhanced

To analyze your customer's experience, consider how five simple questions apply at each link in the chain.

its position as a company that provides unique customer service. Customers may be unhappy with the brands they return, but they are not unhappy with the store.

How is your product repaired or serviced? As many users of high-

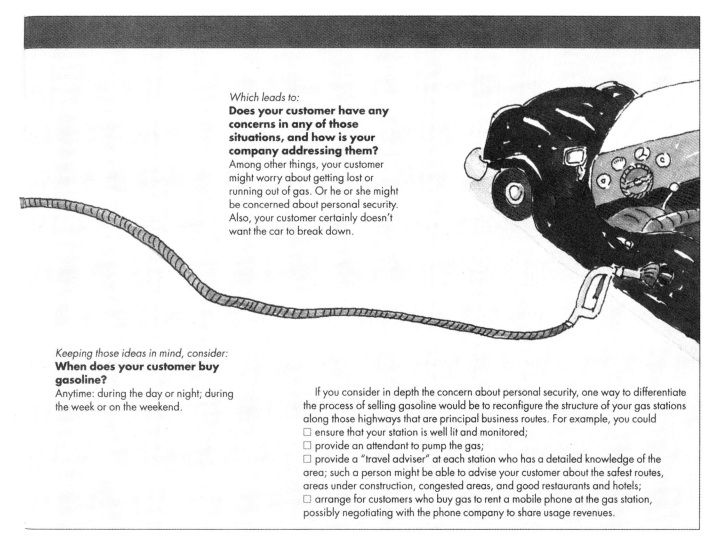

Which leads to:
Does your customer have any concerns in any of those situations, and how is your company addressing them?
Among other things, your customer might worry about getting lost or running out of gas. Or he or she might be concerned about personal security. Also, your customer certainly doesn't want the car to break down.

Keeping those ideas in mind, consider:
When does your customer buy gasoline?
Anytime: during the day or night; during the week or on the weekend.

If you consider in depth the concern about personal security, one way to differentiate the process of selling gasoline would be to reconfigure the structure of your gas stations along those highways that are principal business routes. For example, you could
☐ ensure that your station is well lit and monitored;
☐ provide an attendant to pump the gas;
☐ provide a "travel adviser" at each station who has a detailed knowledge of the area; such a person might be able to advise your customer about the safest routes, areas under construction, congested areas, and good restaurants and hotels;
☐ arrange for customers who buy gas to rent a mobile phone at the gas station, possibly negotiating with the phone company to share usage revenues.

tech products will attest, repair experiences—both good and bad—can influence a lifetime of subsequent purchases.

An ideal solution, used by Tandem Computers—a company that makes computers with parallel central-processing units for applications in which downtime is a major problem—is to try to repair a product even before the customer is aware that such service is needed. Tandem staff members can spot a malfunctioning component through remote diagnostics, send the appropriate part and instructions to the customer by express mail, and walk the customer through the repair process on the phone. This approach has almost completely eliminated expensive and inconvenient downtime for the company's customers; it also has eliminated their need for a costly onsite service force.

Otis Elevator uses remote diagnostics in a different way. In high-traffic office buildings, where servicing elevators is a major inconvenience to occupants and visitors alike, Otis uses its remote-diagnostics capabilities to predict possible service interruptions. It sends employees to carry out preventive maintenance in the evening, when traffic is light.

What happens when your product is disposed of or no longer used? In a world in which it is becoming increasingly economical simply to replace many products as they age rather than spend the money to fix them, what do customers do with the obsolete goods?

Canon offers an interesting example of how a company can differentiate itself at this step in the chain. It has developed a system that allows customers to return spent printer cartridges at Canon's expense. The cartridges are then rehabilitated and resold as such. The process makes it easy for customers to return used cartridges: all they need to do is drop the prepaid package off at a United Parcel Service collection station. At the same time, it enhances the image of Canon as an environmentally friendly organization.

Analyzing Your Customer's Experience

Although mapping the consumption chain is a useful tool in itself, the strategic value of our approach lies in the next step: analyzing your customer's experience. The objective is to gain insight into the customer by appreciating the context within which each step of the consumption chain unfolds. It is crucial to remember that the customer is always interacting with people, places, occasions, or activities. Those interactions determine the customer's feelings toward your product or service at each link in the chain. When they are viewed strategically, they can shape the dynamics of competition for that customer's business.

Essentially, this step involves considering how a series of simple questions—*what, where, who, when,* and *how*—apply at each link in the consumption chain. We have found that the most rewarding way to approach this exercise is to have a group of people from a company start down a path with any of their questions and brainstorm until their ideas dry up. Sometimes a given question will not lead to any particular insight. That's not a problem; the goal is to assemble an inventory of possible points of differentiation. Once the ideas are on the table, you can assess each one and select those that are most promising for your situation.

Candle makers might explore the possibility of offering a complete "candlelight experience."

Blyth Industries, the candle manufacturer we mentioned earlier, provides a good example of how analyzing your customer's experience works in practice. By exploring the options raised by their analysis, Blyth employees were able to take a prosaic product that is easy to imitate and create a profitable competitive advantage. What is important to understand here is that Blyth makes no pretense of being able to create the fabled "sustained competitive advantage"—so beloved of strategy texts—in any single segment of the candle market. Rather, what the company seeks to do is be the first to create and then dominate many small niches in rapid succession over time, gaining economies of distribution and scale by the sheer number of products it has in the marketplace.

Consider some of the possibilities that Blyth employees uncovered when they applied the questions to their business:

What? What are customers doing at each point in the consumption chain? What else would they like to be doing? What problems could they be experiencing? (These problems may not be directly related to your product or service.) Is there anything you can do to enhance their experience while they are at this stage of the chain?

Candles, when you think about it, can play a role in everyday life in a host of different ways. Among other things, they are used to celebrate birthdays, create a festive atmosphere for dinner parties, warm buffet dishes, cope with power outages, and set the mood for romantic evenings. Candles can be purchased in specialty shops, at crafts fairs, in supermarkets, and at card stores. Further, their use can be accompanied by a huge variety of containers, displays, accents, and mood-creating products. All this suggests that candle makers might do well to explore the possibility of offering a complete "candlelight experience" by producing or marketing complementary products as well.

Where? Where are your customers when they are at this point in the consumption chain? Where else might they be? Where would they like to be? Can you arrange for them to be there? Do they have any concerns about their location?

Because candles can have so many uses, it isn't surprising that there are as many potential places for their use. Candles can be found at the beach, on picnics, at proms, at weddings, at home, in restaurants, at children's birthday parties, and in places of worship. what quickly became evident to Blyth was that the concerns and behavior patterns of its customers were likely to be different in each location. That insight suggested the potential for differentiation on the basis of location.

For example, consider how candles are used in the home. Virtually every room in the house has potential: the dining room, living room, kitchen, bedroom, bathroom, and basement can all conceivably provide a setting for candle use, each for a different reason.

Who? Who else is with the customer at any given link in the chain? Do those other people have any influence over the customer? Are their thoughts or concerns important? If you could arrange it, who else might be with the customer? If you could arrange it, how might those other people influence the customer's decision to buy your product?

Honing in on the line of thinking Blyth used about domestic candles, consider the use of candles in the dining room. Who else is going to be there? The other people could be members of the immediate or extended family, business associates, close friends, or a suitor. Each type of person means a possible point of differentiation; each type means a different experience, a different mood, and a different time.

When? When—at what time of day or night, on what day of the week, at what time of the year—are your cus-

tomers at any given link in the chain? Does this timing cause any problems? If you could arrange it, when would they be at this link?

Take the scenario of a dining room with the family. Blyth found that the question *when* uncovered a wealth of opportunities for differentiation. Candles are used in the dining room with the family on birthdays, anniversaries, holidays, and graduation days, and at meals marking other special occasions. Each occasion provides a distinct experience. Important for a candle maker, each also triggers distinct emotions. Blyth employees were able to identify what became several successful new areas of differentiation by exploring how their candles might be designed in special shapes, colors, or scents. They also came up with a variety of ways to package the candles and combine them with such accessories as napkins to suit each situation. Candles intended for use with family members at Thanksgiving, for example, might be scented with cinnamon, colored in tones associated with the holiday, and sold with special holders.

Because there are many holidays and other occasions when families get together in the dining room, you can begin to get a sense of the opportunities available for differentiation. Moreover, the process can be repeated for as many different companions and settings as the imagination of your employees can contemplate. Blyth, for example, also has found a tremendous opportunity to differentiate its prod-

Even a simple product such as gasoline can be differentiated.

ucts for romantic meals. CEO Goergen has worked hard to design scented candles in various shapes in order to influence the ambience of such occasions so that, as he says, "eating becomes dining, and dining becomes romance."

How? How are your customers' needs being addressed? Do they have any concerns about the way in which your company is meeting their needs? How else might you attend to their needs and concerns?

Think about how candles are used outdoors—say, at a company barbecue. Citronella candles come to mind. In addition to creating a festive atmosphere, they are an attractive way to protect people from insect bites.

As we've seen, there is considerable potential for differentiation even in products so simple that at first blush they seem like commodities. Candles are but one. Gasoline is another. (See the exhibit "Is There a Way to Differentiate Selling Gas?") Understanding the customer's experience at any link in the chain for any product offers companies the opportunity to identify and explore many nontraditional ways to create value. The task then becomes selecting from among this wealth of possibilities; considering how each idea meshes with a company's particular skills, assets, and systems; and focusing only on those that can generate a competitive advantage. Each idea also may open up an opportunity to develop a new competence.

Too many companies pursue what seem like great new ideas without carefully assessing whether their organizations are well suited to do so and how quickly competitors can respond. Robert Goergen knows that Blyth Industries has certain strengths its competitors do not, including several unique production techniques and, more important, a deep knowledge of fragrances. Those special strengths, coupled with a solid understanding of customers based on market research, give Blyth an edge. Goergen thus evaluates opportunities for differentiation based on those considerations and moves forward only with the ideas that promise the strongest returns.

Focused Creativity

Virtually every company we have ever worked with has within it scores of people of considerable creativity and imagination. Unfortunately, all too often, the company never benefits because that talent isn't appropriately focused. It may even be squelched by the homogenizing pressures that any large organization tends to impose.

An important benefit of the process

Consider how each idea meshes with your company's skills, assets, and systems.

we've outlined above is that it unlocks the creativity in an organization so that the insights of particular individuals can contribute to a shared understanding of the customer—so that the company, in effect, knows its customers almost better than they know themselves. Companies that do this successfully find themselves deeply attuned to their markets. And, like entrepreneurs, they spend the imagination they have in lieu of the money they may lack to outperform competitors where it counts.

What's in a Brand?

SUMMARY **Consumers and brands have relationships. Nurturing those relationships ensures a company's success. While juggling their many duties, brand managers must keep answering three questions: who buy the brand, what do they want from it, and why do they keep coming back. The answers are partly rational but are also based on emotional "cues" and cultural values.**

Diane Crispell and Kathleen Brandenburg

Diane Crispell is executive editor of American Demographics, *and Kathleen Brandenburg is associate editor of* The Numbers News.

He that steals my purse steals trash," says the villain Iago in Shakespeare's *Othello.* "But he that filches from me my good name . . . makes me poor indeed."

Iago didn't have much of a good name to filch, but businesses should heed his words nonetheless. A business's good name is often a brand name. Inside the customer's mind, a trusted brand is a promise of high quality and good things to come. But a tainted brand name can trigger memories of poor quality and bad service, driving customers away. That's why brand management can make or break a company's reputation.

To businesses, brands mean market share. Packaged-goods marketers know that a name can affect shelf placement in the supermarket. When customers spend an average of only four seconds examining a shelf, this can be important. And because people are willing to spend a little more to get something they trust, branded products can command premium prices.

In the 1990s, established brands face challenges that range from private-label products to deep-discount stores. Their managers must keep up with rapid changes in the way products are distributed, priced, and sold at the retail level. But brand managers' most important goal is protecting the brand's good name. To succeed, they must answer three questions: who buys the brand, what do they want from it, and why do they keep coming back.

WHO BUYS THE BRAND

Most Americans are brand-loyal to something. The annual Monitor poll conducted by Yankelovich Partners of Westport, Connecticut, reports that 74 percent of respondents "find a brand they like, then resist efforts to get them to change." Once consumers are convinced of the quality and value of a particular brand, it takes a lot of money and effort to change their minds.

Many people buy familiar brands even if they believe the product has no actual advantage. Just half of Americans think that specific brands of mayonnaise are different or better

> Only half of Americans think brands of mayonnaise are different, but 62 percent have a favorite brand.

than others and worth paying more for, according to The Roper organization. But 62 percent know what brand of mayonnaise they want when they walk in the store. Another 22 percent look around for the best price on a well-known brand.

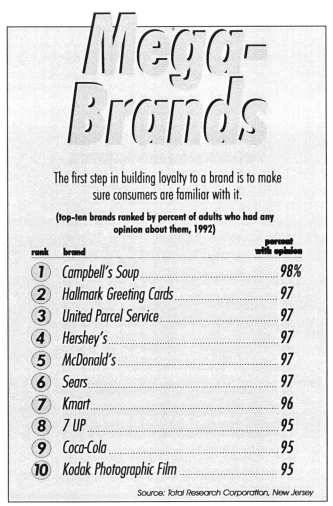

Mega-Brands

The first step in building loyalty to a brand is to make sure consumers are familiar with it.

(top-ten brands ranked by percent of adults who had any opinion about them, 1992)

rank	brand	percent with opinion
1	Campbell's Soup	98%
2	Hallmark Greeting Cards	97
3	United Parcel Service	97
4	Hershey's	97
5	McDonald's	97
6	Sears	97
7	Kmart	96
8	7 UP	95
9	Coca-Cola	95
10	Kodak Photographic Film	95

Source: Total Research Corporation, New Jersey

The same pattern applies to many products, including beer, coffee, and soup.

Brand behavior is complex. Not everyone is brand-conscious, and not all brand-conscious people are truly brand-driven. Depending on the product, 20 to 44 percent of Americans see no difference among brands or any reason to buy higher-priced ones, according to Roper. And in a study conducted by Deloitte & Touche, only about 35 percent of consumers are willing to identify themselves as "label-seekers."

Managers, salespeople, and students are more likely than the average shopper to say that familiar labels are important to them when they shop. Clerical workers, factory workers, and homemakers are less likely to be interested in names. Asian Americans have a high interest in labels, and blacks and Hispanics are slightly more-interested than non-Hispanic whites. Label-seekers have an average amount of education, says Deloitte & Touche, but their household incomes are slightly higher than average.

In many ways, label-seekers are an elite group. They are more likely than average to own compact-disc players, microwave ovens, and home computers. They are also more likely to exercise regularly, participate in sports, and enjoy shopping. In fact, label-seekers list shopping as their fourth-favorite pastime, after TV, music, and reading.

Label-seekers say that a clothing store's selection is the most important reason to shop there, followed by quality and price. For others, selection is the most important criterion for dress clothing, but price is most important for casual clothes and shoes. Label-seekers and others agree that price is the most important thing when shopping for health-and-beauty aids. But label-seekers rank selection second, while nonlabel-seekers mention location. In general, label-seekers see shopping as more of an exciting, emotionally fulfilling experience.

These hard-core brand shoppers are a minority of the population. But all shoppers fit into seven groups based on their definitions of brand quality, according to the Total Research Corporation of Princeton, New Jersey. "Conformists," at 12 percent of the population, choose the most popular brand because they want to belong to the crowd. "Popularity Seekers" (12 percent) go for trendy brands, while "Sentimentals" (12 percent) seek brands that emphasize comfort and good old-fashioned flavor. "Intellects" (17 percent) like upscale, cerebral, and technologically sophisticated brands, while "Relief Seekers" (17 percent) want something that offers escape from the pressures of life. "Actives" (15 percent) look for brands associated with a healthy, social lifestyle, and "Pragmatists" (16 percent) are simply interested in getting value for their money.

The seven groups have different opinions about the quality of particular brands. Among luxury cars, for example, Intellects like the Lexus but give Cadillacs a mediocre rating. Sentimentals prefer Cadillacs and score the Lexus very low. The groups also shift over time in response to economic and social trends. Pragmatists, Conformists, and Actives are currently on the rise, while Popularity Seekers and Sentimentals are declining. Relief Seekers and Intellects are holding steady.

WHAT THEY WANT

Virtually everyone can identify a short list of "megabrands." The most familiar of all brands is Campbell Soup, according to Total Research: 98 percent of Americans have a positive, negative, or indifferent opinion about it. Other highly visible brands include Hallmark, United Parcel Service, Hershey's, McDonald's, Sears, Kmart, 7 UP, Coca-Cola, and Kodak. These names

Best Brands

Many well-known brands also rank high in quality.

(top-ten brands ranked by perceived quality using a 10-point scale, with 10 meaning "outstanding, extraordinary," 1992)

rank	high-quality brands	score
1	Disney World/Disneyland	8.5
2	Kodak Photographic Film	8.3
3	Hallmark Greeting Cards	8.2
4	United Parcel Service	8.2
5	Fisher-Price Toys	8.1
6	Levi's Jeans	8.0
7	Mercedes-Benz Automobiles	8.0
8	Arm & Hammer Baking Soda	8.0
9	AT&T Long-Distance Telephone	7.9
10	IBM Personal Computers	7.9

Source: Total Research Corporation, New Jersey

are cultural icons, and their managers enjoy powerful advantages over

> **When you see a can of Campbell's Tomato Soup, you react in ways that are rational, emotional, and cultural.**

the competition.

When you see a can of Campbell's Tomato Soup, you react in ways that are rational, emotional, and cultural, according to Saatchi & Saatchi Advertising. Your rational mind thinks of tangible product qualities and features, such as the price of soup. Then your emotional side summons up a memory of the warm, comfortable feeling soup gives you. Finally, cultural influ-

ences make you consider the way you will be perceived by those who see Campbell on your pantry shelf.

A brand has many features, and people tend to evaluate the benefits of these features independently, says Saatchi & Saatchi executive vice president Penelope Queen. To understand the rational side, the firm uses a conjoint, or trade-off, analysis technique that measures the relative value of each product attribute in the purchase decision. To understand the murkier emotional and cultural attractions of a brand, Queen conducts psychological interviews that explore societal influences and unconscious emotional needs.

Another ad agency, BBDO of New York, explores brand psychology in its own way. Its "Personal Drive Analysis" found that both Classico and Newman's own spaghetti sauces are associated with upscale sophisticated adults. But people

think of Classico in terms of "Italian" traits such as indulgence and romance, while they identify Newman's own with the actor's individualistic and ambitious personality. BBDO uses this information to ensure that its advertising contains the appropriate emotional "cues" for each brand. Its methods can also reveal new niches by uncovering drives that current brands don't address.

Deep psychological motivations are an important part of why consumers buy, says Queen. But a brand's most powerful advantage is rooted in the human tendency to form habits and stick to routines. People's past experience with a brand is consistently the most important factor in their future brand choices, according to The Roper Organization. In the 17 years that Roper has been tracking the topic of brand choice, price and quality have almost always ranked second and third to past experience.

The reasons for choosing brands do change, albeit slowly. In 1985, quality temporarily moved into second place. In the Roper poll, price regained second place in 1986, and its lead over quality has widened considerably since then. In other words, quality is about as important to consumers as it was 17 years ago, but price is more important.

There are reasons for buying a product that go beyond experience, price, and quality. Recommendations from other people have ranked fourth in all the Roper surveys. Other considerations are how well-known the product is, how it ranks in *Consumer Reports*, and how it affects the environment.

Whether it's a box of detergent or a car, most people will buy the same thing over and over as long as it satisfies their needs. When their needs change, rival brands get a rare opportunity. Often, needs change when lives change. A woman who becomes a single parent may watch every penny and switch to the cheapest detergent she can find. A couple who has a child will replace

Tried It, Liked It

Knowing what to expect is the most common reason for buying a particular brand. Value and quality rank second and third.

(percent of adults who said that specified reasons were most important in deciding to buy a brand, 1992)

- past experience
- price
- quality
- personal recommendations
- well-known/ advertised
- rating in Consumer Reports
- environmental performance

Source: The Roper Organization

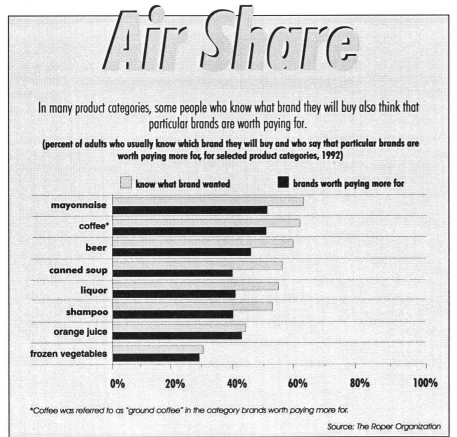

Air Share

In many product categories, some people who know what brand they will buy also think that particular brands are worth paying for.

(percent of adults who usually know which brand they will buy and who say that particular brands are worth paying more for, for selected product categories, 1992)

☐ know what brand wanted ■ brands worth paying more for

- mayonnaise
- coffee*
- beer
- canned soup
- liquor
- shampoo
- orange juice
- frozen vegetables

Coffee was referred to as "ground coffee" in the category brands worth paying more for.

Source: The Roper Organization

their two-seater sports car with a four-door sedan.

Sometimes people in transition switch brands that seem to have nothing to do with the transition. Forty percent of people who move to a new address also change their brand of toothpaste, according to Yankelovich Partners in Westport, Connecticut. "A change of that magnitude opens a person's mind," says Yankelovich senior vice president Watts Wacker. "Everything comes into question."

Most emotional relationships don't last unless both partners are adaptable and accommodating, and the relationship between brands and customers isn't any different. People won't be satisfied with the same skin-care product all their lives, for example. But the brand manager of a skin-care product can keep the relationship alive. One way is by extending the line of products sold under the brand name.

Like people, brands have a life span. They are born, they grow they mature, they reach old age, and they die. One way to delay the process is to give them a makeover. For example, since its beginning, Tide detergent has become at least four products: original powder Tide, Liquid Tide, Tide with Bleach, and Ultra Tide. Each suits a particular market with a particular need.

The danger in line extensions is going too far. Levi's succeeded when it introduced looser-fitting jeans for middle-aged baby boomers, but it failed when it introduced a line of dress suits for men in the early 1980s. Loyal blue-jean buyers thought suits made by Levi's had to be substandard in quality and design. As that perception took hold, Levi's began to lose jeans sales as well. It recalled the upscale line and scrambled to regain its traditional market.

Sometimes an old product can be rejuvenated simply by directing its advertising at a different market. Baby boomers who were raised on sweetened cereals are now health-conscious grown-ups. Kellogg's responded to this shift by repositioning Frosted Flakes as something that is still fun to eat but also good for you. Its advertisements show adults secretly admitting that they love the cereal.

KEEP THEM COMING BACK

Remember the old slogan for Alka-Seltzer: "Try it, you'll like it"? This is the essence of brand advertising. Success depends on finding people who are receptive to change and reaching them with advertising that reflects their attitudes toward the product.

Brand advertising should reflect two broad themes, according to a

> Forty percent of people who move to a new address also change their brand of toothpaste.

two-stage model developed by Larry Percy of Lintas: USA and John R. Rossiter of the Australian Graduate School of Management. The first theme is the reasons people buy (brand awareness), which in this model can be positive or negative. The second is the customer's level of involvement in the purchase decision (brand attitude), which can be high or low. Purchasing aspirin is a low-involvement decision, for example. Buying a house is a high-involvement decision.

Negative motivations include solving or avoiding problems and replenishing supplies of a product. Positive motivations include sensory gratification, intellectual stimulation, and social approval. Buying aspirin springs from a negative motivation, because one buys it to stop pain. But cosmetics and vacations are positive buys.

There are four advertising strategies that match each of the four involvement-motivation combinations, say Percy and Rossiter. For a low-involvement, negative-motivational product like aspirin, advertising should stress the product's problem-solving benefits in a simple, emphatic manner. People don't necessarily have to like aspirin ads, but they must understand the product's benefits. For low-involvement, positive-motivational products like cosmetics, "emotional authenticity" is the key element and single benefit, say the authors. For this reason, the target audience must like the ad.

An automobile is usually a high-involvement purchase, say Percy and Rossiter. As such, its advertising should provide substantial information about the brand. But people buy cars for both positive and negative reasons, and the advertising should reflect this ambiguity. If the target audience needs no-nonsense transportation, the advertising should stress but not exaggerate product benefits while creating an initial positive attitude toward the brand. If the customer is looking for style or power, "emotional authenticity is paramount and should be tailored to lifestyle groups within the target audience." Moreover, "people must personally identify with the product."

In the final analysis, many brands are nothing more or less than an image that may imprint itself in consumers' minds forever. People were still ranking General Electric second in the food-blender market 20 years after it had stopped making them. Now that's brand loyalty.

TAKING IT FURTHER

The Total Research Corporation conducts the Equitrends survey. For more information, contact John Morton; telephone (609) 520-9100. For an insightful analysis of companies that have been successful (or not) with their brands, see *Managing Brand Equity: Capitalizing on the Value of a Brand Name,* by David A. Aaker of the University of California at Berkeley (The Free Press, 1991, $24.95). The Roper Organization conducts periodic surveys about a variety of brand-related attitudes; telephone (212) 599-0700. For Larry Percy and John R. Rossiter's "Model of Brand Awareness and Brand Attitude Advertising Strategies," see the July/August 1992 issue of *Psychology & Marketing* (John Wiley & Sons, Inc.).

MAKING *OLD* BRANDS *NEW*

A good brand doesn't have to go the way of Hai Karate men's cologne or Ajax cleaning scrub.
Most mature brands pack plenty of brand equity and characteristics that can set them apart from
competitors. With astute management, their appeal can shine for new generations of users.

BY BRIAN WANSINK

Burma Shave, Brylcreem, Pepsodent, Ovaltine, William's Lectric Shave, RC Cola, Barbasol, Hai Karate, Black Jack Gum. At one point, these brands were widely recognized and frequently purchased. Many have now faded or become "ghosts" of their former selves. Their numbers are legion. In 1993, Nabisco reported 29 ghost brands; Shering-Plough 17; and Smith-Kline 14, according to Stuart Elliott of the *New York Times*.

While some fading brands are dying because of shifting consumer needs, heavy competition, or waning awareness, others are suffering from marketing malpractice. Many well-trained brand managers believe that brands—like people—follow predictable, irreversible life cycles: they grow, they mature, they decline, and they die. When sales fall, they respond by cutting back on marketing activities and reallocating funds to new brands.

Without ongoing investment of time, thought, or money, a fading brand's sales will continue to drop. This strengthens the original prognosis that there's no help for an old brand,

Brian Wansink, Ph.D., is associate professor of business administration and advertising at the University of Illinois Urbana-Champaign, and director of the Brand Revitalization Consumer Panel. His Brand Lab specializes in research on use of packaged goods and revitalization of mature brands.

> *Altering the characteristics of a brand or changing its packaging are often good ways to sweep away negative attitudes and boost sales.*

thus leading to even less attention and care. Some brands are nurtured back to health when this happens, but many die a lingering death as heavily discounted or regionalized brands.

Lately, however, the $75-to-$100-million price tag on launching a new brand is renewing corporate interest in the less costly option of revitalizing old brands. Not all brands are worthy of a new life. The challenge for brand managers is determining which brands can be revitalized and how best to do it.

THE SECOND TIME AROUND

Many companies take little time or effort to understand the life and death of ghost brands, which is why "brands that fail tell no tales." Yet many mature brands have untapped potential. At the Brand Lab at the University of Illinois, we set out to identify what makes a brand a candidate for revitalization by

NOT JUST FOR THANKSGIVING

(percent increase in average monthly amount used for selected products after viewing "choosing" and "using" advertisements*, 1994)

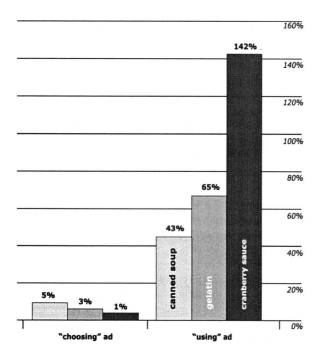

*"Choosing" ads tout common uses for products; "using" ads suggest nontraditional uses. Use was tracked for a three-month period after subjects viewed ads.

Source: experiments by the author

Cranberry sauce gets a big boost in consumption when ads suggested nontraditional uses.

analyzing mature brands that were successfully relaunched, and older brands that are still well liked by consumers.

First, we collected extensive information on 84 brands of consumer packaged goods. This included annual dollar sales, volume sales, and distribution channels, such as grocery stores, mass merchandisers, and drugstores. Then we talked to 360 members of the Brand Revitalization Consumer Panel, a group of primarily female household decision-makers from five states. We asked them a series of subjective questions about their favorite brands among the 84, and what distinguishes them from similar products.

When we matched data from panelists' interviews with objective information on the brands, here's what we learned. In general, brands that have been revitalized were perceived as having meaningful characteristics that set them apart from other brands. They typically have a time-tested heritage or reputation, are widely distributed in grocery stores, drug stores, and mass merchandisers, and are under-advertised and under-promoted compared with other brands in their category. Revitalized brands weren't

the cheapest, either. They tended to be medium- to premium-priced products.

Jeffrey Himmel, chairman and chief executive of the Himmel Group in New York, is a veteran of brand revitalization. His firm has breathed new life into Porcelana fade cream, Topol toothpaste, Doan's Pills, Gold Bond Medicated Powder, and Ovaltine. The best candidates for revitalization, he says, are high-margin products with few shelf-keeping units (SKU). SKUs are assigned to each size and variety of consumer packaged good on the market. Crest toothpaste, for instance, once had more than 60 SKUs. Products that come in multiple variations often have difficulty communicating a focused marketing message. The best brands to revitalize are those that can be contract-manufactured through multiple sources, and can be heavily advertised on radio or television 52 weeks a year, says Himmel.

These criteria have worked well for the Himmel Group. In 1973, it purchased Topol tooth polish for $200,000. Over the next ten years, Himmel built it into a brand with sales of $23 million a year. The same strategy raised Ovaltine from its deathbed to a vital, high margin, market leader.

Once a brand is chosen for revitalization, it's on to the work of getting it back into the minds—and households—of consumers. Brand managers have two opportunities to influence customers: when they choose a brand, and when they use it.

CHOOSING OLD FAITHFUL

Consumers shun old brands for many reasons. Bay Rum might remind a 20-year-old of his feeble grandfather. Aspergum is perceived as a relic by cold sufferers, who assume that modern medicine has come up with a better treatment for sore throats. Yet the underlying reason for rejecting mature brands is unfavorable attitudes toward them. In research with our consumer panel, we often heard that older brands had lost their appeal, lost their identity, and were overshadowed by competing brands.

Altering the characteristics of a brand or changing its packaging are often good ways to sweep away negative attitudes and boost sales. These changes aren't without risk—witness

The best way to jump-start a mature brand is by understanding its uniqueness and equity.

New Coke. But for some brands, a new look on the inside or outside has made a positive difference.

Aqua Velva aftershave lotion retained its trademark scent and color, and started its revitalization by developing a more convenient bottle and a snappier label. Lavoris mouthwash generated sizable sales increases because the clear "crystal fresh" version of its product appealed to young customers who had never used it before. Other successful modifications, such as some done by the Leaf Company (manufacturer of Good & Plenty, Heath bars, Zero, and Payday), involve reverting to original recipes, and extending familiar favorites into new forms, such as bite-size Heath Sensations.

WHEN BIGGER IS BETTER

(units consumed for three products, by size of package, 1996)

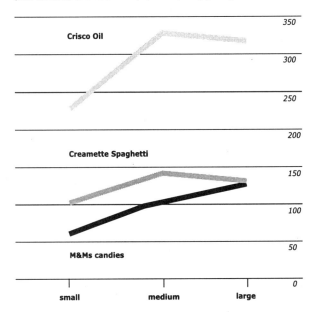

Note: Results are from an experiment conducted with members of the Consumer Brand Revitalization Panel. Units for oil and spaghetti are based on the amount used to make a meal for two; units for M&Ms are amount consumed while watching a video.

Source: experiments by the author

A medium-sized package prompts consumers to use more of the products tested.

Updated formulations or packaging are important, and they may result in modest sales increases. The best way to jump-start a mature brand is by understanding its uniqueness and equity, and making the most of them.

The most significant characteristics that separate one brand from another may not be the most obvious ones. Understanding the deeper meanings of brands to the people who buy them is the focus of a laddering research method developed by Charles Gengler, a marketing professor at Rutgers University–Camden. Consumers are first presented with three brands, including the mature brand being tested, and queried about their preferences.

The researcher then probes responses by asking questions that build on each answer. For instance, if one reason the respondent likes a breakfast cereal is because of its mascot, the next question is, "What is it you like about the mascot?" The respondent might say, "He's always positive and full of energy." The researcher's next question is, "Why is that important to you when eating a breakfast cereal?" to which the respondent says, "It reminds me of being young, and it makes me think the day might be off to a good start." At this point, the researcher has uncovered an underlying emotional, or higher-order, attribute of the brand being tested—it conjures up images of energy and youthful possibilities.

Data from laddering interviews are analyzed to determine the likely importance of various higher-order attributes in brand choice. The results are then compared with customer prototypes to identify the highest-yield consumer segments for targeting.

One company used this technique to generate more sales of a brownie mix. Laddering interviews and analysis revealed that many consumers associate making brownies with being a good mother and with baking for special occasions. The company turned this information into a promotion with a greeting card company. Some kids' birthday cards included a coupon for brownie mix and a recipe for decorating pans of brownies with candy.

When a North American dairy council used the research technique, it learned that current adult milk drinkers tended to have warmer and happier memories of childhood than did non-drinkers. People with fond childhood memories who weren't milk drinkers were an untapped market for the product. The council pitched milk as a comfort food, targeting adults who had the highest potential to become heavy milk drinkers.

Arm & Hammer marketed its baking soda as a deodorizer for refrigerators, freezers, and kitchen sink drains.

Laddering research typically yields many higher-order points of differentiation among brands. So even though it's a rich source of information, brand managers must be careful not to communicate too much information to potential purchasers. Multiple messages delivered in various forms dilute brand equity and confuse consumers, says Kevin Lane Keller, a marketing professor at Duke University. To make the most of a brand's uniqueness, advertising, packaging, and promotions should all emphasize a single, clear, consistent message.

HEY, BUY ME!

Salient brands are the brands people buy. A salient brand is one of which consumers are aware, either by seeing it at the point-of-purchase, or by having it in mind. That top-of-mind awareness is what leads them to put a specific brand on a shopping list or to make a special trip for it.

Trade journals and retail associations consistently report many creative ideas for generating point-of-purchase awareness. The sales-boosting success of many of these ideas confirms what seem like obvious strategies. Bright packages, sale signs, catchy displays, and wide shelf-facing all increase our awareness of a brand. Yet less obvious are recent findings that end-aisle displays and suggestive selling can increase sales, even if the product is not discounted.

A recent study I conducted with Robert Kent and Stephen Hoch demonstrated that ticklers like "Buy 12 Snicker's Bars for your freezer" not only increase awareness, but can nearly double the number of units a shopper intends to buy.

THE MORE WE HAVE, THE MORE WE USE

(average units used daily for selected stockpiled and nonstockpiled products, 1997)

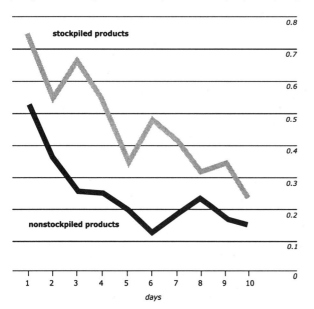

Note: Daily use is the average amount of chips, candy, juice, and granola consumed.

Source: experiments by the author and Pierre Chandon

People tend to eat more of things that are in large supply around the house.

Brands have top-of-mind awareness when they have recently been used, or when recently advertised. Himmel, the brand revitalization pro, attributes his successes to raising top-of-mind awareness for a mature brand, and commanding a large share of the total advertising messages for products in its category.

By focusing on a simple, single-minded point of differentiation, his advertising campaigns use testimonials that are broadcast frequently and consistently. Brands with limited advertising budgets have effectively increased top-of-mind awareness by advertising distinctions on their labels. Trix Cereal, for instance, used a side panel to note complementary products on which Trix could be sprinkled. And Murphy's Oil Soap printed a series of uses for the product under peel-off stickers affixed to its spray bottles.

Research with the Consumer Brand Revitalization Panel shows how important suggestions like these can be. Simply encouraging purchase is not enough. The unfortunate curse that's befallen some brands is that they are "cupboard captives"—owned but not used. Sixty-three percent of the panel households in my studies possessed Tabasco sauce. But 32 percent had had their bottle so long the sauce had turned from red to brown. Similarly, 35 percent had vitamins they had not opened in the past 12 months. An unopened package of cookies lasted more than 6 months in 41 percent of households without children.

NEW USES FOR OLD BRANDS

A brand manager who increases the number of units, such as cans of soup, that a household uses from four to five each year, realizes a 25 percent increase in sales without having to convert a single new user. This is true for both light and heavy users. One way to increase frequency of use is to suggest new uses for a brand.

Numerous old brands have revitalized their sales this way. Consider Arm & Hammer's situation in 1969. Sales were dropping because of a decline in home baking and the introduction of ready-to-bake packaged food products. Revitalization was critical. Arm & Hammer responded by marketing its baking soda as a deodorizer for refrigerators, freezers, and kitchen sink drains. Sales skyrocketed.

The key to effectively advertising a new use for an old brand lies in making new uses appear similar to existing ones. The original use provides an "attitude halo" for the new use, and eases its adoptability.

This was demonstrated in a series of studies in which homemakers viewed a series of advertisements for canned soup, cranberry sauce, and gelatin. The "choosing" soup ad touted soup as hot and nutritious; the "using" ad described soup as a hot and nutritious option for a snack. The "using" ads increased the amount used over a three-month period for the three products tested by an average of 73 percent, or 1.2 units per month.

Perhaps the quickest way to increase usage frequency is to position a brand as a substitute for products in other categories. For instance, advertising campaigns encourage consumers to eat Philadelphia cream cheese instead of butter on bread, to eat Special K breakfast cereal instead of cookies in the afternoon, and to serve Orville Redenbacker popcorn instead of potato chips and peanuts at a party. These attempts are most successful when the substitute is seen as different—but not too different—from the original product. If the substitute brand and the original product are too different, their similarities should be advertised. If they are too similar, their differences should be advertised.

Altering package sizes can also effectively increase use frequency. As a general rule of thumb, if a brand manager is trying to decide which of two packages to introduce—say 20 ounces versus 24 ounces—the larger of the two packages should encourage greater volume consumption per use. In tests of 47 products in various categories, larger packages increased single-occasion usage by 19 percent to 152 percent, with a median increase of 32 percent.

Part of the reason usage acceleration occurs is because larger packages are simply perceived as less expensive to use than smaller packages. Nevertheless, there is a limit to how much spaghetti a household can eat on one occasion, or how much detergent it can use in a week. Once the limit or saturation point is reached, a larger package has no additional impact on use volume.

My Aftershave Belongs to Daddy

Remember the Old Spice mariner, dressed in a burly sailor cap and pea coat with a seagoing burlap sack slung over his shoulder? That's him over there playing beach volleyball. Old Spice aftershave is younger than ever, despite turning 60 this year. It has to be. Successfully selling a mature product to young men means staying contemporary. And for Old Spice, that means body splash and professional beach volleyball tournaments.

"Old Spice users are very, very loyal," says Carol Boyd of Procter & Gamble, makers of aftershave since 1990. The Old Spice fragrance remains attractive after all these years, going head-to-head in blind tests with any designer cologne you care to mention."But the image is an issue that we look at all the time," says Boyd. The same capital a mature brand accrues in name recognition has the potential to trap it in a time warp.

But both Old Spice and another mature aftershave, Aqua Velva, are successfully reaching younger men by keeping to the timeless strengths of the product, expanding the line, and updating their image. Aqua Velva has refocused on its traditional identity as a refreshing, invigorating part of the morning routine. This has been as important as sprucing up its image, says Bob Sheasby, vice president of marketing at the J. B. Williams Company, makers of Aqua Velva.

The brand got off track in the 1970s by trying to compete with the emerging designer cologne market. Television spots featuring likable football star Dick Butkiss chiding quarterbacks for wearing sissy colognes put the brand at a competitive disadvantage by abandoning its fundamental identity as a refreshing toner.

By the early 1990s, "Aqua Velva men" were mature themselves—the typical user was aged 50 or older. Yet in mall-intercept interviews and focus groups, the tried and true Ice Blue fragrance proved as popular as ever. The brand hadn't lost name recognition, either. Even after years of being overshadowed by flashier fragrances, younger men remembered the after-shave. The problem was how they remembered it.

"My dad wore it," many said. For others it was an uncle, the groovy bachelor who drove a sports car.The memories were fond, the scent appealing, but the images dated Aqua Velva as a product of an earlier, older generation. Aqua Velva needed to get groovy again.

In the meantime, a dab or five or ten of CKOne behind a young man's ears has become common on a Saturday night, says Sheasby. But cologne has primarily expanded the fragrance market, not cornered it. In fact, Aqua Velva researchers were encouraged by respondents' preferences in men's daily fragrance. Both men and women said they favor a clean, comfortable scent for every day use. The heavy, spicy, sweet, or predatory smells of Saturday night weren't preferred on a weekday.

Aqua Velva was reintroduced as the refreshing, invigorating, daily slap in the face after the morning shave. It reappeared in a trendier bottle, and the line was expanded to include other grooming products, such as deodorant and body splash. A second flavor, Ice Sport, was introduced, primarily for younger men. At about the same time that researchers for Aqua Velva were hitting shopping malls, Procter & Gamble threw a retirement party for the Old Spice mariner. His replacement sports a T-shirt and base-

ball cap, and commands a sleek racing yacht. He looks more like an Ivy League grad than a rugged sailor. And he's apparently on his way—not to sea—but to the health club. He's traded the burlap sack for a gym bag. Old Spice also extended its line, introducing a successful long-lasting deodorant called High Endurance.

Boyd of Procter & Gamble points to the strong sales of High Endurance as a sign of a successful strategy combining the Old Spice fragrance, new technology, a contemporary product, and youth-oriented advertising. Old Spice claims an easy majority of total aftershave sales, 31 percent for the 12 weeks ending August 1997, according to *Drug Store News*.

The Aqua Velva man these days may be your son, not your father. The average age of Aqua Velva users is quickly falling, says Sheasby of J. B. Williams. The company's new variation on the classic blue tonic, Ice Sport, is making inroads with the 25-plus crowd, he says, while the original Ice Blue is most popular with men aged 25 to 45.

With its new packaging and advertising that communicates exhilaration, Aqua Velva has outperformed many competitors since its redesign more than a year ago, Sheasby says. Dollar sales of Ice Blue and Ice Sport combined were up 21.3 percent in the 12 weeks ending in August 1997, even as overall aftershave sales among the eight major brands declined 3.4 percent, according to *Drug Store News*. Some major brands saw sales tumble up to 28 percent during the period.

We'll have to see which aftershave brands have staying power, and which hit the skids for good. Anyone remember Hai Karate?

—*Kevin Heubusch*

In one experiment, subjects were asked to prepare a meal for two using vegetable oil and spaghetti. The volume of oil used was greater for medium than for small bottles, but it does not increase further with large bottles. Goodies are a different story, though. When subjects munched M&Ms candy while viewing a video, the larger the package, the more they ate.

Packaging can make products seem more convenient, and convenience often makes people use more. Recent research with the Brand Revitalization Consumer Panel suggests that perceptions of convenience are primarily based on the time and effort required to use a product. If it's not possible to reduce the time required or "hassle," perceptions or conven-

ience may be improved by careful selection of a comparison product. For instance, pizza mixes are perceived as 62 percent more convenient when advertisements compare them with scratch pizza rather than frozen pizza.

MAKING THE MOST OF STOCKPILING

The more soft drinks we have at home, the more we tend to drink, right? Not always. A brand that is out of sight is out of mind. While stockpiling increases how frequently people use a brand, it does so only when the brand is salient—that is, when it is either physically visible or on the top of one's mind. Brands are also highly salient and frequently used—shortly after they are purchased. Encouraging stockpiling through promotions or multi-packs increases the frequency of use, but so does any promotion that encourages consumers to frequently purchase a product.

To get consumers to clear stockpiled items out of household inventory and purchase more, marketers must keep their brands on the minds of users. While nearly any type of advertising increases salience, the most effective ads are those that are seen or heard just prior to a usage decision.

Brand managers obviously can't predict when people will stand in front of their cupboards to pick canned vegetables for dinner. Yet there are some windows of opportunity. Coke aired its "Drive-time Drinking" radio ads to encourage commuters to drink Coke while driving home. Similarly, Campbell's Soup raised brand salience by broadcasting "Storm Spot Ads" during inclement weather. Radio's flexibility allowed the ads to be broadcast prior to lunch and to dinner.

There's even a chance to speak to the customer at her cupboard—an ad on a product's package. The audience is captive, the cost per exposure is low, and the opportunity cost of what might otherwise be on the package is often negligible.

Revitalizing old brands is like reopening old mines. Some will be barren, others may hide gold. Academic research shows us that many once-successful brands have something to offer modern consumers, whether it's a brand they once trusted or the nostalgia of years past. The rule to remember is "Never

say die." Fifty years ago, Burma Shave was a proud and prosperous brand. Forty years ago, it was the Edsel-like punch line for jokes. In late 1997, Burma Shave's relaunch was announced with a miner's zeal. Maybe this will be the text of its first outdoor advertisement:

When something's a waste
It's gone in good haste
A good brand though
Should never go
Burma Shave

TAKING IT FURTHER

Data on brand choice and use, and perceptions of mature brands were collected at the Brand Lab at the University of Illinois Urbana-Champaign. Brian Wansink and Cynthia Huffman are conducting ongoing research on brand revitalization. For more information on the Brand Lab, the Brand Revitalization Consumer Panel, and other brand-related research, contact the author at 350 Commerce West, University of Illinois, Champaign, IL 61820; telephone (217) 244-0208. Relevant research reports can be downloaded from http://www.cba.uiuc.edu/~wansink/index.html.

Marketing

Built ᵗᵒLast

Everyone remembers the Edsel—for all the wrong reasons. Here's how to launch a new product with staying power

By Constance Gustke

EACH YEAR SOME 13,000 new products hit the market. Get this: Only 40 percent will be around five years later. Why such a low success rate? "A lot of new products just don't meet consumer needs," says Calvin Hodock. "People fall in love with their own ideas." And all too often that love is blind.

Hodock should know. He heads the steering committee for the American Marketing Association's Edison Awards, which annually recognizes the best new products. Each year the committee screens 500 to 700 products, looking for such qualities as marketplace success, innovation, lasting value, and societal impact. "The more significant the innovation, the more likely the product is to have huge market success," Hodock says.

This year, among the 65 Edison Award winners, Kodak was named New Product Marketer of 1996 for its success in creating and launching the Advantix Photo System, a product judges said met consumer demand while improving ease-of-use of an established technology. (Kodak also supported the launch with the largest advertising campaign in company history.)

As statistics show, though, for every Advantix Photo System there is a Super Combos, the soup-and-sandwich meal launched by Campbell's Soup. While market research found initial consumer acceptance, the product fell flat; it was priced too high, and the quality of the sandwich after it was microwaved was poor.

So what's the secret to launching a product with legs versus a product that lags? According to Hodock, most successful products begin with ideas based on customer demand, and then come to life as both different and better than existing products. They must also have a solid marketing strategy to support their launch.

Jack Hennies, LaunchWorks product manager at marketing consulting firm Maritz Inc. in St. Louis, who helps to create product launch strategies for many of the large consumer-products companies, says the key to a successful launch is measuring all elements of the marketing plan. Too often, Hennies contends, "companies will define what success will look like for the product in terms of sales, not in terms of the individual elements of the marketing program." Hennies says that companies need to know how each marketing element—from dealer meetings to trade and consumer incentive programs to advertising—will affect another element. If the element is a dealer meeting, for example, a company could track dealer buy-in through opinion surveys.

"If companies keep doing the same thing and getting the same results, that's OK if that's what they're looking for," Hennies says. "But most companies need to know if their money is better spent elsewhere."

INFINITI CAPITALIZED ON ITS BRAND EQUITY WHEN INTRODUCING THE LUXURY SPORT UTILITY VEHICLE VERSION OF ITS POPULAR QX4.

As the following stories of new products show, there are several tactics companies can use to increase the odds for a successful launch: diligent market research to find holes in seemingly saturated markets; a corporate ethos that rewards new product innovation and encourages managers to act as

Reprinted with permission from *Sales & Marketing Management*, August 1997, pp. 78-80, 82-83. © 1997 by Bill Communications, Inc.

entrepreneurs; and a marketing effort that supports cross-functional teams and delivers a unified message to the customer.

"Successful companies have a well-defined new-product charter," Hodock says. "They don't enter markets too far removed from their charter. They understand the voice of the customer, as well as create technical breakthroughs."

A CAR LAUNCH
With Infiniti Possibilities

A LITTLE SUCCESS whets the desire for more and more and more. So who could blame the marketing gurus at Infiniti, a division of Nissan, for wanting to capitalize on the ground-breaking rollout of its audacious luxury car, the QX4?

In 1994, five years after the QX4 debuted, Inginiti officials began casting for an add-on to its line. They spied a great opportunity: a luxury sport utility vehicle. The Infiniti marketers believed that by translating the QX4's brand equity to a new niche, Infiniti's core baby boomer market would flock to an upscale sports version.

To nail down specifics, Infiniti director of marketing Steve Kight traveled from Infiniti's headquarters in Gardenia, California, to affluent Westchester County in New York in the winter of 1995 to conduct one-on-one market research with current Infiniti customers who live in that area. "We've found that group dynamics are frequently steered by one or two people," he says. Consequently, Infiniti polls its existing customers during face-to-face interviews and through letters and surveys. Some of the questions asked during the QX4 research included what other car brands customers considered; what existing options they would most prefer; and what new options they would consider buying.

"We're in a brand rather than product business," Kight explains. "In a luxury brand, customers should get everything they want and not make compromises. Our customers told us that they wanted a sport utility with four-wheel drive that drives more like a car than a truck." At the end of the trip, Kight began to picture the new luxury vehicle: priced under $40,000, drives like a car, and has a low step for easy boarding. "Women in particular had a passion about that," he says.

From this description, Infiniti designers worked up five different sport utility designs. Over the next six months, 200 Infiniti and non-Infiniti customers nationwide were polled about the new designs. Participants were selected based on three main criteria: age (35–64), income (more that $125,000 annually), and willingness to buy a luxury car. Next, based on the winning car design, clay and fiber-glass car models were constructed. About 100 customers and a 10-member dealer advisory board provided input at each phase of development. (Some customers' interviews were so thorough they lasted three to four hours.)

By November 1996 Infiniti's new QX4 was a fixture in dealer showrooms nationwide. To promote the launch, Infiniti worked up TV ads and black-and-white print ads for 30 up-scale magazines, including *Smart Money, Forbes,* and *Travel & Leisure,* "to convey the emotion of the car," Kight says. "It's status with a sense of humor. We try to do away with formality." The TV campaign features the QX4 driving up the inside staircase of a luxurious house. Infiniti kicked off the launch with an all-star jazz concert at the Paramount Theater in New York's Madison Square Garden. Kight's marketing team mailed more than 12,000 engraved invitations to customers in the New York area; 4,000 attended.

Beside customers, Infiniti officials made sure not to neglect another key group when launching the QX4: its dealers. Infiniti brought all of its dealers to one Infiniti location, at which they were taken through the vehicle step-by-step, as well as given a chance to drive it. Later, a five-person training team visited the large dealerships to explain sales, marketing, and product specifics.

Kight says that sales have exceeded expectations, averaging 1,600 a month, versus original projections of 1,000. The numbers indicate what it takes to launch a successful product. "It's all a bit like a moon launch. Everything must happen on time: positioning, car design, dealer education, and customer marketing tactics," Kight says, adding: "The secret is that we make sure we understand exactly what our customers want. The QX4 was designed expressly for them."

3M INNOVATES
With the Customer In Mind

3M DID NOT become a global giant with more than $14 billion in annual revenues by doing a few things well; it does a lot of things well. The St. Paul–based company's intense commitment to product innovation largely fuels its success. In the past five years, 3M has plowed about $4 billion into research and development, fueling its 6,500 scientists in laboratories worldwide to develop about 500 new products each year. Company-wide, 3M employees are inspired to think like entrepreneurs with award programs that recognize new-product initiatives. They can also set aside up to 15 percent of their workweek to generate ideas. "The whole company spirit is devoted to

finding the next unique product," says Tom Paul, marketing manager, consumer key accounts.

That innovative spirit was tested in 1993 when 3M sought to push further into the home-care business. The company already enjoyed a strong presence in three market segments: plain sponges, scouring pads, and scrub sponges. Its dilemma: how to grab a foothold in wool soap pads, a niche dominated by titans SOS and Brillo.

3M initially arranged eight focus groups with consumers around the country. At these meetings, consumers frequently complained that using standard wool pads scratched their expensive cookware. This finding produced the idea for the Scotch-Brite Never Scratch soap pad. "Clearly there was an opportunity to update," says Paul, who spearheaded the Scotch-Brite launch. "There hadn't been any serious innovation in wool soap pads for eighty years. We simply needed to learn about consumer willingness to try a new product." Scotch-Brite would be made from gentler minerals than those used by Brillo and SOS, thus reducing the odds of damaging cookware.

In taking the idea from concept to design, 3M assembled a 10-person, cross-functional development team—ranging from manufacturing to marketing. At every step in the development. marketers kept the consumer in mind. They surveyed customers at malls nationwide, asking them to rate the prototype product on a scale of 1 to 10.

Timing was crucial. "Because we're perceived as an innovative leader, we must be the first to market with unique prod-

CORESTATES CELEBRATES ITS COREXCHANGE LAUNCH WITH A PARTY FOR ITS PROSPECTS.

ucts," Paul explains. "And this competitive environment is getting tougher and tougher."

At the same time, 3M didn't want to rush the Never Scratch pads to market and confuse consumers with a product too radically different from Brillo and SOS. That's why 3M first went to market in 1993 with the Scotch-Brite Never Rust wool pad, a product that matched consumers' preference for a wool pad that didn't splinter or rust but was also directly competitive with Brillo and SOS. By 1995, when 3M debuted its Never Scratch version, communicating its benefits to consumers became easier because of the brand recognition the original product had created, Paul says. "Launching each separately would allow us to focus our communication efforts behind each product separately," he says.

Paul declined to give sales figures for the Scotch-Brite Never Scratch wool pads, which are sold through supermarkets and mass merchants. He does say that sales have exceeded 3M's expectations by 25 percent. Paul adds that consumer awareness is good due to a comprehensive advertising campaign. 3M spent "between $5 million and $10 million" on national TV advertising and print ads in women's and food magazines, including such publications as *Good Housekeeping,* Paul says.

CORESTATES BANKS

On Good Marketing

DEVELOPING A SPIFFY, hot, can't-miss new product is great. Until it flops. That fate too often happens when customers don't know a new product exists, no matter how good it is. CoreStates, a Philadelphia-based banking institution that manages $45.5 billion in assets, made certain it would avoid such an outcome when it launched CoreXchange earlier this year.

The marketing for CoreXchange—which essentially is an ATM-like machine that gives shopping mall merchants deposit and cash-exchange abilities right in the mall—began during the product's initial development in early 1996. CoreStates' marketing staff conducted interviews with 50 of its customers who own or

---

Secrets for a Successful Product Launch

WHAT'S A GREAT product Idea without a solid launch strategy? That's right: Just another flop. To help guarantee a successful product launch, be sure to ask yourself these questions before you rush into the marketplace.

INNOVATION Is your product truly new, improved, or otherwise different from anything else out there?

MARKET ACCEPTANCE Is this a product only you and your mother will love, or is there truly a market demand?

QUALITY ASSURANCE Can your company deliver the quality that customers will expect from both your company and its new product?

MARKETING STRATEGY Do you have a formula that examines not only sales results, but also the result of each element of the launch's marketing plan to decide if your money is being best spent to support the launch?

MARKET RESEARCH Have you done your homework? Have you examined which marketing channels will best reach your target customers? Have you used focus groups or test markets to prejudge market acceptance of the product, price, and positioning?

FOLLOW THROUGH Are you prepared to storm the market and not be bullied by the giants who may want to steal your market share with their own versions of your innovative product?

manage retail shops housed in the 300-store King of Prussia Mall outside Philadelphia, the site slated for the CoreXchange introduction. "We asked merchants if they made daily deposits," says Bob Lubonski, CoreStates' vice president of product management. "And we asked them about customer buying patterns."

CoreStates' staff found that stores sometimes had heavier-than-expected customer traffic that could cause them to run out of change or small bills. This finding proved crucial; prior to CoreXchange, merchants had only a four-hour window in the morning (from about 9:30 a.m. to 1:30 p.m.) to get change or conduct other banking business. If they needed change after that time, their best bet was to ask a neighboring merchant.

"Basically, we were looking at the convenience factor," Lubonski says. "[With CoreXchange] we could time transactions to ten minutes and offer an extended deposit time of 9 p.m. Consequently, time of day would no longer be a concern. As long as the mall is open and the merchants have a Core-Xchange card, banking is available to them."

Lubonski realized that offering a product that would add value and convenience for CoreStates' customers was only the first step. Spreading the news was the second.

"Marketing is very important," Lubonski says. "Competitors put their machines into two other local malls, and then they walked away from them. We did a walk through these malls and surveyed twenty merchants there. Only two of the twenty even knew about the [competitor's] system."

To avoid duplicating those results, CoreStates sent a direct mail piece to the King of Prussia Mall's 300 store owners last January (one month prior to the CoreXchange unveiling) inviting them to a breakfast celebrating the launch. Additional mailings were sent to the headquarters of such retail chains as The Gap and CVS. "We did this for more of a heads up than actually expecting that someone from headquarters would fly in for the breakfast," Lubonski says. "But we felt it important to keep them informed of what we were offering." Based on the research from the initial customer interviews, Lubonski chose to include information on the convenience of using CoreXchange in the mailing. About a week after the piece was mailed, marketing staffers followed up with calls to the store owners to remind them of the breakfast and to generate more interest for CoreXchange.

In February the bank debuted CoreXchange with two stand-alone units in the mall; more than 100 store owners attended the breakfast gathering. So far CoreXchange has registered 65 clients, Lubonski says. The break-even goal: 80. According to Lubonski, many of the store managers must get approval to use services like CoreXchange from their owners or corporate headquarters, a process that can take a significant amount of time. But CoreStates officials are pleased with the initial results and plan to introduce CoreXchange in 10 to 15 malls per year for the next three to five years.

Taking Guesswork Out of Pricing

Determining how much to charge for a product or service involves factors that many small firms overlook.

By Roberta Maynard

Wholesaler Danny O'Neill wants to be known by upscale restaurants, coffeehouses, and grocers as a provider of top-quality gourmet coffee. So he works hard at justifying gourmet-level profit margins for his company, The Roasterie, Inc., in Kansas City, Mo.

Says O'Neill: "The better service you can give, the higher the price you can charge, the more you can prepare for the future."

By adopting this simple approach, O'Neill has taken an important first step toward pricing his products effectively. Clarifying a company's positioning strategy—deciding, as O'Neill has, whether to be an upscale niche business, a market leader, a lowest-cost provider, and so on—is an important element of determining pricing. But it's far from the only one.

In fact, the most common mistake made by small companies is their failure to consider the many interrelated factors that should affect pricing decisions, says Dan Roth, manager of business consulting in the Orange County, Calif., office of the Arthur Andersen Enterprise Group, a consulting arm of the Chicago-based Arthur Andersen accounting firm.

Business owners, Roth says, typically price products arbitrarily or base their prices on only one factor, usually their production costs or the price charged by the competition for similar goods.

Pricing, Roth says, should take into account your costs, the expected costs of product updates and new equipment, your objectives for each product (if it's to be a loss leader, for example, or it's a product you expect to phase out), and competitors' offerings. For example: What are they charging? And what are they offering for that price?

Customer perceptions, involvement of distributors and suppliers, government regulations, ethical considerations, and economic conditions also may play roles.

Experts in pricing generally say that the following factors are often the most critical to profitable pricing of products:

Know The Market
Talk with everyone who has a sense of marketplace pricing—distributors, suppliers, salespeople, and customers—and monitor your pricing decisions constantly.

Ellen M. Kruskie, owner of Carolina Petspace, often gets unsolicited feedback from customers, who bring pets to her do-it-yourself pet-washing facility in Raleigh, N.C.

At first, Kruskie says, "my customers told me I [didn't] charge enough." After two years in business, she took their advice and changed the basis of her pricing from what she needed "to keep [her] storefront business afloat," she says, to one that more accurately reflects the value of the service she offers and what customers are willing to pay.

Customers also are good sources of information when you're contemplating adding a service or product. Says Arthur Andersen's Roth: "If I talk to enough people, I'll get a good idea whether there is a demand and what I can charge."

When O'Neill took a page from the book of local breweries and started renting out a room for after-dinner and coffee parties, he called "all the catering people in town" to get a good idea about what he should charge. He learned that his price should reflect the cost of extra trash pickups and additional refrigeration.

O'Neill started the service by establishing a base price and adding per-hour extras for such amenities as staff and condiments. But customers soon let him know that they preferred to pay an all-inclusive price even if it meant paying more for the service.

Know Your Costs
Small firms often have a false sense of what it actually costs them to deliver a product or service. This makes it almost impossible to structure their margins appropriately, says Ed Galvin, a partner in the Chicago office of Coopers & Lybrand's entrepreneurial-advice services.

Often, the problem is an accounting system that doesn't provide sufficient information, says Galvin. An accountant can help determine the key components of product cost and recommend ways to track them. Software can help, too. Companies with yearly revenues in the range of $3 million to $7 million are operating successfully with inexpensive off-the-shelf accounting software and a personal computer, Galvin says.

Unfortunately, Galvin notes, even among small firms with enough information to analyze their expenses accurately, the tendency is simply to match competitors' prices. In their eagerness to record sales, he says, business owners often don't factor into their prices their costs for things such as inventory, packaging, freight, indirect labor, losses from failures and returns, and extensions of customer payment schedules.

Also, a company might customize an order in some way to win the business yet fail to build the customization cost into the price, Galvin says.

Moreover, matching or beating the lowest price isn't always the best strategy. "It can actually work against a service firm, says Herman Holtz, an engineering consultant in Silver Spring, Md. "Customers judge the value of a product by the price when they don't have anything else to go by. Many consultants have told me that when they raised their prices, their sales went up because the customer felt better" about the quality of the service.

Differentiate Your Product

Unless your strategy is simply to be the least expensive among sellers of your product, you can't hope to rise above today's cost-cutting environment without offering something that customers view as superior or unique. Perhaps no one knows that better than Peter J. Kolp, president of Andrews Moving and Storage in Cleveland. Kolp's company has been caught in an industry-wide discounting whirlwind. A moving job that cost $23,000 five years ago can be had

> "The key is to identify what your strengths are compared with competitors'. Do you have a better product, better supply, better delivery time? If you talk about quality, you can usually drive profit up."
>
> —Ed Galvin, Coopers & Lybrand

for about half that today, Kolp says.

Andrews competes with thousands of moving companies, 30 in Cleveland alone. Recent visits to customers made it clear to Kolp that they didn't really differentiate between his company and others. At the same time, he knew that price cuts couldn't go on indefinitely.

After some soul-searching, he says, he decided to "take steps to draw a line in the sand" and develop outstanding service to justify charging higher prices.

"We've got to do whatever is possible so that we can say to our customers that there is a distinguishable difference. We're not going to discount as much as others. We may lose some business, but over the long run, we're going to be better off."

Galvin of Coopers & Lybrand commends what Andrews is now doing: "The key is to identify what your strengths are compared with competitors'," he says. "Do you have a better product, better supply, better delivery time? If you talk about quality, you can usually drive profit up."

As coffee wholesaler O'Neill says: "You can't just say the market is charging $3, so I'll charge $4. You've got to justify that price.

"We deliver for our customers," he says. "There's no fine print with us, and people know that. That's our strategy: to be the best—not the biggest or the cheapest."

The Language of Pricing

Determining your marketing goal for each product or service makes it possible to create a cohesive, overall pricing strategy and to measure results.

Are you considering all the possibilities?

Listed below are the most common terms that describe various pricing tactics. These terms and their definitions were supplied by the Chester Marketing Group, Inc., in Washington Crossing, Pa.

Flexible pricing refers to allowing for price changes to meet changing competitive and marketplace conditions. This usually is necessary in the middle of a product's life cycle.

Skim refers to pricing at an inordinately high level to hit the "cream" buyers. This applies to unique or cutting-edge products.

Slide down means to move prices down over time to tap successive market groups.

Penetration is pricing below the prevailing level to gain market entry or increase market share.

Elasticity is pricing to take advantage of known or perceived price flexibility.

Bundling means pricing several related products and/or services together to provide a competitive advantage.

Price to market refers to a pricing level that is just below where you begin to lose market share.

Psychological pricing means pricing at a level that "sounds" lower than it is; an example would be "$99.95."

Follow means raising or lowering prices when industry leaders do.

Segment pricing refers to pricing the same products differently in different markets.

Cost-plus pricing is built up from a cost "floor," generally on a percentage basis.

Pre-emptive pricing is very low, to discourage competitive market entry by making the market appear unattractive.

Phaseout pricing means pricing high to remove a product from the line.

Loss leader refers to forgoing profit on an item to attract buyers to other, usually higher-priced ones.

Push versus pull is the pricing trade-off between motivating the sales network and pleasing the customer.

Terms and conditions can be components of a pricing strategy. An example is an airline's restrictions for various discount fares for a given flight.

Exploring The Subject Further

These books offer in-depth looks at pricing from different perspectives:

Power Pricing: How Managing Price Transforms the Bottom Line by Robert J. Dolan and Hermann Simon (The Free Press, $40) offers a comprehensive look at competitive-pricing strategies and includes sophisticated mathematical models to determine profit and volume growth.

Price To Sell: The Complete Guide To More Profitable Pricing by Herman Holtz (Upstart Publishing Co., $27.95)

Communicate With Customers

Informing customers of your plans before you raise prices is a good strategy for maintaining business and goodwill, experts agree.

If you plan increases, set a date to impose them and notify customers so they can place an order before the prices change.In fact, Roth advises his clients to increase prices at set times each year. September is a good time, he says, because "most companies have [their] strongest revenues in the third quarter and are more likely at that point to order ahead."

When pet-care entrepreneur Kruskie decided to refine her pricing structure last January, basing prices for dog baths on weight and coat type, she posted a sign in advance of the rate adjustment. In addition, she gave customers a chance to prepay at the old, lower prices while rewarding them with a free wash.

When increases are sudden or likely to continue, good communication with customers is critical. It's a situation O'Neill faced this year when the cost of green coffee rose dramatically.

By mid-March, coffee prices were nearly double what they had been in January. O'Neill found that he "couldn't increase prices fast enough to keep up." He sent a six-page letter to his 300 customers about the cost of coffee.

In it, he explained what The Roasterie was doing to control costs and suggested things customers could do. He included copies of newspaper articles detailing the price increase. O'Neill believes that this approach gave him credibility, and he hasn't lost one customer as a result, he says.

As important as pricing is, it is just one component of a marketing plan, notes Arthur Andersen's Roth. Taking into account many related factors and adopting a long-range view of an industry and business, he says, will help small firms price their products effectively and find new opportunities for profit through pricing.

Roberta Maynard is a business writer in Washington, D.C.

Kamikaze Pricing

When penetration strategies run amok, marketers can

find themselves in a dive-bomb of no return.

by Reed K. Holden and Thomas T. Nagle

Price is the weapon of choice for many companies in the competition for sales and market share. The reasons are understandable. No other weapon in a marketer's arsenal can be deployed as quickly, or with such certain effect, as a price discount. The advantage is often shortlived, though, and managers rarely balance the long-term consequences of deploying the price weapon against the likely short-term gains.

Playing the price card often is a reaction to a competitor and assumes that it will provide significant gain for the firm. Usually, that's not the case. Firms start price wars when they have little to lose and much to gain; those who react to the initiators often have little to gain and much to lose. The anticipated gains often disappear as multiple competitors join the battle and negate the lift from the initial reductions.

Managers in highly competitive markets often view price cuts as the only possible strategy. Sometimes they're right. The problem is that they are playing with a very dangerous weapon in a war to improve near-term profitability that ends in long-term devastation. As the Chinese warrior, Sun Tzu, put it, "Those who are not thoroughly aware of the disadvantages in the use of arms cannot be thoroughly aware of the advantages."

If marketers are going to use low prices as a competitive weapon, they must be equally aware of the risks as well as the benefits (see "The Prisoner's Dilemma"). They also must learn to adjust their strategies to deploy alternatives when pricing alone is no longer effective. Failure to do so has put companies and entire industries into tail spins from which they never fully recover.

EXECUTIVE BRIEFING

Penetration pricing is perhaps the most abused pricing strategy. It can be effective for fixed periods of time and in the right competitive situation, but many firms overuse this approach and end up creating a market situation where everyone is forced to lower prices continually, driving some competitors from the market and guaranteeing that no one realizes a good return on investment. Managers can prevent the fruitless slide into kamikaze pricing by implementing a value-driven pricing strategy for the most profitable customer segments.

Pricing Options

Marketers traditionally have employed three pricing strategies: skim, penetration, and neutral. Skim pricing is the process of pricing a product high relative to competitors and the product's value. Neutral pricing is an attempt to eliminate price as a decision factor for customers by pricing neither high nor low relative to competitors. Penetration pricing is the decision to price low relative to the product's value and to the prices of similar competitors. It is a decision to use price as the main competitive weapon in

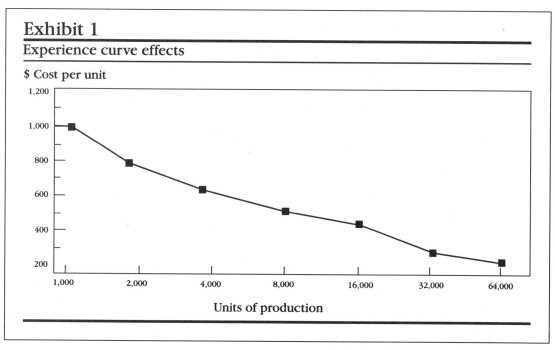

Exhibit 1

Experience curve effects

$ Cost per unit

Units of production

hopes of driving the company to a position of market dominance.

All three strategies consider how the product is priced relative to its value for customers and that of similar competitors. When Lexus entered the luxury segment of the automobile industry, the car's price was high relative to standard vehicles but low relative to Mercedes and BMW. The penetration strategy was defined not by the price but by the price relative to the value of the vehicle and to similar competitive products.

Any of these strategies can be associated with a variety of cost structures and can result in either profits or losses. To understand when each strategy is likely to be successful, managers should evaluate their current and potential cost structure, their customers' relative price sensitivities, and their current and potential competitors. All three areas must be carefully considered before employing any pricing strategy.

Penetration Strategies Can Work

If a firm has a fixed cost structure and each sale provides a large contribution to those fixed costs, penetration pricing can boost sales and provide large increases to profits—but only if the market size grows or if competitors choose not to respond. Low prices can draw additional buyers to enter the market. The increased sales can justify production expansion or the adoption of new technologies, both of which can reduce costs. And, if firms have excess capacity, even low-priced business can provide incremental dollars toward fixed costs.

Penetration pricing can also be effective if a large experience curve will cause costs per unit to drop significantly. The experience curve proposes that, as a firm's production experience increases, per-unit costs will go down. On average, for each doubling of production, a firm can expect per-unit costs to decline by roughly 20%. Cost declines can be significant in the early stages of production (see Exhibit 1).

The manufacturer who fails to take advantage of these effects will find itself at a competitive cost disadvantage relative to others who are further along the curve. This is often the case with new technologies and innovative products, where relatively small increments in units sold yield substantial decreases in unit costs. This is also the case for many new entrants to a market who are just beginning to see experience curve cost reductions.

However, the main ingredient to successful penetration pricing is a large segment of customers for whom price is the primary purchase motivation. This can be the case in business markets where original equipment commodities are sold to the production process of a customer's business, but it rarely occurs in consumer markets where image is an important part of the use of a product.

> The main ingredient to successful penetration pricing is a large segment of customers for whom price is the primary purchase motivation.

When Omega watches—once a brand more prestigious than Rolex—was trying to improve market share in the 1970s, it adopted a penetration pricing strategy that succeeded in destroying the watch's brand image by flooding the market with lower priced products. Omega never gained sufficient share on the lower price/lower image competitors to justify destroying its brand image and high-priced position with upscale buyers. Similar outcomes were experienced by the Cadillac Cimarron and Lacoste clothing.

A better strategy would have been to introduce a totally new brand as a flanking product, as Heublein did with the Popov, Relska, and Smirnoff vodka brands and Intel did with microprocessors in 1988. After the introduction of the 386 microprocessor, Intel adopted a skim price strategy for the high value and proprietary 386 chips. It also wanted to market a circuit in the 286 market that could compete with AMD and Cirrus on a nonprice, value-added basis. The 386 SX was introduced as a scaled down version of the 386, but at a price only slightly higher than the 286. The net result was to migrate price sensitive customers more quickly to the proprietary 386 market with the 386SX, while still capturing increased profit from the high value users with the 386.

In its marketing of the 486, Pentium, and Pentium Pro circuits, Intel continues this flanking strategy with dozens of varieties of each microprocessor to meet the needs of various market segments.

For penetration pricing to work, there must be competitors who are willing to let the penetration pricer get away with the strategy. If a penetration price is quickly matched by a competitor, the incremental sales that would accrue from the price-sensitive segment must now be split between two competitors. As more competitors follow, smaller incremental sales advantages and lower profits accrue to both the initiator and the followers.

Fortunately, there are two common situations which often cause competitors to let penetration pricers co-exist in markets. When the penetration-pricing firm has enough of a cost or resource advantage, competitors might conclude they would lose a price war. Retailers are beginning to recognize that some

> When the penetration-pricing firm has enough of a cost or resource advantage, competitors might conclude they would lose a price war.

consumers who are unconcerned about price when deciding which products and brands to buy become price sensitive when deciding where to buy. They are willing to travel farther to buy the same branded products at lower prices. Category killers like Toys 'R' Us use penetration pricing strategies because they are able to manage their overhead and distribution costs much more tightly than traditional department stores. Established stores don't have the cost structure to compete on this basis, so they opt to serve the high-value segment of the market.

The second situation conducive to penetration pricing occurs when large competitors have high-price positions and don't feel a significant number of their existing customers would be lost to the penetration pricer. This was the case when People's Express entered the airline industry with low priced fares to Europe in the 1970s. The fares were justified with reduced services such as no reservations or meal service. People's also limited the ability of the high value business traveler to take advantage of those fares by not permitting advanced reservations or ticket sales. This was a key element of their strategy: Focus only on price sensitive travelers and avoid selling tickets to the customers of their competitors.

Major airlines didn't respond to the lower prices because they didn't see People's Express taking away their high value customers. It was only when People's began pursuing the business traveler that the major airlines responded and quickly put People's out of business.

The same strategy is being repeated today by Southwest Airlines in the domestic market far more skillfully. Southwest has a cost and route structure that limits the ability of major airlines to respond. In fact, when United Airlines, a much larger competitor, did try to respond with low-cost service in selected West Coast markets, it had to abandon the effort because it couldn't match Southwest's cost structure.

Penetration or Kamikaze?

An extreme form of penetration pricing is "kamikaze" pricing, a reference to the Japanese dive bomber pilots of World War II who were willing to sacrifice their lives by crashing their explosives-laden airplanes onto enemy ships. This may have been a reasonable wartime tactic (though not a particularly attractive one) by commanders who sacrificed single warriors while inflicting many casualties on opponents. But in the business world, the relentless pursuit of more sales through lower prices usually results in lower profitability. It is often an unnecessary and fruitless exercise that damages the entire dive-bombing company—not just one individual—along with the competitor. Judicious use of the tactic is advised; in

The Prisoner's Dilemma

A popular exercise in seminars and executive briefings we hold is to ask executives to participate in a prisoner's dilemma pricing game. Each team must decide whether to price its products high or low compared to those of another team in 10 rounds of competition. The objective is to earn the most money; results are determined by the decision that two competitors make in comparison with each other.

The game fairly accurately simulates a typical profit/loss scenario for price competition in mature markets. The objective is to impart several lessons in pricing competition, the first being that pricing is more like playing poker than solitaire. Success depends not just on a combination of luck and how the hand is played but also on how well competitors play their hands. In real markets, outcomes depend not only on how customers respond but, perhaps more important, on how competitors respond to changes in price.

If a competitor matches a price decrease, neither the initiator nor the follower will achieve a significant increase in sales and both are likely to have a significant decrease in profits. In developing pricing strategy, managers need to anticipate the moves of their competitors and attempt to influence those moves by selectively communicating information to influence competitive behavior.

The second lesson is that managers must adopt a very long time horizon when considering changes in price. Once started, price wars are difficult to stop. A simple decision to drop price often becomes the first shot in a war that no competitor wins. Before initiating a price decrease, managers must consider how it will affect the competitive stability of markets.

Philip Morris discovered this when it initiated a price war in the cigarette business by cutting the prices of its top brands. Competitors followed, and the net result was a $2.3 billion drop in operating profits for Philip Morris, even as the Marlboro brand increased its market share seven points to 29%. The manufacturer of Camels experienced a $1.3 billion drop in profits.

The third lesson from the prisoner's dilemma is that careful use of a value-based marketing approach can reverse a trend toward price-based marketing. This is accomplished through signaling, a non-price competitive tactic that involves selectively disclosing information to competitors to influence their behavior. The steel and airline industries provide prominent examples of the signaling strategy's use. They often rely on announcements that conveniently appear on the front pages of the *Wall Street Journal* to signal competitors of pending price moves and provide them with opportunities to follow. The strategy takes time to implement, but it provides a far better long-term competitive position for marketers who employ it.

Most managers who play the prisoner's dilemma adopt a low-price strategy. This mirrors the real world, where 63% of managers who adopt an identifiable strategy use low price, according to an ongoing research project in which we are engaged. In the game, low-price teams fail to earn any profit in a majority of cases. The strategy works in round one, but competitors quickly learn to respond and both parties end up losing any chance for profit.

Executives rationalize that, if their firm can't make money, competitors shouldn't, either. Managers quickly forget that the objective of this game—and the game of business—is profit. Price cuts in the real world can be devastating. A current example is the personal computer business, where Packard Bell sets the low price standard that many competitors follow.

Packard Bell's management is less concerned with profit than with achieving a volume of sales and market share in a growing industry. But unless the company has operational characteristics that distinguish it from competitors and permit Packard Bell to deliver a quality product at those low prices, its ability to leverage market share will be limited. Analysts estimate that Packard Bell has only made $45 million in net profit over the past 10 years and is staying afloat through loans granted by suppliers and massive cash infusions from its Japanese and European co-owners.

—Reed Holden and Thomas Nagle

as many cases as it works, there are many more where it does not.

Kamikaze pricing occurs when the justification for penetration pricing is flawed, as when marketers incorrectly assume lower prices will increase sales. This may be true in growth markets where lower prices can expand the total market, but in mature markets a low price merely causes the same customers to switch suppliers. In the global economy, market after market is being discovered, developed, and penetrated. High growth, price sensitive markets are quickly maturing, and even though customers may want to buy a low-priced product, they don't increase their volume of purchases. Price cuts used to get them to switch fail to bring large increases in demand and end up shrinking the dollar size of the market.

A prominent example is the semiconductor business, where earlier price competition led to both higher demand and reduced costs. But in recent years, total demand tends to be less responsive to lower prices, and most suppliers are well down the experience curve. The net result is an industry where participation requires huge investments, added value is immense, but because of a penetration price mentality, suppliers can't pull out of the kamikaze death spiral.

There was a time when large, well-entrenched competitors took a long time to respond to new low-price competitors. That is no longer true; domestic automobiles are now the low priced brands, and even AT&T has learned to respond to the aggressive price competition of Sprint and MCI. The electronics, soft goods, rubber, and steel companies that ignored low-price competitors in the 1970s and '80s have become ruthless cost and price cutters. The days of free rides from nonresponsive market leaders are gone.

Another risk comes in using penetration pricing to increase sales in order to drive down unit costs. Unfortunately, there are generally two reasons managers

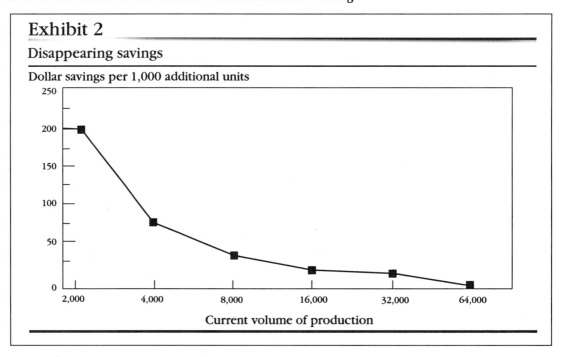

Exhibit 2

Disappearing savings

Dollar savings per 1,000 additional units

[Graph: Y-axis ranges from 0 to 250 in increments of 50. X-axis shows Current volume of production with values 2,000, 4,000, 8,000, 16,000, 32,000, 64,000. The curve starts at approximately 200 at 2,000 units, drops to about 75 at 4,000 units, then to about 35 at 8,000 units, then gradually declines to nearly 0 by 64,000 units.]

Current volume of production

run into trouble when they justify price discounts by anticipated reductions in costs. First, they view the relationship between costs and volume as linear, when it actually is exponential–the cost reduction per unit becomes smaller with larger increases in volume. Initial savings are substantial, but as sales grow, the incremental savings per unit of production all but disappear (see Exhibit 2). Costs continue to decline on a per-unit basis, but the incremental cost reduction seen from each additional unit of sale becomes insignificant. Managers need to recognize that experience curve cost savings as a percentage of incremental sales volume declines with increases in volume. It works great in early growth phases but not in the later stages.

Many managers believe that sales volume is king. They evaluate the success of both their sales managers and marketing managers by their ability to grow sales volume. The problem is that their competitors employ the exact same strategy. Customers learn that they can switch loyalties with little risk and start buying lower priced alternatives. Marketers find themselves stuck with a deadly mix of negligible cost benefits, inelastic demand, aggressive competition, and no sustainable competitive advantage. Any attempt to reduce price in this environment will often trigger growing losses. To make matters worse, customers who buy based on price are often more expensive to serve and yield lower total profits than do loyal customers. Thus starts the death spiral of the kamikaze pricers who find their costs going up and their profits disappearing.

Penetration pricing is overused, in large part, because managers think in terms of sports instead of military analogies. In sports, the act of playing is

enough to justify the effort. The objective might be to win a particular game, but the implications of losing are minimal. The more intense the process, the better the game, and the best way to play is to play as hard as you can.

This is exactly the wrong motivation for pricing where the ultimate objective is profit. The more intense the competition, the worse it is for all who play. Aggressive price competition means that few survive the process and even fewer make reasonable returns on their investments. In pricing, the long-term implications of each battle must be considered in order to make thoughtful decisions about which battles to fight. Unfortunately, many managers find that, in winning too many pricing battles, they often lose the war for profitability.

Value Pricing

To avoid increasingly aggressive price competition, managers must first recognize the problem and then develop alternate strategies that build distinctive, non-price competencies. Instead of competing only on price, managers can develop solutions to enhance the competitive and profit positions of their firms.

In most industries, there are far more opportunities for differentiation than managers usually consider. If customers are receiving good service and support, they are often willing to pay more to the supplier, even for commodities. A client in India produced commodity gold jewelry that was sold into the Asian market at extremely low penetration prices. Because of the client's good relationships with wholesale and retail intermediaries, we recommended a leveraging of those relationships to increase prices to a more reasonable level. Despite much anxiety, the client followed suit and major customers accepted the increases.

Opportunities to Add Value

Marketers often fail to recognize the opportunity for higher prices when they get caught up in kamikaze pricing. To avoid this, they need to understand how their customers value different product and company attributes. The objective is to identify segments of customers who have problems for which unique and cost-effective solutions can be developed. Sometimes it's as simple as a minor adjustment in packaging.

Know what customers want. Loctite Corp., a global supplier of industrial adhesives, introduced a specialty liquid adhesive in a 1-oz. bottle for use in emergency applications. Unfortunately, sales were less than spectacular. After a number of customer interviews, Loctite discovered that the liquid was difficult to apply and the bottle was difficult to carry. What customers really wanted was an easy-to-apply gel in a tube. The product was reformulated to meet these criteria and saw huge success. In the process, Loctite almost doubled the price.

Managers should identify features that they can add more cost effectively than their competitors can. IBM has been under intense price pressure in the personal computer segment. Besides introducing lower-priced flanking products (with limited success), IBM also has introduced computers with more internal memory. This feature had significant appeal because of the higher memory demands of the Windows 95 operating system. The value of this feature was greater than a price cut because IBM is arguably the most cost-effective producer of random access memory in the world. It also forced low-price competitors to incur higher relative costs to match IBM, thereby undercutting their ability to price their PCs below IBM's.

In the process of adding value to their products, firms should remember that value is achieved not only from the products themselves, but from the services associated with their use. The manufacturer of a heavy-duty truck oil broke out of commodity pricing when it began analyzing the oil from its customer's trucks to determine if there were excessively high temperatures or metal in the oil that would indicate a breakdown of the internal components of engines. The service was promoted in a mailer included with each large drum of oil. The cost of this service was minimal, and a large segment of small- and owner-operator customers placed a huge value on it. This tactic helped the firm to differentiate its product with a valued service connected to the product.

Offer complete benefits. Another way to avoid downward pricing is to offer complete product benefits, which is especially useful in the early phases of

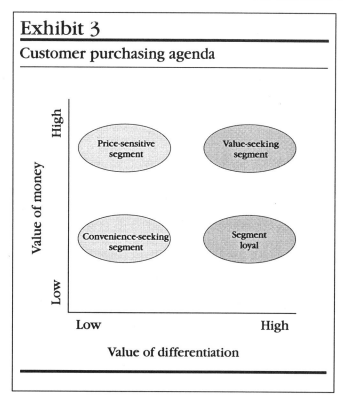

Exhibit 3

Customer purchasing agenda

a new product's life. This tactic is not as effective when products mature and customers no longer need as much service support. However, when customers are still developing their expertise, they require complete systems to achieve the maximum benefit to their organization. This is often an expensive affair that needs to be justified by the future business and profit potential that a customer represents.

When marketers correctly assess this type of situation, they often develop a sustainable competitive advantage that makes them impervious to competitive erosion. This was the strategy that Intel employed when it introduced the 8086 microprocessor to the PC industry in the early 1980s. Although the 8086 was slightly inferior technically to Motorola's 6800, Intel adopted sophisticated customer support programs that permitted new PC manufacturers to introduce new products quickly. This and other services were backed by a strong sales and marketing program that focused on specific customer adoptions. The net result was the beginning of Intel's dominance in PC microprocessors.

> Firms that attract value customers get the loyal buyer as part of the bargain and sell to the price buyer only when it is profitable and reasonable.

Understand customer agendas. Marketers make a serious mistake when they assume that all their customers are willing to sacrifice quality to obtain low prices. A few are, but most really want to get high-quality products at the lowest possible price. The seller of a high-quality product can compete against a low-price, low-quality product by recognizing that, despite the words of the purchasing agent, pricing need not be too aggressive.

Sellers who understand why customers buy their products often find that there is a fairly uniform set of reasons underlying purchasing behavior. Price is often important, but it seldom is the sole motivation. In most business situations, there are four types of agendas with regard to the pricing of products and a buyer's desired relationship with the supplying firm (see Exhibit 3). One of the best ways for marketers to avoid the trap of excessive price competition is to develop market- and customer-level strategies that reflect those behaviors.

> The purpose of sales is not to use a lower price to close a sale, but to convince the customer that the price of a product is fair.

For example, loyal customers highly value specific things that a supplier does for them, such as technical support, quality products, and customer-oriented service agents. These customers are less concerned about the price than about the care they receive. They often have a single supplier and have no intention of qualifying another. Understanding who the loyal customers are and keeping their loyalty is critical.

Conversely, price buyers care little about a long-term relationship with a supplier and want the lowest possible price for products. These commodity buyers have multiple vendors and encourage them to dive into kamikaze price wars. For consumer marketers, price shoppers who switch allegiances at the drop of a coupon provide few incremental dollars to the retailers who cater to them. For business-to-business sellers, these tend to be the buyers who scream loudest and dictate pricing and selling strategies. Unfortunately, the profits they generate rarely justify the attention they demand.

The price buyer's agenda is to get products at the lowest possible prices, so he or she uses tactics that force marketers to employ kamikaze pricing tactics even when it might not be the wisest thing to do. For the marketer, the trick is only to do business with the price buyer when it is profitable to do so and when it doesn't prompt a more profitable customer to purchase elsewhere.

Convenience buyers don't care whose product they purchase, and have little regard for price. They simply want it readily available. This often is the most profitable market segment, provided marketers can deliver their products at the locations preferred by these buyers. Unfortunately, this group exhibits little brand loyalty and provides sellers with no sustainable competitive advantage beyond their distribution systems.

Offer the best deal. Value buyers evaluate vendors on the basis of their ability to reduce costs through lower prices or more efficient operations, or to make the buyer's business more effective with superior features or services. From a customer perspective, this is the place to be; while both price and loyal buying have unique costs, value buying comes with the assumption that these customers are getting the best deal possible, given all factors of consumption. From a marketing perspective, firms that attract value customers get the loyal buyer as part of the bargain and sell to the price buyer only when it is profitable and reasonable.

Organizations that employ kamikaze pricing have a poor understanding of how their products create value for customers. This lack of understanding results in excessive reliance on price to obtain orders. Successful marketers use price as a tool to reflect the value of the product and implement systems in the organization to assure that value is delivered to customers and captured in the pricing.

The Five Cs

"Sell on quality, not on price" was once a popular marketing aphorism. Unfortunately, while product quality can reduce the seller's rework and inventory costs, it does little for customers. Selling the quality of a product is often not enough because buyers have difficulty quantifying its value and may be unwilling to pay for it. By focusing on quality, we miss the opportunity for customers to understand the true value that quality brings to the buyers of our products. Instead, resolving to "sell on value, not on price" focuses on understanding how pricing really should work. To avoid the rigors of price-based competition, marketers should adopt the five "Cs" of the value-based approach:

- Comprehend what drives customer value.
- Create value in product, service, and support.
- Communicate value in advertising.
- Convince customers of value in selling.
- Capture value in pricing strategy.

How a product provides customer value and which value-creation efforts best differentiate a product from the competition must be understood by marketers. When there is additional value that can be created, marketers need to do a better job creating it in their products, service, and support activities. Once a firm provides differentiating value to its customers, the primary responsibility of the marketer is to set up a communications system, including the salesperson, that educates the customer on the components of that value.

The purpose of sales is not to use a lower price to close a sale, but to convince the customer that the price of a product, which is based on its value in the market, is fair. Of course, most sales compensation systems do just the opposite, rewarding salespeople for closing a sale, regardless of the price. Salespeople who lack an understanding of a product's value often bend to a buyer's wishes and match a lower-value competitor's price. Product prices should reflect a fair portion of their value, and they should be fixed so salespeople will have to sell on the basis of value.

Companies that approach pricing as a process rather than an event can effectively break the spiral of kamikaze pricing.

Penetration pricing gains ground in markets against competitors, but extended use of this offensive tactic inevitably leads to kamikaze pricing and calamity in markets as competitors respond, cost savings disappear, and customers learn to ignore value. Good marketers employ such weapons selectively and only for limited periods of time to build profitable market position. They learn how to draw from a broad arsenal of offensive and defensive weapons, understanding how each will affect their overall long-term market conditions, and never losing sight of the overall objective of stable market conditions in which they can earn the most sustainable profit.

Additional Reading

Darlin, Damon (1996), "The Computer Industry's Mystery Man," *Forbes,* (April 8), 42.

Nagle, Thomas and Reed Holden (1995), *The Strategy and Tactics of Pricing.* New York: Prentice Hall.

Reichheld, Frederick F. (1996), *The Loyalty Effect.* Boston: Harvard Business School Press.

Shapiro, Eileen C. (1995), *Fad Surfing in the Boardroom.* Reading, Mass.: Addison-Wesley, Publishing.

Taylor, William (1993), "Message and Muscle: An Interview with Swatch Titan Nicolas Hayek," *Harvard Business Review,* (March–April), 99-110.

Tzu, Sun (1988), *The Art of War,* translated by Thomas Cleary. Boston: Shambhala Publications.

About the Authors

Reed K. Holden is President of the Strategic Pricing Group Inc., Marlborough, Mass., where he has conducted numerous industry seminars in the United States and Asia on pricing and competitive strategy, business market research, and loyal buyer behavior. He also works with corporate clients as an educator and strategic analyst. Reed has more than 11 years of experience as a sales and marketing manager in the electrical and electronics industries. During that time, he specialized in the development and implementation of sales training and industrial marketing programs. He also was an Assistant Professor at Boston University's Graduate School of Management for nine years. He coauthored the second edition of *The Strategy and Tactics of Pricing* and "Profitable Pricing: Guidelines for Management" which was published in the third edition of the *AMA Management Handbook.*

Thomas T. Nagle is Chairman of the Strategic Pricing Group Inc., which helps firms in such diverse industries as telecommunications, pharmaceuticals, computer software, semiconductors, wholesale nursery, consumer retailing, and financial services develop pricing strategies. His seminars are offered in public programs and at major corporations in North and South America and in Europe. The second edition of Tom's book, *The Strategy and Tactics of Pricing: A Guide to Profitable Decision Making,* is used extensively as a text on the subject. He is the author of "Managing Price Competition," published in *MARKETING MANAGEMENT* (Spring 1993), and "Financial Analysis For Profit-Driven Pricing," published in *The Sloan Management Review* (1994). His articles also have appeared in the *AMA Handbook of Business Strategy.* Tom has taught at the University of Chicago and at Boston University and is currently on the executive program faculties of the University of Chicago.

The Stores That Cross Class Lines

Target and Others Find the Magic Mix

By JENNIFER STEINHAUER

COLLEEN McQUISTON is a upper-middle-class home-maker, and she likes to shop accordingly. She buys cosmetics at Foley's, a department store near her home outside Houston, and clothes at Lord & Taylor. She hits Neiman Marcus each year at Christmas. But when she needs a lipstick or guest towels or socks for her children, she is likely to go to Target.

"I'd rather spend $5 on a picture frame at Target than get it at Dillard's for $15," Mrs. McQuiston said. Even as more income flows into her house—her husband is a chemical engineer in the thriving Texas economy—that desire has only grown. "I try to make more of an effort to go to Target," she said. "You can save a lot of money on things that look just as good."

American retailers know that the country is full of Mrs. McQuistons. Middle- and upper-income shoppers, the bread and butter of the retail industry, are shopping their way up and down class lines in unprecedented ways. They shop at Saks Fifth Avenue for a blouse and a costly tube of eye cream, then head to T. J. Maxx the same afternoon for children's clothes or window valances.

Chains like Bloomingdale's, with their commitment to always keeping half the store on sale, have drawn in lower-income shoppers who 10 years ago would not have bothered to come through the doors. But even more striking is the success in recent years of lower-priced merchants, particularly discount stores, in drawing middle- and upper-income shoppers to their aisles.

The epitome of this cross-shopping is Target, the discount chain that has grown in a decade to become the biggest unit of the Dayton Hudson Corporation. The average household income of its shoppers is around $40,000 a year, versus $25,000 to $30,000 for Wal-Mart and Kmart, the country's biggest discounters.

It is not that the affluent have gotten cheap; sales for luxury goods retailers were at a decade high last year. Rather, successful retailers of lower-priced goods have managed to tap into what might be called the Vanilla Candle Syndrome. Tired, overworked Shoppers prefer to save their paychecks for bigger thrills like vacations and massages than to spend them on expensive baby clothes and place mats; and if they cannot afford the vacation or the massage, they go for a scented candle instead.

Indeed, 90 percent of shoppers with household incomes of more than $70,000 a year shop in discount stores, according to a recent survey by WSL Strategic Retail, a consulting group in New York. Five years ago, that percentage was only half as large.

The best of the lower-priced stores allow shoppers to get in and out quickly yet enjoy the sort of service and some of the ambiance offered by department stores a decade ago. Their clothing and housewares shelves offer attractive, inexpensive interpretations of specialty store merchandise, just a few aisles away from the less sexy but all-important items like milk, white T-shirts and potting soil. All this is wrapped in clever advertising that makes people feel that they are part of a big, hip national secret.

"Ten years ago, you had places like Woolworth's where people thought they had to trade courtesy, clean stores and wide aisles for price," said Candace Corlett, a partner at WSL Strategic Retail. "They don't have to do that anymore—thank you very much, Target and Wal-Mart."

Thanks, also, to Old Navy, Home Depot, Ikea and other retailers that manage to move less-expensive goods in a stylish, witty way to all segments of the economic spectrum.

"We have seen a chairman of the board of a major New York company standing in the checkout line next to someone who drives a truck for him," said Bernard Marcus, chairman of Home Depot, the do-it-yourself behemoth based in Atlanta.

Whole shopping centers have been designed with the cross-shopper in mind—places like the Tustin marketplace, a center in the heart of affluent Orange County, Calif., that features T. J. Maxx, Ross Stores, Ikea, Home Depot and Old Navy—and where the average shopper's household income is $60,000.

Marketing experts say the shift in the consumer psyche started with the recession of the early 1990's, when purse-tightening was mandatory, but has persisted through the decade, as shoppers realize that there is no reason to dig their way through crammed department store racks or wait out sales for a simple pair of cotton socks.

"Consumers are looking to buy at the high end, where the value is unambiguous and more fun, or at the lower end, where they can get the best price and be done with it," said J. Walker Smith, a managing partner at Yankelovich Partners, the market research firm.

Stylish . . . and Disposable

The shift has done wonders for the business of Target.

Just a decade ago, it was operating 80 stores from its base in Minneapolis. Now, with 807 stores in 39 states—and in the midst of an aggressive East Coast expansion even as competing discounters go belly up—Target has managed to seduce more-affluent customers like Mrs. McQuiston, who once were but a corporate pipe dream.

The company's success is based as much on what shoppers see—wide aisles, children's shirts priced

at $6 and an easy return policy—as on what they cannot, like Target's obsessive inventory management, close partnerships with key suppliers and a corporate culture that showers respect on shoppers, whom the company refers to as "guests."

"We don't believe that 'trend-right' and 'affordable' are mutually exclusive terms," said Greg Steinhafel, vice president for merchandising at Target, during a recent interview in his office in downtown Minneapolis. "We can bring to the masses tasteful merchandise for a price."

The path of that merchandise to the local Target store might begin in St.-Tropez, France, with a company trend-spotter perched on a pier, camera and telephoto lens in hand, watching the world go by.

Last June, the trend-spotters—people whose job is to find out what colors, styles and moods are hot—camped out in the Riviera resort town, looking at store windows and watching what cafe society was wearing. The verdict: the cargo pant.

The style was ready for 20 test stores by Labor Day, when the trend group returned to Europe. There it was again—that military-style pant with the pockets on the sides of the legs, a style that ended up on major fashion runways last fall. Phase 2 involved sending the cargo pant to the rest of Target's stores, in a variety of fabrics and stylings.

Target's attention to trends goes beyond clothes. The company's trend group goes to all the major food, home decor and apparel trade shows around the world, rubbing elbows with buyers from Pottery Barn, Donna Karan International and Neiman Marcus.

"If they have that certain color, we want it," said Robyn Waters, vice president for trend merchandising at Target. "If there is one item that everyone has, we want to have it, too." Ms. Walters said the company often used the same suppliers as department and upscale specialty stores.

There is no question, however, that the quality of a lot of merchan-

dise at Target does not rise to that of merchandise at fancier stores. Seams tend to fray on some shirts. Bath towels wear quickly. Colors can fade on the plates. The merchandise has to be hip, because that makes its disposable nature easier to take.

"I buy towels for my daughter's room or a serving dish for one season," Mrs. McQuiston said.

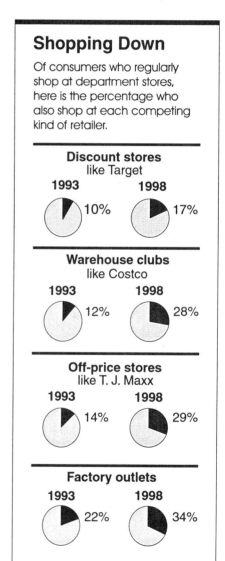

Shopping Down

Of consumers who regularly shop at department stores, here is the percentage who also shop at each competing kind of retailer.

Discount stores
like Target

1993 — 10%   1998 — 17%

Warehouse clubs
like Costco

1993 — 12%   1998 — 28%

Off-price stores
like T. J. Maxx

1993 — 14%   1998 — 29%

Factory outlets

1993 — 22%   1998 — 34%

Source: Kurt Salmon Associates

The New York Times

Target makes it easy for her to return often to spend money in its stores. A wide aisle that the company calls the "race track" runs around each store, and every department is color-coded—in a scheme borrowed from Candyland, the children's board game.

At the checkout, where a retailer's reputation is made or broken, things are carefully organized, too; stations are set up to allow purchases to be scanned, bagged and ready to go in about a minute. "We must be rapid," said Kenneth B. Woodrow, Target's president. "If people have to wait in line, it means we don't respect their time."

Little of this would matter, of course, if the price weren't right. In children's apparel, there are $5 cotton T-shirts with beach images, suspiciously reminiscent of Petit Bateau, the children's clothing line sold in pricey specialty stores. "Our guest has a high level of education and she has money," said Robert Giampietro, vice president for special projects at Dayton Hudson, during a tour of a new Target store in Minneapolis. "She gets the joke."

That joke is most evident in the tongue-in-cheek advertising the company favors. In one ad that has appeared in New York subway stations and newspapers, a stylish woman dressed in black crimps her hair with a waffle iron. The point is that Target has housewares and cool clothes. In another, a lithe model wears an accordion-style lamp shade as a skirt. Yes, the ad conveys, Target sells housewares, and guess what? The chain knows that accordion-pleat skirts are the rage this year.

"This is very important: We're with it and we're current," said Mr. Giampietro, who speaks in rapid-fire sentences while bouncing on the balls of his feet. He wears a watch with the phrase "speed is life" in place of numerals. "And that is better than taking a strategy that we're selling cheap toilet paper."

Stocking and Growing

Mr. Giampietro's kinetic energy cuts through the eerie silence of a Target stockroom. Other retailers' back rooms are often loud and dis-

organized, but Target's are as orderly as the parts of the store that customers see. Few people are even allowed in—Mr. Giampietro was stopped by his subordinates and questioned as he sneaked back for a peek—which means that inventory discrepancies can be traced quickly.

The company knows exactly how much of every item is on every shelf of every store every day, and is obsessive about restocking. The logic is that shoppers who find that their Target is out of toothpaste will not hang around—or return—to see what is new in the towel department.

Suppliers say the chain's sophisticated technology and willingness to venture beyond what is considered traditional discount merchandising, like selling dishes individually as well as in sets make doing business with Target more interesting—and often more lucrative.

"They have the best systems in the business," said Joseph F. Soviero, whose company, Sango America Inc., of Secaucus, N.J., sells ceramics to major department stores, including those of Dayton Hudson. "This enables the merchants to make fast decisions and good ones."

Target's biggest challenge yet is its rollout on the East Coast, where many shoppers have an endless supply chain for everything. In the last year, the company has opened four stores in New Jersey and two in New York, on Long Island, and it expects to open seven more—in New Jersey, on Long Island and in Queens—by the end of the year.

The region has been hard on discounters: Bradlees and Caldor are both operating under Chapter 11 bankruptcy protection, Jamesway liquidated two years ago and Kmart has been struggling with its Manhattan stores.

"On the East Coast, everyone knows some place to get it wholesale, so there is a lot to compete with," said Walter Loeb, a retail consultant in New York. "But I know the stores have found quick acceptance in the area, and that the New

Jersey store was one of their most successful openings ever," he said, referring to the store in Edison.

Target's successful expansion is crucial for Dayton Hudson. The discount chain accounted for about 70 percent of its parent company's $751 million in net earnings last year, and it is being counted on to eventually contribute 85 percent of the profits.

Altogether, the company plans to add about 65 Target stores a year over the next three years, including those planned for the East Coast. Because Dayton Hudson has little debt, it expects to be able to increase earnings at a steady clip even as it spends on new locations.

"They are a benchmark for the industry," Therese Byrne, editor of Retail Maxim, a financial newsletter about the retail industry, said of Target. "In terms of margins, they are two to three times the rest of the discount industry and better than some department stores." Sales in Target stores open at least one year rose an average of 7.3 percent over the last nine months, 40 percent faster than the retail industry average.

Filling the Niche

A few other retailers have managed to tap the same magic. And if their merchandise differs from Target's, their marketing and selling styles are remarkably similar.

Consider Ikea, the Swedish furniture chain. There is nothing inherently special about the most of the retailer's furniture—the mainstays are basics, like white laminated bookcases. But the accents—fun, cheap clocks or lamps—can help a poor college student put together an affordably fashionable room or enable an affluent retired couple to remake a den.

And Ikea's soup-to-nuts warehouses appeal to the time-pressed: They sell everything from kitchen sinks to rugs, and you take it all with you when you leave. "Ikea is offering a solution to decorating problems in a one-stop-shopping environment," said Carol Tisch, the executive editor of HFN, a trade publication for the home furnishings industry. "And they have helped the industry to learn to upgrade the offerings to a broad base of customers."

Old Navy, the lowest-price clothing unit of Gap Inc., sells mainly to families looking for basics that are cheaper than those offered at Gap stores. But college students and urban fashion victims alike flock to Old Navy for faux suede feed-bag purses that they can use for a season and then discard. And buying clothes from grocery bins, as customers do at Old Navy, somehow seems fun.

The commercial real estate industry is keenly aware of the cross-shopping trend.

In Orange County, for example, the Irvine Company, the region's prime developer, found through market research that affluent customers were longing for a discount center but did not like the idea of shopping in an eyesore off a freeway. So starting in 1988, it teamed up with Donahue Schriber, a management company, to open the Tustin Marketplace on 90 palm-fringed acres.

"We felt like there was a niche that was missing here," said Rick Evans, president of Irvine's retail division, which has also developed tony projects like Fashion Island in Newport Beach, Calif. "What has made this center so successful is its ambiance."

It is clear that to entice upper-crust shoppers, stores need the whole package: speed-of-sound checkouts, clever ads, strong fashion and frequent turnover in merchandise.

"People want to feel good rather than look good" these days, said Mr. Smith of Yankelovich. "They figure, 'If it isn't something I want to indulge myself with, then I'll just go to Target. And later, if I am looking for something more enjoyable, I'll go to the Range Rover lot.'"

Value Retailers Go
DOLLAR FOR DOLLAR

If you thought the corner five-and-dime had succumbed to the Wal-Marts of the world, think again. Three hot retailers strike gold with small, "extreme value" stores. **By Anne Faircloth**

The Madison Square shopping center on the outskirts of Nashville has clearly seen better days. A couple of stores sit vacant; the parking lot is far from full. Yet one small, unpretentious storefront is abuzz. At 10 A.M. on a Wednesday morning Dollar General store No. 2392 is doing brisk business on items like 75-cent-a-gallon bleach, $10 cookware sets, and two-for-a-dollar cans of Vienna sausage. John Brown, a maintenance technician at the Nashville airport, is eyeing the $1.50 deodorant. "Sure, it's cheaper here," he says. "They don't call it a dollar store for nothing."

The corner five-and-dime was supposed to have succumbed to the superstore blitzkrieg long ago. But it hasn't worked out that way. Several strong players are proving that there's plenty of money to be made by simply "living off the crumbs of Wal-Mart," says Dan Wewer, an analyst at Robinson-Humphrey. Indeed, the strongest, and many believe the last, growth segment in retailing is the so-called extreme-value category, which includes three of today's hottest retail stocks: Dollar General, Family Dollar, and Dollar Tree.

About as glamorous as three-for-a-dollar paper towels, these stores have nonetheless caught the attention of Wall Street, which believes they are hitting an economic and demographic sweet spot. While in today's category-killer world most suburbanites trek to stores the size of your average island nation to buy everything from linoleum flooring to Barbie dolls, many people are put off by such big-box shopping experiences. In particular, low- and fixed-income customers are drawn to value retailers, which offer easy access, small stores (at an average 6,400 square feet, a Dollar General is about the size of one department in a superstore), and a narrow selection of basics like washing powder

and toothpaste. And, of course, excellent prices; although Dollar Tree is the only real dollar store (everything literally costs no more than $1), all three manage rock-bottom pricing.

According to analyst Barbara Miller of BT Alex. Brown, "Dollar-store customers think Wal-Mart is expensive. They go into these supercenters and ask, 'Do I belong here?' " A small neighborhood convenience store suits these shoppers perfectly. A dollar store is to Wal-Mart what a 7-Eleven is to Safeway—except that in dollar stores, the customer doesn't pay a premium for convenience.

Dollar General and Family Dollar, the grandes dames of this niche, have been around since the 1950s, yet today's numbers indicate that there's never been a better time to be in this business. About 40% of the country's households earn less than $25,000—the target income level of these two chains. And thanks in part to the recent increase in the minimum wage—20% over the past two years—these folks have more money to spend. And they will buy, says Miller. "These customers spend every extra dollar they have."

She estimates that households earning $30,000 or less drop a whopping $55 billion each year on basic consumables—canned meat, snacks, cleaning supplies, and health and beauty aids. This sales potential has not been lost on the dollar stores, which have significantly boosted their offerings in these categories. Last year value retailers as a group rang up $8.3 billion in total sales; of that, $3.8 billion was generated by consumables. There is a lot of room left for growth.

As major discounters continue to shift toward the supercenter format, broadening their customer base and increasing their offerings of higher-priced goods, they create an opening for value retailers to snap up

The Rise of Value Retailers

Family Dollar
Dollar General
Dollar Tree
S&P 500

Index: 12/31/96=100

FORTUNE CHART

5/28

1997 1998

Value Retailing's Big Three

A look at the numbers behind the leaders in Wall Street's favorite new retailing category

Retailer	Sales 1997	Income 1997	Same-store sales growth	Number of stores	New stores for 1998	Number of states	Average store size	Sales per sq. ft.	Average sale total
Dollar General	$2.6 billion	$145 million	8.4%	3,360	500-525	24	6,400 sq. ft.	$141	$7.90
Family Dollar	$2.0 billion	$75 million	9.3%	2,970	350-400	38	6,500 sq. ft.	$127	$8.04
Dollar Tree	$635 million	$48 million	7.8%	924	205	28	3,900 sq. ft.	$224	$5.50

shoppers from the low-income segment. In other words, for every middle-class mom Kmart attracts with its Martha Stewart bedding, it alienates a minimum-wage worker struggling to make ends meet on $5.15 an hour. By 2002, Miller predicts, value retailers will rack up $10.3 billion in consumables sales and total sales of $19.4 billion—18% compound annual growth over five years.

Martha Stewart would feel decidedly out of place in your average dollar store. Most have bare-bones fixtures—products like detergent are often stacked on the cardboard cartons they come in—and a cash-and-carry checkout (no credit cards). In keeping with the low-budget format, value retailers tend to go into locations left vacant by other tenants at rents of around $3 to $4 per square foot, less than half the discount-store average.

Thanks to these controlled costs, Miller estimates that in its first year of operation, a Dollar General produces a return on investment in excess of 50%, which in turn creates considerable cash flow. The company is thus able to sustain rapid growth—500 new stores slated for 1998—while incurring minimal debt. Family Dollar, which has never carried long-term debt, has a return on investment of 35% per unit as a result of lower sales. Still, that has been enough to fund a debt-free expansion into 38 states, with 350 to 400 new stores planned for the next fiscal year.

It's remarkable that in a niche so small, two such similar companies have competed successfully against each other for 40 years while overlapping significantly: In over half the towns where there's a Dollar General, there's also a Family Dollar. It works because these little stores draw from a very small radius, often less than three miles. Therefore, a town of 7,000 can easily support both.

Nevertheless, in the past five years Dollar General has emerged as the clear winner in the dollar-store wars, surpassing Family Dollar in both number of stores (3,360 vs. 2,970) and revenues ($2.6 billion vs. $2 billion). Along the way, its stock increased sixfold since 1993 and is currently trading around $40. Key to its success was Dollar General's recognition in the late '80s of the importance of everyday low prices, a concept pioneered by Wal-Mart. Although the company now offers goods at prices other than a dollar, more than 1,500 items are still sold at that price point, and others are fixed at prices between $1.50 and $20. This strategy has allowed Dollar Gen-

eral to eliminate advertising circulars, once the backbone of its business.

Cal Turner Jr., CEO of the Nashville-based chain, has spent his life courting the low-income customer. His father opened the first Dollar General in 1955. But Cal Jr. had a hankering to enter the ministry and today, at 58, looks every inch the lanky Southern Baptist preacher. His mission, however, is Dollar General: "I've had more of an impact on people in this business than I ever would have had from the pulpit."

Family Dollar was slower to act on the pricing and merchandising trends that drove Dollar General's growth. The retailer, based in Charlotte, N.C., emerged from a prolonged slump in 1994 when it phased in everyday low prices and cut circulars—which cost $2 million to produce each time—from 22 to nine this year. As a result, its ad budget has shrunk to less than 1% of sales for 1998. Following Dollar General's lead, it has shifted its merchandise mix from clothes to household basics—a move that is paying off in strong same-store sales: 9.3% growth last year. Apparel and other soft goods account for just 34% of sales. Shoppers replenish cleaning supplies and food more frequently than they do clothes; therefore, although prices are lower, traffic and sales are up. The stock, responding to the turnaround, has doubled in the past year, from $8 to $16.

Much of the credit goes to President Howard Levine, 38, who in 1996 returned after a nine-year hiatus to the company his father founded. Leon Levine, 60, who remains chairman and CEO, has long been respected and feared as a merchant. He understood that to sell merchandise at Family Dollar's low price points, you had to first buy it at the right price. A trade publication described him as possessing "bargaining skills that would put a . . . bazaar trader to shame."

In the early '80s, Procter & Gamble refused to cut Family Dollar a deal on Pampers diapers, arrogantly assuming that the store could not do business without the brand. Family Dollar dropped Pampers and continued to feature its own private label. Even though today vendors like P&G can no longer afford to ignore the buying power of extreme-value retailers, "we still don't sell Pampers," chuckles Howard.

Dollar Tree is the type of single-price-point store that's long been considered a glorified junk shop, packed with closeout goods nobody wants. Yet since going public in March 1995, Dollar Tree stock is up more than sevenfold, from $6.67 to $51. Last year the company made $49 million on sales of $635 million and now operates 924 stores, with 205 to open in 1998. Wall Street loves Dollar Tree's store economics—it boasts a return on investment of nearly 100% per unit, allowing the company to open hundreds each year through cash flow alone.

How does a company get returns like that when it sells everything for $1? Rather than focusing on schlocky closeouts, Dollar Tree strikes relationships with first-run vendors—often producers of so-called parallel brands—so instead of Fantastik, Dollar Tree sells Fabulous. It imports 40% of its merchandise directly, eliminating the costly middleman, and relies on closeouts for less than 15% of the mix.

With its slightly more upscale real estate—25% of its stores are in shopping malls—Dollar Tree targets a higher-income customer than the other value retailers. By locating stores alongside Wal-Marts and Targets, Dollar Tree is going after their $35,000 to $40,000 household-income demographic. It lures these customers to make impulse purchases with what analyst Jim Stoeffel of Smith Barney calls the "wow factor"— the excitement of discovering that an item costs only a dollar. Just 30% of its merchandise mix consists of core consumables; the rest is a hodgepodge of toys, garden tools, holiday decorations, and ceramic angels.

Still, the same trends that have played so favorably for Dollar General and Family Dollar have worked for Dollar Tree as well. CEO Macon Brock emphasizes the convenience aspect: "You can find every category we sell at Wal-Mart, but you'll pay more, and it will take you longer to find it and longer to pay for it," he says.

Brock estimates that there is room for at least 3,000 stores in Dollar Tree's existing 28-state base. The other players, too, see room for a lot more outlets. Dollar General has six stores on an 18-mile stretch of highway in Orlando—each is generating $1 million in sales, above the company average of $900,000.

For now, no one seems eager to go after value retailers' small-box, convenience-oriented turf. This fall Wal-Mart intends to open three prototype small-format convenience stores that will include drive-through pharmacies; however, Turner dismisses these stores as "a different animal." Indeed, at 40,000 square feet, they can hardly be considered as accessible as the dollar-store format. Pat McCormack, who covers Wal-Mart for BT Alex. Brown, believes the discount giant is hardly worried about the extreme-value segment. Dollar General's total revenues equal one week's sales for Wal-Mart, he points out.

And yet the dollar stores are pesky creatures. Argues Tom Tashjian, an analyst at NationsBanc Montgomery: "They are taking a nickel here and a quarter there from everybody"—the local variety stores, traditional discounters, grocery stores, and drugstores. The danger, he says, would be to "steal too many nickels from any one of those competitors. Then someone would retaliate." For now, they have stayed safely under the big players' radar by offering value to a segment of the population that traditional discounters have largely ignored. As Sam Walton was fond of saying, the customer votes with his feet, and low-income shoppers are clearly casting their lot with the dollar stores.

Retailers With a Future

Five benefits distinguish companies that compete on value.

Leonard L. Berry

America is "overstored," with too many retailers competing for too few customers. From 1968 to 1993, square footage for U.S. shopping centers increased 216%—four times the growth in retail sales during this period. Many retailers operating in America today are casualties waiting to happen, poised to be among the thousands of retail failures that occur annually in the United States (12,952 in 1995).

But it's the mediocre retailers that need to fear hypercompetition the most. High-performance retailers—retailers with a future—just keep growing while mediocre competitors, with no special competence or flair, struggle to survive. Retailers with a future know they must compete on value, not price. The single biggest mistake many of America's retailers are making today is assuming that value and price mean the same thing to consumers. They do not. Price is only a part of value.

To consumers, value is the benefits received for the burdens endured. Potential benefits include quality merchandise, caring personal service, pleasant store atmosphere, convenience, and peace-of-mind. Burdens include both monetary costs (price) and non-monetary costs, such as store employees who know little about the merchandise and don't care, slow checkout, inadequate parking facilities, and sloppy, unattractive, or poorly merchandised stores.

Retailers become, and stay, successful with a strong benefits-to-burdens offer. They maximize the most important benefits to targeted customers and minimize the most critical burdens. They compete on value, not solely on price—or not on price at all. Gasoline is the classic commodity product, yet a minority of these customers buy strictly on price. In 1994, Copernicus, a marketing research and consulting company, did a national study of the purchase decision criteria gasoline customers use and found that only 20% simply wanted the lowest price. The other 80% wanted a reasonable price plus other benefits, such as personal service when needed, clean rest rooms, pay-at-the-pump convenience, good lighting after dark, and a convenience store on the premises.

Competing on Value

Price is price; value is the total experience. If customer service is generally poor and merchandise looks the same from one store to another, then most consumers will indeed want the lowest price because they have no reason to pay more. But offer them a fulfilling shopping experience,

> **Price is price; value is the total experience.**

and you build a company with a future. That's what Home Depot does. And Victoria's Secret. And Starbucks Coffee. And Pier 1 imports. And Sears, resurrected at the 11th hour by new leadership.

None of these companies competes strictly on price. Home Depot gives customers the confidence to be do-it-yourselfers. Victoria's Secret turns an awkward product category once called "foundations" into a romantic, sexy category called "intimate apparel." And while Victoria's Secret was reinventing lingerie as

---

EXECUTIVE BRIEFING

Retail failure rates are high with no relief expected. Yet, despite hypercompetition in many markets, some retailers are performing well. What they have in common is compelling value for customers created through a bundle of benefits that outweighs shopping burdens. Retailers who offer a dominant merchandise assortment, fair prices, respect for customers, time and energy savings, and fun can engender the type of loyalty that secures their future.

---

a fashion category, Starbucks was transforming coffee into a fashion beverage. With exciting products from all over the world, Pier 1 turns each store visit into an adventure. And Sears didn't jump-start its comeback with a price message; it invited consumers to try the "softer side of Sears."

Retailers with a future are led by executives who have a good answer to the question: "What do we want to be famous for with customers?" Great retailers are famous with customers for delivering a valuable bundle of benefits, a bundle that customers depend on receiving. Competitors might match the prices, but they won't be able to duplicate the entire bundle.

To compete on value, retailers need to include at least five types of benefits in their bundles: (1) a dominant merchandise assortment, (2) fair prices, (3) respect for customers, (4) time and energy savings, and (5) fun (see Exhibit 1)

Dominant Assortments

One of the most powerful forces for change in retailing is the emergence of category killers—retailers that stock a complete merchandise assortment for the category in which they compete. Category killers like CompUSA, Office Depot, and Bed Bath and Beyond offer consumers a one-stop shopping alternative to limited-assortment competitors. In effect, the influence of category killers has raised customers' expectations of retail merchandising practices.

The used-car lot with 50 or 75 vehicles for sale is acceptable until the customer experiences CarMax, which offers over 500 used cars. The mall bookstore with 15,000-20,000 titles is just fine until a book lover experiences a Barnes & Noble super-store with more than 100,000 titles. The department store appears to have an adequate lingerie selection until Victoria's Secret opens in the same mall and presents new possibilities. The traditional pet store with a few thousand stockkeeping units looks and feels like a pet store is supposed to look and feel until a Petsmart store arrives in the market with 25,000 square feet of bright, airy shopping space, 12,000 SKUs, an in-store kiosk offering an additional 80,000 SKUs, and a full complement of in-store services, including pet grooming, a veterinarian clinic, and a pet adoption center.

Retailers with a future invest in category dominance with maximum merchandise breadth and depth for their chosen business. They don't just dominate with vast assortments but dramatize their dominance with sensory merchandising, interactive technology, unique departments, and special services. When consumers enter Victoria's Secret, they experience an impressive visual display of merchandise, sensuous aroma, and the sounds of the London Philharmonic Orchestra. At CarMax, customers sit down at a computer with a salesperson to identify the cars on the lot that meet their specifications. Not only does Comp USA sell more than 200 children's software titles, it also designed a special Compkids section where children play with computers and sample the software.

Retailers with a future use assortment dominance to generate in-store excitement, offer so much merchandise that customers can comparison shop without going to another store, and commit to the best in-stock performance of all competitors. And, by carrying goods and services complementary to the core line, they sell a total solution to the customer's problem. Home Depot, for example, sells material for building a deck, the know-how to build it, and the plants and fertilizer to landscape it.

Becoming an assortment dominator is more about attitude than store size or format. A 3,000-square-foot bookstore can reinvent itself as a seller of children's books, videos, and educational toys and become an assortment dominator. The attitude is that no competitor will have a better selection—or present it in a more compelling manner. Sears currently is expanding separate specialty store chains to sell furniture and hardware, a strategy that frees up more of the existing department store space for apparel and housewares—the "softer side of Sears." The specialty store strategy is enabling Sears to achieve more assortment dominance in both soft goods and hard goods.

Assortment dominators are top-of-the mind, first-choice outlets for one or more categories of merchandise. Although specialists in every category they feature, they are not necessarily specialty stores in the traditional sense. They are killers—big-store killers, medium-store killers, small-store killers, catalog killers—no matter what the case.

Pricing Fairness

Many retailers today engage in unfair and confusing pricing practices that erode their credibility and drain profits. The three-level "strawman" pricing scheme is typical of such practices: A phony "regular price" to be quickly lowered, the "sale price" at which most of the merchandise is expected to be sold, and deeper markdowns to clear slow-selling merchandise. In one survey, 75% of respondents said department stores purposely priced merchandise high only to mark it down for an advertised sale. Retailers with a future reject trickery and price products at an everyday level that represents good value for customers. Their prices earn the customer's trust, not destroy it.

Pricing fairness does not necessarily mean the *lowest* price. Even though some successful retailers promise everyday lowest prices in their promotions, very few companies can actually employ this strategy because it requires a cost structure significantly lower than that of competitors. And most executives know they can't back up this kind of promise because a competitor with a lower price always lurks around the corner. In his book, *Customers for Life,* automobile retailer Carl Sewell claims that someone can always charge a dollar less—because they are smarter than you and control their costs better, or dumber than you and don't know what their costs are.

Instead, most retailers with a future follow the principles of everyday *fair* pricing:

- Most of the merchandise is sold at regular (non-sale) prices that represent a good value for customers. The retailer strips waste from operations and gives customers their money's worth.

- Sales promotion events are legitimate, meaning that the merchandise on sale is marked down

from its regular price, rather than being marked down from an inflated, phony price.
- Prices are easy for customers to understand. They are communicated in a simple, straightforward manner without any hidden charges.

Taco Bell, which brought value pricing to the fast-food sector, is an everyday fair-pricer. Taco Bell's strategy is to offer the best value fast meal whenever and wherever customers are hungry. To implement this strategy, Taco Bell discarded traditional business approaches that gave the consumer only 27¢ worth of food for each dollar. Through machine-made tacos, off-site production, more training, more empowerment, and less employee supervision, Taco Bell now gives its customers more than 40¢ worth of food per dollar.

In a recent speech, Taco Bell chairman John Martin explained: "Imagine a dollar bill. If consumers give you 100 pennies, what do they get back? They get 27¢

EXHIBIT 1

Retailers with a future

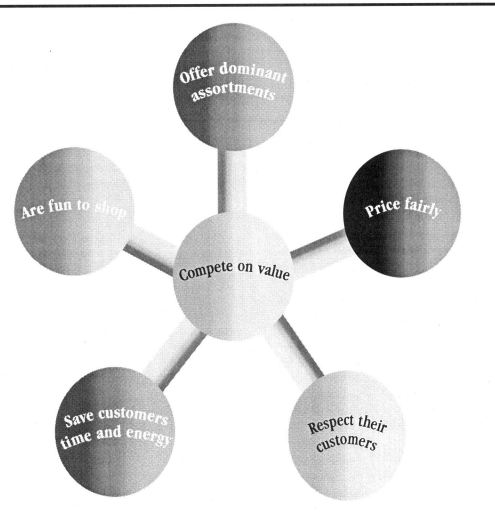

worth of food, 8¢ worth of advertising, 13¢ worth of overhead, 11¢–12¢ worth of occupancy costs, and so on. We say, instead of giving them 27¢ worth of food, let's give them 40¢ worth of food. If you're going to do that, then you've got to get this other stuff down. Of this other stuff, what is important to customers and what is not?"

As recently as 1990, Taco Bell assigned one supervising manager for every five restaurants. Multiple field management layers have since been eliminated and today supervising managers are responsible for 30 or more points of distribution. Store construction and operating costs have been significantly reduced by centralizing food preparation and reconfiguring restaurants from 70% kitchen/30% seating to 70% seating/30% kitchen.

Everyday fair pricing works best in conjunction with other strong benefits. Barnes & Noble superstores have a dominant book assortment, architecturally innovative store designs, spacious and comfortable interiors, responsive customer service, front-of-store parking convenience, coffee bars, and fair pricing. The pricing is straightforward, typically 10% off the publisher's list price on all hardback books, 20% off paperbacks on the *New York Times* bestseller list, and 30% off hardbacks on the *Times* list.

Respect for Customers

Having formally studied quality of service in America for more than 12 years, I am convinced that a *customer-respect deficit* exists in U.S. service businesses, including retailing. Customers are the lifeblood of every retail company, yet all too often they are treated badly. Something as basic as respect can influence a company's competitiveness because it sends a clear message to customers: Respectful service signals customers that a company is worthy of their loyalty; disrespectful service signals that they should take their business elsewhere.

The sidebar ["Common Customer Service Complaints"] presents 10 of the most common complaints customers express about service firms. Each of these is linked to disrespect—from cheating customers ("True Lies") to ignoring them ("Misplaced Priorities"). Disrespectful service is so common that customers notice, and remember, when a company treats them well. Retailers with a future respect their customers' time, desire for a courteous, professional service experience, and demand for fair treatment.

Some retailers treat customers as if they were houseguests. They prepare for their guests' arrival, plan special surprises to delight their guests, and make their guests feel welcome and comfortable. By investing in respectful service and making it a priority, retailers with a future turn a business basic into a customer draw.

Tattered Cover. One of America's most successful independent book retailers, Tattered Cover operates two stores in Denver. The main store is in a four-story, 40,000-square-foot building. Customers love this store because it feels like home, with wooden bookshelves, antique furniture and desks, and "151 comfy chairs and couches," as one employee puts it. Customers are encouraged to touch the books and may sit and read all day if they wish. They can sit in a church pew in the religion section and relax on a psychiatrist's couch in the psychology section.

Tattered Cover's culture is to put customer and book together. On a slow day, Tattered Cover will handle 300 special orders; on a fast day, up to 650. "Diligence and doggedness are what we do best," says owner Joyce Meskis. "We search for the elusive title wanted by the customer." General manager Linda Millemann adds: "We have always been willing to special order. Managers from other stores say, 'Well, you are big enough to do that,' but that is how we got big."

The company's employees are trained to be nonjudgmental about customers' purchases. "People buy sensitive books. It's the customer's right to read what he or she wants," floor manager Sidney Jackson explains. This nonjudgmental attitude is reinforced by the wide variety of publications in stock—about 220,000 different books and approximately 1,300 newspapers and magazines.

Tattered Cover's competitive advantage is the atmosphere of trust and community that pervades the stores. Check-writing customers are not asked to furnish identification and all employees get a key to the store on their first day of work. Meskis started this practice in 1974 when she bought the store and continues it to this day, even though the company now has more than 400 employees. The key symbolizes to employees that Tattered Cover is their store. Employees also are allowed to borrow any of the books in inventory, a policy that creates more informed floor personnel and symbolizes complete trust.

The respect shown employees encourages the respect they provide to customers, which fosters intense loyalty to the store. Indeed, it is the way human beings are treated at Tattered Cover that sets this retail company apart.

Royers' Round Top Cafe. Round Top, Texas, a town with 88 residents, is not exactly a prime setting for a retail success story. Yet, Royers', a 38-seat restaurant, attracts 300–400 customers on a typical Saturday, many of whom travel from Houston, 80 miles away. The draw is wonderful food, world-class pies (it's a nickel extra if you don't have ice cream with the pie), and respectful service.

Customers wait for their tables on the front porch, where they help themselves to beer and wine on the honor system. Once seated, customers are never rushed through the meal. "Eating is an event that should be enjoyable and relaxing," says owner Bud Royer. "I absolutely will not let the floors be swept until the customers at the last table walk out the door. I don't want that last table to feel like we are rushing them because we want to go home."

The restaurant accepts no credit cards but does not turn away customers without cash. The customer eats, takes the bill home, and mails in a check. No one has failed to pay the bill yet. The customer-respect deficit in retailing creates an opening for retail companies that are prepared to treat customers well. Size-of-company is not important; size-of-commitment is. To assess your company's commitment, consider the "Customer Respect Checklist."

Save Customers Time and Energy

Studies consistently report that consumers perceive their free time is dwindling. In a series of studies by the Americans' Use of Time Project, national samples of adults were asked whether they "always," "sometimes," or "almost never" felt rushed to do the things they have to do. In the 1992 survey, 38% of the sample indicated they "always" felt rushed, up from 32% in 1985 and 22% in 1971. The perception of time poverty is greatest for consumers who combine work, marriage, and parenthood. In the latest study, nearly two out of three working mothers (64%) reported always feeling rushed.

Perceived time scarcity contributes to stress. In a 1991 survey by Hilton Hotels, 43% of the sample agreed that they often feel under stress when they do not have enough time. In the 1993 National Study of the Changing Workforce, 80% of respondents said their jobs require them to work very hard, 65% said they must work very fast, and 42% said they feel "used up" by the end of the day. From a 1994 study reported in *American Demographics* comes the finding that 60% of Americans feel under great stress at least once a week, and 19% feel this way almost every day.

Too little time and too much stress have a negative impact on personal energy levels, which is not conducive to a leisurely visit to the shopping mall. Consumers now visit malls less frequently and visit fewer stores in less time when they do go. A 1994 national poll conducted by Maritz Marketing Research found that one-third of adult shoppers reported shopping at malls less frequently than just a year earlier, citing limited money and time as the main reasons.

Yankelovich Partners asked consumers in a survey what they would do on a free Saturday or Sunday. Sixty-nine percent said they would watch television and 46% said they would take a nap. A hidden competitor for stores is the increasingly appealing idea of staying home. In Yankelovich's annual *Monitor* study, consumers are asked what is important in deciding

Common Customer Service Complaints

True Lies: Blatant dishonesty or unfairness, such as service providers selling unneeded services or purposely quoting fake, "low-ball" cost estimates.

Red Alert: Providers who assume customers are stupid or dishonest and treat them harshly or disrespectfully.

Broken Promises: Service providers who do not show up as promised. Careless, mistake-prone service.

I Just Work Here: Powerless employees who lack the authority—or the desire—to solve basic customer problems.

The Big Wait: Waiting in a line made long because some of the checkout lanes or service counters are closed.

Automatic Pilot: Impersonal, emotionless, no-eye-contact, going-through-the-motions non-service.

Suffering in Silence: Employees who don't bother to communicate with customers who are anxious to hear how a service problem will be resolved.

Don't Ask: Employees unwilling to make any extra effort to help customers, or who seem put-out by requests for assistance.

Lights On, No One Home: Clueless employees who do not know (i.e., will not take the time to learn) the answers to customers' common questions.

Misplaced Priorities: Employees who visit with each other or conduct personal business while the customer waits. Those who refuse to assist a customer because they're off duty or on a break.

—*Len Berry*

where to shop. "Makes it easy to shop" was rated important by 55% of the respondents in 1988 and by 67% in 1993.

Retailers with a future save customers time and energy. They invest in making their stores easy to get to and easy to get through and/or making shopping possible without going to a store at all. They compete on convenience, offering maximum access, one-stop or no-stop shopping, logical store design, quick transactions, and no-hassle returns.

Walgreen. With nearly $500 in sales per square foot (compared to the drugstore industry average of $300), the country's largest drugstore chain focuses on making its stores easy to get to and get through. Walgreen's targeted customer is the high-frequency shopper who visits a drugstore more than five times a month. Although these shoppers represent just 10% of the population, they account for 50% of Walgreen's sales.

High-frequency customers buy general merchandise as well as pharmaceuticals in drugstores, and the key to attracting them is convenience. Walgreen's strategy is to blanket markets with freestanding stores that are easily accessible—stores on the "corner of Main and Main"—and provide ample parking, drive-through

Customer Respect Checklist

✔ Do we trust our customers? Do we operate our business to effectively serve the vast majority of customers who are honest, or to protect ourselves from the small minority who are not?

✔ Do we stand behind what we sell? Are we easy to do business with if a customer experiences a problem with our offerings? Do we have a sense of urgency to make the customer whole? Are front-line employees empowered to respond appropriately to a problem? Do we guarantee the goods we sell? Do we guarantee our service?

✔ Do we stress promise-keeping in our company? Is keeping commitments to customers—from being in-stock on advertised goods to being on time for appointments—deemed important in our company?

✔ Do we value our customers' time? Do we anticipate periods of maximum demand for our offerings and staff accordingly to minimize customer waiting? Are our facilities and service systems convenient and efficient for customers to use? Do we prepare new employees to provide efficient, effective service before putting them in front of customers? Do we teach employees that serving customers supersedes all other priorities, such as paperwork or stocking shelves?

✔ Do we communicate with customers respectfully? Are our signs informative and helpful? Are our statements clear and understandable? Is our advertising above reproach in its truthfulness and taste? Are our contact personnel professional in appearance and manner? Does our language convey respect, such as "I will be happy to do this" and "It will be my pleasure?" Do we answer and return telephone calls promptly—and with a smile in our voice? Is our voice-mail system caller-friendly?

✔ Do we respect all customers? Do we treat all customers with respect, regardless of their appearance, age, race, status, or size of purchase or account? Have we taken any special precautions to minimize discriminatory treatment of certain customers?

✔ Do we thank customers for their business? Do we say "thank you" at times other than after a purchase? Do our customers feel appreciated?

✔ Do we respect our employees? Do our human resources policies and practices pass the employee-respect test? Do our employees, who are expected to respect customers, experience respectful treatment themselves? Would employees want their children to work in our company when they grow up?

—Len Berry

pharmacy windows, wide aisles, low shelves, excellent in-store signage, and scanner-based checkouts.

Intercom, a satellite-based computer system linking all Walgreen stores, maintains customers, prescription records for timely use in emergencies. Where state law allows, customers can obtain a refill at any Walgreen's store. A customer living in Texas who forgets her medicine on a trip to Arizona need only visit an Arizona store for a refill. Walgreen's customers can reach a pharmacist 24 hours a day via a toll-free 800 number, and the company will send the prescription via overnight mail. Through Intercom, Walgreen can provide a patient's prescription records to hospital emergency rooms 24 hours a day, seven days a week.

Once the customer's name, address, and prescription information are put into the Intercom system, a label and receipt are printed automatically. Refills require no new information, and Intercom can supply customers a printout of prescription purchases for their tax and insurance records. Walgreen is currently rolling out Intercom Plus, its "next generation" pharmacy system that will improve customer service and productivity further and enable prmacists to provide more counseling to patients.

Fun to Shop

Consumers who are selective in their shopping choices are unlikely to spend time in undifferentiated and lackluster stores. Retail dullness—merchandise sameness, boring displays, worn and tired stores, and/or an absence of in-store events—is a losing strategy in today's and tomorrow's marketplace.

The pace of sensory stimulation is so great today that many consumers are easily bored. Their reality is global travel, 50-plus television channels in the home, multimedia computers, on-line access to virtually any kind of material on the Internet, innovative marketing campaigns from companies such as Nike, and innovative retailing from companies such as Warner Brothers Studio Stores. Consumers today are used to being entertained and they expect it in exchange for their time, effort, and money. As the worlds of retailing and entertainment continue to merge, dull retailers will fade into oblivion.

Whether selling computers or cars, food or footwear, books or bracelets, retailers with a future make shopping fresh, stimulating, and exciting. They keep new merchandise flowing into the store so regular shoppers can always discover something new. They directly appeal to the customers' appetite for sensory adventure, entertain customers while they educate them, and dazzle them with the dramatic.

West Point Market. An outstanding specialty food store in Akron, Ohio, that has been in business nearly 60 years, West Point Market is the quintessential sensory retailer. Flowers are everywhere: in front of the store, in the parking lot, at the store entrance, in the aisles. The property has more than 80 trees, the delivery truck is painted with dancing vegetables, merchandise signs are hand-drawn in soft colors by an artist, exits are marked by handcarved wooden signs, and colorful balloons decorate the entire store. And there's more:

- Information and recipe tags on West Point's shelves educate shoppers on how to use the products: "This creamy mild cheese with caraway seeds slices well for ham sandwiches on hearty rye."
- The market's "Customers of Tomorrow" program includes kiddie shopping carts and cookie credit cards (good for a free cookie on each store visit).
- Rest rooms feature classical music, almond soap, indirect lighting, and, of course, fresh flowers.
- Product tasting and in-store demonstrations are common. As many as four events—one chef cooking pasta, another preparing salsa recipes, and another preparing a cold pasta with a new avocado dressing, plus a bread sampling table—might occur simultaneously on a Saturday.

Everyone in this store is smiling—customers and employees alike—because West Point Market makes food shopping fun.

The Container Store. A highly successful chain based in Dallas, The Container Store sells merchandise designed to help people organize their homes and their lives. Every conceivable product to bring efficiency to a kitchen, organize a closet, or tidy an office is available at The Container Store. There is no "back of the store" here; every corner is beautifully merchandised. Employees sit in the store aisles assembling components into finished products while customers gather around to watch, chat, and learn more about the product. Unique merchandise, a bright and airy decor, live product demonstrations, and happy, helpful employees all make The Container Store fun for shoppers.

Barnes & Noble. Customers frequently take their time strolling through this bookseller's super-stores, perusing the well-stocked magazine section, sitting in a chair to read or people-watch, enjoying a coffee at the in-store Starbucks, perhaps meeting a friend, and then finally purchasing some books. At Barnes & Noble, customers can have a literary and social experience in one store visit.

In a 1995 speech, Leonard Riggio, Barnes & Noble chief executive said "The store is the principal message. Too many retailers devote too much attention to advertising, instead of creating great stores. . . . Bookstores never again will be considered sleepy places." Poverty of time and energy is not an issue for Barnes & Noble because shopping these stores is not a chore; the company sells a product—books—that offers busy consumers a sense of stability and relaxation in stores that are entertaining.

Value Compels

Surviving hypercompetition in American retailing requires an unprecedented level of strategic and operating excellence. Only the fittest of America's retailers can feel any security whatsoever about the future. Retail fitness is defined by the value delivered to customers. Value is not price, nor is it one of anything else; value is a compelling bundle of benefits well worth the customers' money, time, and effort.

America's consumers, increasingly selective and expectant, can find many sources of compelling retail value. They have no reason to patronize mediocre retailers that offer nothing special. Every retailer needs to ask and honestly answer this question: If our company were to disappear from the landscape overnight, would customers really miss us? For retailers with a future, the answer is a resounding "yes." Like salt, they have no satisfying substitute.

About the Author

Leonard L. Berry holds the JCPenney Chair of Retailing Studies, is Professor of Marketing and Director of the Center for Retailing Studies in the College of Business Administration at Texas A&M University, College Station. He is also editor of the "Arthur Andersen Retailing Issues Letter" and was AMA President for 1986–87. His books include: *On Great Service: A Framework for Action* (New York: The Free Press, 1995); *Delivering Quality Service: Balancing Customer Perceptions and Expectations* (New York: The Free Press, 1990); *Marketing Services: Competing Through Quality* (New York: The Free Press, 1991); and *Service Quality—A Profit Strategy for Financial Institutions* (Homewood, IL: Business One Irwin, 1989). Len has twice won the highest honor Texas A&M bestows on a faculty member: the Distinguished Achievement Award in Teaching (in 1990) and the Distinguished Achievement Award in Research (in 1996). He is a member of the board of directors of CompUSA and Hastings Books, Music, and Video Inc. In 1995, he was elected as a public member of the board of directors for the Council of Better Business Bureaus.

THE NOSTALGIA BOOM

Why the old is new again

To viewers watching the ad for the new Volkswagen Beetle, it is like squinting into the past. A vague image begins as a small circle set against a stark white background. As the picture sharpens, the circle becomes a flower—with seven daffodil-yellow New Beetles as its petals. The cute-as-a-Bug cars drive away, and a zippy black Beetle careens into view and skids to a stop. The tag line: "Less flower. More power."

Welcome back to the '60s—except this time, the revolution will be televised by Madison Avenue. Volkswagen's Flower Power commercial is only the first in a barrage of ads about to hit the airwaves as the German auto maker launches a new and improved version of the venerable Beetle to America after a 20-year absence. Volkswagen's strategy is simple: It plans to sell its back-to-the-future car by wrapping it in the symbols of the not-too-distant past.

Volkswagen is not the only marketer mining the warm associations of boomer youth and the Age of Aquarius to sell consumer goods. These days, nostalgia marketing is everywhere, from almost forgotten brands such as Burma Shave to jingles that borrow from classic rock. Pepsi uses the Rolling Stones' *Brown Sugar,* while James Brown's *I Feel Good* helps sell Senokot Laxatives. Hollywood is awash with remakes of movies and TV shows plucked from an earlier era. Even retired slogans and mascots are being resurrected. Maxwell House has dusted off "Good to the last drop," while

Charlie the Tuna is swimming his way through Starkist tuna ads once again.

Consumers can't seem to get enough of these airbrushed memories. Middle-aged boomers obsessed with their youth and movin' down the highway toward retirement clamor for retro roadsters such as the Porsche Boxster. Walt Disney Co. developed an entire town, Celebration, Fla., on the notion that Americans are pining for the look and feel of 1940s neighborhoods. Baseball fans step back in time by piling into Cleveland's Jacobs Field and Oriole Park at Camden Yards—new ballparks designed to look like they've been around since the turn of the century. Meanwhile, kids have reclaimed mom and dad's bell bottoms and platform shoes and brought back Diane Von Furstenberg's wrap dress.

No one, though, has as much riding on the nostalgia wave as Volkswagen. Its U.S. market share having withered to less than 1%, VW is wagering $560 million that its spunky little car can revive its fortunes. It's a very calculated bet. The new, postmodern Beetle has been reinvented with a message that slyly assuages end-of-the-millennium angst with a harkening back to the Summer of Love. The new version, which is about to hit the showrooms, comes with all the modern features car buyers demand, such as four air bags and power outlets for cell phones. But that's not why VW expects folks to buy it. With a familiar bubble shape that still

makes people smile as it skitters by, the new Beetle offers a pull that is purely emotional. "If you sold your soul in the '80s," tweaks one ad, "here's your chance to buy it back."

STRESS RELIEF? Why the intense yearning to turn back the clock? The faster we hurdle toward the millennium, it seems, the more we're reaching desperately backwards toward the halcyon days of mid-century, days of postwar prosperity and quaint notions of revolution that nowadays seem astonishing in their innocence and idealism. In their place have come growing anxiety about aging and a fear of hanging on in today's increasingly stressful society.

Americans are overwhelmed, social experts say, by the breathtaking onrush of the Information Age, with its high-speed modems, cell phones, and pagers. While we hail the benefits of the wired '90s, at the same time we are buffeted by the rapid pace of change. "We are creating a new culture, and we don't know what's going to happen," explains futurist Watts Wacker, co-author of *The 500-Year Delta.* "So we need some warm fuzzies from our past."

Just take a stroll through the supermarket. Shelves are now brimming with packaged goods that look as if they're from another era. After Coca-Cola Co. recreated a plastic version of its famous contour bottle in 1994, sales grew by double digits in some markets, says Frank P. Bifulco, vice-president for marketing

Even today's youth are adopting icons
of a time before most of them were born

of Coca-Cola USA. Necco wafers are enjoying a comeback—sales are up 25% in the past two years—thanks in part to a packaging redesign that harkens back to its roots. "There has been a flurry of clients coming to us and saying, 'We want that handcrafted look,' " says Jack Vogler, partner at SBG Enterprise, a San Francisco packaging-design house that recently restored the old packaging of the Sun-Maid raisin girl and Cracker Jack's Sailor Jack and Bingo.

Even old ads are being recycled to woo wistful customers. Sales of Maxwell House have perked up since it began including archival footage of percolating coffee pots in its ads. It's a startling departure from the modern image Maxwell House projected in the early 1990s as hip upstarts such as Starbucks Corp. became all the rage. "Consumers are not in a real experimental time now," says Richard S. Helstein, vice-president for advertising at Kraft Foods Inc. "They are looking for brands they can depend on—brands they grew up with."

Successes such as these have advertisers jumping on the bandwagon—even when they don't have archives to pillage. In February, Ford Motor Co. began airing a commercial commemorating how Henry Ford put America on wheels. The spot includes what appears to be grainy, historic footage of a Model T puttering down a long-ago Main Street. But the sepia-toned scene was actually shot last year on a Hollywood back lot and was given a vintage look by using a 1920s hand-cranked camera, old emulsion film, and special editing.

Why recreate history? Ford is hoping that consumers will equate longevity with quality. "People really respond to it. They say, 'This is a company that has lasted through a couple of world wars,' " says Bruce Rooke, executive creative director at Ford's agency, J. Walter Thompson Co.

Indeed, social experts say much of the appeal of nostalgia stems from a longing for a return to simpler times. Despite a robust economy, Americans remain an anxiety-ridden bunch. Not all the riches of a long bull market can make up for the rigors of overbooked working parents forced to reduce family life to an exercise in time management. Divorce rates remain high, job security is down, and saving enough to send the kids to college or for retirement can seem overwhelming. Is it any wonder that a new survey from Roper Starch Worldwide shows that 55% of Americans believe the "good old days" were better than today? That's an about-face from attitudes of a generation ago, when 54% of those surveyed in 1974 told Roper they believed there was no time better than the present.

GOLDEN MEMORIES. Naturally, baby boomers, ever powerful in their numbers, are driving this return to roots. The Roper survey identifies the most longed-for age as the 1950s, 1960s, and 1970s. "The '50s and '60s were a time of very high expectations for baby boomers," says J. Walker Smith, a partner with the Yankelovich Partners consumer-research firm. "But life didn't turn out to be the 1964 World's Fair."

In fact, life went on, and aging is yet another force at the root of nostalgia marketing. The oldest of the boomers are in their 50s and are resisting the aging process with the vigor they once reserved for protesting the war. While they snap up vitamins, diet pills, and other tonics touted to stop the clock, marketers are counting on the appeal of nostalgic products to salve the wounds of growing old. If nothing else, familiar products and jingles give boomers the chance to act and feel young. "Boomers are saying, 'Maybe my parents were old at 50, but I'm not,' " says Rick Adler, president of Senior Network Inc., a marketing consultant firm.

That's certainly a big reason why Dennis J. Berger, 52, waited six months to take delivery of his white $65,000 Porsche Boxster, a retro roadster styled like the 1950s vintage Porsche favored by movie stars like James Dean. "It opened up a memory of when I was a teenager in New Jersey," says Berger, vice-president of Allied Plastics Co. in Jacksonville, Fla. "This car reminds me of the '50s, when there wasn't a care in the world."

Yet the nostalgia phenomenon is not simply about America reliving a Golden Age. It is also about reinterpreting it. We may look back through rose-colored glasses, but few want to live in the past for the sake of authenticity. The new retro ethos has a thoroughly modern cast. Log Cabin syrup brought back an old-timey label but sports a convenient squeeze-top bottle. When Coke redid its famous hourglass bottle, it made it in today's popular big-gulp sizes. And movie remakes come complete with the latest in special effects. "Americans want that Victorian house with the wraparound porch, but it had better be wired for all the latest technology," says Carolyn E. Setlow, senior vice-president at Roper.

Such reinterpretations are particularly popular among younger, Generation-X consumers. While they've adopted many products and fashions from the 1960s and 1970s as their own, they often update them with an ironic twist. And it has little to do with longing for an era they never experienced. "I see it more as rediscovering than retro," says 20-year-old Matthew Levy of New York City. "I don't want to be my father. I want to rediscover things he forgot about when he was out climbing the corporate ladder." Case in point: cigars. Both he and his dad smoke them. But Levy says his generation has reinvented the product to suit its lifestyle. "Where my dad smoked cigars, they didn't allow women. No one my age would go for that."

Too much of a good thing? Ad shops fear overkill

The vintage-style stadiums that have risen across the country embody this marriage of past and present. Camden Yards and Jacobs Field look like ballparks from a bygone era. Coming to New York might be a re-creation of the old Brooklyn Dodgers' home turf, Ebbets Field. But this time, it would house the New York Mets. On the inside, these faux-historic stadiums are ringed with the luxury suites that make corporate customers comfortable and owners rich. Even regular fans are rewarded with wider seats and broad concourses dotted with more concession stands and restrooms than real old ballparks ever had. "People will go to see a place once because it's historic," says HOK Sport Senior Vice-President Joseph E. Spear, the architect of Camden Yards and Jacobs Field. "But they don't come back unless they have a good time."

POWER SUNROOF. The Beetle comeback is also based on a combination of romance and reason—wrapping up modern conveniences in an old-style package. Built into the dashboard is a bud vase perfect for a daisy plucked straight from the

1960s. But right next to it is the high-tech multi-speaker stereo—and options like power windows, cruise control, and a power sunroof make it a very different car than the ratty old Bug. So, too, does the sticker price. While a new Bug cost just $1,800 in 1968—$8,300 in today's dollars—a typically equipped new Beetle will run about $16,500.

But if the Beetle, like us, has grown up, Volkswagen is hoping it will still spark the same emotions as its younger self. With its simple design and no-frills engineering, the original Beetle was the antithesis of Detroit's gas-guzzlers. As boomers by the tens of thousands bought their first cars, it blossomed into an unlikely icon. By 1968, its peak year, VW sold 423,000 Beetles in the U.S. Cheap to own, easy to fix, and giddy fun to drive, the Beetle personified an era of rebellion against conventions. Says John Wright, a pop-culture expert at the Henry Ford Museum in Dearborn, Mich.: "When people look at Volkswagen, it looks at youth."

But youth fades, and by the late 1970s, the Bug had faded, too. VW

was never the same after it dropped the Beetle from production for the U.S. in 1978. By 1993, says Jens Neumann, a member of Volkswagen's board of managers, with less than 1% of U.S. auto sales, "we were just about to drop out of this market."

MYSTERY MARKET. Instead, VW Chairman Ferdinand Piëch decided to make an almost quixotic bid to recapture its former glory. In 1993, he ordered up a prototype of a new Beetle in what was essentially a last-ditch effort to jump-start sales. The concept car was launched at the 1994 auto show in Detroit—and promptly stole the show as car shoppers and reporters mobbed the VW display. Crowds packed in several people deep just to get a look at the yellow Bug. The wildly enthusiastic reaction from the public astounded even VW execs. "We were, to say the least, overwhelmed," says Piëch.

Still, VW is walking softly into the market. It plans to build just 100,000 Beetles a year at its plant in Puebla, Mexico, with half of those targeted for the U.S. and Canada. Company execs refuse to be pinned down on the Bee-

Rock On!

In the battle to win the hearts and minds of aging boomers, more and more marketers are turning to old rock and pop hits

BRAND	ARTIST	SONG
Toyota	Sly and the Family Stone	Everyday People
AT&T	Elton John	Rocket Man
Senokot Laxative	James Brown	I Feel Good
Pepsi	The Rolling Stones	Brown Sugar
Microsoft	The Rolling Stones	Start Me Up
Ford	The Who	I Can't Explain
Intel	Bee Gees	Stayin' Alive
Levi's	The Partridge Family	I Think I Love You
Burger King	Squeeze	Tempted

tle's target market, saying only that it is designed for "optimists." Yet it's clearly aiming wide. While many of its ads sport jokes targeted at the previous Beetle generation, others are aimed squarely at Gen-X.

Early signs are that VW could have a cross-generational hit on its hands. Dealers across the country have been inundated with inquiries on the new Bug, and many now have long waiting lists. Jeff La Plant, sales manager for Volkswagen of Santa Monica, says he has already gotten orders from 100 customers. "It's like you have a rock star here and everybody wants an autograph," La Plant says. "I've never seen a car that had such a wide range of interest, from 16-year-olds to 65-year-olds."

Greg Stern, a 47-year-old film producer in Santa Monica, is No. 1 on La Plant's list. Describing the car as—what else—"way cool," he's in line for a silver or white model. "In 1967, my Dad got me a VW. I loved it. I'm sure the new one will take me back," says Stern. "I'm getting the New Beetle as a surprise for my daughter, but I'm sure I'm going to be stealing it from her all the time."

Like Volkswagen, others have discovered that a history of warm memories is an exploitable asset these days. The Nickelodeon cable channel's Nick at Nite proved such a hit recycling sitcoms that it spawned TV Land and a host of other imitators. Burma Shave is banking almost entirely on its nostalgic appeal as it returns to store shelves after a 30-year absence. The shaving cream's legendary rhyming roadside signs, last seen in 1964, will return this summer. And they may even begin showing up in the supermarkets and Wal-Marts where Burma Shave is now sold, says brand manager Steve Cochran. "Those signs evoke a lot of nostalgia about driving along the highway on vacation," he says.

At least Burma Shave's history is real. As nostalgia becomes ever more important as a marketing tool, companies are increasingly willing to fake it. Four years ago, Gap Inc. launched the Old Navy casual clothing chain with a series of old-timey black-and-white ads and store decor that recalled the '50s. "We used nostalgia in the very beginning to give credibility to the brand, so that it didn't feel like it was coming from nowhere," explains Richard Crisman, Old Navy's senior vice-president for marketing. Since then, Old Navy has modernized its marketing with new campaigns emphasizing value and fashion. But many of the original decor touches remain—all 300 stores sport a '50s Chevy pickup truck, for example, and the New York flagship store features a '50s-style diner.

HEY, IF IT WORKED BEFORE . . .

His goofy bowl-cut hairstyle is gone, and the suit is blue instead of red. But six years after ending a 35-year TV run, Captain Kangaroo is back—and so are Mr. Greenjeans and Mr. Moose. Starting last fall, a recast Captain welcomed a new generation of preschoolers to the Treasure House.

As they say in Hollywood: When in doubt, recycle. Although remakes and sequels have always played a big role in Tinseltown, never before have so many producers devoted so much time to story lines pilfered from the past. "Just about every studio is dredging up something from its library," says Dean Devlin, producer of the upcoming *Godzilla* movie.

WARM MEMORIES. In the past three years alone, Universal has made big, live-action movie hits out of *The Flintstones* and *Casper*. Walt Disney Co. had a smash in the live-action updating of *101 Dalmations*. Plenty more is on the way, including summer films based on the '60s shows *Lost in Space* and *The Avengers*. Meanwhile, TV remakes of *The Love Boat, Fantasy Island,* and *The Hollywood Squares* are in the works. This month, Paramount will re-release *Grease*.

Why the deluge? Larry Jones, general manager of Viacom Inc.'s Nick at Nite and TV Land oldie channels, believes it "reflects a need for people to get back to a time when life was simpler." Jones should know: The highly successful diet of *Hogan's Heroes* and *I Love Lucy* reruns his channels serve up has launched a host of copycats.

But warm memories are just part of the trend. Another prime driver is money. The film and TV industry spends millions each year developing projects that never make it to the screen. A remake or sequel is a known quantity that many in the increasingly risk-averse industry assume will have built-in audience appeal.

Still, not all oldies are reborn as goodies. Last year's Tinseltown bombs include movies based on *McHale's Navy, Flipper, Sergeant Bilko,* and *Mr. Magoo*. In February, Universal Pictures flopped with a sequel to the 20-year-old *The Blues Brothers* movie. These failed largely because they didn't offer anything new. "It can't look so much like the original that it looks like it should be on late-night TV," says Devlin.

Indeed, Hollywood is discovering that remakes require plenty of modern-day gimmickry. Paramount Pictures turned *Mission: Impossible* into an $189 million blockbuster by signing Tom Cruise and loading the film with special effects. The studio's 1996 film of *The Brady Bunch* scored by portraying the wholesome, bell-bottom-clad 1970s family as 1990s misfits. "You have to have a unique gimmick or people aren't going to buy your film no matter how familiar they might be with it," says *Brady Bunch* producer Alan Ladd Jr.

That's why King World Productions Inc. paid a reported $3 million bonus to get Whoopi Goldberg to sit in the center square for its redo of the game show *The Hollywood Squares*. To turn Generation Xers onto their *Lost in Space* movie, New Line Cinema hired popular actors such as *Friends'* Matt LeBlanc.

To see how oldies can work in the right setting, just look at CBS: Catering to its aging boomer viewers, it has boosted Friday ratings by adding new versions of *Candid Camera* and *Kids Say the Darndest Things* to the lineup. It's tried. It's true. Best of all, it packs the house.

By Ronald Grover in Los Angeles

DRAMA FLOP. For Old Navy, the tactic paid off. But not all efforts to manufacture nostalgia have been so successful. Executives at fast-food chain Kentucky Fried Chicken Corp. learned that you can go too far. Three years ago, they decided the brand needed some advertising help from founder Colonel Harlan Sanders. KFC's research showed that consumers still trusted the colonel. The problem: Sanders died in 1980, and KFC could not find old film clips of him that would work in a modern commercial. "Nothing was sound-bitey enough," explained Peter J. Foulds, KFC's advertising vice-president.

So KFC dressed up an actor in the colonel's starched white suit and broadcast black-and-white TV commercials that pretended to show the founder spouting his special brand of homespun wisdom. But the attempt to recreate history didn't wash, and KFC was roundly criticized for defaming the dead. After less than a year, the ads were pulled. Still, KFC hasn't given up on using the colonel altogether. Instead, the company decided the best—and safest—way to evoke his memory was to enlarge his image on buckets of chicken.

Celebrities who are dead, however, are hotter than ever in commercials. Ironically, one factor behind the wave of dead celebs who have come back to endorse products is sophisticated technology. Computer-generated imagery has made it appear that Fred Astaire had a new dancing partner—Dirt Devil vacuum cleaners. Lucille Ball sells diamond rings for Service Merchandise Co. And Ed Sullivan is back from the beyond to unveil one more phenom to the world: the Mercedes-Benz sport-utility. "Who is Mr. Introduction-to-America more than Ed Sullivan?" says Mike Jackson, president of Mercedes-Benz of North America.

If only reviving a dying brand were as easy. A&W Restaurants Inc., once famous for carhops on roller skates, is attempting to reverse more than two decades of decline by overhauling its restaurants in a 1950s rock 'n' roll image. A&W Chairman Sidney Feltenstein, a former Burger King Corp. marketing executive, hopes the retro appeal will help them stand out in a crowded segment. Feltenstein says McDonald's Corp. and Burger King can fight over the kids; he's aiming for adults. So far, the makeover appears to be working: At one redone A&W in Dearborn, Mich., middle-age diners dominate the lunchtime crowd. "It reminds you of your youth," says salesman Kirk Pettit, 38, as Beach Boys music wafts from an old Wurlitzer jukebox. Overall, sales at the remodeled stores are up 20% over 1996.

So is nostalgia just the latest hype from Madison Avenue? Or is it the zeitgeist of a culture? While it clearly hits a chord, some worry that overkill can't be far off. "The grainy black-and-white commercials are the shaky camera of the late '90s," scoffs Martin Horn, Chicago-based research director at DDB Needham Worldwide Inc. "We in the ad business slide into derivative behavior." Also dubious is John K. Grace, executive director of Interbrand, a New York-based brand consultancy, who believes American culture in the late '90s lacks distinc-tion, so young and old alike are clinging to the sights and sounds of the past until something better comes along. He compares it to the quiet 1950s, which led to the tumultuous 1960s: "There are no cultural hooks for youth to grab on to today, so they find comfort in what was. But nostalgia can't be sustained."

But others say advertisers are only reflecting Americans' deeper longings to take control of their lives by reconnecting with their idealized past. "If you want to understand values, study our advertising," says Seymour Leventman, a sociology professor at Boston College. He believes the nostalgia craze will only grow as trend-setting baby boomers age.

That's why the New Beetle just might be a tonic for the times. It is our romantic past, reinvented for our hectic here-and-now. "The Beetle is not just empty nostalgia," says Gerald Celente, publisher of *Trends Journal*. "It is a practical car that is also tied closely to the emotions of a generation."

To unleash that emotion, VW's staid German executives flew to Atlanta to stage a love-in to introduce the Love Bug last month to 300 journalists from around the world. Young women in tie-dyed T-shirts handed out daisies and peace medallions in a psychedelic rock hall. VW's Piëch marveled at his little car's enduring appeal. "It is different, and it makes you feel different," he said. "It's like a magnet." Different, yet deeply familiar—a car for the times.

By Keith Naughton and Bill Vlasic in Detroit, with bureau reports

Good Service, Good Selling

Kristin Anderson and Ron Zemke

Sales and service are not separate functions. They are two sides of the same coin. Even if your title is customer service representative and a coworker is a sales associate, you both have the same ultimate goal: satisfying the customer. It wasn't always this way. In days gone by, sales and service personnel used to be adversaries.

Sales and marketing people viewed their counterparts in service and operations as "those guys who never want to help me make a sale and who screw it up after it's a done deal."

Service and operation folk, for their part, tended to view sales and marketing people as "those people in suits who write outlandish ads, make ridiculous promises to close the sale and leave us holding the bag with customers."

In today's world, sales, marketing, service and operations share a common goal: creating and retaining customers. To achieve that goal we have to combine good service with good selling. Consider the case of Edgar Pinchpenny III, the unhappy owner of a Model 412-A Handy-Andy Cordless Electric Screwdriver. (You know he's unhappy because he is waving the 412-A around and demanding his money back.)

Using your very best "Knock Your Socks Off Service" skills (listening, questioning, problem solving), you determine that Pinchpenny is upset because the 412-A needs frequent recharging and isn't very powerful. But you also know that the 412-A was built for small repair jobs around the house. It absolutely was not designed for the industrial strength sort of work Pinchpenny is trying to get out of it. That's why your company also sells the much more expensive 412-C Turbo-Andy, the best professional power screwdriver in the industry and the perfect tool for Pinchpenny's job.

Better service at the time of the original sale *might* have matched Pinchpenny with the more appropriate tool. But what should you do about the situation now? Consider which of these four possible actions you would recommend:

- **Option 1.** Tell Pinchpenny that if he hadn't been so cheap in the first place, he wouldn't be standing there screaming himself into a coronary.
- **Option 2.** Explain the limitations of the 412-A and the benefits of the 412-C to Pinchpenny, and recommend that he consider buying up.
- **Option 3.** Apologize to Pinchpenny for the inconvenience and explain the difference between the two models. Then offer to personally make an exchange on the spot and to give him a discount on the 412-C to compensate for being inconvenienced.
- **Option 4.** Apologize for the salesperson's stupidity, offer Pinchpenny an even exchange—the old, abused 412-A for a shiny new 412-C at no additional cost—throw in a free set of your best stainless screwdriver bits *and* offer to wash Pinchpenny's car.

We pick Option 3 as the best course of action: It shows concern, re-

---

THE ART OF SERVICE RECOVERY

The word recovery means to "return to normal"—to get things back in balance or good health. In service, good recovery begins when a customer service representative recognizes (and the sooner the better) that the customer has a problem.

The service recovery process includes the following steps. Not all are needed for all customers. Use what you know about your company's products and services, and what you can discover about your customers' problems, to customize your actions:

1 Apologize. It doesn't matter who's at fault. Customers want someone to acknowledge that a problem occurred and to show concern over their disappointment.

2 Listen and empathize. Treat your customers in a way that shows you care about them as well as about their problem. People have feelings and emotions. They want the personal side of the transaction acknowledged.

3 Fix the problem quickly and fairly. A "fair fix" is one that's delivered with a sense of professional concern. At the bottom line, customers want what they expected to receive in the first place, and the sooner the better.

4 Offer atonement. It's not uncommon for dissatisfied customers to feel injured or put out by a service breakdown. Often they will look to you to provide some value-added gesture that says, in a manner appropriate to the problem, "I want to make it up to you."

5 Keep your promises. Service recovery is needed because a customer believes a service promise has been broken. During the recovery process, you will often make new promises. When you do, be realistic about what you can and can't deliver.

6 Follow up. You can add a pleasant extra to the recovery sequence by following up a few hours, days or weeks later to make sure things really were resolved to your customer's satisfaction.

—K. A. and R. Z.

From *Marketing Forum*, December 1997, pp. 2-3. Excerpted from *Delivering Knock Your Socks Off Service*, 2nd ed., published by AMACOM. © 1998 by Performance Research Associates Inc. Reprinted by permission.

sponsiveness and good salesmanship. It doesn't unduly punish Pinchpenny for the human error involved in the original purchase—whether his or ours. Nor does it unduly reward him for his argumentative and unpleasant return behavior.

Option 2 is a narrow, old-fashioned, service-as-complaint-department response. It isn't likely to keep Pinchpenny as a long-term customer. Options 1 and 4 are the kind of answers suitable for companies where frontline people are specifically recruited with IQs approximately equal to their shoe sizes.

When Selling Is Not Good Service

There are three situations in which selling is not good service:

• **When there are no alternatives.** The customer's needs cannot be met by any product or service you offer, regardless of how well you can fix the problem, answer the question or explain the current product or service.

• **When there is no slack.** You know how to solve the problem, but the customer came to you mad, has stayed mad and obviously wants to stay mad. There is very little chance

to make the customer unmad, let alone sell an upgrade or a switch to a different model.

• **When there is no point.** An upgrade or add-on would be totally illogical, unrelated or inappropriate to the situation, as in, "Would you like some garlic bread to go with your cappuccino this morning?"

When Selling Is Good Service

There are five situations in which selling is good service:

• When the product or service the customer is using is wrong, but you know which model, system or approach will better fit his needs and are in a position to get it for him.

• When the product or service the customer acquired from your company is right but some other part, piece, program or process is needed before your product or service will perform properly: "Your computer operating system is Version 4.9. Our software is designed for the new 5.0 operating system. I do know of an upgrade for the 4.9 that might work."

• When the product or service in question is out of date: "I can send you a new widget and walk you through the repair when you receive

it. I also think it would be a good idea to consider a newer model that will do the job better. The Laser XJ7 has improved circuitry . . ."

• When an add-on feature will forestall other problems: "I see you decided against extended warranty protection. Since you've had two problems during the warranty period, I wonder if you shouldn't reconsider that decision?"

• When changing the customer to a different product or service will be seen as value-added or TLC: "This checking account requires a very high minimum balance. That's what caused the service charge you are concerned about. I'd like to recommend a different plan that I think will fit your needs better and save you from incurring future charges."

If it says Customer Service on your name tag, then serving the customer is your full-time occupation. But remember: Even if nothing in your job description hints at a sales responsibility, you are a part of the sales and marketing team.

Kristin Anderson and Ron Zemke are, respectively, principal and president of Performance Research Associates Inc., Minneapolis.

Rebates' Secret Appeal to Manufacturers: Few Consumers Actually Redeem Them?

By WILLIAM M. BULKELEY
Staff Reporter of THE WALL STREET JOURNAL

Rebates are booming—mainly because of a little-discussed marketers' secret: Most people never cash them in.

The coupons are showing up on everything from computers to shredders to dishwashers and baby seats. **Office-Max** Inc., an office-supply chain, sells 217 different products that carry them.

But while the coupons do spur sales, "the whole point behind rebates is to entice purchases and hope [consumers] don't remember to submit" their claims, says Charles Weil, president of Young America Inc. His company mails out 30 million rebate checks a year on behalf of companies like **PepsiCo** Inc., **Nestle SA** and OfficeMax.

Rebates originated in the 1960s and boomed in the late 1980s and early 1990s when liquor bottles and cigarette cartons carried $1 and $2 mail-in rebates. But those promotions, which sometimes required such exertions as soaking off labels to document purchases, soon lost their allure. At the same time, scamsters discovered they could submit dozens of rebate forms for every offer, souring some marketers on the approach.

But now rebates are back. The Postal Service has cracked down on rebate fraud. And the money at stake is rising because computer and electronics makers have caught the bug.

Cox Direct Inc., a direct-marketing company based in Largo, Fla., says that 76% of surveyed packaged-goods companies used money-back offers in 1996, up from 66% in 1995. NCH NuWorld Marketing Ltd., the nation's biggest coupon processor, says the use of traditional cents-off coupons is down, but its mail-in rebate business is increasing, especially for higher-price items. And

Young America, which was acquired three months ago by a leveraged buyout arm of **Bankers Trust New York** Corp., says its business is growing 25% annually thanks to ever more complex rebate and premium programs.

Manufacturers like rebates because they let them offer price cuts to consumers directly. With a traditional price cut, retailers can keep the price on the shelf the same and pocket the difference.

Rebates can also be rolled out and shut off quickly. That lets manufacturers fine-tune inventories or respond quickly to competitors without actually cutting prices. Because buyers fill out forms with names, addresses and other data, rebates also set off a gusher of information about customers.

But the best reason of all to offer rebates is that many consumers never bother to redeem them, allowing manufacturers to offer, in effect, phantom discounts. Many fliers prominently advertise low prices, noting the requirement to send in for rebates in microscopic letters. "That allows the retailer and manufacturer to advertise a very hot price when the costs aren't very high," says Wes Bray, a partner in Market Growth Resources Inc., a consulting firm. "Not many consumers redeem them—5% to 10% maximum."

Consumer advocates, meanwhile, hate rebates. "We feel companies should give a more honest reduction in the price," says Linda Colodner, executive director of the National Consumers League, a Washington, D.C., group. Her own son missed out on a $50 rebate offer for a cellular phone he gave her for Christmas because he failed to send in the proof of purchase in time to meet a Dec. 31 deadline, she says.

And rebates can generate enormous ill-will for companies that mishandle them. Bill Berdux, a California marketing executive, put up a "CompUSA Rebate Problems and Complaint" Web page criticizing the computer retailer after he failed to receive a $30 rebate for computer disks. After he posted an account of his experience, dozens of other frustrated customers sent him their sagas, which he also posted." "I got e-mail from all over the country. People are vengeful and nasty," he says.

James Halpin, president of CompUSA, which is based in Dallas, says he isn't familiar with Mr. Berdux's situation, but says the company provides a toll-free number for complaints.

Kevin O'Leary, president of **Learning** Co., a Cambridge, Mass.-based maker of educational software, says the economics of rebates "are quite attractive" since the company pays out rebates to 8% to 10% of the customers eligible for its $10 offers, and 20% of the $20 offers. "Since we started, our market share has gone from 18% to 28%," Mr. O'Leary says.

Big $50 rebates have become commonplace in the modem industry. When manufacturers cut prices, they have to reimburse retailers for modems still on store shelves that were purchased at a higher wholesale price. "Rebates mean they don't have to do price protection," says Jennifer Glickman of ARS Research Inc., a Dallas market-research firm.

Rebates also offer research possibilities. Last summer, **Sharp Electronics** Inc. offered a $500 rebate on its $4,695

projection TV. The company didn't want to just cut the price, fearing added sales wouldn't make up for the price cuts. When sales jumped beyond expectations. Sharp cut the list price to $3,995 permanently.

Some newer rebate programs are designed to build customer loyalty. Office-Max, an office superstore chain based in Cleveland, recently introduced a service in which its customers fill out a single form to accompany their rebate receipts and proofs of purchase from the store each month. OfficeMax then mails the material to Young America, which sends back rebate checks.

Michael Feuer, OfficeMax's chairman, says the plan is especially appealing to small businesses, which wouldn't bother with one-product rebates but can get back several hundred dollars a month.

Global Advertising And The World Wide Web

W. Wossen Kassaye

State-of-the-art cyberspace technology is truly a wonder. Consumers can sit down to visit any Web site at any time and browse through documents, download programs, place an order for a product, receive advice from customer service, and much more. Geography, distance, and time zones are no problem. Language barriers are also becoming less of a concern in consumer global shopping. MediaVision Co. has introduced software designed to translate English text on the Web into Japanese automatically. International Communications Inc. has launched a nine-language Web site for Europe, Asia, and the Americas (http://www.intl.com), thereby enabling each region to access the same information in its language of choice.

The potential to reach so many diverse markets makes the Web immensely attractive for global advertising. In fact, Web advertising is touted as already significant and growing. As firms large and small rush "to have a presence in cyberspace," the number of World Wide Web sites is increasing at an unprecedented rate. So is the number of consumers attracted to it. The biggest growth in Web advertising revenues is expected to take place in North America, followed by the EU and the Pan-Pacific Region. In its place of birth, the United States, Web advertising is already a two-year-old phenomenon. Advertising revenue estimates range from $20 million for all of 1996 to $157.4 million just for the first nine months of the year!

This prospect notwithstanding, compared to television and radio there are lots of things about the Web that can fit into the category of "at least not yet." It hardly fits the bill of a medium that reaches every household, or even most of them. Often the connection is not very reliable. Web addresses are often incomplete. It is not accessible to everyone, nor is it fully and truly interactive. Security protection is also a serious problem.

Mystified and nonplused, advertisers nonetheless continue to hold high expectations about what the Web can possibly offer—if not now, then some day soon. They must beware, though. Because hype has

> ## Can advertising live up to its hyped potential on the Web?

taken over reality, some of their expectations may be misplaced. Surveys by such firms as Dataquest (1995) show the dilemma businesses can face and the questions they must answer. In what ways is the Web different from traditional media? Is it appropriate for every firm? And if it is to be used, how can the Web complement other aspects of a firm's marketing strategy?

CHANGES IN MARKETING ENVIRONMENT FAVORING THE WEB

The World Wide Web is already being put into an impressive array of uses. Voice profile for messaging (VPM) protocol, religious outreach programs, and direct marketing (such as Levi Strauss) are just a few examples. International companies have begun using it to countervail local laws against pornographic materials and gambling. The UK firm SSP International Sports Betting (http://www.ssp.co.uk) is

From *Business Horizons*, May/June 1997, pp. 33-42. © 1997 by the Foundation for the School of Business at Indiana University. Reprinted by permission.

making legalized betting accessible on the Web to consumers in Japan, which does not allow gambling on its soil. Up to now, SSP's 2,000 or so customers have been placing their bets over the phone or via fax. Now the Web should help cement the company's relationship with its customers.

Irrespective of the region or global market, the demographics of Web users are compelling. In the United States, most users tend to be under 50 years of age and college educated. Males make up the majority (from 66 to 82 percent, depending on the survey). These statistics mirror the findings of a recent survey by International research instituteS (IriS), reported in Business Wire, of 18 nations spanning North America, Australia, Asia, and the EU. According to that survey, however, only a relatively few consumers have ventured into the Internet, let alone the Web.

The penetration has been highest in the workplace and lowest in the household. At one end of the spectrum, with more than 10 percent of firms accessing the Web for business communication and information, Sweden and Finland lead in workplace use, followed by the United States (9 percent) and Australia (8 percent). At the other end, with usage rates equal to or less than 2 percent, penetration is lowest in France, Italy, Cyprus, Portugal, Spain, and Greece. At the household level, penetration is highest among consumers in the United States and Canada (8 percent), and lowest in Portugal and Spain (less than 1 percent). EU member states such as Germany and the Netherlands fall in between. Japan, surprisingly, is slightly behind the EU; and South Korea is a year or two behind Japan. The adoption rate disparity may be explained by differences in presumed Web attractiveness as an advertising vehicle (**Figure 1**).

Motives, Criteria, And Decisions In Using The Web

The decision to adopt the Web is often dictated by different drives, urges, wishes, or desires. Regardless of the motives, however, the popularity of the medium has been largely influenced by two major factors: (1) changes in market forces, and (2) decline in traditional media influence among the young. The Web's attractiveness to people of all ages is also growing by the day.

Before launching a Web ad, the advertiser must carefully assess whether the decision to adopt the Web is favored by market forces, the firm's own target market characteristics (consumer demographics and habits), and its expertise in Web technology. If the firm cannot build its own Web page in-house, its relationship with its agency and the agency's overall expectations of the medium are important considerations that need not be overlooked. The agency may be expected to ascertain market facts, help the client decide on the Web, and, if necessary, help it navigate the process.

Characteristics Of Market Forces Supporting The Web

As shown in Figure 1, changes in macroenvironmental factors, such as economic climate and workplace transitions, have also influenced the Web and are creating tremendous growth opportunities for software, broadcast, and communications companies. For example, one telephone line per residence is no longer adequate for some households, what with their fax machines, the Internet, and so on. So telephone companies in many metropolitan areas are adding new exchanges and area codes at an increasing rate. In the Boston area alone, NYNEX is introducing three more area codes to accommodate growing requests for multiple telephone lines.

AT&T, MCI, Sprint, and all of Ma Bell's offspring have devoted resources to the Internet. Computer and software companies such as Apple and Microsoft are also rethinking their strategies. At Microsoft, on-line expansion plans have been abandoned in favor of Internet-related strategies. Apple's recovery strategy in Europe focuses on the Internet, specifically on a device similar to WebTV called Machine D that can be connected to a telephone line and television set. Likewise, Microsoft and NBC have jointly formed MSNBC to tap into the growing market.

No doubt the overall bullish atmosphere surrounding the Web continues to fuel greater global interest in it. Both Pacific Internet and Europe Online are engaged in consortia to create a regional Internet backbone. Using Hong Kong and Singapore as regional hubs, Pacific Internet is teaming up with Internet Initiative (Japan), Hong Kong Supernet, and Sumitomo (Japan).

From an advertising perspective, perhaps the single most important boost to the Web has come from the new economic realities. No longer do companies need full control over manufacturing and warehousing as long as they can coordinate all the activities to bring about exchange. In addition, the possibility of global reach via the Web has figured largely in the quest for a new approach. With employment anxieties heightened because of corporate downsizing, the Net has become the lifeblood of contact with the external world for those who choose to work from home and those who have decided to go it alone after losing their employment. Being in the know and aware of the technological revolution, middle and senior managers who left corporations seem to have embraced the Web in their new endeavors. Other major market forces that favor the Web include the increase in home-based businesses, the popularity of virtual corporations, the pressure to cut costs and increase accountability, and changing consumer characteristics. Vis-a-vis these trends, traditional media have not fared as well as advertisers had hoped.

Figure 1
Driving Forces In Web Ad Development And Effectiveness

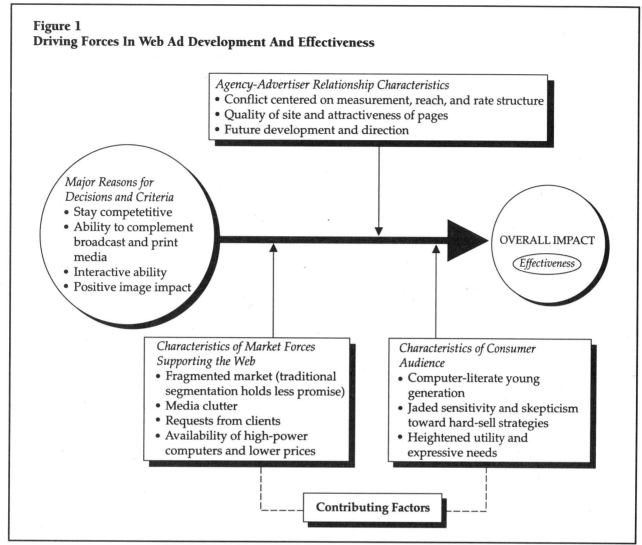

Characteristics Of Consumers Using The Web

Research suggests that the Web is most attractive for reaching the under-35 cohort—"Generation X." Armed with an estimated $200 billion in annual spending power, and comprising nearly 75 percent of current Web users, this demographic group constitutes a formidable force. With their aversion to newspapers and their addiction to and fascination with electronic media, especially computers, the Web has become almost a natural medium for them. Not only do they type quickly on the keyboard, they seem to be equally at ease in communicating that way. Most significant, they have been primarily responsible for building the sites, preparing the banners, and popularizing the Web.

Knowing how consumers look at the Web is important in creating fresh and contemporary perspective. This is particularly true for Generation X, especially the 18- to 29-year-olds. Despite having grown up on an electronic diet, of late this group has become weary and cynical of at least one medium, television, both in terms of show structure and ad presentation.

Generation X-ers, unlike Baby Boomers, don't take to traditional "linear storytelling," in which an audience is "dragged up the inclined plane of tension." "Thanks to years of channel-zapping and joy-sticking," says Trip Gabriel of the *New York Times*, "they do not care about the dramatic arc of any one show, but instead like to flip among several at once." They also view traditional media advertising with some skepticism. Suspicious of hype, they want the messages to be simple, honest, straightforward. But no messages should appear to be directed at them.

When the U.S. Department of Defense discovered that 82 percent of its active duty population was addicted to electronic media, it went in search of something other than on-base communication to reach Generation X-ers. It opted for sponsorships and organized prize giveaways to generate favorable word-of-mouth, and found the approach effective in appealing to the demographic group. Back in the private sector, Coors Brewing's television campaign targeting "X-ers" was changed to feature the CEO, Peter Coors himself, offering the straightforward, honest talk the group is presumed to prefer.

HOW THE WEB DIFFERS FROM OTHER MEDIA

Web advertising is much like television, newspaper, and radio advertising in its intended purpose to inform, augment sales, and improve product and image. Because of the nature of each medium, however, there are important differences.

Traditional media differ from the Web in their accessibility, market size, and the critical mass they reach. TV and radio ads tend to concentrate on a well-defined geographic domain. On the Web, however, the market could well be global, and the market segment less well-defined. The contrast is the highest between the Web and traditional media when it comes to the potential for interactivity. Still another difference is in the penetration level of each medium and, consequently, the clutter that accompanies the specific medium.

In terms of ease, availability, and familiarity, television and radio still maintain the upper hand. Broadcast ads tend to have a relatively long life, compared to the short life of Web ads. Some have recommended this as a prerequisite for attracting visitors. "A good Web site is never the same," reports Collopy (1996). "Not only does it change continually, but the experience depends on the clicker. You provide a large quantity of experience, and the user dictates it."

The need, then, to change Web sites quite often and with relative ease is now seen as an essential part of the planning process in Web advertising. With more than 300,000 registered Web sites and the number of ads growing exponentially, the significance of this issue may dissipate—not because it is not a problem for advertisers, but because there are so many ads. Chances are visitors will not remember most of them. The biggest problem may prove to be clutter.

The Web has the potential to overcome at least one limitation of traditional broadcast media: lack of access on demand. The user can click on any Web site, access its home page, and browse through layer upon layer of information at any time. No longer is the ad presented only when the sender desires. Once the information is stored and updated to make it relevant, the user decides on both the extensiveness of the search and the particular attributes or issues pursued. This makes the Web the most convenient information source for those within its link.

Something Old, Something New

The attractiveness of the Web rests in its ability to forge a new medium by combining so many. And although the formats and arrangements, including multimedia possibilities, are somewhat new, the Web still has the advantage of appearing familiar. The advent of WebTV is making the transition somewhat easier for households. The number of users is likely to grow with the convergence of various technologies. In the immediate future, anyone with touch-screen technology can potentially access information from any place equipped for it. Unleashing such interactivity will likely increase the power and potential of the Web as an advertising medium. Though not all users or visitors may be active shoppers, the few who are could make the Web cost-effective and desirable.

Distribution: Reaching Global Markets

Through supportive formats and contents, a company may provide a consistent and integrated brand image for its global consumers. Whether in information distribution or retrieval, firms are beginning to see the Web as an effective yet reasonably cheap medium with immense communication capabilities. First, the cost to the sender is perceived as minimal. In addition to its ability to provide content that can be customized to the users' needs, the Web is seen as instrumental in reducing telephone and other communication expenses. Second, the Web is a relatively cheap medium with potential for global reach. With the interest in global markets taking center stage, more and more firms are keen on tapping its huge potential. Although these markets may be far apart, firms expect to draw on the shared interests of Web users globally hoping to leverage product offerings aggressively and improve images worldwide. Overcoming their inability to determine the effectiveness of traditional media, the Web may also make it easier for advertisers to predict the advertising/sales relationship.

One major problem, however, irrespective of whether consumers access the Web via computers or television sets, is telephone ownership. Telephones around the world, on average, are owned by only 7 percent of the population: this limits the number of people who can access the Web. The question then rises: Does the Web provide a better fit for some companies and or industries than others?

JUSTIFYING WEB PARTICIPATION

Advertising on the World Wide Web makes sense under the following scenarios:

1. For a regional or global company, as opposed to one with a state or local franchise. *Objective: Better global reach.*

2. For a situation or market segment in which the match between customers and the medium is particularly strong. *Objective: Best customer fit.*

3. For a company or product category that lends itself best to the unique features of the Web and/or where the medium can give a product distinct advantages. *Objective: Best product fit.*

4. For a company that has a conspicuous brand name and unique brand image that can be accentuated or complemented by a Web presence. *Objective: Image maximization.*

5. For competitive reasons, such as keeping up with the competition or perceived industry norms, or to create an image of being technologically up-to-date. *Objective: Me-too approach and/or concern for image.*

Each of the above can be analyzed and evaluated separately. For practical purposes, however, we concentrate on three generic objectives that apply to most firms: (1) brand equity, or image advantage among consumers, (2) global operations and presence, and (3) consumer characteristics and expected fit with the Web (see Figure 2). Differences in participation levels may be explained by evaluating these factors in a matrix format along dimensions of fit between (a) consumers and product/industry, and (b) industry and market. Based on WebTrack's InterAd Database, Figure 2 shows how various industries rate on these major categories.

Figure 2
Evaluation Matrix: Web Ad Participation Based On User Demographics And Other Criteria

INDUSTRIES (Percent of monitored firms with Web Sites)*	*Brand Equity (Image Advantage)*	*Company Presence*	*Consumer Characteristics (Media/Customer Match)*
High Web Participation:			
Telecommunications (45%)	Strong	Regional/Global	Average
Computers and Office Equipment (42%)	Strong-Moderate	Global manufacturing	Strong; Ideal match (esp. among Gen.Xers)
Electronic Entertainment Equipment (25%)	Strong (brand image)	Global operations/ Regional manufacturing	Strong-Ideal
Publishing and Media (22%)	Moderate	Regional/National (state or local markets)	Average-Weak
Financial Services (19%)	Limited	Regional/National	Good-Average
Insurance and Real Estate (14%)	Moderate-Limited	Few National/Regional (several statewide markets)	Average-Weak
Low Web Participation:			
Food and Food Products (4%)	Strong-Moderate	Regional/Increasingly global	Weak
Retailing (4%)	Moderate-Weak	Regional/Some global (presence and sourcing)	Weak
Building Materials (4%)	Strong-Limited	Regional/National	Average-Weak
Drugs and Remedies (4%)	Strong-Moderate	National (extensive global competitiveness)	Average-Weak
Apparel and Footwear (3%)	Average-Weak	National presence/ International sourcing	Weak
Toiletries and Cosmetics (1%)	Strong-Moderate	National (increasingly global presence)	Average-Weak

Source: WebTrack's InterAd Database (http://www.webtrack.com). Webtrack monitors more than 2,500 companies with media budgets exceeding half a million dollars, as well as some 4,000 brands (The Net, 1996).

High Level Participation

The most Web-oriented industries in the hierarchy of current participation levels are telecommunications (45 percent) and computers and office equipment (42 percent). Further down are electronic entertainment equipment companies (25 percent), publishing and media companies (22 percent), financial services (19 percent), and insurance and real estate firms (14 percent).

As shown in Figure 2, almost all industries with high participation have a high regional and/or global presence. For these firms, using the Web appears ideal; it complements their global presence. Insurance and real estate firms have only national, regional, and

> *"The balance of advantage in using the Web rests on the medium's power to enhance the image of a company or its brands."*

sometimes statewide markets. Clearly, for most firms in this group the Web appears ideal only if they plan to do business regionally or globally. The same seems to hold true when using the Web in search of image advantages among consumers for industries as diverse as financial services, insurance, and real estate.

In terms of expected fit between the Web and users' demographics and psychographics, the Web may not necessarily be ideal for all communication firms; it appears ideal for on-line businesses and somewhat reasonable for companies in the publishing and media, financial services, and insurance and real estate fields. For those in electronic, entertainment equipment, computers, and office equipment industries, the fit is strong particularly with Generation X-ers.

Low Level Participation

The least Web-oriented industries include food and food products, retailing, building materials and drugs and remedies. Only 4 percent of the companies in each of these industries currently participate in WWW

advertising. Among apparel and footwear companies, the participation rate is even lower at 3 percent; in the toiletries and cosmetics industry, it is only 1 percent. Nevertheless, efforts are under way to boost the participation levels of companies in these industries. In alliance with grocery stores, Peapod now enables households to order supplies through the Web; Streamline Inc. is attempting to do the same thing for a much larger assortment of goods, including laundry services.

Because of either sourcing or direct market penetration, food and retailing seem to have a sizable regional and limited global presence. Building materials firms have a strong regional and/or national presence. Drugs and remedies face extensive global competition, but tend to concentrate on national markets. Firms in the apparel and footwear industry engage in international manufacturing and outsourcing; very few have a global presence. Toiletries and cosmetics have a national and, increasingly, a global presence. Based on global presence alone, the Web seems ideal for almost all firms in this group, and more so for those in retailing and food. At this point, however, their participation is minimal.

The balance of advantage in using the Web rests on the medium's power to enhance the image of a company or its brands. This opportunity provides for a more integrated and polished look for a firm globally. Given their prominence in traditional media, then, it is surprising that firms in such industries as drugs and remedies, toiletries and cosmetics, and food and food products do not actively advertise on the Web. One reason could be that, because of their lifestyles, current Web users are not seen as constituting an ideal market for these products—a fact that could change with the growing popularity of the Web and the ability of companies in these industries to use their Web pages as virtual stores. It could also be that many have adopted a "wait and see" attitude, or their sites are still under construction.

Overall Evaluation

Distinctly, it appears that the decision to use the Web is not necessarily based on systematic evaluation of users' demographics and psychographics and/or the benefits to be derived from such efforts. It is not driven by specific objectives such as sales. Nor does it appear to be driven by systematic efforts to create a fit between the medium and market(s) or consumer(s). Instead, the decision seems to be based on creating a certain image for the advertiser. Three desirable images stand out: (1) to be seen as the first in the industry, (2) to be seen as a technologically oriented company, and (3) to be seen as comparable to, if not better than, the competition.

A THREE-PHASE APPROACH TO ADVERTISING ON THE WEB

Given the problems discussed and acknowledging the evolutionary nature of Web technology, implementing Web advertising may be better served by adopting a three-phase process. This would involve: (a) the decision on whether or not to launch a Web site, (b) selecting the appropriate Web strategies, and (c) planning for strategic integration with other media.

The rationale is straightforward. First, a lack of objective evaluation about the Web may lead to problems of image and "information overkill." Such problems can be avoided. Second, if what is expected from Web advertising cannot be articulated in broad terms and systematically evaluated in terms of deliverability by the medium, there may be no point in using the Web. Early pruning would save the company undesirable branches. Combined, these activities may enable a firm to measure whether the communication is on target.

Making The Decision

The initial phase—deliberation and decision—should focus first on determining whether a firm may benefit from Web advertising. Specifically, the decision has to be based on (1) an evaluation of the company's objectives, (2) the possibility of reaching identified target markets using the medium, and (3) the perceived need to meet the competition headlong, or leapfrog over it, and the anticipated benefits of such a strategy.

Once it has been determined that using the Web as an advertising vehicle could indeed benefit a company in achieving its objectives, management's attention should turn to learning about the Web. Companies have to address at least three important issues before they decide to advertise on the Web, much less launch a Web site.

First, they need to understand what the Web involves: how it works, and so on. And they must realize that Web advertising requires long-term commitment to the medium and short-term dynamics in information display.

Consider Volvo's dilemma. Lured by the double prospect of reaching a market segment that was likely to buy the automobile and creating a first mover advantage, the firm became one of the first to advertise its wares on the Web. Instead of new clients, however, Volvo attracted existing customers who wanted to use the site as a forum for their complaints. The company found itself overwhelmed; it had not anticipated such strong negative reaction. The choice was difficult: Maintaining the site could bring more business in the future; allowing it to go on could chip away the prospects the company was seeking. Eventually, cowed by the negative reaction, Volvo decided to fold its Web site.

Companies should also remember that the Web's access rules and requirements are completely different from those for broadcast media. There is also a difference in the set of skills required for production. For the Web, the important skills center around computer graphics and the Web's unique languages, such as Hyper Text Markup (HTML) and Virtual Reality Markup (VRML), rather than copy. To be sure, pictures are important for television, but the skills that are emphasized most tend to be holistic, broad, and word-related. TV's objective is to persuade. In contrast, examination of Web ads shows that most of them display as much information as physically possible, without regard to persuasive power or profile fit. Customers themselves have to "custom fit" the information.

> *"Web advertising requires long-term commitment to the medium and short-term dynamics in information display."*

Second, a company needs to define and list what is expected of the medium and determine whether the Web could deliver on those expectations. The most difficult task in doing so is translating the company's objectives into actionable Web specifics or expectations. Unless the tasks are explicitly translated into Web advertising objectives, the pages may end up containing too much information. This is likely to happen if advertisers see the Web as a conduit of information. Simply transplanting television ad objectives into Web objectives does not seem to suffice either. Web ads are dictated by different dynamics. Television—as with radio, newspapers, and magazines—relies on "in-your-face" advertising and intrusions into a person's consciousness. Web advertising, with the exception of banner ads using "push" technology offered by the likes of Marimba and PointCast, attempts to establish a presence and name recognition via site(s) or through the banners of search directories. Users have full control over the types of ads they want to see. This is an important distinction with serious implications for Web ad preparation and execution as well as customer service.

Third, firms need to assess whether they have the commitment—manpower, time, and financial resources—needed to stay the course once they have decided to adopt the Web. Lack of commitment is likely to result in typical Web sites that disappointingly lead nowhere, or constantly inform the visitor that they are under construction. Roughly, some 10 to 15 percent of Web sites seem to fall into this category. Perhaps caution is needed most regarding what a Web site entails. Web sites are never truly finished; they require constant and dynamic changes to attract visitors. As Guy Kawasaki (1996) notes, "A good Web site is a process, not an event."

Selecting Appropriate Web Strategies

New orientation. Not since the advent of television has a technology altered so dramatically the advertising orientation of firms. Almost everyone—ad agencies, PR agencies, marketers, advertisers—ha[s] been forced to re-examine the role of advertising in the new medium. This re-orientation should urge management to focus on the dramatic changes under way (both in equipment and software developments), as well as stay apprised of options and new possibilities.

Attracting visitors to the site. No matter how attractive or jazzy-looking, if the Web site does not pull in visitors, the effort is for naught. The trick is to make people—albeit the right kinds of people—curious about a site. Some unique features of the Web make this task difficult. It does not have prime-time shows or unique programming features. Some look for entertainment on the Web, but there is no comprehensive listing of what is being featured where—no *TV Guide* for the Web. Even avid users have to be pulled in from the outside either through other sites, word of mouth, or traditional media. Advertising one's addresses on a regular basis in both print and broadcast media is one practical way to attract customers. Another way is to make such information a regular feature in product packaging and labeling.

If too many people are attracted to a Web site, however, the time it takes to get in may become a source of frustration for visitors. If the problem persists, they may stop visiting the site altogether. The experience of America On-Line attests to this. When AOL switched to a flat fee, the number of callers increased dramatically, leading to a momentary crash and subsequent customer and legal problems. During the last presidential election, CNN experienced a similar problem. It was momentarily unable to support all the callers, leading to long delays and slow responses. Such problems may be overcome by having multiple sites, one for each sub-segment. This, however, makes it difficult to promote one generic URL for a company, not to mention the additional costs of maintaining multiple sites. Moreover, the bottleneck problem is really one of insufficient servers and phone lines.

Creating the appropriate links. Links add depth and spice to a Web site. By adding relevant points of connection to other Web sites or sources of information within a company's own site, links may provide more complete information to visitors. But if there are too many links, the user may be overwhelmed. Not being linked to the appropriate sites or companies could also be detrimental to a marketing effort. So the *type* of link is also important. To reduce the clutter and possible information overload, the links must be simple, direct, and relevant.

Besides links, the time it takes to load the information and display it on the screen is important. The more animated, graphic-oriented, and jazzed-up the program, the more time it takes to load. If loading takes too long, visitors may be discouraged from returning to the site.

Reaching global consumers. Localization is a logical next phase in the development of a medium with a truly global reach. Two factors have already facilitated this process: (1) setting up delivery and service capabilities in new markets, and (2) creating multilingual Web sites. Many companies with Internet experience have begun to expand into other markets.

Through localization, international consumers can view Web information in their language of choice, dramatically increasing a company's sales effort in the global marketplace. A prime example is the realization at such companies as International Communications, a firm engaged in applying software in the information technology industry, that English-only Web sites translate into lost revenue from international consumers. The company sees multilingual Web sites as a powerful and cost-efficient medium for reaching international consumers. Such a move is under way in the EU, Japan, and elsewhere.

Integrating Web Advertising With Other Strategies

The third and final phase is integration: deciding how best to integrate existing media activities with the new Web efforts. Two levels are identified. The first is integration between and among Web efforts, which focuses on the need to integrate the various links and assure an effective exposure to a company or brand. The second is between Web advertising effort(s) and all other efforts, including sales promotions, television/radio advertising, print advertising, and so on.

Integrating marketing communications is always a cumbersome task. Web ads need it most to create synergy with other media. So far, perhaps because of the emergent nature of the technology and the decision of companies to go it alone, bypassing ad agencies, the focus given to an integrated approach appears minimal. Displaying Web addresses in advertisements is better than nothing at all; however, to engage in fully integrated marketing communications, firms have to determine how Web ads complement other media efforts. Case after case suggests that this connection is amiss.

Even at IBM, which has long subscribed to integrated marketing communications, Web ads are not fully integrated with the rest of the company's marketing effort.

An integrated approach implies that the company has an overall communication strategy for each target market. Given the fragmentation of markets and the multiplicity of media being employed, integrated communications should also mean a comprehensive strategy based on a process rather than on an unintegrated, one-time approach. Moreover, such a process should have a triple focus: the integration of the message with (1) media vehicles used, (2) target market expectations, motives, and needs, and (3) various functions performed by the firm-advertising, public relations, sales promotions. Combining these focuses will help a company get the most out of its Web ads and benefit from the synergy so generated. Of course, the individual efforts must be meaningful by themselves. But they should also have the power to reinforce all other efforts when put together. When a firm succeeds in achieving this objective, the overall effect will be greater than each of the functions and the advertising vehicles by themselves.

If it is axiomatic in business that visibility translates into market share, claiming a stake on the World Wide Web has become analogous to homesteading with the intent to own the territory someday. Although not all participants appear to benefit from their Web ads, many do. The Web is also changing the way companies prepare ads and handle customers' queries. Nevertheless, because it serves only a few distinct groups and not all customers, the Web is not about to replace customer service or other media advertising—at least not yet.

The Web should be used in creating an integrated message strategy that has a greater overall impact than when each vehicle, with its message for the target market, is independently selected. Notably, various forms of communication play different strategic roles in providing clarity, consistency, and maximum reach. Using different media vehicles may create synergy in that the coverage mutually reinforces the effort.

References

John Barnes, "Net Gains," *Marketing Week*, July 28, 1995, pp. 33–38.

David Bowen, "Is Anybody Out There? One Day Companies Will Have To Relocate In Cyberspace," The Independent, March 10, 1996, p. 1 (Business).

Hiawatha Bray, "For Advertisers, Web Offers Wide Audience, Pinpoint Accuracy," The *Boston Globe*, May 5, 1996, p. 41 (Economy).

Business Wire, "Web Site Bridges Language Barriers: International Communications Launches World Wide Web Site In Nine Languages," June 11, 1996.

Business Wire, "Centigram Supports Universal Messaging Standard Protocol With Other Voice Messaging Industry Leaders . . . ," April 29, 1996.

Business Wire, "WebMate Technologies Announces International Subsidiary," May 30, 1996.

Business Wire, "Surfing The 'Net' Not Yet A Global Activity, Says International Study," June 11, 1996.

Trisha Collopy, "Ad Agencies Dive Into Web," *Baltimore Business Journal*, January 26, 1996, p. 13.

Dataquest, Inc., "Turbo Data-Draft," August 1995.

Dataquest, Inc., "User And Distribution Studies," November 1995.

Trip Gabriel, "Decoding What 'Screen-Agers' Think About TV," *New York Times*, November 25, 1996, p. 1.

Jonathan Gaw, "Looking For Ways To Profit From On-Line Marketing: Advertisers Searching For Answers On How To Reach Growing Audience," (San Jose) *Star Tribune*, April 30, 1996, p. 1D.

Mike Hewitt and Jenny Simmons, "Start Me Up . . . (But Not Too Quickly . . .): Launching of Microsoft Network in the UK," *Marketing*, September 7, 1995, pp. 22+.

W. Wossen Kassaye and Joseph P. Vaccaro, "The Prevalence Of Barter In Television: An Empirical Study," *Journal Of Media Planning*, Spring 1992, pp. 51–58.

W. Wossen Kassaye and Joseph P. Vaccaro, "TV Stations' Use Of Barter To Finance Programs And Advertisements," *Journal Of Advertising Research*, May–June 1993, pp. 40–48.

Guy Kawasaki, "Four Things To Ask Your Webmaster," *Forbes*, May 6, 1996, p. 126.

J. Lien, "Netscape To Set Up Asia-Pac HQ Within Next Three Months," *Business Times*, February 6, 1996, p. 1.

Marcia MacLeod and Rod Newing, "Directory Of Internet Service Providers Across Europe," *Financial Times*, March 6, 1996, p. vii.

Michele Marchetti, "Talkin' 'Bout My Generation," *Sales & Marketing Management*, December 1995, p. 64.

G. A. Marken, "Getting The Most From Your Presence In Cyberspace," *Public Relations Quarterly*, Fall 1995, pp. 36–37.

Walter S. Mossberg, "Going On-Line Is Still Too Difficult To Lure A Mass Audience," *Wall Street Journal*, February 22, 1996, p. B1.

Kathleen Murphy, "New Survey Attaches Hard Numbers To Growing Area Of Web Advertising," *Web Week*, December 16, 1996, p. 1, citing estimates by the Internet Advertising Bureau.

"New Products: Software Program Translates English Text On The Internet," *Asian Wall Street Journal Weekly*, October 2, 1995, p. A18.

William D. Novelli, "One-Stop Shopping: Some Thoughts on Integrated Marketing Communications," *Public Relations Quarterly*, 34, 4 (1989–90): 7–9.

Chris Oakes, "Commercials In The Age Of Point And Click: Advertising On The Web," *The Net*, November 1995, p. 45–49.

"Psychological Profiling To Aid The Interactive Marketeer," *New Media Age*, August 17, 1995, p. 15.

Joan E. Rigdon, "Hip Advertisers Bypass Madison Avenue When They Need Cutting-Edge Web Sites," *Wall Street Journal*, February 28, 1996, p. B1.

Mimi Fronczak Rogers, "Tune In, Turn On And Drop In . . . To The Web," *Prague Post*, March 20, 1996.

Jenna Schnuer, "At-Home Surfers Dive Into The Net," *The Magazine for Magazine Management*, September 15, 1995, p. 39.

Waichi Sekiguchi, "South Korea Gets Late But Quick Start On Internet," *Nikkei Weekly* (Asia & Pacific), December 25, 1995, p. 21.

Ben Sullivan, "Apple Pares To Internet Core," *Budapest Business Journal*, May 20, 1996, p. 23.

"UK Bookie Brings Sumo Betting To Japan On Web," *New Media Age*, December 7, 1995, p. 3.

"Universal News Services, "AT&T Teams With Silicon Graphics To Provide Enterprise Internet And Intranet Solutions," June 5, 1996.

"World Watch; International Business/The Pacific," *Los Angeles Times*, May 30, 1996, p. 4D.

W. Wossen Kassaye is an associate professor of marketing at Bentley College in Waltham, Massachusetts.

Unit Selections

Key Points to Consider

❖ What economic, cultural, and political obstacles must an organization that seeks to become global in its markets consider?

❖ Do you believe that an adherence to the "marketing concept" is the right way to approach international markets? Why or why not?

❖ What trends are taking place today that would suggest whether particular global markets will grow or decline? Which countries do you believe will see the most growth in the next decade? Why?

❖ In what ways can the Internet be used to extend a market outside the United States?

 **Links** | **www.dushkin.com/online/**

These sites are annotated on pages 4 and 5.

It is certain that marketing with a global perspective will continue to be a strategic element of U.S. business well into the next decade. The United States is both the world's largest exporter and largest importer. In 1987, U.S. exports totaled just over $250 billion—about 10 percent of total world exports. During the same period, U.S. imports were nearly $450 billion—just under 10 percent of total world imports. By 1995 exports had risen to $513 billion and imports to $664 billion—roughly the same percentage of total world trade.

Whether or not they wish to be, all marketers are now part of the international marketing system. For some, the end of the era of domestic markets may have come too soon, but that era is now over. Today it is necessary to recognize the strengths and weaknesses of our own marketing practices as compared to those abroad. The multinational corporations have long recognized this need, but now all marketers must acknowledge it.

International marketing differs from domestic marketing in that the parties to its transactions live in different political units. It is the "international" element of international marketing that distinguishes it from domestic marketing—not differences in managerial techniques. The growth of global business among multinational corporations has raised new questions about the role of their headquarters. It has even caused some to speculate on whether marketing operations should be performed abroad rather than in the United States.

The key to applying the marketing concept is understanding the consumer. Increasing levels of consumer sophistication is evident in all of the world's most profitable markets. Managers are required to adopt new points of view in order to accommodate increasingly complex consumer wants and needs. The markets of the late 1990s will show further integration on a worldwide scale. In these emerging markets, conventional textbook approaches can cause numerous problems. The new marketing perspective that is called for by the circumstances of the next century will require a long-range view that looks from the basics of exchange and their applications in new settings.

The selections presented here were chosen to provide an overview of world economic factors, competitive positioning, and increasing globalization of markets—issues to which each and every marketer must become sensitive. "So You Think the World Is Your Oyster" suggests that although there is money to be made in exporting, cracking the global market takes considerable work. In "Are You Smart Enough to Sell Globally?" Lambeth Hochwald reflects on the necessity of researching an international market before doing business there. The final article reveals how marketeers can successfully extend their markets outside the United States in the years ahead.

Global Marketing

SO YOU THINK THE WORLD IS YOUR OYSTER

Sure, there's money to be made in exporting. But cracking the global market takes work

Winnebago, a town of nearly 2,000 nestled in the fertile blue-earth plains of southern Minnesota, might not seem like an obvious place to look for globetrotters. But there sits Meter-Man Inc., where 25 employees make agricultural measuring devices. In 1989, the 35-year-old company began exploring the idea of exporting and three years later began shipping products to Europe. Today, a third of Meter-Man's sales are in 35 countries throughout Europe, South America, the Far East, South Africa, and Israel. The company expects international sales to account for about half its business by the turn of the century. "When you start exporting, you say to yourself, this will be icing on the cake," says James Neff, director of sales and marketing. "But now I say going international has become critical to our existence."

Meter-Man is far from alone. With the collapse of communism, the embrace of freer markets by much of the developing world, the completion of the North American Free Trade Agreement, and the conclusion of the Uruguay Round of the General Agreement on Tariffs &

Trade, world trade in the 1990s is growing twice as fast as the overall world economy. These days, America's highly competitive manufacturers are grabbing a growing share of global merchandise trade. What's more, the U.S. is also the world's top service exporter. With the ranks of the middle class swelling around the world, governments everywhere deregulating their service industries, and the rapid spread of information technology, everyone from graphic designers to software developers to investment bankers is finding increasing opportunities abroad.

True, big companies still dominate international trade. Yet the share of small and midsize manufacturers that sold 10% or more of their products abroad rose from 27% in 1994 to 51% last year, according to a survey by Grant Thornton, the accounting and consulting firm.

Ah, the joys of the global economy. A diversified stream of revenue. The promise of fatter profits. Dinner with customers in London and Buenos Aires. Research shows that U.S. exporters enjoy on average faster sales growth and employment

gains than nonexporting companies, says Andrew Bernard, economist at Massachusetts Institute of Technology. And owners aren't the only ones who benefit: Wages for workers in jobs supported by exports are 13% to 16% higher than the national average. "Over time, you learn that the more people you can trade with, the more money you can make," says Abby Shapiro, head of International Strategies Inc., an electronic publisher of global business information.

Sounds terrific, doesn't it? But the risks from exporting are just as impressive. Fluctuating currencies. Impenetrable cultures. Faraway customers. Delayed payments. Byzantine business practices. "Small business sees the growth prospects outside the U.S., but the international market can burn and kill you in terms of cost," warns Browning Rockwell, president of Horizon Trading Co., an international trading company based in Washington. Adds Roger Prestwich, director of education at the Minnesota Trade Office: "Just because the U.S. is part of a global economy doesn't mean all—or any—of the 200-plus countries in the world are interested in your products."

CRITICAL FACTORS. How can a small-business owner succeed overseas? Consultants, financiers, and small-business owners with export experience cite several critical factors. Do lots of homework at the beginning. Plan on investing heavily in your overseas expansion. Tap into a network of professional consultants well versed in the quirks of international trade. And understand that going global is a long-term commitment. The typical small business should expect to spend anywhere from $10,000 to $20,000 just to do basic market research, take in a trade show, and fly overseas to visit a country or two. And it may take as long as three years to see any return on its investment.

Market research is increasingly easy to come by. Much of the information is available for free or at a low cost. Federal, state, and local governments, which have become near-zealots in their fervor to get small business to think globally, can be a great resource. Private companies are eager to teach small businesses everything from the basics of trade finance to unusual foreign business customs. Trade associations, meanwhile, believe a vital part of their mission is to help their members join the world economy. And many colleges and universities are expanding their course offerings on doing business abroad. "All over the country, more and more institutions are coming up with an exporting program," says E. Martin Duggan, president and chief executive of the Small Business Exporters Assn., a nonprofit trade association in Annandale, Va.

The Internet offers an easy portal into the many export programs offered by the federal government, nonprofit organizations, and the private sector. Click on the Commerce Dept., the Small Business Administration, the Export-Import Bank, or the U.S. Business Advisor, and you can study the basics of exporting, learn how to apply for loan guarantees, get country and industry data, download customs and export-loan documents, and find links to trade resources elsewhere on the Net.

Private companies and nonprofit groups are also working hard on developing programs that will allow for finance, insurance, freight forwarding contracts, and other export business to

be done over the Web. Horizon Trading's Rockwell, for instance, created a company called Trade Compass three years ago after he saw how the Net could expedite cross-border transactions. "People will call up and say, 'I want to export blue jeans to Mexico. What do you

---

TEN KEY QUESTIONS FOR NOVICES TO ASK

1 Is the product or service needed in other countries? What information is required to make an intelligent decision about that, and how will you get it?

2 Will your product or service have to be adapted for international markets? How difficult will this be, and how much will it cost?

3 How committed are management and stakeholders to going global? What expertise exists on staff, and what additional resources will you need?

4 How will you market your product or service internationally? How much investment will be needed, and what resources are available to help you?

5 How will international sales be financed?

6 How will you ensure getting paid for international sales?

7 What about communication? Will you need to translate sales literature? Will you need to learn another language?

8 How will you learn about differing customs which could affect your company, product, or way of doing business?

9 How long will it take to see a profit from international sales? Is entering the international marketplace worth the perceived risks?

10 What agencies, groups, or others can provide assistance to your company on the various facets of the exporting process? How much will this expertise cost?

DATA: MINNESOTA TRADE OFFICE, BASED ON SURVEY OF SMALL BUSINESSES THAT EXPORT

---

think?' " says Eileen Cassidy, director of the SBA's Office of International Trade. "The first thing I say is, 'do you have a computer with an Internet connection?' "

Still, the electronic world is only one avenue. State governments began embracing the global economy during the tumultuous 1970s and early 1980s, especially in the Rust Belt states of the Midwest and the former agricultural states of the Southeast. Today, every state actively devotes resources to promoting exports. State trade agencies run classes and seminars on the basics of exporting for small businesses, and they offer lots of information on market prospects and industry competition overseas. State governments, on their own or linked to a federal program, offer loan guarantees and export insurance

for small business. Most states also host overseas trade delegations and aid local company participation in international trade shows.

Federal- and state-sponsored export councils and trade missions offer another route for gathering information. Take the experience of Lucille Farms Inc., a manufacturer and marketer of cheese products in Montville, N.J. Its chief executive, Alfonso Falivene, wants his company to wade slowly into the international arena. He recently joined the U.S. Dairy Export Council established by the Commerce Dept. Council members have taken trips overseas to study trade prospects and dairy competitors. Its meetings offer a forum for dairy people to share their experiences and frustrations. In addition, "I have stacks of information in my office," says Falivene. "If I had to go out and get the information on my own, it would cost me thousands and thousands of dollars."

Many small-business exporters say trade shows are among the most valuable ways for a company to gain market intelligence, establish contacts, and swap global war stories with like-minded entrepreneurs. Meter-Man participated in a huge agricultural trade fair in Paris when it decided to expand into Europe. Over the course of five days, company executives held 21 meetings with potential customers and distributors. One contact from those meetings is now a major Parisian distributor of its measuring devices.

Which markets make the most sense to target? Obviously, it depends on what industry you're in and what your analysis of particular countries shows. Perhaps your software package or new drug will sell well in Spain but not in Italy, or flourish in Australia but fall flat in Southeast Asia. In general, trade experts say the bigger opportunities for small business probably lie in the rapidly expanding areas of Latin America and the Far East. And of course, with their proximity and market size, Canada and Mexico are popular export spots. But no matter how grand the market research suggests your prospects may be, keep your ambitions in check. "The big mistake we see is people taking a shotgun approach," warns one old hand at the small-business exporting game. "We take a rifle approach. We concentrate on one area before we move to another one."

Once you've done your homework, chosen your market, and developed a few contacts overseas, you'll need some professional help to navigate your way through unfamiliar business terrain, such as trade finance, international law, documentation, and local customs. Thanks to an alliance among the SBA, the Commerce Dept., and the federal bar association, new exporters can get a free consultation with an international attorney drawn from the Export Legal Assistance Network (ELAN). To get the name of the ELAN regional coordinator in your area, contact your local SBA district office, or call the Small Business Answer Desk at 800 8-ASK-SBA.

MAZE OF RULES. Service-sector firms, especially, seem to rely on joint ventures and other cooperative arrangements to smooth their way into a local market. The knowledge of local institutions is often invaluable in dealing with the bewildering maze of local rules and regulations that typically envelop banking, insurance, telecommunications, education, health care, and other service industries. "You can't just take a successful American practice or service overseas without making real adjustments for the local market," says Joseph Hartnett, director of international services for the central U.S. at Grant Thornton. "How you sell will be different."

Edaw Inc., a well-known landscape architecture firm in San Francisco, has built up an international business over the past 15 years. The 450-employee company first gained a strong reputation in the U.S. so that when an overseas company wanted to tap into American expertise and talent, Edaw was on the short list of contacts. It also had one or two people willing to take long flights, eat lousy food, and stay in hotel after hotel. In Europe, Australia, and Asia, the company has linked up with local partners, and it is buying a majority position in a Hong Kong company. "You have to go with local, recognized partners that are well-entrenched," says Jim Heid, partner and director of development at Edaw. "It's almost impossible to build up a business by sending a bunch of expatriates overseas."

It's also essential to line up enough financing to see you through the inevitable bumps in the export road. Taking on overseas customers brings with it the risk of political upheaval and currency

fluctuations. What's more, it typically takes overseas companies longer to pay their bills, so new exporters often find their cash flow dwindling. The government offers a vast array of working-capital, loan-guarantee, and insurance programs for small-business exporters. The Ex-Im Bank, for instance, long criti-

---

THE INTERNET GUIDE TO SMALL-BUSINESS EXPORTING

The easiest way to tap into exports is to mine the rich lode of the Net. These sites hold plenty of value—and most have links to additional information.

WWW.EMBPAGE.ORG. Embassy home page is a window to embassies and consulates around the world.

WWW.EXPORTHOTLINE.COM. Contains thousands of market research reports, a trade library, market intelligence on 80 countries, and plenty of links.

WWW.NEMONLINE.ORG/ELAN. Site lists international trade attorneys tied to the Export Legal Assistance Network, which provides free consultation to small companies exploring exports.

WWW.EXIM.GOV. The Export-Import Bank of the U.S. is focusing more on small business these days.

WWW.FITA.ORG. Industry trade associations are valuable sources on exporting. The Federation of International Trade Associations offers links to local, regional, and national associations that promote exports.

WWW.ITA.DOC.GOV. The International Trade Administration of the Commerce Dept. boasts critical trade information and statistics, addresses, and phone numbers of export-assistance centers in each state around the country, and country data and analysis.

WWW.SBA.GOV. The Small Business Administration offers a wealth of basic information, resources, a guide to its various export support programs (such as loans and working-capital guarantees), and plenty of links to export information elsewhere on the Web.

WWW.TRADECOMPASS.COM. Trade Compass offers exporting information, international business Web links, and online resources.

WWW.TRADEPORT.ORG. A site with lots of information on all aspects of small-business exporting.

WWW.TSCENTRAL.COM. Trade Show Central has information on more than 30,000 trade shows, conferences and seminars worldwide.

DATA: BUSINESS WEEK

---

cized for being a banker solely for multinationals, is now eagerly wooing smaller companies. Its working-capital guarantees, with roughly 95% going to small exporters, reached $378 million last year, up from $181 million in 1994.

International transactions can be paid for in a variety of ways. The most common is the irrevocable letter of credit (LOC). The typical LOC costs $200 to $300, including the bank's examination fee, which can range from 0.10% to

0.25% of the sale. In essence, an LOC substitutes the bank's balance sheet for the customer's balance sheet once the transaction is confirmed. Problem is, many of the nation's banks don't offer LOCs, and some of those that do prefer not to do business with small exporters. The best places to start your search are with large regional or money-center banks, or the local offices of major international banks.

KEY QUESTION. Bankers can help out in other ways, such as advising on the structure of overseas contracts and directing you to public or private insurance for transactions. "The biggest problem at many companies I see is a lack of coordination between sales and finance," says Jeanne Derderian, in charge of business development for exporting at Chicago-based LaSalle National Bank, a subsidiary of the Dutch banking behemoth ABN AMRO Group. "Salesmen are out there making promises on what the terms will be and later on the finance people say, we can't do that."

Still, the key question is whether you will get paid by someone thousands of miles away. If an LOC isn't practical, try to protect yourself with an up-front payment. Edaw, for instance, often finds itself in intense competition with other international firms under tight deadlines, with no time for lawyers to review complicated contracts. To protect itself from currency moves, political uncertainties, and other risks, it requires 20% to 40% of its fee up front. It credits that to the overall invoice, before its architects ever get on an airplane.

Better yet, take things slowly. When it comes to relying on an agent, a broker, or a joint-venture partner in overseas markets, a hasty choice can turn out to be ruinous. "I see it all the time," sighs Mark Levine, director of customs and duties practice at Coopers & Lybrand. "People think they are getting a reputable agent or broker, and they are just a fly-by-night operator."

Super Vision International Inc., an Orlando-based maker of fiber-optic lighting, initially does business only with the largest companies in a country, often subsidiaries of U.S. multinationals. "If you are going into a new country, you don't have the revenues to knock on every door. So deal with the top players, who are reliable and justify your time and flights," says CEO Brett Kingstone. Over time, Super Vision nurtures a relationship with a local distributor, which then becomes Super Vision's conduit to smaller companies in a country. The recipe seems successful: Super Vision now gets about two-thirds of its revenues from overseas, much of it from developing countries.

Even with good planning and international savvy, going abroad is no cakewalk. Take the experience of California auto dealer Anthony A. Batarse Jr. In 1992, his four auto dealerships were pulling in about $17 million. He heard that the government of Cameroon was looking to spend $24 million on 500 customized vehicles and a service center.

Batarse wasn't afraid of an international deal—the El Salvador native's father had been an exporter. Over two years, he got financing from the Ex-Im Bank and the State Dept.'s blessing. He even checked Cameroon's human rights record with Amnesty International. He took out his savings, refinanced his house, and mortgaged a couple of other buildings he owned. He sent engineers to Cameroon to start preliminary work on the service center and ordered the special cars from General Motors Corp. Then the State Dept. reversed itself, citing Cameroon's credit record and the risk that the vehicles would be used by abusive police. Batarse was forced to sell two of his dealerships to repay the $750,000 he had spent and is still in the red. "It almost put me out of business," he says.

Of course, luck knows no borders. When Meter-Man's Neff flew to a trade show in Barcelona a few years ago, he found himself sitting next to a man from Paraguay who was headed for the same show. The two struck up a relationship, and his travel companion ended up ordering about $200,000 of Meter-Man's product and is now a major South American distributor. "All the classes in the world don't get you sitting next to a guy interested in your product," says Neff. "I've tried drumming up business the same way another 50 times, but it hasn't worked again," he laughs. Whether doing business in Tuscaloosa or Timbuktu, success is a cross between hard work and good fortune.

By Christopher Farrell in St. Paul, Minn., with Edith Updike in New York

Are You Smart Enough to Sell

GL●BALLY?

How to research an international market before doing business there

BY LAMBETH HOCHWALD

BURT CABANAS HAS ONE PIECE OF ADVICE for companies planning to expand internationally: Research, research, research. "We went into Thailand initially without doing research and that was a mistake," says Cabanas, president and CEO of Benchmark Hospitality Inc., which develops and manages conference centers, conference hotels, and resorts. In addition to Thailand, Benchmark (based in Woodlands, Texas) has properties in Japan and the Philippines, and is analyzing six additional countries. "We made many assumptions about how we would do marketing in ways that were a few degrees off target," Cabanas explains. "We were told by U.S. companies that if we were going to do business [in Thailand], we should be in Bangkok, and we spent a tremendous amount of time getting a presence there. We then found out we could have been just as successful outside the city. Taking someone else's word for it rather than doing the research set us back a year and a half."

Sure, it's a good sign if your company is ready to expand globally. But before you conquer the world, it's critical to launch a well-crafted international market-research campaign. Simply put, you have to do your homework. (Just ask those companies that rushed into Asia right before the region's economy collapsed.) "So much of the market research you do depends on the product you're selling," says Scott Haug, practice director at Towers Perrin Sales Management Practice in Los Angeles. "There's a language issue and cultural issues— things that offend local sensibility. It's also not just how big the market is, but how fast it's growing. You have

to tap into the psyche of the customer, which varies from country to country. Plus, if you're going up against the strongest [local] brand, you need to begin brand building right away."

> **The first step is finding potential franchisees abroad who have sufficient capital and management personnel to manage the franchise.**

Ruth Stanat, president of SIS International Research in Fort Wayne, Indiana, and author of *Global Gold* (Amacom, 1998), recommends dividing market research into two phases. The first phase is conducted from company headquarters (cost: between $10,000 and $20,000), and includes tapping into the U.S. Department of Commerce's country trade reports and databases. The second step is doing in-country field research (cost: between $50,000 and $80,000), which usually involves conducting focus groups, in-depth interviews with prospects, and telephone surveys—all initiated with the goal of assessing risks and forecasting market demand.

Even after discovering that a good customer base exists, a company has to become expert in a country's business environment: examining its political and economic condition (including local tariffs and trade regulations), and the short- and long-term growth potential. "One of the biggest mistakes is having a knee-jerk reaction to international expansion," Stanat says. "Instead, take the time for critical analysis."

As the stories of the following three companies indicate, opening international operations can challenge even the most adept manager.

Firsthand Research

When it comes to selecting the right overseas markets, Bill Edwards believes it's best to send his own operations staff and marketing specialists to explore countries where his company wants to do business. The company,

> "The research is critical because bankers want to know how much you know about the local economy and area demographics before they'll move forward."

Alphagraphics, a corporate design, copy, and print services firm based in Tucson, Arizona, currently operates in 24 countries in Asia, Eastern Europe, and Latin America.

The first step is finding potential franchisees abroad who have sufficient capital and management personnel to manage the franchise. Staffers initially conduct on-line research, search U.S. Department of Commerce sources, examine referrals by other franchisees, and check into queries made to Alphagraphics via the Internet. The company then sends staffers overseas to size up the contenders. Once Alphagraphics managers meet the potential franchisee, they research the financial status of the prospective "partner," says Edwards, senior vice president of the international division.

"Most market research firms don't know our business and tend to classify us as a quick-print shop versus a high-end business," Edwards says. "They tend to be expensive as well, to the tune of up to $25,000 for basic market research, and frankly I can put my own people in-country for less than that, even if they stay for months at a time."

The company currently is researching 10 additional countries in Western Europe, and Edwards is well aware of how long it might take to get there. "International market research can take between

FIVE STEPS TO CONDUCTING INTERNATIONAL MARKET RESEARCH

STUDY, STUDY, STUDY A company wouldn't dive into a new U.S. market without first thoroughly examining it. This is even more important when expanding internationally. Ignore assumptions and hearsay about a market; instead find out firsthand what the market conditions and potential are.

SIZE UP THE MARKET In addition to one-on-one customer interviews, use off-the-shelf research data to determine what customers want, buy, and need, says Deven Sharma, a vice president at management consulting firm Booz-Allen & Hamilton Inc. in New York. For any product segment, there is some industry data on how big a market is in a given country, Sharma says. "This data is readily available in all countries except for the ones that haven't emerged, like Cambodia, which is still tough."

CHECK YOUR ASSUMPTIONS Most people would think Central America isn't a profitable market, says Bill Edwards, senior vice president of the international division of Alphagraphics design and printing company, which operates in 24 countries and is researching 10 others. "Most think it's too poor and that there's not enough substantial business there to support a company like

ours. That's false. We've been open for two years in Honduras and Guatemala, and El Salvador and Panama are next. If you have assumptions about a region of the world, check it out yourself or hire a firm to do it. Don't be sure your initial assumptions are right on."

BE CREATIVE "It's worked for us to hire MBA students to do the ground research so you have an idea of where to focus your professional energy," says Greg Brophy, president of Shred-It, an industrial shredding company that only has spent between $5,000 and $7,000 on research per country. "They gave me an understanding of the market before I hired any market researchers."

ASK THE RIGHT QUESTIONS Ruth Stanat, president of SIS International Research in Fort Wayne, Indiana, and author of Global Gold (Amacom, 1998), says that there are five must-ask questions when hiring an international research firm: Do you have people in the country who can do the work? How long have you been doing this kind of work? How many studies have you done in my industry, product area, and the country I'm looking into? How do you supervise and quality control the project? And, how much will this cost? —L.H.

six months and four years," he says of his efforts, from the company's first foray into Hong Kong in 1986 to the bulk of the company's international expansion, which started in 1992. "We sold our first store to an American who owned a print shop in Hong Kong," he says. "We didn't even have an international group to handle overseas expansion."

With an established overseas presence, potential franchisees know what they're getting if they hook up with Alphagraphics, and Alphagraphics has a more efficient prospecting perspective. "If there's a very obvious need, and it's a rapid growth market for high-tech services, we can tell who our customers are going to be and quickly find a partner." Edwards says. "In some markets, it's hard to convince locals that the concept will work. In those places, we're very careful to take as much time as necessary to find a partner."

A Thorough Approach

Greg Brophy had a hunch that international companies would need his industrial-strength shredding machines. He just had to decide which country to target with his mobile shredding and recycling service, aimed at businesses, hospitals, banks, and government agencies eager to destroy anything from paper to computer disks to license plates.

Brophy, president of Shred-It, in Mississauga, Ontario, started examining foreign markets four years ago by hiring a German MBA candidate and phoning chambers of commerce and economic development offices in the cities he was interested in prospecting. "We spent five months researching the general European market," Brophy says. "The research is critical because bankers want to know how much you know about the local economy and area demographics before they'll move forward."

The MBA candidate Brophy hired (he found him by placing a few calls to top universities in Germany) was eager to amplify his studies by doing international market research. "I had this graduate student begin the research in Germany, and then he came to Canada and worked here for four months," Brophy says. "I had him put together binders with competitive analyses of how many firms were doing the same sort of work we do. And since we care about companies with fifteen-plus employees who might need our mobile shredders, he did a count of companies in every city we wanted to be in."

With this analysis in hand, Brophy then hired two research firms in France and England (referred to him by the company's Canadian research firm) to collect data on the potential of doing business there. "I wanted to make sure the numbers were right," he says. "If you get the data from two firms, you know you're pretty close."

So far, Brophy's analysis has been on target. The company has grown to more than 54 offices in the U.S. and Canada as well as Argentina, Belgium, Hong Kong, and Luxembourg, with market research for each country costing $5,000 to $7,000. And Brophy's research strategy works today with one final step: He heads overseas himself to find out whether Shred-It's style will work in a particular country. "We have very defined systems, and in Europe, local companies kept asking me how I knew our system would work there," he says. "That's why I do all-day sales presentations with clients once the initial research is done. In a way, my best market research is my face-to-face contacts with local company representatives."

Using Local Talent

It's impossible to sell successfully in a country without having an intimate knowledge of its business culture. That's why Burt Cabanas tries to enlist the support of nationals to help navigate the complexity of that country's mores when looking to open a Benchmark property. He's added government officials to his board as well as board members from completely different U.S. companies with overseas offices. Grasping a country's culture, Cabanas believes, is more important than absorbing reams of hard data about its market.

> "If you have a brand name that's recognized internationally, you have a lot of ease of entry because there's already a perception of what that brand name means."

"First, we look at the corporate presence in a city in order to decide if it's appropriate to put a conference center there," he says. If so, Cabanas needs to choose the right staff to manage it. So, when Benchmark either builds a new conference center or converts an existing hotel to a conference center, the corporate philosophy is to split key positions between executives from the country and transferred U.S. personnel.

This approach was particularly critical in early 1997 when the company converted an existing hotel outside of Bangkok (in nearby Ayutthaya) into a conference hotel. To prepare for that opening, Benchmark established an office in Thailand and hired a vice president, Thomas Cole, to evaluate whether a conference center for the small-meetings market would succeed there, and gain the company a foothold in Asia. Although Cole is American, he's written a book on Thai culture and understands the nuances of life there, Cabanas says. Benchmark also formed a corporation that has Thais on its board of directors, including the country's supreme commander of the armed forces. "Although General Somchai Dhanarajata doesn't know the hotel business, we realized that government and military personnel are key figures to help us understand how the country does business."

In addition, Cabanas used a local marketing firm to analyze the depth of the meetings market in Bangkok. The entire research effort cost $200,000. "You want the research to be in-country, because there's a uniqueness to how the economy of the culture runs," he says. "It's also easier to get information quicker if we have someone there with contacts in that country. The Internet is a great source for data, but we're more interested in knowing how open the door is for us to do business and how deep the market is."

STUDY GUIDES

■ The Green Book, published by the American Management Association, lists all market research firms and those with international capabilities. www.greenbook.org
■ Esomar, the European Society of Opinion and Market Research, has a worldwide listing by company. www.esomar.nl
■ The U.S. Department of State's Web site offers commercial guides to almost every country in the world, compiled by the local embassies. www.state.gov.

The timing of research and the time it takes to market successfully abroad all depends on the strength of your brand, adds Cabanas, who says it took 10 years to get a feel for how a conference center would be received in Japan, five years for Thailand, and one year for the Philippines. "If you have a brand name that's recognized internationally, you have a lot of ease of entry because there's already a perception of what that brand name means," Cabanas says. "In our case, we're a small company and our benchmark of conference center development isn't as well-known, so we had to take the time to introduce the concept of our company."

Benchmark has continued to expand, and is studying Cairo, Mexico, Milan, and South America. "We're still in the early stages for all of the countries except Egypt," says Cabanas, who is evaluating a total of six countries. "We're just probing around and testing the temperature and culture of the possible facilities there, but we always connect immediately with someone who knows the country thoroughly. That's the best market research we can do."

Writing for a global audience on the Web

By Laura Morelli

By the end of this year, an estimated 97.3 million people will have access to the World Wide Web. That number is expected to swell to a staggering 319.8 million in just four years, according to estimates from International Data Corp. in Framingham, Mass. As international boundaries dissolve and new marketing opportunities abound on-line, customers from Australia to Zaire will flock to your company's Web site.

Or will they? Unfortunately, the World Wide Web silences the "If we build it, they will come" mantra. Building a site that's accessible to a global audience means more than simply establishing a presence on the Web. It means revising your on-line communications strategy.

You must write lively copy that takes into account the cultural and linguistic makeup of your potential audience, and then use graphics effectively. Here are some guidelines to get you started:

❑ Use simple language and avoid complicated sentence structures.

Your prose should not sound child-like or patronizing; strive for clear, concise language by choosing a shorter word over a longer one, for example, whenever possible. Keep the tone simple and straightforward.

Instead of: "Sales have been driven by a number of factors, including an improving economy and careful monitoring of prices by managers to help ensure the product not only remains competitive but makes a real comeback," write, "Though an improving economy has been key to the product's comeback, other factors have helped drive sales. First, managers have monitored prices carefully to ensure that the product remains competitive."

> ❝ **The World Wide Web silences the 'If we build it they will come' mantra. Building a site that's accessible to a global audience means more than simply establishing a presence on the Web. It means revising your on-line communications strategy.** ❞

❑ Use the active voice.

Active voice, which helps achieve concise copy, is especially important on the Web where readability is essential.

For example, instead of: "The ad was designed by the creative team," write, "The creative team designed the ad."

❑ Avoid culturally specific idioms or references.

Expressions such as "putting all your eggs in one basket" or "looking for a needle in a haystack" may not understood by all your readers. Watch for sports metaphors that do not transcend national or cultural borders, such as "scoring a touchdown."

❑ Avoid humor.

Humor is rooted in cultural norms. No matter how clever your tagline or cartoon seems, it likely will elude, and possibly offend, a percentage of your audience.

❑ Consider dates, time and geography.

If you write Oct. 4, 1998, as "10/04/98," Europeans will understand April 10, 1998. If weights, measures or temperatures form part of your message, provide both American units and metric equivalents. Consider expressing time in military format (16:00 for 4 p.m.) to avoid confusion.

With the exception of such major cities as New York, Hong Kong or London, don't assume your audience will know the location. Write "Kansas City, Mo., U.S.A.," instead of simply "Kansas City."

❑ Define acronyms and abbreviations.

Remember that acronyms such as TQM may not be clear to all your readers. If a name is long or cumbersome, spell it out in the first reference with the acronym in parentheses, then abbreviate all subsequent instances.

For example, write "Efficient Consumer Response (ECR)" the first time, then simply "ECR" thereafter.

❑ Consistency is key.

Consistency is the essence of all corporate communications, but it bears repeating for the purposes of the Web. Use the same tense throughout your site, and refer to products, events and people in the same way every time.

If your Web site consists of sections written by different people, hire an experienced editor to make the site speak in "one voice" so it will project a unified corporate image.

❑ Use graphics to assist in communicating written concepts.

Never underestimate the power of graphics, which are especially important in the face of language barriers. Europeans understand the universality of graphical communication—long ago, they replaced "hot" and "cold" with red and blue dots on the restroom faucets in places such as international airports.

In your Web site, for example, replace the link "Contact us" with an image of an envelope. Use other internationally understood graphical icons for ease in navigating your site.

❑ Double-check photographs and illustrations.

Always avoid representing cultural stereotypes or metaphors. Remove any pictures that include hand gestures, no matter how benign they may seem to you.

For your site to be truly global, it must be multilingual. It's true that English is the global language of business, and there's a strong bias toward English on the Web. An estimated 55 million English speakers currently access the Internet, including residents of North America, Britain, Australia, New Zealand and India. Still, potential customers among the 9 million Japanese speakers, 6.9 million German speakers and 5.3 million Spanish speakers on-line should not be dismissed.

Many companies provide polyglot Web development, which goes beyond simple translation into the target languages. If many of your customers are overseas, it pays to have your site "localized," so that it reflects not only the native language but the local norms of weights and measures, time, currency and so on. Localization is essential if you want your customers abroad to find you using keyword searches in their native languages, and order your products in their currency.

Seeking examples of effective global sites on the Web? Look not to corporate America but to papal Rome. At the Vatican home page (http://www.vatican.va), everything is in place: Concise text, effective graphics, six different languages and links to sites of specialized interest. And if you're surprised about who's leading the way in international marketing on the Internet, don't be. After all, the Catholic Church has been in the global communications business longer than any of us.

Laura Morelli is president of WordQuest Communications LLC in West Simsbury, Conn., which provides corporate writing services and communications training to global businesses.

This glossary of marketing terms is included to provide you with a convenient and ready reference as you encounter general terms in your study of marketing that are unfamiliar or require a review. It is not intended to be comprehensive, but taken together with the many definitions included in the articles themselves, it should prove to be quite useful.

acceptable price range The range of prices that buyers are willing to pay for a product; prices that are above the range may be judged unfair, while prices below the range may generate concerns about quality.

adaptive selling A salesperson's adjustment of his or her behavior between and during sales calls, to respond appropriately to issues that are important to the customer.

advertising Marketing communication elements designed to stimulate sales through the use of mass media displays, direct individual appeals, public displays, giveaways, and the like.

advertorial A special advertising section in magazines that includes some editorial (nonadvertising) content.

Americans with Disabilities Act (ADA) Passed in 1990, this U.S. law prohibits discrimination against consumers with disabilities.

automatic number identification A telephone system that identifies incoming phone numbers at the beginning of the call, without the caller's knowledge.

bait and switch Advertising a product at an attractively low price to get customers into the store, but making the product unavailable so that the customers must trade up to a more expensive version.

bar coding A computer-coded bar pattern that identifies a product. *See also* universal product code.

barter The practice of exchanging goods and services without the use of money.

benefit segmentation Organizing the market according to the attributes or benefits consumers need or desire, such as quality, service, or unique features.

brand A name, term, sign, design, symbol, or combination used to differentiate the products of one company from those of its competition.

brand image The quality and reliability of a product as perceived by consumers on the basis of its brand reputation or familiarity.

brand name The element of a brand that can be vocalized.

break-even analysis The calculation of the number of units that must be sold at a certain price to cover costs (break even); revenues earned past the break-even point contribute to profits.

bundling Marketing two or more products in a single package at one price.

business analysis The stage of new product development where initial marketing plans are prepared (including tentative marketing strategy and estimates of sales, costs, and profitability).

business strategic plan A plan for how each business unit in a corporation intends to compete in the marketplace, based upon the vision, objectives, and growth strategies of the corporate strategic plan.

capital products Expensive items that are used in business operations but do not become part of any finished product (such as office buildings, copy machines).

cash-and-carry wholesaler A limited-function wholesaler that does not extend credit for or deliver the products it sells.

caveat emptor A Latin term that means "let the buyer beware." A principle of law meaning that the purchase of a product is at the buyer's risk with regard to its quality, usefulness, and the like. The laws do, however, provide certain minimum protection against fraud and other schemes.

channel of distribution *See* marketing channel.

Child Protection Act U.S. law passed in 1990 to regulate advertising on children's TV programs.

Child Safety Act Passed in 1966, this U.S. law prohibits the marketing of dangerous products to children.

Clayton Act Anticompetitive activities are prohibited by this 1914 U.S. law.

co-branding When two brand names appear on the same product (such as a credit card with a school's name).

comparative advertising Advertising that compares one brand against a competitive brand on a least one product attribute.

competitive pricing strategies Pricing strategies that are based on a organization's position in relation to its competition.

consignment An arrangement in which a seller of goods does not take title to the goods until they are sold. The seller thus has the option of returning them to the supplier or principal if unable to execute the sale.

consolidated metropolitan statistical area (CMSA) Based on census data, the largest designation of geographic areas. *See also* primary metropolitan statistical area.

consumer behavior The way in which buyers, individually or collectively, react to marketplace stimuli.

Consumer Credit Protection Act A 1968 U.S. law that requires full disclosure of the financial charges of loans.

consumer decision process This four-step process includes recognizing a need or problem, searching for information, evaluating alternative products or brands, and purchasing a product.

Consumer Product Safety Commission (CPSC) A U.S. government agency that protects consumers from unsafe products.

consumerism A social movement in which consumers demand better information about the service, prices, dependability, and quality of the products they buy.

convenience products Consumer goods that are purchased at frequent intervals with little regard for price. Such goods are relatively standard in nature and consumers tend to select the most convenient source when shopping for them.

cooperative advertising Advertising of a product by a retailer, dealer, distributor, or the like, with part of the advertising cost paid by the product's manufacturer.

corporate strategic plan A plan that addresses what a company is and wants to become, and then guides strategic planning at all organizational levels.

countersegmentation A concept that combines market segments to appeal to a broad range of consumers, assuming that there will be an increasing consumer willingness to accept fewer product and service choices for lower prices.

customer loyalty concept To focus beyond customer satisfaction toward customer retention as a way to generate sales and profit growth.

demand curve A relationship that shows how many units a market will purchase at a given price in a given period of time.

demographic environment The study of human population densities, distributions, and movements that relate to buying behavior.

derived demand The demand for business-to-business products that is dependent upon a demand for other products in the market.

differentiated strategy Using innovation and points of difference in product offerings, advanced technology, superior service, or higher quality in wide areas of market segments.

direct mail promotion Marketing goods to consumers by mailing unsolicited promotional material to them.

direct marketing The sale of products to carefully targeted consumers who interact with various advertising media without salesperson contact.

discount A reduction from list price that is given to a buyer as a reward for a favorable activity to the seller.

discretionary income The money that remains after taxes and necessities have been paid for.

disposable income That portion of income that remains after payment of taxes to use for food, clothing, and shelter.

dual distribution The selling of products to two or more competing distribution networks, or the selling of two brands of nearly identical products through competing distribution networks.

dumping The act of selling a product in a foreign country at a price lower than its domestic price.

durable goods Products that continue in service for an appreciable length of time.

economy The income, expenditures, and resources that affect business and household costs.

electronic data interchange (EDI) A computerized system that links two different firms to allow transmittal of documents; a quick-response inventory control system.

entry strategy An approach used to begin marketing products internationally.

environmental scanning Obtaining information on relevant factors and trends outside a company and interpreting their potential impact on the company's markets and marketing activities.

European Union (EU) The world's largest consumer market, consisting of 16 European nations: Austria, Belgium, Britain, Denmark, Finland, France, Germany, Greece, Italy, Ireland, Luxembourg, the Netherlands, Norway, Portugal, Spain, and Sweden.

exclusive distribution Marketing a product or service in only one retail outlet in a specific geographic marketplace.

exporting Selling goods to international markets.

Fair Packaging and Labeling Act of 1966 This law requires manufacturers to state ingredients, volume, and manufacturer's name on a package.

family life cycle The progress of a family through a number of distinct phases, each of which is associated with identifiable purchasing behaviors.

Federal Trade Commission (FTC) The U.S. government agency that regulates business practices; established in 1914.

five C's of pricing Five influences on pricing decisions: customers, costs, channels of distribution, competition, and compatibility.

FOB (free on board) The point at which the seller stops paying transportation costs.

four I's of service Four elements to services: intangibility, inconsistency, inseparability, and inventory.

four P's *See* marketing mix.

franchise The right to distribute a company's products or render services under its name, and to retain the resulting profit in exchange for a fee or percentage of sales.

freight absorption Payment of transportation costs by the manufacturer or seller, often resulting in a uniform pricing structure.

functional groupings Groupings in an organization in which a unit is subdivided according to different business activities, such as manufacturing, finance, and marketing.

General Agreement on Tariffs and Trade (GATT) An international agreement that is intended to limit trade barriers and to promote world trade through reduced tariffs; represents over 80 percent of global trade.

geodemographics A combination of geographic data and demographic characteristics; used to segment and target specific markets.

green marketing The implementation of an ecological perspective in marketing; the promotion of a product as environmentally safe.

gross domestic product (GDP) The total monetary value of all goods and services produced within a country during one year.

growth stage The second stage of a product life cycle that is characterized by a rapid increase in sales and profits.

hierarchy of effects The stages a prospective buyer goes through when purchasing a product, including awareness, interest, evaluation, trial, and adoption.

idea generation An initial stage of the new product development process; requires creativity and innovation to generate ideas for potential new products.

implied warranties Warranties that assign responsibility for a product's deficiencies to a manufacturer, even though the product was sold by a retailer.

imports Purchased goods or services that are manufactured or produced in some other country.

integrated marketing communications A strategic integration of marketing communications programs that coordinate all promotional activities—advertising, personal selling, sales promotion, and public relations.

internal reference prices The comparison price standards that consumers remember and use to judge the fairness of prices.

introduction stage The first product life cycle stage; when a new product is launched into the marketplace.

ISO 9000 International Standards Organization's standards for registration and certification of manufacturer's quality management and quality assurance systems.

joint venture An arrangement in which two or more organizations market products internationally.

just-in-time (JIT) inventory control system An inventory supply system that operates with very low inventories and fast, on-time delivery.

Lanham Trademark Act A 1946 U.S. law that was passed to protect trademarks and brand names.

late majority The fourth group to adopt a new product; representing about 34 percent of a market.

lifestyle research Research on a person's pattern of living, as displayed in activities, interests, and opinions.

limit pricing This competitive pricing strategy involves setting prices low to discourage new competition.

limited-coverage warranty The manufacturer's statement regarding the limits of coverage and noncoverage for any product deficiencies.

logistics management The planning, implementing, and moving of raw materials and products from the point of origin to the point of consumption.

loss-leader pricing The pricing of a product below its customary price in order to attract attention to it.

Magnuson-Moss Act Passed in 1975, this U.S. law regulates warranties.

management by exception Used by a marketing manager to identify results that deviate from plans, diagnose their cause, make appropriate new plans, and implement new actions.

manufacturers' agent A merchant wholesaler that sells related but noncompeting product lines for a number of manufacturers; also called manufacturers' representatives.

market The potential buyers for a company's product or service; or to sell a product or service to actual buyers. The place where goods and services are exchanged.

market penetration strategy The goal of achieving corporate growth objectives with existing products within existing markets by persuading current customers to purchase more of the product or by capturing new customers.

marketing channel Organizations and people that are involved in the process of making a product or service available for use by consumers or industrial users.

marketing communications planning A seven-step process that includes marketing plan review; situation analysis; communications process analysis; budget development; program development integration and implementation of a plan; and monitoring, evaluating, and controlling the marketing communications program.

marketing concept The idea that a company should seek to satisfy the needs of consumers while also trying to achieve the organization's goals.

marketing mix The elements of marketing: product, brand, package, price, channels of distribution, advertising and promotion, personal selling, and the like.

marketing research The process of identifying a marketing problem and opportunity, collecting and analyzing information systematically, and recommending actions to improve an organization's marketing activities.

marketing research process A six-step sequence that includes problem definition, determination of research design, determination of data collection methods, development of data collection forms, sample design, and analysis and interpretation.

mission statement A part of the strategic planning process that expresses the company's basic values and specifies the operation boundaries within marketing, business units, and other areas.

motivation research A group of techniques developed by behavioral scientists that are used by marketing researchers to discover factors influencing marketing behavior.

nonprice competition Competition between brands based on factors other than price, such as quality, service, or product features.

nondurable goods Products that do not last or continue in service for any appreciable length of time.

North American Free Trade Agreement (NAFTA) A trade agreement among the United States, Canada, and Mexico that essentially removes the vast majority of trade barriers between the countries.

North American Industry Classification System (NAICS) A system used to classify organizations on the basis of major activity or the major good or service provided by the three NAFTA countries—Canada, Mexico, and the United States; replaced the Standard Industrial Classification (SIC) system in 1997.

observational data Market research data obtained by watching, either mechanically or in person, how people actually behave.

odd-even pricing Setting prices at just below an even number, such as $1.99 instead of $2.

opinion leaders Individuals who influence consumer behavior based on their interest in or expertise with particular products.

organizational goals The specific objectives used by a business or nonprofit unit to achieve and measure its performance.

outbound telemarketing Using the telephone rather than personal visits to contact customers.

outsourcing A company's decision to purchase products and services from other firms rather than using in-house employees.

parallel development In new product development, an approach that involves the development of the product and production process simultaneously.

penetration pricing Pricing a product low to discourage competition.

personal selling process The six stages of sales activities that occur before and after the sale itself: prospecting, preapproach, approach, presentation, close, and follow-up.

point-of-purchase display A sales promotion display located in high-traffic areas in retail stores.

posttesting Tests that are conducted to determine if an advertisement has accomplished its intended purpose.

predatory pricing The practice of selling products at low prices to drive competition from the market and then raising prices once a monopoly has been established.

prestige pricing Maintaining high prices to create an image of product quality and appeal to buyers who associate premium prices with high quality.

pretesting Evaluating consumer reactions to proposed advertisements through the use of focus groups and direct questions.

price elasticity of demand An economic concept that attempts to measure the sensitivity of demand for any product to changes in its price.

price fixing The illegal attempt by one or several companies to maintain the prices of their products above those that would result from open competition.

price promotion mix The basic product price plus additional components such as sales prices, temporary discounts, coupons, favorable payment and credit terms.

price skimming Setting prices high initially to appeal to consumers who are not price-sensitive and then lowering prices to appeal to the next market segments.

primary metropolitan statistical area (PMSA) Major urban area, often located within a CMSA, that has at least one million inhabitants.

PRIZM A potential rating index by ZIP code markets that divides every U.S. neighborhood into one of 40 distinct cluster types that reveal consumer data.

product An idea, good, service, or any combination that is an element of exchange to satisfy a consumer.

product differentiation The ability or tendency of manufacturers, marketers, or consumers to distinguish between seemingly similar products.

product expansion strategy A plan to market new products to the same customer base.

product life cycle (PLC) A product's advancement through the introduction, growth, maturity, and decline stages.

product line pricing Setting the prices for all product line items.

product marketing plans Business units' plans to focus on specific target markets and marketing mixes for each product, which include both strategic and execution decisions.

product mix The composite of products offered for sale by a firm or a business unit.

promotional mix Combining one or more of the promotional elements that a firm uses to communicate with consumers.

proprietary secondary data The data that is provided by commercial marketing research firms to other firms.

psychographic research Measurable characteristics of given market segments in respect to lifestyles, interests, opinions, needs, values, attitudes, personality traits, and the like.

publicity Nonpersonal presentation of a product, service, or business unit.

pull strategy A marketing strategy whose main thrust is to strongly influence the final consumer, so that the demand for a product "pulls" it through the various channels of distribution.

push strategy A marketing strategy whose main thrust is to provide sufficient economic incentives to members of the channels of distribution, so as to "push" the product through to the consumer.

qualitative data The responses obtained from in-depth interviews, focus groups, and observation studies.

quality function deployment (QFD) The data collected from structured response formats that can be easily analyzed and projected to larger populations.

quotas In international marketing, they are restrictions placed on the amount of a product that is allowed to leave or enter a country; the total outcomes used to assess sales representatives' performance and effectiveness.

regional marketing A form of geographical division that develops marketing plans that reflect differences in taste preferences, perceived needs, or interests in other areas.

relationship marketing The development, maintenance, and enhancement of long-term, profitable customer relationships.

repositioning The development of new marketing programs that will shift consumer beliefs and opinions about an existing brand.

resale price maintenance Control by a supplier of the selling prices of his branded goods at subsequent stages of distribution, by means of contractual agreement under fair trade laws or other devices.

reservation price The highest price a consumer will pay for a product; a form of internal reference price.

restraint of trade In general, activities that interfere with competitive marketing. Restraint of trade usually refers to illegal activities.

retail strategy mix Controllable variables that include location, products and services, pricing, and marketing communications.

return on investment (ROI) A ratio of income before taxes to total operating assets associated with a product, such as inventory, plant, and equipment.

sales effectiveness evaluations A test of advertising efficiency to determine if it resulted in increased sales.

sales forecast An estimate of sales under controllable and uncontrollable conditions.

sales management The planning, direction, and control of the personal selling activities of a business unit.

sales promotion An element of the marketing communications mix that provides incentives or extra value to stimulate product interest.

samples A small size of a product given to prospective purchasers to demonstrate a product's value or use and to encourage future purchase; some elements that are taken from the population or universe.

scanner data Proprietary data that is derived from UPC bar codes.

scrambled merchandising Offering several unrelated product lines within a single retail store.

selected controlled markets Sites where market tests for a new product are conducted by an outside agency and retailers are paid to display that product; also referred to as forced distribution markets.

selective distribution This involves selling a product in only some of the available outlets; commonly used when after-the-sale service is necessary, such as in the case of home appliances.

seller's market A condition within any market in which the demand for an item is greater than its supply.

selling philosophy An emphasis on an organization's selling function to the exclusion of other marketing activities.

selling strategy A salesperson's overall plan of action, which is developed at three levels: sales territory, customer, and individual sales calls.

services Nonphysical products that a company provides to consumers in exchange for money or something else of value.

share points Percentage points of market share; often used as the common comparison basis to allocate marketing resources effectively.

Sherman Anti-Trust Act Passed in 1890, this U.S. law prohibits contracts, combinations, or conspiracies in restraint of trade and actual monopolies or attempts to monopolize any part of trade or commerce.

shopping products Consumer goods that are purchased only after comparisons are made concerning price, quality, style, suitability, and the like.

single-channel strategy Marketing strategy using only one means to reach customers; providing one sales source for a product.

single-zone pricing A pricing policy in which all buyers pay the same delivered product price, regardless of location; also known as uniform delivered pricing or postage stamp pricing.

slotting fees High fees manufacturers pay to place a new product on a retailer's or wholesaler's shelf.

social responsibility Reducing social costs, such as environmental damage, and increasing the positive impact of a marketing decision on society.

societal marketing concept The use of marketing strategies to increase the acceptability of an idea (smoking causes cancer); cause (environmental protection); or practice (birth control) within a target market.

specialty products Consumer goods, usually appealing only to a limited market, for which consumers will make a special purchasing effort. Such items include, for example, stereo components, fancy foods, and prestige brand clothes.

Standard Industrial Classification (SIC) system Replaced by NAICS, this federal government numerical scheme categorized businesses.

standardized marketing Enforcing similar product, price, distribution, and communications programs in all international markets.

stimulus-response presentation A selling format that assumes that a customer will buy if given the appropriate stimulus by a salesperson.

strategic business unit (SBU) A decentralized profit center of a company that operates as a separate, independent business.

strategic marketing process Marketing activities in which a firm allocates its marketing mix resources to reach a target market.

strategy mix A way for retailers to differentiate themselves from others through location, product, services, pricing, and marketing mixes.

subliminal perception When a person hears or sees messages without being aware of them.

SWOT analysis An acronym that describes a firm's appraisal of its internal strengths and weaknesses and its external opportunities and threats.

synergy An increased customer value that is achieved through more efficient organizational function performances.

systems-designer strategy A selling strategy that allows knowledgeable sales reps to determine solutions to a customer's problems or to anticipate opportunities to enhance a customer's business through new or modified business systems.

target market A defined group of consumers or organizations toward which a firm directs its marketing program.

team selling A sales strategy that assigns accounts to specialized sales teams according to a customers' purchase-information needs.

telemarketing An interactive direct marketing approach that uses the telephone to develop relationships with customers.

test marketing The process of testing a prototype of a new product to gain consumer reaction and to examine its commercial viability and marketing strategy.

TIGER (Topologically Integrated Geographic Encoding and Reference) A minutely detailed U.S. Census Bureau computerized map of the U.S. that can be combined with a company's own database to analyze customer sales.

total quality management (TQM) Programs that emphasize long-term relationships with selected suppliers instead of short-term transactions with many suppliers.

total revenue The total of sales, or unit price, multiplied by the quantity of the product sold.

trade allowance An amount a manufacturer contributes to a local dealer's or retailer's advertising expenses.

trade (functional) discounts Price reductions that are granted to wholesalers or retailers that are based on future marketing functions that they will perform for a manufacturer.

trademark The legal identification of a company's exclusive rights to use a brand name or trade name.

truck jobber A small merchant wholesaler who delivers limited assortments of fast-moving or perishable items within a small geographic area.

two-way stretch strategy Adding products at both the low and high end of a product line.

undifferentiated strategy Using a single promotional mix to market a single product for the entire market; frequently used early in the life of a product.

uniform delivered price The same average freight amount that is charged to all customers, no matter where they are located.

universal product code (UPC) An assigned number to identify a product, which is represented by a series of bars of varying widths for optical scanning.

usage rate The quantity consumed or patronage during a specific period, which can vary significantly among different customer groups.

utilitarian influence To comply with the expectations of others to achieve rewards or avoid punishments.

value added In retail strategy decisions, a dimension of the retail positioning matrix that refers to the service level and method of operation of the retailer.

vertical marketing systems Centrally coordinated and professionally managed marketing channels that are designed to achieve channel economies and maximum marketing impact.

vertical price fixing Requiring that sellers not sell products below a minimum retail price; sometimes called resale price maintenance.

weighted-point system The method of establishing screening criteria, assigning them weights, and using them to evaluate new product lines.

wholesaler One who makes quantity purchases from manufacturers (or other wholesalers) and sells in smaller quantities to retailers (or other wholesalers).

zone pricing A form of geographical pricing whereby a seller divides its market into broad geographic zones and then sets a uniform delivered price for each zone.

Sources for the Glossary:

Marketing: Principles and Perspectives by William O. Bearden, Thomas N. Ingram, and Raymond W. LaForge (Irwin/McGraw-Hill, 1998); *Marketing* by Eric N. Berkowitz (Irwin/McGraw-Hill, 1997); and the *Annual Editions* staff.

AE Article Review Form

We encourage you to photocopy and use this page as a tool to assess how the articles in **Annual Editions** expand on the information in your textbook. By reflecting on the articles you will gain enhanced text information. You can also access this useful form on a product's book support Web site at **http://www.dushkin.com/online/**.

NAME: _____ DATE: _____

TITLE AND NUMBER OF ARTICLE: _____

BRIEFLY STATE THE MAIN IDEA OF THIS ARTICLE: _____

LIST THREE IMPORTANT FACTS THAT THE AUTHOR USES TO SUPPORT THE MAIN IDEA:

WHAT INFORMATION OR IDEAS DISCUSSED IN THIS ARTICLE ARE ALSO DISCUSSED IN YOUR TEXTBOOK OR OTHER READINGS THAT YOU HAVE DONE? LIST THE TEXTBOOK CHAPTERS AND PAGE NUMBERS:

LIST ANY EXAMPLES OF BIAS OR FAULTY REASONING THAT YOU FOUND IN THE ARTICLE:

LIST ANY NEW TERMS/CONCEPTS THAT WERE DISCUSSED IN THE ARTICLE, AND WRITE A SHORT DEFINITION:

ANNUAL EDITIONS revisions depend on two major opinion sources: one is our Advisory Board, listed in the front of this volume, which works with us in scanning the thousands of articles published in the public press each year; the other is you—the person actually using the book. Please help us and the users of the next edition by completing the prepaid article rating form on this page and returning it to us. Thank you for your help!

ANNUAL EDITIONS: Marketing 99/00

ARTICLE RATING FORM

Here is an opportunity for you to have direct input into the next revision of this volume. We would like you to rate each of the 41 articles listed below, using the following scale:

1. Excellent: should definitely be retained
2. Above average: should probably be retained
3. Below average: should probably be deleted
4. Poor: should definitely be deleted

Your ratings will play a vital part in the next revision. So please mail this prepaid form to us just as soon as you complete it. Thanks for your help!

We Want Your Advice

RATING | **ARTICLE**

1. The Future of Marketing: What Every Marketer Should Know about Being Online
2. Everything New Is Old Again
3. The Secret's Out
4. Envisioning Greenfield Markets
5. The Emerging Culture
6. Marketing Mix Customization and Customizability
7. Marketing Myopia (with Retrospective Commentary)
8. Customer Loyalty: Going, Going . . .
9. Customized Customer Loyalty
10. Customer Intimacy
11. Wrap Your Organization around Each Customer
12. Innovative Service
13. How You Can Help Them
14. Service Is Everybody's Business
15. Whatever It Takes
16. The New Hucksterism
17. Metaphor Marketing
18. Finding Unspoken Reasons for Consumers' Choices
19. The New Market Research
20. A Beginner's Guide to Demographics
21. Tapping the Three Kids' Markets

RATING | **ARTICLE**

22. Culture Shock
23. What Your Customers Can't Say
24. The Joy of Shopping
25. The Very Model of a Modern Marketing Plan
26. Discovering New Points of Differentiation
27. What's in a Brand?
28. Making Old Brands New
29. Built to Last
30. Taking Guesswork Out of Pricing
31. Kamikaze Pricing
32. The Stores That Cross Class Lines
33. Value Retailers Go Dollar for Dollar
34. Retailers with a Future
35. The Nostalgia Boom
36. Good Service, Good Selling
37. Rebates' Secret Appeal to Manufacturers: Few Consumers Actually Redeem Them
38. Global Advertising and the World Wide Web
39. So You Think the World Is Your Oyster
40. Are You Smart Enough to Sell Globally?
41. Writing for a Global Audience on the Web

(Continued on next page)

ANNUAL EDITIONS: MARKETING 99/00

NO POSTAGE
NECESSARY
IF MAILED
IN THE
UNITED STATES

BUSINESS REPLY MAIL
FIRST-CLASS MAIL PERMIT NO. 84 GUILFORD CT

POSTAGE WILL BE PAID BY ADDRESSEE

**Dushkin/McGraw-Hill
Sluice Dock
Guilford, CT 06437-9989**

ABOUT YOU

Name _____   Date _____

Are you a teacher? ☐   A student? ☐
Your school's name

_____

Department

_____

Address _____   City _____   State ____   Zip ____

School telephone # _____

YOUR COMMENTS ARE IMPORTANT TO US !

Please fill in the following information:
For which course did you use this book?

_____

Did you use a text with this *ANNUAL EDITION*? ☐ yes ☐ no
What was the title of the text?

_____

What are your general reactions to the *Annual Editions* concept?

_____

Have you read any particular articles recently that you think should be included in the next edition?

_____

Are there any articles you feel should be replaced in the next edition? Why?

_____

Are there any World Wide Web sites you feel should be included in the next edition? Please annotate.

_____

May we contact you for editorial input? ☐ yes ☐ no
May we quote your comments? ☐ yes ☐ no